.E'S SO FIN
.N WHITENI
.E AND CLASS

Reproduced by kind permission of PRIVATE EYE / S J Russell.

She's So Fine:
Reflections on Whiteness, Femininity, Adolescence and Class in 1960s Music

Edited by

LAURIE STRAS
University of Southampton, UK

ASHGATE

© The Editor and Contributors 2010

First published in paperback 2011

All rights reserved. No part of this publication may be reproduced, stored in a retrieval system or transmitted in any form or by any means, electronic, mechanical, photocopying, recording or otherwise without the prior permission of the publisher.

Laurie Stras has asserted her right under the Copyright, Designs and Patents Act, 1988, to be identified as the editor of this work.

Published by
Ashgate Publishing Limited
Wey Court East
Union Road
Farnham
Surrey, GU9 7PT
England

Ashgate Publishing Company
Suite 420
101 Cherry Street
Burlington
VT 05401-4405
USA

www.ashgate.com

British Library Cataloguing in Publication Data
She's so fine: reflections on whiteness, femininity, adolescence and class in 1960s music. – (Ashgate popular and folk music series)
  1. Women singers–Great Britain–History–20th century. 2. Women singers–United States–History–20th century. 3. Popular music–1951–1960.
  I. Series II. Stras, Laurie.
  782.4'2164'082-dc22

Library of Congress Cataloging-in-Publication Data
She's so fine: reflections on whiteness, femininity, adolescence and class in 1960s music / [edited by] Laurie Stras.
    p. cm. – (Ashgate popular and folk music series)
  Includes bibliographical references and index.
  ISBN 978-1-4094-0051-6 (hardcover : alk. paper) 1. Popular music–United States–1961–1970–History and criticism. 2. Popular music–Great Britain–1961–1970–History and criticism. 3. Women singers–United States. 4. Women singers–Great Britain. 5. Sex role in music. 6. Femininity in music. 7. Girl groups (Musical groups) I. Stras, Laurie.
  ML3470.S53 2009
  [e-uk–]
  781.64082'09046–dc22

2009053202

ISBN 9781409400516 (hbk)
ISBN 9781409436652 (pbk)

Bach musicological font developed by © Yo Tomita

Printed and bound in Great Britain by the
MPG Books Group, UK

*To my mother and my sister,
and to Pete, Joe and Jim,
the best back-up a girl singer could have.*

Contents

List of Figures and Tables	*ix*
List of Music Examples	*xi*
Notes on Contributors	*xiii*
General Editor's Preface	*xv*
Acknowledgments	*xvii*

Introduction: She's So Fine, or Why Girl Singers (Still) Matter   1
Laurie Stras

PART I "NOW THAT I'M NOT A KID ANYMORE": AMERICAN GIRLS' VOICES IN THE 50s AND 60s

1   Voice of the Beehive: Vocal Technique at the Turn of the 1960s   33
     Laurie Stras

2   Vocal Decorum: Voice, Body, and Knowledge in the Prodigious
     Singer, Brenda Lee   57
     Robynn J. Stilwell

3   "He Hit Me, and I was Glad": Violence, Masochism, and
     Anger in Girl Group Music   89
     Jacqueline Warwick

PART II "EVERYTHING'S COMING UP ROSES": BRITISH GIRLS IN THE MID-60s

4   Dusty's Hair   113
     Annie J. Randall

5   Brit Girls: Sandie Shaw and the Women of the British Invasion   137
     Patricia Juliana Smith

6   Mary Hopkin and the Deep Throat of Culture   163
     Sarah Hill

viii   *SHE'S SO FINE*

PART III   GIRLS ON TOP:
ROCK CHICKS AND RESISTANCE AT THE END OF THE 60s

7   Whose Tears Go By? Marianne Faithfull at the Dawn and
     Twilight of Rock Culture   183
     Norma Coates

8   Bold Soul Trickster: The 60s Tina Signifies   203
     Susan Fast

Response   235
Martha Mockus

Select Bibliography   239
Song Title Index   251
Subject and Name Index   255

List of Figures and Tables

Figures

2.1	Brenda Lee performing as a child in a party dress © Michael Ochs/ Michael Ochs Archives/Getty Images	77
2.2	Brenda Lee performing in her early teens © Michael Ochs/ Michael Ochs Archives/Getty Images	80
2.3(a)	"Sweater girl" pose for schoolgirl Brenda Lee	82
2.3(b)	An early 1950s ad, which demonstrates the iconicity of the pose	83
4.1	Dusty Springfield as a teenager, aka Mary O'Brien (Rex USA)	115
4.2	Publicity photo of Dusty Springfield, 1964 (Pictorial Pictures)	115
4.3	Cover of how-to book for girls, *Your Hairdo*, 1966 (Scholastic Books)	118
4.4	Newspaper article on Dusty's wigs (from a fan's scrapbook, reproduced courtesy of *Dusty Springfield Bulletin*)	119
4.5	Martha Reeves and Dusty Springfield © Rex Features Ltd. Used by permission	125
4.6	*Record Mirror*'s report of Dusty's forced departure from South Africa, 1964 (from a fan's scrapbook, reproduced courtesy of *Dusty Springfield Bulletin*). Permission received from publisher, Paul Howes	128
6.1	Mary Hopkin, cover girl (published in the second issue of *Asbri*, 1969)	173
6.2	"School Days": Mary Hopkin, second from right (published in the second issue of *Asbri*, 1969)	173
8.1	Album, Ike and Tina Turner, *Outta Season* (Blue Thumb LBS83241, 1969)	204
8.2	Irish McCalla as *Sheena, Queen of the Jungle* (Nassour Studios, Inc., 1955)	227
8.3	Kay Aldridge in *The Perils of Nyoka* (Republic Pictures, 1942)	228
8.4	Ike and Tina Turner in 1966 © GAB Archive/Redferns/ Getty Images	230
8.5	Tina Turner in the late 1960s © Bob Gruen/www.bobgruen.com	231

Tables

4.1   *A Girl Called Dusty* (UK release, April 1964, Philips BL7594)   121
4.2   *Ev'rything's Coming Up Dusty* (UK release, October 1965,
       Philips BL1002)   121

Disclaimer

Every effort has been made to trace all the copyright holders, but if any have been inadvertently overlooked, the publishers will be pleased to make the necessary arrangement at the first opportunity.

List of Music Examples

1.1 "You Are My Sweetheart" (Dixon, Gathers, Pought, Pought, and Webb): The Bobbettes [Atlantic 2027, 1959], excerpt — 45

1.2 "He's Gone" (Richard Barrett and Arlene Smith): The Chantels [End 1001, 1957], excerpt — 46

1.3 "I Saw A Tear" (Stan Green and Shirley Reeves): The Shirelles [Scepter 1207, 1960], excerpt — 48

2.1(a) "Your Cheatin' Heart" (Hank Williams): title phrase, as sung 1 by Hank Williams (MGM 11416) — 78

2.1(b) "Your Cheatin' Heart" (Hank Williams): title phrase, as sung 1 by Brenda Lee (Decca MCL 1792) — 78

6.1 "Tro, Tro, Tro" (Pete Seeger): Mary Hopkin [Cambrian CEP414, 1967], opening phrase — 170

6.2 "Turn! Turn! Turn!" (Pete Seeger): Mary Hopkin [Apple 2, 1968], opening phrase — 170

Notes on Contributors

Norma Coates is Assistant Professor at the University of Western Ontario, Canada, jointly appointed in the Faculty of Information and Media Studies and the Don Wright Faculty of Music. Her work includes several articles on gender and rock music, and rock music on network television. Her book about rock and roll music on American network television from Elvis Presley to MTV is forthcoming from Duke University Press.

Susan Fast is a musicologist in the department of English and Cultural Studies at McMaster University, Canada. Her research focuses on constructions of identity in popular music performance. She is author of *In the Houses of the Holy: Led Zeppelin and the Power of Rock Music* (Oxford, 2001). Her publications include articles on Live Aid and cultural memory, constructions of authenticity in U2, feminism and rock criticism, and on the mass-mediated benefit concerts that appeared after the terrorist attacks of 9/11. Her current project, funded by the Social Sciences and Humanities Research Council of Canada, investigates gender, race and normative genre boundaries in rock music.

Sarah Hill is Lecturer in Music at Cardiff University, Wales, UK. She is the author of *'Blerwytirhwng?' The Place of Welsh Popular Music* (Ashgate, 2007), co-editor of *Peter Gabriel: From Genesis to Growing Up* (Ashgate, 2009), and is currently working on a cultural history of popular music in San Francisco, 1965–69.

Martha Mockus teaches in the Women's Studies Program at Hamilton College, New York where she held the Jane Watson Irwin Chair, 2006–08. Her research and publications focus on musical performance as a form of queer and feminist critique.

Annie J. Randall is Associate Professor of Musicology at Bucknell University, USA; she is co-editor for Wesleyan University Press's Music/Culture series. She recently completed *Dusty! Queen of the Postmods*, a book on the music and transatlantic reception of Dusty Springfield (Oxford University Press, 2008). Past publications include *Music, Power, and Politics* (Routledge, 2005) and *Puccini and The Girl: History and Reception of* Girl of the Golden West (University of Chicago Press, 2004).

Patricia Juliana Smith is Associate Professor of English at Hofstra University, USA. She is the author of *Lesbian Panic: Homoeroticism in Modern British Women's Fictions* (Columbia University Press, 1997) and editor of *En Travesti: Women, Gender Subversion, Opera* (with Corinne E. Blackmer, Columbia

University Press, 1995) and *The Queer Sixties* (Routledge, 1999). She has published numerous articles on British literature and culture, popular music, opera, and film. She is currently writing *Britannia Waives the Rules: The Permissive Society in 1960s British Literature and Culture.*

Robynn J. Stilwell is Associate Professor of Music at Georgetown University, USA. Her publications include articles in *Beethoven Forum, Popular Music & Society, Acta Musicologica, Music & Letters* and *Screen*, and chapters in books on film, popular music, and French popular culture. She has co-edited several volumes on musicals and film music, and is currently writing on the voice in the musical underscore, particularly its implications for representations of gender and power.

Laurie Stras is Senior Lecturer in Music at the University of Southampton, UK; with Deborah Roberts, she is co-director of the early music ensemble, Musica Secreta. She is the author of numerous articles and chapters on sixteenth-century Italian music, and on the early twentieth-century American jazz vocal group, the Boswell Sisters.

Jacqueline Warwick is an Associate Professor of Music at Dalhousie University, Canada. She is the author of *Girl Groups, Girl Culture: Popular Music and Identity in the 1960s* (Routledge, 2007).

General Editor's Preface

The upheaval that occurred in musicology during the last two decades of the twentieth century has created a new urgency for the study of popular music alongside the development of new critical and theoretical models. A relativistic outlook has replaced the universal perspective of modernism (the international ambitions of the 12-note style); the grand narrative of the evolution and dissolution of tonality has been challenged, and emphasis has shifted to cultural context, reception and subject position. Together, these have conspired to eat away at the status of canonical composers and categories of high and low in music. A need has arisen, also, to recognize and address the emergence of crossovers, mixed and new genres, to engage in debates concerning the vexed problem of what constitutes authenticity in music and to offer a critique of musical practice as the product of free, individual expression.

Popular musicology is now a vital and exciting area of scholarship, and the *Ashgate Popular and Folk Music Series* presents some of the best research in the field. Authors are concerned with locating musical practices, values and meanings in cultural context, and draw upon methodologies and theories developed in cultural studies, semiotics, poststructuralism, psychology and sociology. The series focuses on popular musics of the twentieth and twenty-first centuries. It is designed to embrace the world's popular musics from Acid Jazz to Zydeco, whether high tech or low tech, commercial or non-commercial, contemporary or traditional.

Professor Derek B. Scott
Professor of Critical Musicology
University of Leeds

Acknowledgments

This book was written by a girl group, albeit one that has made only a few live appearances, has no name (although The Prof-ettes might work) and has cut no records. Our collaboration began as a study panel, organized by Annie Randall, at the 2002 US branch meeting of the International Association for the Study of Popular Music in Cleveland, OH, which was so stimulating we persuaded Annie to host a symposium the following year at Bucknell University. A further panel session, organized by Susan Fast, followed at the 2003 Houston meeting of the American Musicological Society. We are, of course, grateful to the organizers of the conferences, and in particular to Bucknell's Assistant Vice President for Academic Affairs, Jim Rice, for giving us a platform and allowing us time and space to air our ideas. We have acknowledged our intellectual debts in our individual chapters; but collectively we are also deeply grateful to our anonymous readers who commented so wisely and generously on the draft.

During this entire period and beyond, we conducted an email discussion on topics ranging from female baritones, Eurovision and the ideal syllabus for a course on twentieth-century girl singers to the effects on the skin of prolonged exposure to baked beans and whether or not it was appropriate to dance the Pony to "I Feel The Earth Move." This conversation is the backing track to the whole volume—in each essay, if you listen hard enough, you should be able to hear the shoo-wops and doo-langs of the other members of the group. And while I happily claim responsibility for the material discussed in the introduction, especially if anyone takes exception to it, I am equally delighted to acknowledge that it has been hugely informed and enriched by the opinions and wisdom of my co-contributors.

Introduction

She's So Fine, or Why Girl Singers (Still) Matter

Laurie Stras

On June 25, 2004, the sun was setting over more than 80,000 people at the culmination of the highest-grossing festival event yet staged anywhere in the world, the final Red Hot Chili Peppers concert in London's Hyde Park. Standing in the crowd with my eleven-year-old son I witnessed something I really had not expected: the performance of not one, but two, fragments of girl group classics by one of the most historically and overtly male-identified rock groups of the previous twenty years. Both were sung alone in a fragile falsetto by guitarist John Frusciante: the Shangri-Las' "Remember (Walkin' in the Sand)" was third in the set; the Chantels' "Maybe" came a little while later.

The girl group songs had a particular function in the structure of the overall performance—as quiet interludes, they eased transitions and allowed the ear to rest, simultaneously erasing the audience's aural memories of what had just been played and heightening curiosity for what would come next. Moreover, they complemented other aspects of homage during the gig that highlighted the band's eclectic sense of pedigree—Flea's Coltrane-inspired improvs, Chad Smith's medley of best-loved drum riffs, covers of Joy Division's "Transmission," 45 Grave's "Black Cross," Looking Glass's "Brandy" and, on a previous night, Donna Summer's "I Feel Love." Even so, by virtue of their incongruity there must have been more to their inclusion. The Red Hot Chili Peppers is not the first male band to cover girl group songs, even without overt irony—although many web-posting Frusciante fans appear to believe that "Remember (Walkin' in the Sand)" is an Aerosmith song.[1] But by making these songs a feature, the Peppers may also have purposefully exposed some of the raw musical materials used in their well-publicized and self-avowed millennial gender re-positioning, away from their youthful socks-on-cocks hyper-masculinity towards a more balanced, and perhaps inevitable, mature embracing of their feminine side. Look, they seemed to be saying, we're not just about funk and jazz and metal and rap; we value the Chantels and the Shangri-Las for what *they* have taught us about music, too.[2]

---

[1] Aerosmith's cover was released on *Night In The Ruts* (CBS 83681, 1979).

[2] This self-consciously informative strategy replayed in their 2006 tour, when the later 60s influences on the album *Stadium Arcadium* (Warner Bros 44222, 2006)—particularly

I admit to having gone to bed that night with joy in my heart at the thought of Arlene Smith being paid reverence by a guitar god, and with another welcome reassurance that my then current project—the essay that is included in this book—was truly relevant to the understanding of contemporary pop and rock, and, more broadly, popular culture as a whole. And I still have an irrational need for that reassurance, for as a working musician I long lived with the ignominy of being "just the girl singer," regardless of whether or not I was playing an instrument as well. Perhaps worse—in a group of female musicians where I did not play—I was "just the singer." Let me say this but once: girl singers are important. Chronically undervalued and dismissed both inside and outside the business as musically incompetent, intellectually challenged eye-candy, they have been the butt of musicians' jokes literally for centuries (I know a good one told by the Duke of Mantua in 1581). Girl singers tend to get short shrift, professionally and critically; and because of this historical reluctance to acknowledge that girls can have musical skill, talent and/or even genius, attempts to explain their undeniable appeal frequently relegate it to the animal—*it's sexy*—or to lowest common denominator commerciality—*it's pretty, but it isn't art*. Nonetheless, girl singers matter: if they didn't, we wouldn't listen to them or buy their records. We wouldn't use them to sell products from soft drinks to deodorant, we wouldn't—at a particular age, at least—seek to emulate them, we wouldn't remember their songs as clearly or as fondly as we do once we reach adulthood, and we certainly wouldn't parody them.

"What do you call a girl that hangs around with musicians?" "A singer"

Before going any further, it might be wise to at least try to pinpoint what distinguishes the girl singer from a woman who sings, and the girl group from women who sing. The latter is perhaps the simpler. The girl group is an identifiable community, a gang, a clique: its lyrical conversations can mimic the interaction between teenage girlfriends; its visual and vocal uniformity underline its cohesion as a social set, its appeal is directly expressed towards other girls. Musically, it is defined by its almost exclusive reliance on others for the practical realization of the performance or recording.[3] Oddly, even a mixed-voice group—such as the

---

the lush vocal harmonies à la Crosby, Stills and Nash—were heralded by Frusciante's solo performance of Simon and Garfunkel's "For Emily, Whenever I May Find Her."

[3]   Jacqueline Warwick provides this definition in the preface to her book *Girl Groups, Girl Culture* (New York and London, 2007), p. ix: "Girl group music as I define it comprises several distinct elements: an emphasis on the concerns and interests of teenage girls in its lyrics (i.e., boys, the strictness of parents, etc.); material prepared for the most part by professional songwriters; origins in the recording studio and dependent upon professional session musicians; an instrumental sound often dominated by orchestral instruments rather than the minimal rock'n'roll band lineup of guitar, bass guitar, and

INTRODUCTION

Exciters, the Essex, and the Ad Libs—can, to some commentators, qualify as a girl group, as long as the material and approach are right: the lead voice is always a girl; the guy(s) are part of the clique, they assist in the comment and response to the girl's story, and they are never the love interest.[4] As a culture, we are able to make these distinctions almost subconsciously. Although we may not have thought before about precisely what a girl group is, we nonetheless recognize one when we see or hear one: B*witched is a girl group; Sweet Honey in the Rock is not. Girl groups can launch solo careers (Diana Ross, Patti LaBelle, Beyoncé) but like male vocal groups they are not necessarily personality-specific: the Shangri-Las recorded as a quartet, but performed as a trio; the Blossoms recorded songs credited to the Crystals; even high-profile groups such as the Supremes had singers come and go.[5]

As the old joke shows, musicians may think they know what a girl singer is, but the matter is slightly more complicated than that. Like girl groups, a girl singer relies on others to make her voice heard, in the band and in the recording studio. Hers is a performative role: she takes instruction from the band or bandleader, but she is in front of the band. When she is singing, her focus is entirely on the audience—and the audience's focus is entirely on her. She is not expected to make music with the band, as much as sing over them. More than a musician, she is a commodity, and so *available*—either as a sexual partner or as a best friend/role model/big (or little) sister.[6] I frequently return to the quandary posed to me by a

---

drum kit; and above all, the audibly adolescent voices of girls interacting in dialogues between lead and backing vocalists."

[4] "Evidently, the exclusion of male voices was not what defined a girl group; there had only to be a girl lead singer with a story of romance to tell, and a group of mates, perhaps including a boy, to tell it to. The token male of the girl groups was a confidant, part of a closeted female society who shared the lead singer's emotional ups and downs with her, rather than a symbol of love's young dream in his own right; and so in the early days of girl-group music, he did not seem in the least out of place lurking amongst the petticoats of the chorus line;" Charlotte Greig, *Will You Still Love Me Tomorrow? Girl Groups From The 50s On ...* (London, 1989), p. 67.

[5] The Spice Girls are perhaps an exception to this trend, as their publicity and group personae was so heavily based upon the individual personae of its members: Sporty, Scary, Baby, Posh and Ginger Spice. When Ginger (Geri Halliwell) left the group in 1999, there was never a plan to replace her. But just how far beyond individual personalities the girl group is traditionally situated is illustrated by Phil Spector's comment to Al Aronowitz, reported in the *Saturday Evening Post* in 1963 ("handling" presumably means manipulating personnel): "A singer doesn't last long, three years, maybe—Presley's the exceptional phenomenon. A group, you can keep it sustained close to three years if you handle it properly."

[6] This might suggest that the girl singer is commodified for exchange between men, between men and other women, or even between herself and other women, so stretching Irigaray's model of woman as a commodity for exchange solely between men; see Luce Irigaray, *This Sex Which Is Not One*, trans. Catherine Porter (Ithaca, NY, 1985), p. 31. However, Irigaray later writes, "Just as commodities cannot make exchanges among

student some years ago: "Is the girl half of a duo still a girl singer?" It vexes me still, even after the class debate and much pondering afterwards, but I am inclined to say, "Not always," and if I weren't hedging my bets like a born educator I would probably say, "No." Girls performing in duos with a male singer do not tend to interact with the audience in the same way the solo girl singer does. Cher was Sonny's wife; Shirley and Lee were "the Sweethearts of the Blues"; these relationships take precedence over our relationship with them. They are promised or taken by another, their primary focus is not the audience but their partner; so while these singers might *be* girls, they don't function as girls.[7]

The language we choose to label the girl singer reveals all. Although "girl" and "woman" denote vague chronological or biological stages of female development, they also have important subjective connotations depending on the attitude of the viewer.[8] A girl singer may clearly be "all woman," but even if she possesses the near cartoon proportions of Jayne Mansfield, when she gets on stage she is still a girl singer: curiously subjugate, but also paramount; necessary for the spectacle but not for the craft. Furthermore, from the onset of rock and roll until very recently (when in the mid-1990s childbearing and children became a distinct fashion statement) there was a lingering sense that only the young and, if not virginal, at least unfecundated should strut their stuff—hence the brouhaha that greeted the heavily pregnant Neneh Cherry after her mini-skirted appearance on the BBC's *Top of the Pops* in 1989. We do not want girl singers to be women.[9] The reason for this is simple: "girls" are much easier to objectify than women—that's why

---

themselves without the intervention of a subject that measures them against a standard, so it is with women. Distinguished, divided, separated, classified as like and unlike, according to whether they have been judged exchangeable. In themselves, among themselves, they are amorphous and confused: natural body, maternal body, doubtless useful to the consumer, but without any possible identity or communicable value" (p. 187). The "subject" is the producer/record company/music business who sets the standard for value—in terms of the singer's desirability, musically and visually. The girl singer as a commodity may be consumed by other women, but it is men who determine the marketplace.

[7] This exclusivity is not present in single-sex duos. We do not care, when they are performing, at least, about the relationship between the Judds, the Everly Brothers, or Sam and Dave. Nor is it present when the male half of the duo is not a singer. Whatever the bond between Yazoo's Vince Clark and Alison Moyet, or the Ting Tings' Jules De Martino and Katie White, we understand the singer's primary relationship—in performance, at least—is with us, the audience.

[8] And perhaps also the singer: in 1992, at the age of 64, Rosemary Clooney released an album on the Concord Jazz label called *Girl Singer*; seven years later she published a memoir of the same name. Despite her advanced years, she clearly self-identified strongly with the term.

[9] This seems also to fit within Irigaray's model of *virgin, mother* and *prostitute* as the social roles imposed on women: "The virginal woman, on the other hand, is pure exchange value," Irigaray, p. 186.

we have cover *girls*, dancing *girls* and *Girl* Fridays.[10] Women—that is, girls who have undertaken some kind of rite of passage, however culturally defined—are no longer commodities; they do not represent something that is available. Even in the post-feminist era, girls only become women when they stop engaging with the objectification. We almost never hear tell of "women singers," except as a self-conscious strategy that, following traditional feminist practice, pointedly avoids the pejorative subtext of "girl."

Like the office girl, the girl singer is at the bottom of the professional heap. She becomes a woman musician only when she proves herself artistically equal to her male colleagues (by whatever means, but usually by outdoing them on a massive scale), when she takes musical responsibility for herself by no longer relying on the men around her, or appears to be beyond the crass manipulation of the industry by embracing an alternative socio/political cause. And yet, the girl singer has a privileged place, a pedestal all of her own, even if she is not elevated for the purposes of respect or protection so much as sensory consumption. She is an object of desire and an icon of possibility, be it sexual, aspirational, or even nostalgic in nature.

As befitting such prominent players in popular and mass culture, books about girl singers geared to the fan or the so-called lay reader are plentiful, particularly of the authorized, and unauthorized, biographical ilk. Books about individual girl groups are much fewer and further between. Although the commercial machines surrounding contemporary groups such as the Spice Girls or the Corrs may throw up a variety of publications from sticker books to picture biographies, books on individual groups from previous generations are conspicuous by their absence: by my reckoning, only the Spice Girls, the Supremes, the Marvelettes and the Andrews Sisters have full-length treatments in print—this in comparison to a host of books on male groups. There is a small handful of books that deal with the girl group phenomenon as a whole, and some chapters within books on broader topics such as women in rock or histories of pop singing, but considering the vast industry that publishes on rock and popular music, the field is pitifully small.[11]

---

[10]   "Originally feminists expressed dislike of the word 'girl' for much the same reasons that black men refuse to answer to 'boy'. An adult woman is called a 'girl' in order to emphasize her inferior status … . English men have not quite shed their repellent habit of referring to the women who work for them as 'girls', as if insisting upon their junior, inferior status, no matter what their age. In Australia men used to refer to their secretaries as 'their girls' as in 'Ring my girl, she'll take care of it.'"; Germaine Greer, *The Whole Woman* (London, 2000), pp. 404–05.

[11]   Book-length treatments include Alan Betrock, *Girl Groups: The Story of a Sound* (London and New York, 1982), a narrative account of American groups; John Clemente, *Girl Groups: Fabulous Females That Rocked The World* (Iola, WI, 2000), an encyclopaedic resource, with discographies and potted histories; Greig, *Will You Still Love Me Tomorrow?*, is a more journalistic review, with substantial interview material. David Freeland's *Ladies of Soul* (Jackson, MS, 2001) is a collection of oral histories, mainly of singers more strongly identified with soul, but includes chapters on Carla Thomas and Timi Yuro. There are

Within the academy, girl pop singers have fared somewhat worse than they do even in the wider world; in fact, they might be seen to be suffering from a triple threat. As women, they tend to be but footnotes to male-centered histories of popular culture and popular music, but (with the notable exception of Madonna, the Riot Grrrl movement, and a flurry of articles on the Spice Girls in the late 1990s) unless they are also songwriters they are equally disdained by most gender studies, even within musicology. Not only do they bring with them the baggage of their critical and professional dubiousness, but also they are frequently considered as subjects unsuitable for positive critique, as in many cases they appear to embody all that feminist thinking and scholarship seeks to debunk. There are some outlying areas of cultural criticism, particularly those theoretically allied to studies of fandom/fetishism, that have attempted to think seriously about girl singers, but even as this work is essential and welcome, via the sometimes circular logic of the academic study of difference it nonetheless has counterproductive potential: as icons of Otherness, girl singers simultaneously can be celebrated and their power denied—rather like placing a few startling sentences in a centered box on a page of otherwise continuous text. So until very recently few academic articles, and even fewer books, have discussed girls' contributions to pop music as integral parts of popular culture and social history on their own terms.[12] This is not to say that there is not a significant contingent of scholars who know that they should know more about the impact of girls in pop, especially those of the 1950s and 1960s, but acknowledging a lacuna (or series of lacunae) is very different to being motivated enough to address that lack, and to recognizing the full implications of continuing to shrug the shoulders and saying, "yup, there's something missing."

The one body of so-called mainstream academic work that has dealt anything more than passing critical attention to 60s girl singers and groups are those articles

---

chapters on girl groups in Susan Douglas, *Where The Girls Are: Growing Up Female with the Mass Media* (London, 1995); Gillian Gaar, *She's a Rebel: The History of Women in Rock and Roll* (Seattle, 1992); Anthony Gribin and Matthew Schiff, *The Complete Book of Doo-Wop* (Iola, WI, 2000); Lucy O'Brien, *She Bop II: The Definitive History of Women in Rock, Pop and Soul* (London, 2002); Barbara O'Dair (ed.), *Trouble Girls: The Rolling Stone Book of Women in Rock* (New York, 1997); Jay Warner, *American Singing Groups: A History 1940–1990* (New York, 1992).

[12]   Barbara Bradby, "Do-Talk and Don't-Talk: The Division of the Subject in Girl-Group Music," in Simon Frith and Andrew Goodwin (eds), *On Record: Rock, Pop and the Written Word*, (London and New York, 1990) pp. 341–68; Patricia Juliana Smith, "'Ask Any Girl': Compulsory Heterosexuality and Girl Group Culture," in Kevin Dettmar and William Richey (eds), *Reading Rock and Roll: Authenticity, Appropriation, Aesthetics* (New York, 1999), pp. 93–124; Cynthia Cyrus, "Selling an Image: Girl Groups of the 1960s," *Popular Music* 22/2 (2003): 173–93; Jacqueline Warwick, "'He's Got the Power': The Politics of Production in Girl Group Music," in Sheila Whiteley, Andy Bennett, and Stan Hawkins (eds), *Music, Space and Place: Popular Music and Cultural Identity* (Aldershot: 2004), pp. 191–200; Warwick, *Girl Groups, Girl Culture*.

INTRODUCTION

that point out their influence on more prestigious male artists or repertoires.[13] Why we (and yes, I just did this myself at the beginning of this introduction, so I can say "we") choose to do this is not necessarily because we suffer from a behind-every-great-man mentality that suggests girl singers are worthy of notice just because they inspired the Beatles, or the Peppers, or even Aerosmith. We may not feel that this is the best way to argue them into the canon, or that it's worth bothering to do so, either because the constructedness of the canon seems suspect to us, or because we realize that it would be an uphill struggle against an impossibly steep gradient. But even if we kick our kitten heels—or our Doc Martens—and say, "Canon formation? How twentieth-century!" the legacy of our academic training is mighty strong. In order to have our work taken seriously, we are obliged to site it within the context of that which has gone before, we must proceed from the known to the unknown, and quite simply the only "known" out there is the male-centered History of Rock. More prosaically, it is a strategy that just might gain the attention of a wider readership from the outset. And, ultimately, girl singers don't live in a vacuum: they sing and develop alongside male musicians, hence overlap and inspiration are inevitable, and it is quite right and proper to evaluate them. But, like difference, influence or genealogy cannot be the only lens through which we view girls in pop.

The 60s girl pop singer is, without a doubt, an enduring icon of popular culture, with references cropping up in all manner of other forms of entertainment and media from the Sesame Street Squirelles singing "My Boyfriend's Back (And Front)" to the Chorus in Disney's film *Hercules* (1997), the lead singer of which is clearly drawn to resemble Diana Ross.[14] The use of musical and visual styles can seem indiscriminate; for instance, in spring 2006, there were at least three national ad campaigns on UK terrestrial television using girl group pastiches: for fabric softener, car insurance and residential mortgages. Broadway-shows-turned-Hollywood-musicals *Dreamgirls* (2006) and *Hairspray* (2007) have retold stories of the 1960s music business, retrospectively examining issues of race, class and gender with pathos and humor. British singers Amy Winehouse and Duffy summoned comparisons in 2008: looking and sounding respectively like Ronnie Spector's and Dusty Springfield's faerie love-children, their records

---

[13] Including, but not limited to: Barbara Bradby, "She Told Me What to Say: The Beatles and Girl Group Discourse," *Popular Music and Society* 28/3 (2005): 359-90; Ian Inglis, "'Some Kind of Wonderful': The Creative Legacy of the Brill Building," *American Music* 21/2 (2003): 214–35; Warwick, "You're Going To Lose That Girl. The Beatles and the Girl Groups," in Yrjö Heinonen, Markus Heuger, Sheila Whiteley, Terhi Nurmesjärvi and Jouni Koskimäki. Jyväskylä (eds), *Beatlestudies 3. Proceedings of the Beatles 2000 conference*, Department of Music, Research Reports 23 (University of Jyväskylä, 2001): 161–7; Greg Panfile, "Boys will be Girl Group, or the Johnettes," in *Soundscapes—Journal on Media Culture* (1999), http://www.icce.rug.nl/~soundscapes/ (accessed ?).

[14] The Squirelles were introduced in 1993 to help correct the gender balance of the Sesame Street Muppets; "Media Column," *Education Week*, July 14, 1993.

also reverently reference the girl group genre. In the same year, on the other side of the Atlantic, country singer Shelby Lynne released an entire album of Dusty Springfield songs, *Just a Little Lovin'*. Neo-girl groups, such as the Dansettes in the US and the Pipettes in the UK, knowingly use retro fashions, graphics and musical arrangements to invoke the era of their mothers'—or more correctly, grandmothers'—youth. But there is also still a taste for the real thing. Many original members of 60s girl groups still tour the festival circuit singing their hits to new generations. Re-release labels Rhino Records (US) and Ace Records (UK) both produced monumental collections of both rare and not-so-rare girl group singles, Rhino in particular seeming to have invested a great deal of publicists' time and money in creating as big a splash for the release as possible.[15] And, as if finally to recognize the importance of girl groups to not just popular culture, or mass culture, but Culture with a capital C, London's Victoria and Albert Museum launched a major exhibition in 2008 called "The Story of the Supremes," which toured the country after a six-month installation. As the song says, pretty girls are everywhere, indeed.

But the girl singers of the 1960s are more than just a show business convention, or a stylistic referent for historically aware or musically curious male rock groups; they have an importance that we ignore at our peril if we seek to understand our contemporary social dynamics. They were feminine archetypes for millions of adolescent baby-boomers on either side of the Atlantic: what girls were (or thought they should be), and what boys thought that girls were (or that they should be). As Barbara Bradby has noted, the girl talk of the 60s girl singers was revelatory to both sexes; through their music, girls actively initiated a dialogue with, and required a response from, boys.[16] The popularity of girl singers allowed young African American women, and young working-class white women, to be socially visible for the first time, and on a grand scale. For better or worse, the models for behavior and attitude projected by 60s girl singers shaped the generation that produced both second-wave feminism and the feminist backlash; and without the practice run girl singers gained in the media, later feminist voices, both black and white, would not have been heard quite so loudly or effectively.[17]

It would be wrong to suggest that girl groups, and especially girl singers, emerged—like Venus—as new, never-before-seen entities in the wake of rock and roll's tidal wave in the late 1950s. Throughout the twentieth century, young (and not so young) women had careers as soloists with dance bands and jazz combos, as stage comediennes, in harmony groups and in male/female duos, from Ruth Etting, Ethel Waters, the Brox and Boswell Sisters through the canary era of Ella Fitzgerald, Anita O'Day and Billie Holiday that also produced latter-day

---

[15]   *One Kiss Can Lead To Another: Girl Group Sounds Lost & Found* (four disc set) (Rhino Records 74645, 2005); *Early Girls, Volumes 1–4* (Ace Records, 1995–2005) and *Where the Girls Are, Volumes 1–6* (Ace Records, 1997–2004).

[16]   Bradby, "She Told Me What to Say."

[17]   Douglas, 83–98.

comediennes like Doris Day and Rosemary Clooney. Yet the rock and roll era did produce something new: teenage girl singers who sang like, about, and for teenagers. Although the history of 50s and 60s girl singers is not explicitly told in any of the essays in *She's So Fine*, what appears to be a truth emerges from them; namely, that girl singers were almost universally denied agency in their own careers, and it was only those who seized opportunity, or who fought for a career on their own terms, who had any chance (but by no means a guarantee) of success beyond a few years, or even a few records. For many members of girl groups, that membership granted them little more than a few months' stardom and a few years' hard graft, with no financial reward or security at the end of it all. We may have a sense that solo singers fared better, for we can all think of women—indeed most of the women in this book—whose careers extended into the next decade and beyond; and we can all name members of girl groups who have transcended group status and found success on their own. The reality may be that girl groups are essentially unsustainable (*pace* Phil Spector's and Berry Gordy's respective attempts to make the Crystals and the Supremes into concepts into which any number of anonymous singers could be inserted) because too many variables—too many life events and personal decisions—come into play. Furthermore, if the constituent audience for the girl group is the teenage girl, then the life of the relationship between group and audience is self-limiting, for eventually the teenage girl becomes a woman, with different priorities, emotional needs, dilemmas and demands. Girl groups do not speak of or to women—name me a girl group song that discusses the proper bedtime for a five-year-old, keeping house on five dollars a week, or what a girl could possibly do with an education once she got it.[18]

Solo singers, on the other hand, have much more potential to be flexible. The solo girl singer who is not a one-trick pony—at least in musical terms—and who can retain the support of her record company, can ride the rapidly changing fashions in pop music through adapting her repertoire and her performance style; Madonna appears to do this effortlessly (although surely a great deal of effort is involved). Moreover, the girl singer can go into acting, she can host TV shows, she can even mature with her audience as well as develop a relationship with a new generation, if her material and her image are carefully chosen and crafted. But the career trajectory for the girl singer is not always straightforward: Cilla Black, Diana Ross, Lulu and Cher may have been more or less continuously employed at the top end of show business for forty-odd years and have had top 10 singles in the 2000s, but they have all diversified into other forms of entertainment: TV and radio compering, film, stage musicals. Frequently, careers are revived or prolonged by a collaboration with a currently successful artist or group: Diana Ross with Westlife; Dusty Springfield with the Pet Shop Boys; Lulu with Take That and

---

[18]   The exception that proves the rule is, of course, LaBelle—first the Ordettes, and then Patti LaBelle and the Bluebelles—who, under the guidance of Vicki Wickham, relaunched themselves in the UK in the 1970s as a female rock group, singing about racism, politics and sex from an adult perspective.

Ronan Keating; Sandie Shaw with the Smiths; Tina Turner with any number of white male rock artists. Others, such as Darlene Love and Janis Ian, have grafted away for decades away from the limelight, developing and retaining audiences outside the mainstream pop charts. Some have battled—successfully (Sandie Shaw) and unsuccessfully (Ronnie Spector)—for control of their catalogues or at least some share of the royalties accrued by their hits. But most have simply had to get on with life, as shown by John Clemente's potted "where-are-they-now" biographies, which list subsequent occupations as diverse as dental hygienists and bank executives: girls may just want to have fun, but a woman's work is never done.[19]

Good girls: Doxa and conformity in the 50s and 60s

This book began its long road to publication in 2002, when Annie Randall suggested to some colleagues that it would be good to put together a panel on 60s girl group pop for the annual meeting of the US branch of the International Association for the Study of Popular Music, which was held in Cleveland. For most of us, it was an opportunity to explore something we had not looked at before, or which had been tangential to our previous scholarship: only Patricia Smith and Jacqueline Warwick had published previously on the subject. We each had ten minutes: a riotous hour ensued, with much laughter, singing along and begging (on the audience's part) to just hear a *little* bit more of that track, *please* … . Perhaps the venue helped solidify the notion in our minds that this work was worth continuing: a few blocks away stood the Rock and Roll Hall of Fame, that bastion of the male popular music canon, where we had to search long and hard to find the few items of girl group/ girl singer memorabilia on show (at that time, only the Shirelles, the Supremes, Martha Reeves and the Vandellas, Aretha Franklin, Dusty Springfield, Tina Turner, and Brenda Lee were inductees—since then, only the Ronettes and Wanda Jackson have been added). Although there was no attempt to coordinate our contributions, we found—both at the conference and in our subsequent email conversation and symposium meeting—that certain themes kept cropping up. Stated most broadly, these themes are gender, race, class, and adolescence; but more specifically, we seemed all to be grappling with the spaces in which these issues intersected in the pop music of the late 1950s and early 1960s, especially in the English-speaking ambit of the US and the post-Empire British Commonwealth.

Gender, race, adolescence, and class are four distinct yet interconnected axes of identity that themselves are and have been fundamental to the identity of British and American teenage girls; any consideration of their music must confront these constructs as they are embodied and projected by British and American girl singers. Each category relies upon the others for its production: the perception of femininity is inflected by youth, race and manners; race can be implied by conventions of femininity and "breeding," as well as certain adolescent behaviors; class may

---

[19] Clemente, *passim*.

be articulated through performances of femininity, ethnicity, and maturity; the experience of adolescence, socially and biologically, is largely determined by gender, class, and race. The interconnectedness and interdependence of these constructs typically cause them to become conflated, or to obscure each other—only meticulous and patient enquiry can tease out the strands of identity that they produce. Moreover, after many years of theoretical discourse to encourage such a view, there is a strong tendency to see these categories as primarily indicative of difference. Yet whilst categories of gender, race, age, and class undeniably signify difference for those who are held beyond their borders, for those who self-identify within them they are as much or more about conformity. And, indeed, the formation of identity—either group or individual—involves not just the processes of identification and differentiation, but also a considerable amount of what Susan Friedman calls "play," exploring what lies between the boundaries of the binaries that separate Us from Them.[20]

If for a moment one considers these categories from the perspective of sameness rather than difference, as a function of and determined by a self-forming group, their boundaries become better viewed as fluctuating rather than permeable. For instance, Ruth Frankenberg says whiteness, as an articulation of race, is "more about the power to include and exclude groups and individuals than about the actual practices of those who are to be let in or kept out," and the same may well hold true for the other three constructs.[21] So while the acquisition of certain traits, or the ability to perform them well enough to be accepted within a group, is a matter for the individual, the success of his or her enterprise is a matter of the group's agency alone. Moreover, the desire to be different (or differentiated) may fuel a group's formation, but it is the desire for conformity that sustains its power balance, both within its community and against those that it excludes. Anyone who has had experience of girls' cliques at school will know how this works. The clique decides what's "in"; someone wishing to join the clique will do whatever she can to meet the criteria. If the clique wants her, it will accept her; if it doesn't, it will find some new criterion on which to reject her. Conversely, if the clique decides it wishes to admit someone new, regardless of who she is, what she looks like, or what she does, it may change its criteria in order to make her "fit."

If we recognize that notions of gender, race, age, and class are contingent upon each other, we must also recognize that they are themselves contingent upon temporal and geographical factors; what constitutes belonging to any category of inclusion varies with time and place. Again, for instance, Frankenberg signals her collection's intention to displace whiteness as "the unmarked marker" and to engage critically with the variability in the construction of race in different locations

---

[20] Susan Friedman, *Mappings: Feminism and the Cultural Geographies of Encounter* (Princeton, 1998), pp. 74–6.

[21] Ruth Frankenberg, "Introduction: Local Whitenesses, Localizing Whiteness," in Ruth Frankenberg (ed.), *Displacing Whiteness: Essays in Social and Cultural Criticism* (Durham, NC, 1997), p. 13.

and eras. Our other constructs also have normative paradigms that may be seen to be equally "local" and equally slippery.[22] While there are many similarities and common experiences to be found for young women of the 1950s and 1960s living in the US and Britain, it is as well to be aware of some important differences. In biological terms, adolescence may have arrived at approximately the same age for 1950s British and American youths. However, British teenagers who, by dint of economic status or ability, did not go on to further or higher education, were expected to enter the world of work upon leaving school at fifteen, while their American counterparts were much more likely to stay on at school until seventeen or eighteen.[23] At the beginning of the 1950s (before the scale and the permanence of non-white immigration had registered with those who would eventually object) social and economic status in Britain were less inflected by race than they were by ethnicity within British borders: southern Home Counties origin took precedence over northern or Celtic roots.[24] And although skin color may have been a prime determinant in the US, ethnicity—especially when articulated through religion—and regionality also informed social and economic status, particularly in local constructions.[25] Jewish, Catholic, Eastern European, Mediterranean, and Southern American "white trash" communities hovered around the boundaries of what Frankenburg calls *doxa*[26]—the norm, the "national/natural state of being"—at some times excluded and at others embraced.

Because doxa is normal, it is invisible; it is the unmarked, default setting. Doxa is the fantasy absolute against which deviance can be measured by those it includes or those who seek inclusion. For our British and American teenage girls in the late 1950s and early 1960s, doxa meant white (non-white always being determined by a discrete racial or ethnic marker, yet solely *defined* by exclusion from dominant white culture, therefore made up of an indeterminate number and type of racial/ethnic groups) and "respectable," that is, aspiring or belonging to a

---

[22] Ibid., pp. 1–33.

[23] "Only about 14 percent of British 15–18-year-olds were in school in 1950, whereas the United States was graduating 59 percent of its youth from high schools and 75 percent were enrolled in high schools." Claudia Goldin and Lawrence Katz, "Why the United States Led in Education: Lessons from Secondary School Expansion, 1910 to 1940," Working Paper 6144, NBER Working Paper Series [USA] (National Bureau of Economic Research, 1997), p. 20, n. 11.

[24] The only significant non-Celtic or Anglo-Saxon ethnicity—the Jewish community—was by the late 1950s largely assimilated into the middle classes; Todd Endleman, *The Jews of Britain* (Berkeley, 2002), p. 240. The Afro-Caribbean community was tiny by comparison, its youth representing only 2 per cent of the school population in 1964; see *The Moving Here* project, http://www.movinghere.org.uk/galleries/histories/caribbean/growing_up/education.htm#, UK National Archives (accessed October 8, 2008).

[25] Categories of ethnicity and their boundaries are discussed in a number of specific and more general texts on whiteness; a good summary may be found in Richard Dyer, *White* (London and New York, 1997), particularly pp. 48–60.

[26] Frankenberg, p. 16.

socio-economic group not marked by either great deprivation or great wealth, but which embraced certain values regarding feminine virtue that were specifically bound up with economic and social behaviors.[27] Whilst acknowledging the distinct differences between British and American understandings of class, within this group in both societies expectations and aspirations for girls' and women's behaviors were broadly the same: marriage and domestic competence (if not aptitude) were expected, women's first responsibility was to home and family, and if as wives they had to work, they should strive to do so in strictly segregated jobs that did not compromise their respectability.

Drawing again on the experiences of my own family, I might offer for comparison the experiences of my American mother, Judy, and my British mother-in-law, Eunice, both of whom came from families that might be considered to be "lower middle class" in the US and "upper working class" in the UK—not quite blue-collar but certainly the first generation not to be so. They are remarkably similar, despite not being entirely contemporaneous (my mother married in 1959, Eunice in 1948). Both women completed secondary education; my mother also went to university on a scholarship, graduating Phi Beta Kappa.[28] In their early twenties, both married officer engineers who would leave national service to enter industry, so both married into the professional middle class. Both had their first child within a year of marriage, and went on to have a second soon after. Both women went to work—my mother as a teacher, Eunice as a secretary. Eunice quit work once she was married, but my mother did not immediately, as by this time she was also a "graduate wife"—but she was only working for what she and her friends called their PhT's ("Putting Him Through") and quit when my father finished his master's degree. Both Mom and Eunice were raised with the expectation of exactly this kind of "career path," although both also had to acquire and utilize further skills that would increase their respectability: for instance, Eunice clearly worked hard to moderate her London East End accent and saw herself as a professional City girl; my mother studied Amy Vanderbilt (as did I!) to learn how to set the table for multiple courses when my father brought his boss

---

[27] For a more nuanced discussion, see Karen Brodkin, *How the Jews Became White Folks and What That Says About Race in America* (New Brunswick, NJ, 1998) in Chapter 3, "Race, Gender and Virtue," pp. 77–102; "White women were by presumption good women; they either did not work for wages or they did so in ways that preserved their femininity and respectability—not least, by being separated from their male peers and nonwhites. White women were presumed to be good women and thereby deserving of male protection, but their virtue was contingent on the extent to which they fulfilled the ideals of dependence upon, and domestic service to, men and stayed in their proper place of heterosexual domesticity. If they left 'home,' they too risked losing their privileges" (p. 101).

[28] Phi Beta Kappa is a prestigious academic honor society, the oldest in the US, which "celebrates and advocates excellence in the liberal arts and sciences" through inviting for induction "the most outstanding arts and sciences students at America's leading colleges and universities," http://www.pbk.org (accessed March 3, 2008).

home for dinner. Curiously, here their stories differ: accent was and is not a great indicator of status in local hierarchies in the US, so my mother's teaching-honed elocution was perfectly adequate for social advancement; Eunice had learned the art of elegant dining from her grandmother who had been in domestic service (for the nobility, she *always* stressed), and who regularly set her own Sunday lunch table in Manor Park as carefully as if it were in a stately home.

The point of this small excursion is to illustrate that although the class systems of the UK and the US were and are very different (even if East Coast, and particularly Southern East Coast, hierarchies are somewhat similar to the British, based as much on family history as wealth or profession), at a local level in both countries the mechanics of social aspiration and advancement, and the experience of young women whose lives were governed by doxa in the decade or so after the war, weren't that far apart. The urge towards self-improvement was powerful; if you wished to advance, you aspired to conform to doxa, and once there, you realized that doxa in itself was aspirational—and so never quite attainable. You might be among those who set the standard locally—so you could be part of a group that included or excluded—but there was always another tier to which you could rise. This speaks volumes to the condition of female adolescence, which has been described as "a set of discourses on self-monitoring—on analyzing yourself in relation to other girls to identify and verify the kind of girl you are and your relations to dominant models for women and femininity."[29] And while it has been acknowledged that working-class girls of whatever race share more experiences among themselves than they do with girls of their own race in higher-status, higher-income groups, and so feel less pressure to conform to notions of idealized femininity than their middle-class counterparts, in this post-war period the *only* way for women to advance economically (and therefore socially) was to conform, and the pressure to advance economically was felt keenly by all.[30]

But how did girls know to what they should conform? It's a moot point. The slipperiness of post-war doxa is highlighted and complicated by the fact that our chosen timeframe is bisected by a cluster of events that impinged radically upon it. As Wini Brienes puts it: "Perhaps John Kennedy's assassination is as accurate a dividing line as any other, but so could be the 1964 murders in the South of young civil rights workers …, the escalation of the war in Vietnam, the Beatles' explosion onto the American scene, or the 1963 publication of Betty Friedan's *The Feminine Mystique*."[31] In Britain at the beginning of the 1960s, British neo-Nazis and white supremacists joined forces to form the British National Party, the National Socialist Movement, and the paramilitary group Spearhead, targeting the black,

---

[29] Catherine Driscoll, *Girls: Feminine Adolescence in Popular Culture and Cultural Theory* (New York, 2002), p. 169.

[30] Jill Taylor, Carol Gilligan and Amy Sullivan, *Between Voice and Silence: Women and Girls, Race and Relationship* (Cambridge, MA, and London, 1995) p. 40.

[31] Wini Breines, *Young, White and Miserable: Growing Up Female in the Fifties* (Chicago and London, 1992), p. xii.

Jewish, Cypriot, Maltese and Irish communities with diatribe and violence. Then in 1963, the Profumo Affair rocked the establishment: Christine Keeler, a working-class, white, teenage girl (who, moreover, had West Indian lovers) conducted simultaneous liaisons with a Cabinet minister and with a Russian diplomat. The scandal contributed to the downfall of the Conservative government the following year. On both sides of the Atlantic, these events were symptomatic of, triggered by, or themselves set in train, significant social upheaval, made manifest by instabilities in doxa, not just in terms of race but also of gender, age, and class.

What's so sweet about sweet sixteen? Teen identity and girl singers

The repertoire and genre generally referred to as "girl group music" came into being in the late 1950s and had faded, or at least transformed, by the end of 1964; its demise could be seen as emblematic of the changes being wrought in British and American societies. As such it flourished at a time when doxa was relatively stable and therefore invisible, but when femininity was circumscribed by fairly rigid, and highly visible, codes.[32] This dichotomy of marked and unmarked, visible and invisible, created tensions: the overarching normality of whiteness and respectability obscured the implausibility and even impossibility of so-called normal female beauty and behavior (such as is determined by income) portrayed in contemporary mass culture on both sides of the Atlantic. Adolescent girls were bombarded by the mixed messages, but nonetheless struggled against sometimes almost insurmountable difficulties to mould themselves into the ideal.[33] It is apt that the near-twin paragons of young girls' aspirations and fantasies, the American Barbie and the British Sindy, were both launched in this period (and still survive today); toys with "emphatic femininity" that "may feel real enough to serve as touchstones or role models ... as emblems of who [girls] want to be,"[34] but which also "can only continue to articulate gender norms by being unfixed, by emphasizing the mobility of such norms."[35] The dolls embodied a fixed ideal of emerging womanhood for the English-speaking world, and the paraphernalia around them imbued them with the values of middle-class respectability, but

---

[32] An important distinction needs to be drawn here between contemporary (i.e. 1950s and 1960s) interpretations of "middle class" in the UK and the US. While the UK was—and to some extent still is—mired in a complex class hierarchy that depended much on parents and parentage, post-war America fostered the growth of an economic middle class that was marked by its relative permeability (exceptions made, of course, for non-whites and poor white southerners). When using the term here, I wish also to embrace what was known as "the affluent working classes" in the UK—a stratum that would have been considered middle-class in the US.

[33] Breines, pp. 95–101.

[34] Mary Rogers, *Barbie Culture* (London, 1999), p. 19.

[35] Driscoll, p. 100.

girls of any racial or ethnic background could use them as tools of fantasy either to identify with and imagine themselves as the norm, or to insert that feminine paradigm into any situation, however ostensibly inappropriate.

It is generally accepted that the concept of the teenager is American, gradually exported to first the English-speaking world, and then globally, perhaps a product of the pre-war American project of free secondary education that allowed adolescence to take place at least partially unhindered by the responsibility of work. One of the questions we asked ourselves in the long email conversation that accompanied the preparation of these essays was whether "white" was an inevitable but invisible corollary of "teen" in the 1950s and 1960s. The erasure of non-doxa experience from historical accounts of the American teenager is common, with two exceptions: the participation of African American teenagers in the Civil Rights movement; and their innovation in the arena of popular music— although this generally occurs only in relation to white teenagers' adoption of non-white music as an act of rebellion.[36] This could be explained, however, by observing that the teen experience captured and promulgated by the mainstream media in 1950s and early 1960s America (and which was then emulated in Britain) was almost exclusively doxa—white and respectable. In Britain, much the same situation obtained; non-doxa communities—including the Celtic ethnicities—were rarely represented in popular culture. Even the critical and uncompromising strand of social "kitchen sink" realism that produced dramas such as John Osborne's *Look Back in Anger* (1956) and Shelagh Delaney's *A Taste of Honey* (1958) had Anglo-Saxon protagonists, however low their status.[37] Many studies of emerging teen culture published in hindsight tend to use popular media for their analytical material and as evidence, so it is not surprising that histories present such a monochrome tale.

Explicitly or implicitly, the practice of equating "teen" with "white teen," or assuming the experience of white, respectable or aspiring-to-respectable teenagers was broadly replicated for adolescents from other ethnic and economic groups, was and is easy, if incorrect.[38] But on the other hand, it is equally incorrect to say

---

[36] For instance, this is the case in an otherwise excellent book by Thomas Doherty, *Teenagers and Teenpics: The Juvenilization of American Movies in the 1950s* (Philadelphia, 2002).

[37] At first glance, one might perceive that Shelagh Delaney's play *A Taste of Honey*, written when she was 18 and first produced by Joan Littlewood's Theatre Workshop in London in 1958, is a product of a teenager writing about teen problems. However beguiling a thought, and however pertinent the play's issues would be to a teenager—interracial sex, homosexuality, pregnancy outside marriage, family conflict—the play does not treat them primarily from the point of view of adolescence. Rather Jo and Geoffrey's predicaments are adult ones, perhaps intensified by their lack of experience, but not characterized solely by it.

[38] See, for instance, Thomas Hine, *The Rise and Fall of the American Teenager* (New York, 2000), pp. 185–87: "Demure behavior, modesty, and virginity at marriage were expected of young women of English stock, as they were of the Irish, Jews, Italians, and

that non-doxa adolescents refused or were unable to engage, identify with and aspire to the paradigms presented to them by the media—in fact, sometimes quite the opposite happened. This was not just a matter of young girls attempting to conform to impossible beauty standards.[39] If the media showed teens sitting at the counter in soda shops, then that's where teens should sit; and if the teen experience on show was not differentiated by color, then all teens (of whatever color) would have felt encouraged to identify with and feel an entitlement for that experience. Perhaps it was precisely this sense of identification, the impulse towards sameness, that led young African Americans to participate so readily in civil rights protests and non-violent anti-segregation actions, as they would wish for themselves the experience the media told them was appropriate for people of their age.

In terms of girl singers and girl groups, stressing the commonality of teenager-hood is to recognize that all girls were subject to the same commercial conditioning, and moreover that their status as entertainers made them part of the very industries that were creating and engaging "teen" as a commercial market and a commodity itself. The easy fit between the girl singer and some form of idealized teenage femininity on both sides of the Atlantic is demonstrated by the marketing paraphernalia of Barbie and Sindy: in 1961, two years after her launch, Barbie released her own album of six songs on three 45rpm singles, *Barbie Sings*, while Sindy's 1963 launch was accompanied by a promotional single and TV advertisement campaign featuring a Breakaways-like girl group wailing, "Sweet Sindy, the name is Sindy!". It is quite clear that from the time of the Shirelles' "Will You Love Me Tomorrow," frequently cited as the "breakthrough" girl group record, the visual codes and behaviors broadcast by both black and white girl groups kept well within doxa. In her article on the visual management of girl groups, Cynthia Cyrus claims that the common strategy was to present a "race- and class-*neutral*" [my emphasis] image to encourage a feeling of conformity and belonging in the groups' target consumers, adolescent girls.[40] However, on closer examination, the attributes she lists are far from neutral, as they emphasized white European beauty norms and financial comfort: for African Americans these included straightened hair, clothes that demonstrated a high disposable income and charm school diction and manners.[41] The Ronettes may have been "fabulous"

---

nearly everyone else … . Their mothers, whether Irish, Italian, Jewish, or Yankee, wanted to maintain their daughters' marriageability by protecting their virtue and reputation." What does this say about African American (and even Southern white) young women? Nonetheless, personal memoirs of African American adolescents show a sometimes quite different experience during their teen years; see Breines, pp. 13–17, 148–51 and elsewhere.

[39]   See Breines, pp. 95–99, for a discussion of non-white teenage girls' attempts to conform to standards of white beauty.

[40]   Cyrus, p. 190.

[41]   These same strategies had been used several decades earlier by TOBA performers the Whitman Sisters, who groomed their chorus girls in manners, deportment and dress so

and dangerous, but one of their early records, "Good Girls," betrays an alternative agenda: "Always be a lady—you can mash potato but forget the gravy." Even the Shangri-Las' teen tantrums and street-wise image spoke more of their suburban (they came from Cambria Heights, an upwardly-mobile enclave of Queens, New York), aspirational privilege to rebel by slumming it than it did of them not being well brought up in the first place. Their lyrics strengthen the implication: they are good girls attracted to the "good bad, not evil" guy ("Give Him a Great Big Kiss"); their rejection of the values of their upbringing breaking the heart of their perfect mother ("I Can Never Go Home Again"). The performance of femininity and respectability are central to the girl group's relationship to doxa; and the ability of doxa to fluctuate in both directions, and indeed its moral underpinning, is emphasized by the way these groups are presented: non-whites, if they make an effort, might just be included; whites, if they make mistakes, might just get themselves excluded.

Theorizing the way identification between artists and audience took place, Cyrus points out that the emerging scholarship on girl group music (she cites Douglas, Smith, and Pegley and Caputo) emphasizes the scholars' own identification with the groups and their lyrics, especially in terms of how music helped teen girls express, and then cope with, their daily dilemmas.[42] Certainly girl groups and their music helped cement the identity (or as Cyrus puts it, the "multiplicitous identity") of the teenage girl, but almost as certainly they did more than simply express the problems. Girl group songs could well have helped make teen angst seem normal—not just allowed but *de rigueur* if you were to be a real teenager. And the issues these songs treat—boyfriends, parental relationships, friends, looks, staying respectable—are issues of privilege: not insignificant, mind you, and no less important to those who had to deal with them, but certainly not about putting food on the table or keeping body and soul together.

What kind of girl (do you think I am)? Lenticular logic and masquerades

What kind of unholy confusion must have been wrought by the messages delivered to young girls in the baby-boom era? Get good grades! (But don't act too smart.) Get a good education! (But don't expect to use it.) Buy this! (But be thrifty.) Bake a cherry pie! (But don't eat it, you'll get fat.) Always look as attractive as you can!

---

that they would not incur accusations of inappropriate behavior; Nadine George-Graves, *The Royalty of Negro Vaudeville: The Whitman Sisters and the Negotiation of Race, Gender and Class in African American Theatre, 1900-1940* (New York, 2000).

[42] Cyrus, pp. 173–74. Cyrus cites Douglas, *Where the Girls Are*; Smith, "'Ask Any Girl'," and Karen Pegley and Virginia Caputo, "Growing Up Female(s): Retrospective Thoughts on Musical References and Meanings," in Philip Brett, Gary Thomas and Elizabeth Wood (eds), *Queering the Pitch: The New Gay and Lesbian Musicology* (New York and London: Routledge, 1994).

(But don't let any man touch you.) Get your boyfriend to commit to marriage! (But don't go all the way until *after* the wedding.) Wini Breines's memoir of being "young, white and miserable" documents the contradictions faced daily by both white and non-white teenage girls, struggling amidst the images foisted upon them by commercial culture and the traditional expectations of British and American society. She concludes that the most successful, indeed essential, strategy for girls was to dissemble—actively to pretend to be doing/thinking one thing while actually doing/thinking another.[43] Although deception has been a mainstay of entertainment since ancient classical theatre (and probably before), it is clear from the popular movies and songs of this era that there was a strong fascination for multiple identities and layers of truth—think of "The Great Pretender," "Cryin' in the Rain," and any number of Doris Day films. Girl singers, of course, are expected to masquerade—a theme thoroughly explored in one of the seminal rock and roll films, *The Girl Can't Help It* (1956). And the masquerade becomes less onerous when it is shared—so a girl in a girl group (or a fan of a girl group) who adopts a group identity does not have to pretend that this is who she really *is*, just who she is choosing to be right now.

With girl groups and girl singers (as with Barbie and Sindy) there is a capacity for multiplicity, and from their audiences there is a general willingness to go along with the proposition that the image presented—the one you are to accept—is, if not a lie, at least not the whole truth. It is a pact between the viewer and the viewed: the image, regardless of how obviously "made up" it is, renders invisible what's underneath. Since Susan Douglas told us "Why the Shirelles Mattered" in *Where the Girls Are*, it has become almost a feminist commonplace that the music of the girl singers and groups of the late 1950s and 1960s contained and explained the swirling tensions of teenage libido, under a façade of clean skin, perky hairdos and matching dresses. But the pact did not just obscure burgeoning sexuality, it also rendered other markers unreadable, making crossovers and experimental play between the boundaries easier, less detectable, more palatable.[44] This is what Tara McPherson, in her examination of another type of female masquerade, calls "lenticular logic," after the technology behind those nifty little postcards that change image when you tilt them.[45] Both images are printed on the card, but it is nigh on impossible to see them both at the same time. So, the whiteness of the Angels' skin may well have obscured the blackness of their music; the middle-

---

[43] Breines, p. 124.

[44] "With puberty, girls face enormous cultural pressures to split into false selves. The pressure comes from schools, magazines, music, television, advertisements and movies. It comes from peers. Girls can be true to themselves and risk abandonment by their peers, or they can reject their true selves and be socially acceptable. Most girls choose to be socially accepted and split into two selves, one that is authentic and one that is culturally scripted"; Mary Pipher, *Reviving Ophelia: Saving the Selves of Adolescent Girls* (New York, 1995), p. 38.

[45] Tara McPherson, *Reconstructing Dixie: Race, Gender and Nostalgia in the Imagined South* (Durham, NC, and London, 2003), pp. 25–28.

class indicators enveloping the Supremes certainly obscured both their lower-class beginnings in the Detroit projects as well as the blackness of their skin.[46] The success of the logic may be reflected in the fact that, unlike masculine rock and roll, there seems to be little evidence that much girl singer/girl group pop was regarded as dangerous or subversive by the parents' generation.[47] But in practice, it had the effect of a slow-burning fuse towards social and political dynamite, as the voices it amplified were decidedly non-doxa in origin.

McPherson has shown how lenticular logics have worked in regional southern American society to complicate the dynamics of race and gender, and it is a simple matter to extrapolate her theories onto American singers, but almost as surely the same logics were at work in the UK, if perhaps negotiating different boundaries. Charlotte Grieg notes that the Beverley Sisters broke through class barriers when, as working-class Londoners, they became the darlings of the BBC's light entertainment programming.[48] This may be an over-simplified view—British television was never an exclusively middle-class profession. Nevertheless, the Beverleys' urban accents did not qualify as the BBC's preferred Received Pronunciation, and to hear such a clear marker of working-class status outside the realm of character comedy, and from the mouths of women, to boot, must have ruffled a few feathers. However, they used many of the same strategies Cyrus identifies for groups of a decade later—always immaculate, tastefully dressed by top designers, dazzlingly blonde, never being seen wearing anything but identical outfits and hairstyles—to create a comforting, conforming image. Their glamorous appearance, and the fact that they were so clearly an "act," gave them a little more license to perform material that would have been otherwise unacceptable for middle-class women, including the typically suggestive songs of their music hall roots (their parents had been a successful musical comedy duo). Perhaps most incongruously, they recorded a cheeky calypso number, "He Like It! She Like It!" in 1951, which was promptly banned for broadcast. Stylistically the Beverleys could have claimed Yankee inspiration, as the song was an American import, originally recorded by Louis Prima in 1946. Moreover, their obvious models the Andrews Sisters had had a huge hit with "Rum and Coca-Cola" in 1943. But calypso in Britain was very much more strongly identified with black West Indians who had arrived on the SS

---

[46]   Cyrus, p. 180; Douglas, p. 76.

[47]   "Only some subcultures are perceived as being subcultural ... . Groups of girls also challenge dominant identifications through their diverse affiliations, and if brought to the attention of an analyst they ... might evidently form subcultures. But girls' cultural groups are rarely seen as subcultures and within such groups they are generally marginal to its perceived rebellions. Donna Gaines sees girls within her subject group acting/identifying 'as they always have ... . They were defined by who they were, but what they wore, by where they were seen, and with whom' (93). 'Girls' seems both not specific enough for subcultural identity and so homogenous it overwhelms other possibilities for one"; Driscoll, pp. 209–10, quoting Gaines, *Teenage Wasteland: Suburbia's Dead End Kids* (New York, 1991).

[48]   Greig, pp. 88–91.

Empire Windrush in 1948, so in recording and performing "He Like It! She Like It!" the Beverleys were decidedly pushing the boundaries for nice white girls, by both using a black-identified form and embracing its risqué humor.

As I wrote the last paragraph, a part of me was howling derision at myself, saying, "That's really stretching it, lady—how could blackness ever be part of the Beverley Sisters' act?" But this is what lenticular logics do—they make such preposterous juxtapositions seem, well, normal. And, of course, they are: normal because they are the stuff of playing beyond the boundaries, seeking points of commonality, as Susan Friedman would have it that all humans do; and normal because they are really quite commonplace cultural manifestations. But it seems that the safety net for such excursions is woven from the strong fabric of doxa, a mingling of the fibers of gender, race, age, and class, and consequently of conventional hetero- and monoracial sexuality, and of tightly proscribed sexual values. The net had the capacity to conceal whatever contradictions lay behind it, and the girl singers and girl groups of the 1950s and 1960s could wrap themselves in it, even as they pushed at/played beyond its limits—or in other words, behaved like teenagers. When the net is no longer there and when the lenticular logic is removed, as when girl group songs are performed by men ("Leader of the Pack" performed by British gay icon Julian Clary is a good example), the genre and the repertoire are shown for what they were, a place for contesting and questioning, challenging and posturing. That this work took place behind a veil of respectability, which had the power to include by rendering differences invisible, is surely a major reason for the genre's seemingly contradictory historic importance as a fostering ground for feminine and racial equality.

Past, present, and future—a context for *She's So Fine*

1960s pop is a vast uncharted ('scuse the pun) terrain for the card-carrying boffin, although you'd hardly know if from the way music history has heretofore been written. I have said before that girls and women rarely feature as major figures in the canonic histories of popular music, and this is as much an issue of genre as it is of gender or race. Notwithstanding the pompadoured and quiffed gender havoc of rockabilly and skiffle in the 1950s, the 1960s saw popular music—particularly that marketed for specific musical consumption rather than as part of "variety"—gradually filter out into distinct genres for distinct constituencies: white boys had rock; black boys and girls had soul and blues, and white girls had ... well, what? Pop, a genre supposedly without authenticity or meaning, tainted with the same consumerist, vacuous brush that tainted its target audience, teenage girls. It's worth noting, too, how age, class and race work in terms of performers and genre by the mid-60s. The black girls of Motown were groomed to become "women," regardless of their age, but white women, as opposed to girls, were largely confined to "low class" country and western or counterculture folk.[49] Pop, at least in the 1960s, was the *only* arena of popular music available to respectable white girls in which to develop.

Catherine Driscoll has noted that when the Birmingham School first began to describe and analyze youth culture (again, in the magic year of 1964), the analyses were solely focused on cultures of young men, thereby shaping subsequent discourse to exclude female or feminine youth.[50] She says:

> Youth as a struggle with hegemonic tendencies has seemed to be more easily identified in the cultural activities of young men, and feminist cultural studies thus inherits from cultural studies (as well as feminism) a tendency to represent and discuss girls as conformist rather than resistant or at least to study them almost exclusively with reference to that division.

As a result, rebellious boy countercultures have been valorized and conformist girl cultures devalued, as much in popular music studies as anywhere else, where the history of rock as revolution predominates. Pop and its attendant girl-space, with their alleged emphasis on conformity and concomitant lack of authenticity, have been noted as a phenomenon but one that always seems to operate as a foil to prove rock's ultimate superior cultural worth.

But what if girl cultures are, in fact, resistant, regardless of whether they resist in the same overt way as boy cultures do? The Spice Girls' message of girl power voiced resistance, but was decried as being anything but by feminists and die-hard misogynists alike. But it was certainly received as resistance—Germaine Greer cites a conference in 1998, which found that "whereas half the space in school playgrounds used to be taken up by a self-selecting group of boys playing football, girls' clapping and dancing games were taking over."[51] Driscoll comments that the Spice Girls "constitute an acceptable interest and means of grouping for many girls[, but] they also suggest [a] powerful self-interest" and also suggests that "the attribution of stupidity to Spice Girls fandom resembles that attributed

---

[49]   This would seem to support the view that white middle-class women were not expected to be seen or to seek work outside the home and that class unites more than race in terms of socio-economic expectations for women; see Brodkin, pp. 77–102, and Taylor, Gilligan and Sullivan, pp. 40, 43.

[50]   Driscoll, p. 11: "The Birmingham School talked about new youth and new youth cultures, under which rubric they almost exclusively discussed boys or young men. This focus not only marginalizes girls within the new field of youth culture studies but consequently erases the significance of modern girls to early twentieth-century cultural analysis. In the first half of the twentieth century girls were repeatedly, and even obsessively, associated with the rise of mass culture and accompanying cultural changes, and this continued in the second half of the century despite the dominant association of youth studies and youth culture with young men."

[51]   Greer, p. 409.

INTRODUCTION

to Beatlemanics."[52] The fact that even feminists couldn't agree over whether the Spice Girls were the saviors or destroyers of feminism (if they are authentic, then God help us; if they are not, we are equally doomed) means there was and is still much to be discussed over the power and potential of girl pop. With its lenticular logics and manipulation of doxa, 1960s girl pop is just as much a site of tension between conformity and resistance, as much a barometer of social change as is 1990s pop. This collection aims to open the repertoire up for debate.

She's So Fine sits astride a range of concerns and provides a range of methodologies, often working through close readings, through which to account for girl singers and girl groups within an academic framework. As we have sought to convey and discuss audiovisual experience without audiovisual aids, by concentrating on some of the better-known artists from the period, we hope our readers are able to summon up much of the material we consider in the mind's eye and ear. Our "texts" cover a wide array of primary source materials: recordings; telecasts; interviews, both published and personal; biographies and autobiographies; images; journalism; criticism; fan material and even artifacts. There is a strong bias towards examining music and musical elements in this book, not just because most of us trained as musicians and musicologists, but also because most available writing on girl singers and girl groups is either historical or biographical journalism, or concentrates heavily on visual/textual analysis of image and lyrics, bypassing musical—and especially the vocal—content. Before one can begin to describe the interplay between the sonic and the visual, so vital to the understanding of how popular music works—and the management of which is so crucial to adolescence—there needs to be a way to talk about and to value the sonic. That being said, music can be approached from many different angles: between us we teach or have taught in historical musicology, music performance, music analysis, communications and media, English, cultural studies and women's studies programs. Each approach on its own may illuminate only one or two facets of the phenomenon, but if they are placed together a fuller picture, with finer nuances, should emerge. Clearly, we each hope that our individual essays will contribute something of value to our home disciplines, but also we see the book as a whole contributing to the multidisciplinary, scholarly literatures on gender and race.

Collectively, however, we have an even greater purpose. We would like to think of this volume as the beginning of a re-evaluation—with the emphasis on value—of the very premises of 1950s and 1960s pop. *She's So Fine* sets out many important issues and arguments, yet there is so much more to say than a book of 100,000-odd words can contain. For instance, in 2007, two books on Phil Spector appeared, bringing a total of nine books on one girl group producer listed on amazon.co.uk, yet there are no books on the Ronettes, apart from Ronnie Spector's autobiography.[53] However, as Darlene Love said to Spector, "If it's all about your

---

[52]   Driscoll, p. 273.

[53]   Mick Brown, *Tearing Down The Wall of Sound: The Rise and Fall of Phil Spector* (London, 2007); Mark Ribowsky, *He's a Rebel: Phil Spector—Rock and Roll's Legendary*

music, why aren't you making instrumentals?"; so naturally, our first directive would be that more scholar hours should be devoted to the investigation of girls' and women's voices, solo or in concert.[54] There are many fine pop singers and wonderful girl groups from both sides of the Atlantic—Connie Francis, Timi Yuro, the Dixie Cups, Alma Cogan, Helen Shapiro, the Breakaways—who peopled our email conversation and whose records we shared when we got together, who don't even get a mention in the finished script. We simply could not subject everyone we would have wished to include to the fine detail of academic scrutiny. So while we may rue our inability to share our collective thoughts on Ann-Margret or the Chiffons, we can only hope that eventually there will be a *She's Even Finer* or *She's So Fine, Too* to expand on what we've done here.

Book-length studies of individual groups and artists would be particularly welcome, especially those that made the transition from "girl" to "woman" in the public eye. Some major figures almost self-select: the Shirelles, the Ronettes, the Supremes, the Shangri-Las, Aretha Franklin, Diana Ross, Dionne Warwick, Carole King, Brenda Lee. These would require a multidisciplinary approach, not least as the frequently portfolio career of the girl-singer-turned-into-something-else (Lulu, Cher, Cilla, Diana Ross) can be viewed from many different angles: musical, visual, cultural, commercial. Books that take on singers who crossed genre (Tina Turner, Patti LaBelle, Darlene Love) or who became important songwriters (Ellie Greenwich, Carole King, Lesley Gore, Janis Ian) might be weighty tomes, indeed, but that is no reason not to attempt them. A serious study on how girl groups and girl singers fit into the commercial structure of the music business, and indeed the wider entertainment business, needs to be conducted—they may have been viewed as disposable and ephemeral, but they were nevertheless hugely important for it in terms of financial gain.

There is clearly a great deal more to be said about the broader issues in this book—gender, race, class, and age—as they are articulated in sound and image, as well as what Jacqueline Warwick calls "the politics of music production in the girl group genre" and "the issues surrounding girls and public space."[55] The history and status of backing groups, and the complex issues of race and gender they raise, constitute a massive area for further exploration: not only—as Lou Reed would have it—the "colored girls that go do-do-do" but also groups like the Vernon Girls, whose role on UK television in the 1950s "positioned women in an anonymous, corporately owned, and sexually objectified collective on a weekly basis."[56] There is the knotty question of the exclusive nature of the male/female

---

Producer (2nd ed.; New York, 2007); Ronnie Spector, *Be My Baby: How I Survived Mascara, Miniskirts, and Madness, or My Life as a Fabulous Ronette*, (New York, 1990).

[54]   Rob Hoerburger, "Power of Love," *Guardian Weekend*, July 24, 1993; reported in O'Brien, *She-Bop II*, p. 71.

[55]   Warwick, *Girl Groups, Girl Culture*, pp. x, xii.

[56]   Freya Jarman-Ivens, "Introduction," in Freya Jarman-Ivens (ed.), *Oh Boy! Masculinities and Popular Music,* (New York and Abingdon, 2007), p. 2.

duo, and the potentially intricate gender dynamics of mixed-sex groups. And one might ask why there is an almost complete lack of mixed-race girl groups, not just in this era but up to the present day.[57] Like Captain Kirk and Lieutenant Uhura's kiss, interracial mingling in the girl group could only happen in late 1960s fantasy, with the inclusion of the devastatingly smart, songwriting multi-instrumentalist (yet curiously primarily depicted holding a tambourine) Valerie Brown—yes, Brown—in the cartoon series *Josie and the Pussycats*. With time, we hope that scholarship that takes pop music, and girls' music, seriously will be able to look at these issues as part of an informed and credible debate.

Tell me what (s)he said: The essays in *She's So Fine*

The eight essays that make up the main body of *She's So Fine* fall into three loosely-bound and roughly chronological groups: in the first, "Now That I'm Not a Kid Anymore: American Girls' Voices in the 50s and 60s," three essays look at girl singers in the US during the first half of our timeframe; in the second, "Everything's Coming Up Roses: British Girls in the Mid-60s," three more essays concentrate on British (but mostly not English) artists who flourished after the American girl group phenomenon had dwindled. The final section, "Girls on Top: Rock Chicks and Resistance at the End of the 60s," looks at two singers, one British and one American, one white and one black, whose strategies for professional (and personal) survival necessarily involved coming to terms with the constructed nature of their public/performance personae. The chronological ordering is convenient, but not essential: all of the essays consider their subjects not just as history, but also as part of the active, continuous formation and reformation of culture, revealing significant connections and resonances with contemporary artists and repertoires.

The opening three essays in the collection coincidentally are those that focus most strongly on girlhood and adolescence, in both physical and social contexts. My own is first—not by design, but because it (chrono)logically sits before the rest. Moreover, for those reading cover to cover, it works to invoke the collective sound of our girls' voices, to help the mind tune in to the musical world of the volume. I examine the development of the girl pop singer sound from the point of view of vocal technique, for although it is through the visual images and the production that we understand the constructed message of a record, it is through the voice

---

[57]   There are notable late-century exceptions, for instance the Spice Girls, the Pussycat Dolls and the Sugababes, but most female involvement in mixed-race popular music-making has been as singers—mostly as backing singers but occasionally as solo singers—in mixed-gender groups. In particular, PP Arnold (Small Faces/The Nice) and Madeline Bell (Blue Mink), both African American singers, found success in the late 1960s working with white male or mixed-race groups in the UK. In the early 1970s, Chaka Khan replicated this with Rufus in the US.

that we believe we are connecting with the singer herself. Vocal technique (or its apparent lack) can work to construct a vocal identity, and the teen girl singers who emerged in the late 1950s and early 1960s—by design or default—used specific techniques to create a new teen vocality that was quite different from the sound produced by girl singers of previous generations. This vocality, like the visual images created for the groups and the lyrics they sang, was recognized and owned by the teen girl audience; and like the fashions, the dances and the language, by and large it could be imitated by fans. As such, it was an important facet of the identification processes examined and celebrated in other girl group scholarship.

Robynn Stilwell's contribution focuses the investigation of vocality on close readings of Brenda Lee's singing style as she developed from a prodigious eleven-year-old into a fully matured artist—at sixteen. Her essay highlights the tensions and contradictions put in train when a child, however gifted, performs material that invokes experiences that are socially unacceptable for her age. Having established rockabilly as "androgynous, infantile and sexualized, sinful and sanctified" she argues that Lee—a poor white southern American girl—was a perfect match for the genre. By allowing these binary opposites to co-exist, and reading them through a doubled vision—like McPherson's lenticular logic— Stilwell challenges previous readings of Lee, showing her to be far from either a "blank slate" on which (male) producers could write, or a Lolita figure who both knew and understood what she was singing about. Stilwell demonstrates that the seemingly intractable contradictions in Lee's music, image and career can be explained and understood, if not resolved, by considering together her musical heritage, her physical development, the influence of her southern upbringing and the commercial pressures brought to bear on her performances as she matured. Furthermore, Stilwell's essay highlights the dilemmas inherent in any interaction with any adolescent (be that by an academic, a parent, a consumer, or even another adolescent), who is in the process of learning the performative cues of adulthood. There is always the possibility of dissonance between cues that are intentional, and those that are mimicked; between those that are biological, and those that are cultural; between what we see and what we hear.

In a more troubling challenge to doxa, Jacqueline Warwick's essay confronts superficial interpretations of girl group music, revealing the uncomfortable and sometimes even shocking undercurrents to be found in a genre often dismissed as trivial. She interprets the music—lyrics, melody and harmony, arrangements— and the image—choreography, fashion, presentation—of girl groups within the framework of the self-discipline and repression visited upon teenage girls in the 1950s and 1960s, stating that "girl group songs are not normally thought of as 'angry music,' but themes of conflict, rage and even violence run through this repertoire." Analyzing works such as "Nowhere to Run" and the infamous "He Hit Me, and It Felt Like a Kiss," Warwick shows that girl group songs do much more than simply provide a soundtrack to the teenage dating game; they graphically illustrate the strategies girls employed to deal with anger and conflict with others, and within themselves. The last section of the essay deals with contemporary performance of anger by girl musicians, focusing not just on Riot Grrrls but also on more mainstream pop artists such as Christina Aguilera and Britney Spears, positing that girls in pop "provide the script" for their fans, and thereby perform a valuable social function by establishing "a vocabulary for 'nice' girls to express their anger in a socially sanctioned way."

The title of the second section of the book, "Everything's Coming Up Roses" is intended to be not a little ironic and to highlight the slipperiness of race and doxa in the UK, as the women it examines were largely seen (especially in the US) as archetypical English Roses, although the majority of them were of Celtic descent. It cannot go unnoticed that both Smith's and Hill's essays underline the concurrence of being chosen to represent Britain in the Eurovision Song Contest with the effective end of a girl singer's pop career. The section opens with an essay on the most iconic British female singer of the decade, Dusty Springfield. Annie Randall rightly notes that Dusty is "one of the most fascinating artists of her era" by virtue of "the spectacular collision … at the intersection of gender, race, nation, and sexuality" that manifests itself in her music. Randall uses the concept of "signifyin(g)," well developed in the criticism of African American music played by African Americans, to explain how Dusty was able to emulate and then re-interpret Motown artists' recordings, coining the term "Dustifyin(g)" to encapsulate her very original contributions to the sound of 60s soul. In a deft theoretical move, she shows that although both Dusty's image and the blackness of her music were indisputably and openly constructed, they were both also taken at face value by her fans to represent "the real Dusty." Again, the concept of lenticular logic can enrich this reading—although we know that "the real Dusty" was neither blonde, nor English, nor straight, nor called Dusty, nor was she born into African American musical culture, we cannot see "the real Dusty" while focusing on her constructed image and listening to her music. Randall closes her essay by concentrating on Dusty's voice, and it is perhaps her voice that enforces the lenticular image: at a very basic level we do not, and cannot, hear her voice—or indeed any voice—as constructed; the voice has the power to disconnect with construct and context, and we are led to believe that the voice connects us with the "real" person.

Randall's essay draws in part on a chapter by Patricia Juliana Smith that examines Dusty's "camp masquerade" during the years she was crowned "the White Queen of Soul."[58] One of the few scholars who has previously published on 60s girl music (and, in fact, one of only three who have published more than once on the subject), for this collection Smith chose to look at some of the girls, now women, who might have been termed the Princesses of Pop, whose careers and output have been overshadowed by Dusty's. Smith uses performance analyses to show how the Brit Girls' music differed fundamentally from that of their American

---

[58] Patricia Juliana Smith, "'You Don't Have to Say You Love Me': The Camp Masquerades of Dusty Springfield," in Patricia Juliana Smith (ed.), *The Queer Sixties* (New York and London, 1999), pp. 105–26.

28 *SHE'S SO FINE*

predecessors—particularly in terms of the way they negotiated gender. She also engages in critical biography to highlight the ways our four parameters—race, gender, age and class—affected both the girls' careers and their subsequent impact and longevity. Finally, Smith highlights the role of personality in the creation and maintenance of British stardom, and shows how the close connection of the audience with the personal lives of these women worked, frequently in negative ways, to determine the course of their professional lives.

The last essay in this middle section goes deeper into the issue of ethnicity within Britishness touched upon in the previous two chapters. Sarah Hill's account of Welsh singer Mary Hopkin's cross-over into a specifically Anglophone milieu examines closely the gendered positioning of a subaltern community, culture and musical tradition within the dominant Anglophone culture, drawing parallels with Hopkin's own passive position in relation to her male, English patrons. Drawing on the work of Suzanne Cusick, she compares the "penetration" of a subaltern culture by a dominant culture with the linguistic "penetration" executed when a non-English speaker adopts English as her performing language as part of a process of building a successful musical career. Hill problematizes Hopkin's characterization as "England's sweetheart," noting that such a designation is ultimately patronizing, and shows how a dogged insistence on the part of the media for maintaining her passive persona contributed to the erasure of Hopkin's agency in her own work.

The first chapter in the final section, "Girls on Top: Rock Chicks and Resistance at the End of the 60s," might well have fit in the preceding section, as it takes as its focus Marianne Faithfull. Norma Coates explains how Faithfull's manufactured image merged with and then obscured her "real" self—a similar story to others told in previous chapters, but perhaps with more devastating personal consequences for the singer. The implications of class and gender within rock culture and its mythology are carefully explored, using Faithfull's unique position—a member of two aristocracies, one hereditary (if devalued) and the other (counter)cultural—however constructed, to show how a double standard operated, and still operates, towards the hapless girl singer. Coates contrasts the development and debauching of Faithfull's "persona" (an analytical term derived from performance studies, signaling the self as perceived by the audience) in and by rock culture, with the concomitant rise and canonization—in both senses of the word—of the Rolling Stones', and in particular Mick Jagger's, persona. She then charts Faithfull's restoration to rock respectability through her deliberate, and now positive, manipulation of her history, and her understanding and embrace of the persona as an effective means of artistic representation.

The essays close with Susan Fast's analysis of the first decade of one of the longest careers in girl-singer-dom, that of Tina Turner (although one should recognize Tina's uneasy fit with the concept of girl).[59] The chapter nonetheless has much to say about whiteness—and blackness—in Tina's image and performance.

---

[59] She is in a visible relationship, but Ike still makes her *available*: "In her case, the qualities of a woman's body are 'useful'. However, theses qualities have 'value' only

Like Randall, Fast uses the model of signifyin(g) to show how Tina emulated, parodied, validated and destabilized normative male practices in rock and roll music, and how her image simultaneously complicated white culture's ideals of feminine beauty and black exoticness. Fast's essay is necessarily wide-ranging, and incorporates nuanced and complex discussions of covers as authenticating practice, of live versus studio performance, of parody and of masculinized femininity. Again we can see lenticular logics at work, as Tina's "wild woman" persona belied its own origin in paradigms of whiteness; and her exuberant celebration of womanhood, "Bold Soul Sister," is shown to be a trenchant and incisive parody of the hyper-alpha-male James Brown.

Although most of us were babies, not teenagers, in the 1960s, each of the contributors to *She's So Fine* writes from the heart about the music and the singers that have shaped our lives. In the best tradition of feminist criticism—and touching on the tenets of narrative ethnography—our work draws on our own experiences and our interaction with our subject for its inspiration. When we had the chance to present our topics to each other at the Bucknell University symposium on girl groups, there were moments that revealed just how close the material of our essays intertwined with our personal histories, moments that nonetheless could never translate onto paper. When Annie Randall displayed a photo of Dusty from 1967, resplendent in back-combed blondeness and false eyelashes as long as her arm, she announced, "*This* could be a picture of my third-grade teacher!" I hooted with laughter and squealed back, "No, Annie, it's a picture of my mom!" The standard response to a personal quandary has become, "What would Dusty do?" Even if we were only little girls when these singers were making records, their images of young womanhood were what we aspired to be. My older sister and I took turns with who was to be Cilla and who was to be Lulu in our imaginary *Top of the Pops*; a few years later, we played Josie and the Pussycats in the back yard with her best friend. And I know I'm not the only one among us who took the step beyond the hairbrush-in-front-of-the-mirror stage, and sang these songs in public as part of my professional engagement with the repertoire. But this affection, or even attachment, has taken us beyond the subjective discourse of our fandom; we have written these essays not only to further our own and others' understanding, and to model critical approaches for the re-discovery and re-evaluation of the repertoire, but also, most simply, to reaffirm and amplify why—and how—girl singers still matter.

---

because they have already been appropriated by a man ... . Prostitution amounts to *usage that is exchanged*." Irigaray, p. 186.

PART I
"Now that I'm not a Kid Anymore": American Girls' Voices in the 50s and 60s

Chapter 1
Voice of the Beehive:
Vocal Technique at the Turn of the 1960s[1]

Laurie Stras

This essay is about the vocal technique of popular girl artists in the late 1950s and early 1960s.[2] I realize that "vocal technique" and "1960s girl singers" might not be concepts immediately or even easily associated. One could argue that many girl pop singers in the early 1960s made hit records despite having little grasp of good vocal technique; or in other words, "Any three girls could reproduce the simple harmonies and effects of the teen sound in an empty subway tunnel."[3] However, these are not statements of fact but superficial truisms that at the very least need testing and/or qualifying. In the context of pop singing, what *is* good vocal technique? In the early 1960s, what was it "good" for? Something significant happened at the turn of that decade to change the sound of girls' vocals forever, and it was not just a matter of genre or interpretation; the differences in basic vocal production between the majority of young female popular singers of the 1950s and those of the 1960s are stark. This essay attempts to describe some of the differences, and then poses some theories as to why and how changes took place.

So what did the 1960s girl singer sound like? Aida Pavletich, in her 1980 book on women in popular music, *Rock-A-Bye Baby*, thinks they sounded as if they didn't "have too much 'up there'." To Pavletich, the 1960s girl singer appealed to

---

[1]   I am deeply grateful to my co-contributors for their generous comments and hilarious singing stories; to singing and teaching colleagues John Potter, Deborah Roberts, Louise Gibbs and Keith Davis for their equally generous and sometimes equally hilarious insights; to Anna Barney for her engineer's knowledge of the workings of the female voice; but the most heartfelt thanks go to those students who trusted me with their voices and who allowed me to learn with them, in particular Molly, Sarah, Frances, Savi and Natasha.

[2]   Throughout this essay, I will try to explain technical terms in non-technical language as well; however, for many of the embellishments and affectations of pop singing, there is no accepted academic (or even professional) terminology. Readers curious about the realization of these "tricks" are encouraged to find a place where they will not be disturbed or overheard, and to try and reproduce them for themselves.

[3]   Aida Pavletich, *Rock-a-Bye, Baby* (Garden City, NJ, 1980), p. 78.

her teen audience because she "spoke to their needs in their gee-whiz language, and in their voices, the 'dumb' girl sound."[4] She elaborates:

> The Teen Angels had the very essence of the "dumb" sound ... . It was a nontechnique that sprang up naturally but was difficult for a trained singer to obtain ... . The young girl groups sounded "dumb" because they could not float a note on a column of air to achieve a full-voiced sonority; they sang like children. They also sounded dumb because they could not phrase or pronounce their lyrics properly ... . The evanescent "dumb" sound was not bound by the rules of logic, and at times amounted to baby talk.[5]

Pavletich experiences the vocal qualities of teen girls as somehow undesirable, aberrant, or indicative of a lack of application or intelligence: they sounded like children (but they shouldn't have); they were not eloquent (but they should have been); and perhaps most importantly, she perceives that those qualities could have been, and should have been, permanently eradicated by training.

Yet in her chapter devoted to explaining "Why The Shirelles Mattered," Susan Douglas recounts her teenage recognition of girl group music as "the voices of teenage girls singing about—and dignifying—our most basic concern: how to act around boys when so much seemed up for grabs." She says that on the seminal recording "Will You Love Me Tomorrow," "[Shirley] Owens's alto voice vibrated with teen girl angst and desire, grounding the song in fleshly reality."[6] She goes on to describe Owens's voice using adjectives that in 1961, the year of the record's first release, might more readily have been used to describe the tonal range of an operatic contralto—"earthy," "provocative," "haunting," "sensual"—making her seem more like Kathleen Ferrier than a schoolgirl from Passiac, New Jersey. But Douglas does not just claim this affective quality for Owens as a critic, she speaks as a member of the Shirelles' constituent audience trying to account for, and to celebrate, the profundity of her youthful experience of girl group songs.

Presumably these women are of roughly the same generation, but what Pavletich decries, Douglas cherishes; it is difficult to credit, but they are describing the same voices. Douglas values these voices in a social context regardless of their place in any kind of artistic hierarchy; Pavletich devalues them in a critical context of accomplishment, regardless of their commercial appeal or cultural importance. Most American or British female baby-boomers (even tail-end baby-boomers like myself) will appreciate and maybe even applaud Douglas's point of view; but any trained singer who has had either to try to reproduce this sound professionally or

---

[4]   Ibid. Pavletich's terminology may have its roots in contemporary criticism, see Al Aronowitz, "The Dumb Sound: Pop Before the Beatles." *Saturday Evening Post*, August 1963, reproduced on *Rock's Back Pages*, http://www.rocksbackpages.com/.

[5]   Pavletich, p. 76.

[6]   Susan J. Douglas, *Where the Girls Are: Growing Up Female with the Mass Media* (London, 1995), pp. 84–85.

to work with it in others as a teacher could also understand why Pavletich feels the way she does. Pavletich responds most favorably to singing as skill and craft, Douglas to the bodily communication of the girl herself.[7]

The teenage singing voice

The voice is a fundamental element of the human identity, both as means of communication and expression of the self, and as a means by which the self is recognized by others. As we learn to speak and to listen, we also learn to control, manipulate and interpret vocal qualities, both consciously and subconsciously, as means of representation that do not rely on language. The meanings we place on them are to only a certain degree culturally determined; as vocal production can be affected by emotional or physical state (in particular through respiratory rate and muscular tension) such qualities as croakiness, stridence, whininess, even breathiness and breathlessness can transcend linguistic boundaries without translation. Good vocal technique is, therefore, at least partially a matter of control over vocal quality as a conveyor of meaning; for many repertoires this includes the maintenance of the voice in an optimal condition for maximum control. As singers learn to sing, either in lessons or through experience, they refine their voices to suit the repertoire they want to perform. For those genres in which tunefulness is a desirable quality (however a culture might define "tunefulness"—but in these genres I would include most Western repertoires), that refinement will comprise the control of tone, focus and pitch accuracy at least, and probably also vibrato and phrasing. These abilities are only rarely to be found in the inexperienced singer; crucially, they are also those most difficult to predict and maintain consistently during puberty and early adolescence.[8] Furthermore, a voice that sounds out of control does not necessarily communicate to the listener *why* it is out of control: it could be because of incompetence (Pavletich), passion (Douglas) or illness—or simply because it reflects the physical state of the body producing it.

Research shows that the vocal folds of children and adult females operate in a similar way, but in the teen years the voice is wayward.[9] This waywardness is better accepted for teen boys, as it is more easily understood as part of a

---

[7]   One might see in these two viewpoints the opposition of *pheno-song* and *geno-song* described by Roland Barthes in "The Grain of the Voice," in Simon Frith and Andrew Goodwin (eds), *On Record: Rock, Pop and the Written Word* (London and New York, 1990), pp. 293–300.

[8]   Susan Monks, "Adolescent Singers and Perceptions of Vocal Identity," *British Journal of Music Education* 20/3 (2003): pp. 243–56.

[9]   Ibid., p. 244. In literature on the vocal tract and in singing pedagogy, the term "vocal folds" is now used in place of the older term "vocal cords." A detailed discussion of the physiology of the vocal tract is out of place here, but a hugely simplified visual metaphor may help lay readers. If one compares the vocal tract to the neck of a balloon, the folds meet

developmental process ("voice-breaking") that leads to the adult male voice. For girls, however, whose adult voices do not differ substantially from those of childhood, what is actually development can sound like aberration. The voices of the 60s girls groups were, with one or two notable exceptions, almost all pubescent or adolescent. These voices *by their nature* were liable to sound out of control, at least occasionally. Structural and/or hormonal changes to the vocal tract and soft tissues can temporarily affect a girl's ability to sing in tune, within her "normal" range, without cracking between registers, or to sing to the ends of phrases. Sudden growth can cause postural difficulties that affect breathing and it can also temporarily narrow the ear canal, with consequences for tuning and articulation; diction can also suffer as a result of dental maturation or orthodontic work. The susceptibility of the immune system to hormonal fluctuation, changing environments and different patterns of activity may account for the apparently increased numbers of coughs and colds experienced by teenagers, with concomitant effects on their ability to control tone, focus and pitch.

Of course, a girl would have to be extremely unlucky to suffer every one of these setbacks simultaneously, and some girls may only experience one or two of them to a noticeable degree. A young singer with an exemplary technique and uncommonly good physical fortune (and perhaps a protective commercial machinery that kept her from any damaging exposure during vulnerable moments) might even appear to survive the upheaval of teen growth with no discernable ill effects on her singing. However, the rise in popularity of the girl groups forced into the limelight many teenage singers that were not so fortunate, either in terms of the physical properties of their vocal tracts or their innate technical abilities; and in their voices we hear the results of strategies designed to cope with or disguise their fragile grasp on vocal control. Technically and physically reckless to the point of foolhardiness (in terms of what singing teachers call "vocal health"), these strategies nonetheless produced the sound now instantly recognizable as the teen pop voice.

When I started teaching pop singing at Southampton University in 1997, I found that I had three basic kinds of teenage student: the Christine Daaes, the Cathy Seldons and the Lena Lamonts.[10] The Christines—those who had previously received classical, or more specifically bel canto, training—tended automatically to drop their larynxes and to place their voices cranially; they began by hooting

---

in a similar way to the sides of the balloon's neck when stretched, forming sound when air is forced between them.

[10]   I use these fictional singers —from the film versions of *The Phantom of the Opera* (2004) and *Singing in the Rain* (1955) respectively—very loosely to characterize broad general categories, hoping that readers will have some passing familiarity with the vocal stereotypes they represent. The actresses playing Christine (Emmy Rossum) and Cathy (Debbie Reynolds) were teenagers at the time of filming. British readers might also take the 1970s child star Lena Zavaroni as a point of comparison for the Lena type who has undergone strenuous "stage" vocal training.

down the microphone, their openly-resonating, highly-focused pure vowel sounds producing a rather disagreeable distortion through the amplification.[11] The Cathys had also learnt about placement (either through training or experience), but they found it easier to move it around their faces and throats, so producing a more speech-like and varied focus. They could relax the larynx, allowing it to rise or drop with a more flexible approach to tone. Good breathing technique—again, either taught or acquired—provided the consistent airflow and subglottic pressure (better understood as "breath support," the workings of the intercostal or chest muscles maintaining the air in the lungs under pressure) necessary to control the focus and projection of the voice. The Cathys might "belt" or "croon," but the production was basically the same, the tonal and dynamic differences produced by varying the focus, the breath support and the speed of airflow across the folds.

The Lenas fixed their larynxes in a high position, and it seemed the only way they could get their voices to project above a certain pitch was to tighten the focus even more and almost literally squeeze the sound out through their noses. Some of them had been taught to sing this way by vocal coaches intent on quickly producing voices that would carry adequately for stage work. Most either could, or soon were able to, focus the lower range where the resonance occurs in the chest, creating a pleasant, warm and comfortable sound. As the pitch got higher the resonance should naturally have risen into the head, but they did not want to let go of that weighty sound; nor did they find it easy to relinquish its power (as it contains fewer harmonic partials, the head voice is naturally quieter). So instead of relaxing and finding a new place for the sound—and hence needing to learn how to control the changeover in register—they would lock the position of the larynx by tightening the muscles in the folds, the neck and the tongue, and then force the air out under great pressure. This resulted in the sound of a voice being heaved up against an obstacle, and then pushed out through the nasal passages.[12] Each voice had a point beyond which it would not go; when the pitch got too high and the tension in the muscles too great, the voice would crack and break into an unfocussed higher register, an event that could be painful to all concerned, both physically and aesthetically.

As a teacher, this rather desperate subjugation of the vocal tract made me doubly unhappy because, exposed to too much tension and pressure, the Lenas' vocal

---

[11]   The position of the larynx can be seen from outside the body, roughly indicated by the Adam's apple. Vocal placement is the term used for a fairly abstract and widely debated concept, nonetheless widely understood by singers to help them differentiate between the various places in the body where one can feel the voice resonate. Logically, lower pitches tend to resonate in lower spaces in the body, middling pitches in the jaw and sinuses; voice teachers sometimes recommend that the highest notes be "floated" out of the top of the head.

[12]   Monks describes a similar habit in her young classical singers: "A common feature of young singers is to 'create' a clearer, brighter tone by pushing the voice, pressing the larynx into a higher or lower position to tighten the vocalis muscle [i.e. the muscle located in the vocal folds] rather than using better breath control to clarify the vocal sound by controlling air flow." Monks, "Adolescent Singers," p. 245.

folds would eventually become inflamed, probably also causing the development of nodules (small polyps), and could ultimately stop working altogether.[13] But some of these girls seemed actually to *like* the noise, and what was even odder was that it sounded relatively authentic for the pop repertoire they wanted to sing; in fact, I had a tough job convincing one or two to carry on working beyond this point to develop a less perilous technique. I realized then that this was also the early 1960s sound I once struggled to reproduce as a session singer. Furthermore, Pavletich is right: it *is* difficult for a trained singer to subject her voice to this kind of abuse. Psychologically and physiologically, one has to forget everything one has learned about "good technique"; but the physical challenge is a matter of voluntarily (that is, against what has become second nature, if not nature itself) getting the right mix of high larynx position, upper chest resonance and breath pressure, then blocking it all down with the musculature.

Both the Christines and the Cathys had "good vocal technique," inasmuch as they sang in a way designed not to inflict catastrophic damage, but the example of the Christines' initial struggles instantly provides another answer to my fundamental questions—"good vocal technique" differs depending on the context, and a classical technique that opens vowels by dropping the larynx and takes the voice into the top of the head cavity for resonance has little currency in pop. The Cathys and the Lenas both could have been said to have had control over their voices; however, the Cathys' control derived from learning to manage the infinite possibilities of vocal production, whereas the Lenas controlled their voices by limiting those possibilities. The Lenas' approach almost served to accentuate their teenage susceptibility, the inflexibility of the control making the voice all the more vulnerable, especially when that control failed. The Cathys, on the other hand, were better placed to cope with the occasional blip caused by the physical development of their bodies, smoothing over or disguising as much as possible any signs of immaturity.

Singing teenagers before 1960

The teen girl singer did not, of course, materialize magically at the turn of the 1960s, although it would be fair to say that before the late 1950s, girls younger than seventeen or eighteen, and therefore still in the midst of the most dramatic hormonal and structural changes of puberty and adolescence, were not commonly among those commanding major recording contracts and musical/theatrical careers. The exceptional few—for instance, Judy Garland and Deanna Durbin in the 1930s, Julie Andrews in the 1940s and Brenda Lee in the mid-1950s—clearly possessed technical and musical abilities more than adequate to overcome whatever temporary difficulties their physical development may have presented.

---

[13]   Merideth Bunch, *Dynamics of the Singing Voice* (Vienna and New York, 1982), pp. 71, 116.

But they were not child stars in the same sense as, say, Shirley Temple or Baby Rose Marie; they were prodigious, not simply precocious. They sang mature songs and mature lyrics with mature-sounding and technically accomplished voices; it seems that for successful teen singers before the turn of the 1960s, good vocal technique allowed them to sound like, and compete commercially with, grown women.[14] Their youth was indeed stressed as part of their media image, and the public was encouraged to be fascinated by how adult they sounded for their age, but they occupied no clear novelty niche in the musical market. The records of Garland, Durbin and, to some extent, Lee (Andrews didn't record until she was in her twenties) shared a repertoire with and were sold alongside those of older singers. Furthermore, if their voices had betrayed their ages too readily, there would certainly have been an uncomfortable tension between the image their voices projected and the subject matter of the Tin Pan Alley material the pre-rock and roll record business traditionally promoted.

The potential for this kind of uneasy incongruity is demonstrated by the 1956 hit version of "Tonight You Belong to Me" by the sister duo, Patience and Prudence, aged eleven and fourteen at the time of recording.[15] The girls' musician father, Mack McIntyre, chose the song for them; he also set up the session with Liberty Records. It is a novelty record to be sure, for no attempt seems to be made to disguise the age of the singers; in fact, they are made to sound almost younger than they really are. The voices are breathy, unfocussed and unsupported, and the singers are clearly unable to use any sophisticated vocal coloring. Although much of the vocal is delivered in two-part harmony, the girls have the security of singing both parts in unison on different takes. The impression of both naivety and the physical weakness of childhood is strengthened by the girls' apparent need for frequent breaths in the middle of phrases, even in the middle of words. The absence of "good vocal technique" here unambiguously conveys childishness, rather than precocity. This quality may well have sold the record to many who thought it cute, but the overall effect could become distinctly creepy if one considered too closely the implications of those young voices singing, "I know with the dawn that you will be gone, but tonight you belong to me." However, any possible discomfort is at least partially mitigated by the well-balanced, multi-tracked unison voices singing in harmony. Although primarily a production consideration intended to

---

[14] Both Garland and Durbin made their first commercial releases in 1936. Garland's was Benny Goodman's "Stompin' at the Savoy," with Bob Crosby and the Bobcats (Decca 61165). Durbin's was Luigi Arditi's vocal waltz, "Il bacio," a tour-de-force for coloratura soprano, backed by Gus Kahn's "Someone to Care for Me"; she sang both songs in the film *Three Smart Girls* (Decca 61481/2, 1936). Andrews made her Royal Variety Performance debut in 1948 at the age of 13, singing another coloratura aria, the polonaise "Je suis Titania" from Ambroise Thomas's opera *Mignon*. In 1956, Decca released ten-year-old Brenda Lee's first single, Hank Williams's "Jambalaya" (Decca 30050).

[15] Billy Rose and Lee David's song was originally recorded by the matinee tenor "Whispering" Gene Austin in 1927.

fill out the sound of the voices and to take the edge off the inaccurate tuning, the choral effect it creates also diffuses the contact between the singers and the listeners, lessening the impact of lyrics that suggest a degree of sexual intimacy utterly unsuitable to pubescent American girls.

Nevertheless, what stops "Tonight You Belong to Me" being completely intolerable in terms of its moral messages is the implication of innocence in the voices; by virtual of their childish noise, Patience and Prudence do not sound as if they are in any way complicit in potential underage shenanigans. However, when a young voice is technically accomplished, that layer of inappropriate meaning is bound to be exposed. Like Patience and Prudence, Dodie Stevens was barely in her teens when she made her only hit, "Pink Shoelaces," in 1959, but as a singer she was more like Garland and Lee—a twelve-year-old with a big, skillfully-controlled voice and a carefully styled delivery. Yet when considered from the perspective of the singer's age, the record is perhaps even more disturbing than Lee's rendition of "Bigelow 6-200" (discussed by Robynn Stilwell in her chapter in this book). Stevens uses both chest and head registers (the latter in a falsetto riff after the chorus) with a focused and confident tone; her voice is also flexible enough to produce rapid, understated and almost instrumental inflections that echo Plas Johnson's dirty tenor sax solos on the backing track. Her vocal is single-tracked, accentuating its directness and "authenticity": but what makes her performance worryingly precocious is the first two spoken verses, in which she switches tone between a perky conversational narrative in the first three lines to an altogether more suggestive purr on the fourth, more personal comment:

> (Verse 1) Now I've got a guy and his name is Dooley
> He's my guy and I love him truly
> He's not good lookin', heaven knows
> *But I'm wild about his crazy clothes*
>
> (Verse 2) He takes me deep-sea fishing in a submarine
> We go to drive-in movies in a limousine
> He's got a whirly-birdy and a twelve-foot yacht
> *Ah, but that's-a not all he's got*[16]

In those fourth lines, the voice drops back into her throat, and she covers the tone with a breathiness that contrasts abruptly with the clean and direct sound of her previous speech. Small rockabilly-styled glottal catches give the lines extra rhythmic definition, but she also draws out the softer consonants to make a further syncopation between the start of the sound and when it is released: "w-w-wild," "cr-r-azy," "th-that's-s-s-a not." There is nothing childish about this delivery—it is womanly and knowing, and every bit as sophisticated as the activities that she

---

[16] "Pink Shoelaces," words and music by Mick Grant © 1959, reproduced by permission of Ardmore & Beechwood Ltd, London W8 5SW.

tells us about (and, we are led to believe, the ones she omits). Clearly, we are not meant to hear Stevens's adolescence. Later in the song we learn that Dooley is old enough to be enlisted, and when he finally speaks, he does so in a booming, Big Bopper bass. This clinches it—Dooley is an adult and, at least for the duration of the record, we can (and should) believe that Dodie is as well.

In her book on girl groups, Charlotte Grieg remarks on how the teenage girl in the 1950s had little space between childhood and adulthood to express herself.[17] She says, "in the fifties, more than before the war, girls were being subjected to intense pressure to grow up quickly. In a sense there were no real teenage years for girls, only a sudden leap from being children to having children, from leaving home to making a home." In performance terms, Patience and Prudence and Dodie Stevens are on either side of the gap; while the physical age difference between them is infinitesimally small, the ideological distance between their records is hopelessly vast. The musical gulf that separates them is the space that commentators like Charlotte Grieg and Susan Douglas identify as having been subsequently carved out and filled by the singers of the girl group era seemingly on behalf of the hapless 50s teenager, giving a voice to her issues through their lyrics, and a fashion image that distinguished her from her mother and her little sisters. Neither the McIntyre girls nor Stevens adequately express the reality for teen girls in the 50s, who by and large suffered the double frustration of parents whose moral attitudes and own adolescent opportunities were inevitably shaped by the social conditions of Second World War, and (because of the earlier onset of puberty, attributable in part to the increase in affluence of post-war society) a longer period between reaching physiological sexual maturity and the age at which it was socially acceptable to do anything about it.[18]

Of course, the outward signs of the clothes, the hair and the lyrics of this new generation of teen girl singer were vital to establishing her social identity, but she also began to be able to claim her vocal identity, singing in a voice that was in the process of development, with all the technical vulnerability that might entail. As I have described, the inexperienced, developing female voice is most vulnerable at

---

[17] Charlotte Greig, *Will You Still Love Me Tomorrow? Girl Groups From The 50s On ...* (London, 1989), p. 26.

[18] The recognition of this tension is by no means confined to retrospective analysis. In 1952, the Unesco Conference in Paris concluded: "All societies tend to delay and regulate heterosexual activities; but while sex gratification may be discouraged or prohibited, the achievement of physical maturity is not delayed. Hence one of the major developmental problems of the young, often vexed by distorted attitudes acquired in childhood, and by the fears and inhibitions of adults, is that of acquiring a fully adjusted sexual self, able to accept and control one of the most powerful of all the drives of the personality." This conclusion is given in an analysis of letters sent into the agony column of an unnamed weekly periodical for teen girls between 1953 and 1955. The author also reports: "Marriages are today taking place earlier, so that the responsibilities of wife and mother may follow close upon adolescence," corroborating Charlotte Greig's statement. See James Hemming, *Problems of Adolescent Girls* (London, Melbourne and Toronto, 1960), pp. 25, 69, 88–104.

the point where the lower register begins to give way to the higher. Pushed beyond the comfortable upper end of that range, extreme tension and pressure on the folds causes the voice to crack, break and squeak, and accurate intonation becomes very difficult. The perils of negotiating registral change can be compounded by the unpredictable physiology of the adolescent vocal tract; so in the same way that pubescent boys gain control over their speech and singing by learning to use only their chest voice, girls of a similar age may also attempt to limit themselves to the lower range when singing, coincidentally perfect for singing pop.[19]

Precisely when and why the lower range became the norm for female popular singers is difficult to pinpoint; however, it is possible to trace the concern for a microphone-friendly vocal technique back to the early days of radio, when "singers—especially sopranos—accustomed to projecting their voices on a stage often blew the tubes on radio transmitters when they used the same vocal force in front of a microphone."[20] In the early 1920s "The First Lady of Radio," Vaughn De Leath, sang primarily in a light head voice, but by the 1930s her popularity had been eclipsed by a newer generation of hot jazz singers—led by Ethel Waters and Connie Boswell—who could sing softly and intimately in a lower range. In the 1950s, virtually all female popular singers were at their best in a mid-to-low range (just barely above the high baritone/tenor male singer); in swing girl groups such as the Andrews Sisters, and in the later barbershop-influenced Chordettes, the lead was almost invariably placed in the middle. The female head voice in pop practice became a falsetto—an advanced technique reserved for scat divas like Ella Fitzgerald and Annie Ross, country yodellers like Patsy Cline or exotic specialty acts like Yma Sumac. The listening public were used to hearing female vocals at conversational pitch, so one of the primary identifying traits of a younger voice—the vulnerable upper register—was simply not exposed in the mainstream pop output of the decade. As Arlene Smith of the Chantels explained, the high female voice "was considered unrecordable" and unfashionable.[21] But that was all about to change.

The teen voice and doo-wop

Girl group music has its roots, socially and musically, as a female counterpart to the almost exclusively male preserve of doo-wop. Different theories have been

---

[19] Susanne Cusick comments on the cultural differences between speech and song, and how they are negotiated differently by the sexes in puberty; see Cusick, "On Musical Performances of Gender and Sex," in Elaine Barkin and Lydia Hamessley (eds), *Audible Traces: Gender, Identity and Music* (Zurich and Los Angeles, 1999), pp. 32–3.

[20] Susan J. Douglas, *Listening In: Radio and the American Imagination ... from Amos 'n' Andy and Edward R. Murrow to Wolfman Jack and Howard Stern* (New York, 1999), p. 87.

[21] Greig, p. 16.

advanced to explain why, initially, the ratio of boys' to girls' singing groups was so large. It seems that the teen phenomenon of group singing appealed primarily to boys; it created a gang to which they could belong, and (crucially) they saw it as a way of getting girls to notice them.[22] Girls may also have felt the need to belong and the need to be noticed, but their opportunities to gather were more constrained; as Shirley Alston explained, the Shirelles formed "like a street-corner group, only being girls, we weren't allowed on the corner, so we'd go down to the basement of Beverly's house."[23] But it is also likely that girls' physiology prevented them from taking a more prominent role in the emerging 1950s vocal groups.

Doo-wop has a fairly open-voiced texture with a high lead and a low bass clearly distinguished from the other parts, rhythmically and spatially. Any aspiring female group wanting to sing a cappella would need a bass, but it is relatively rare to find a teenage girl with a truly powerful bottom register—though some of the first doo-wop girl groups to record, such as the Hearts and the Deltairs, had them.[24] The lead in a girls' doo-wop arrangement could not easily sit in the middle of the female range—either there would not be enough space in the range above or below in which to fit in the other parts, or there would be too many voices competing at the same pitch. So either the lead had to drop into the lower voices, with the arrangement rhythmically fitting around it, or one girl needed to sing both high and strong. The Bobbettes and the Chantels, the two earliest of the new girl groups to hit the mainstream charts in 1957, found their solutions at these opposite ends. The Bobbettes' Reather Dixon and Emma Pought together produced a strong tenor sound; Arlene Smith, on the other hand, was clearly a soprano.

The Bobbettes initially used two lead singers most of the time singing in unison, so that they had a ready-made double-tracked sound that boosted volume and masked poor intonation. They were marginally younger than the Chantels, the five girls ranging in age between eleven and fifteen when they made their first record, "Mr. Lee." Like Patience and Prudence much of their early and most successful material had a novelty character; when performing live, their energetic stage routines depended as much on "street" choreography and comedy as they did on the girls' singing.[25] They appeared in publicity photos with their hair short and wearing white cotton, tier-skirted dresses, emphasizing—or at the very least not attempting to hide—their girlhood. Their musical image was equally, and

---

[22] Anthony J. Gribin and Matthew M. Schiff, *The Complete Book of Doo-Wop* (Iola, WI, 2000), pp. 185–6.

[23] Gerald Early, *Tuxedo Junction: Essays on American Culture* (Hopewell, NJ, 1989), p. 98, cited in Jeffrey Melnick, "'Story Untold': The Black Men and White Sounds of Doo-Wop," in Mike Hill (ed.), *Whiteness: A Critical Reader* (New York and London, 1997), p. 140.

[24] Gribin and Schiff, p. 100. Neither group had a significant impact on the R&B charts, although the Hearts did place in 1955 with their first release, "Lonely Nights."

[25] John Clemente, *Girl Groups: Fabulous Females That Rocked The World* (Iola, WI, 2000), p. 39.

disarmingly, "honest," probably because they were encouraged to write their own material. Little in their early songs demanded (or demonstrated) technical sophistication or even a strong commitment to "nice" singing; the technical skill in their voices was not directed towards creating an aesthetically beautiful sound, but to the use of clever and energetic vocal tricks, such as rhythmically punchy diaphragm shouts and gospelly, guttural growls. The overall effect of listening to the Bobbettes' early records is an aural equivalent of watching a particularly skilled group of children in the playground work through complicated skipping rhymes and steps.

As the girls grew more physically, emotionally and professionally mature, their songs and arrangements changed, the high-energy patter giving way to more tender ballads arranged in a more traditional doo-wop sound. The tenor leads took turns as solo voices, and one of the sopranos provided high and fluty falsetto descants. In "You Are My Sweetheart" a wordless, sung bass line is featured along with the descant, while the inner parts harmonize lightly note-on-note with the lead (Example 1.1). Effectively, the singers are using all the range available to them, but while the middle voices are difficult to age simply by listening to them, the outer voices sound stretched, struggling for both intonation and tone. Frequent breaks in these outer lines allow the singers to catch their breath; for different reasons, both extremes require extra regulation of airflow, and neither singer here is in complete control. And perhaps more importantly, the lead here is still not exposing the most vulnerable parts of her voice, but sings comfortably in the mid-range.

The Chantels were considerably more successful than the Bobbettes in the charts, their more sophisticated sound giving them something greater than just novelty appeal. Their material was dominated by smooth 12/8 ballads that required sustained, ornamented lines from a strong doo-wop lead. Arlene Smith perhaps belonged more to the Brenda Lee/Dodie Stevens camp: a girl naturally blessed with a good instrument, but one who also had consummate stylistic control. Her most instantly noticeable vocal attribute was, of course, her range. She said, "I was singing in a key … that people supposedly wouldn't listen to. Everyone else was singing mid-range to low—I came out screechy and high. I remember hearing Carla Thomas singing in my register just after we got started, and I was outraged! People were really catching on to my thing."[26] Smith's passaggio (or the point at which her voice "breaks" from chest to head) is much higher than usual for a woman, appearing to rest at the top of the treble staff between f^2 and g^2—a good octave above the majority of female voices, and still at least a fourth above those who have worked their chest voice upwards through practice and determination.[27] She *had* had some vocal training in her school church choir along with her fellow group members, from which she probably developed her acute (and very mature)

---

[26] Greig, p. 16.

[27] For a discussion of the female "belt," see Stephen Banfield, "Stage and Screen Entertainers in the Twentieth Century," in John Potter (ed.), *The Cambridge Companion to Singing* (Cambridge, 2000), pp. 65–67.

Example 1.1 "You Are My Sweetheart" (Dixon, Gathers, Pought, Pought, and Webb): The Bobbettes [Atlantic 2027, 1959], excerpt

awareness of tone, placement and breathing. However, commentators seem to have been slightly sidetracked by her choral background, hearing in her sound the effects of being trained to sing Gregorian chant.[28] Whilst there are solid reasons to attribute some of the melodic style of her early, self-penned tunes (such as "Maybe," "He's Gone," and "The Plea") to chant practice, her vocal approach is almost entirely derived from the practice of the doo-wop high tenors, many of whom used falsetto in combination with their "normal" voices.[29] Smith's high break made her head voice strongly reminiscent of male falsetto, and like her male doo-wop counterparts she had developed a significant overlap between the two registers, giving her a choice of registral placement for most of her lead range. In Example 1.2, the bridge of the Chantels' first release, "He's Gone," downwards stems represent notes taken in chest voice, and upwards stems those in falsetto.

---

[28] Greig, p. 11; Lucy O'Brien, *She Bop II* (London, 2002), p. 69.

[29] Clemente, p. 10. Clemente gives no supporting evidence for his claim, but Jacqueline Warwick has suggested "The Plea" is melodically structured according to chant procedure; see Warwick, *Girl Groups, Girl Culture: Popular Music and Identity in the 1960s* (New York and London, 2007), p. 16. For a discussion of doo-wop tenor styles, including falsetto, see Gribin and Schiff, pp. 31–34.

Example 1.2 "He's Gone" (Richard Barrett and Arlene Smith): The Chantels [End 1001, 1957], excerpt

Her registral virtuosity is, true to doo-wop styling, even more impressive in the context of the ornaments and phrasing she adds to the melodic line.

The vocal affectations of both doo-wop and rockabilly rely on this kind of flexibility and precision; the unhappy "break" of the inexperienced singer becomes a percussive and rhythmic effect in the throat of the experienced, along with other art-singing no-no's such as swooping (approaching a note from underneath can make it easier to hold in the chest voice without breaking), glottal stops and myriad catches, sobs and sighs. At times, these sounds can infiltrate the vocal line to the point of obscuring the lyrics. When Arlene sings "I really love you, with all my heart and soul, come back to me, and I'll never let you go," almost every other syllable, even those with initial consonants, is articulated in the throat: consummate, assured doo-wop. It is highly significant that the vocal style was developed and honed by teenagers. While the most successful teen doo-wops—and along with Smith, here we might include Frankie Lymon (Smith's acknowledged model) and Little Anthony—were anything but out of control, their highly stylized technique suggests or even overplays the vulnerable vocality "normal" to their age, hypervocalizing emotion through those distinctive gestures. The effect is intensified by a tendency in doo-wop songs to mismatch lyrics to melodic and rhythmic patterns that place the stresses on the wrong syllables, a feature that develops further in the teen girl repertoire.[30] If the sound could be

---

[30] Pavletich, p. 76. Pavletich recognizes this tendency as part of the "dumb" style, yet does not trace it back further into the predominantly male doo-wop repertoire where it certainly exists.

reproduced visually, the stumbling, hiccupping delivery of the doo-wop would be seen as almost a photographic negative of "normal" vocal eloquence. What we are intended to hear, and to believe, is that the voice that breaks or fails at a linguistic or musical level does so because of the singer's inability to control not the voice, but the physical manifestations of a heightened emotional state.

In some ways it is unfortunate to compare the Bobbettes with the Chantels. Each group had its strengths, and what the one did well, the other did less convincingly. The Chantels' first album contained only one up-tempo number, "Come My Little Baby," a pop rhumba clearly modeled off of the Bobbettes' whooping and calling, complete with the double lead voices (neither of which was supplied by Smith, whose sound surely must have been thought too mature). All of the eleven other songs are 12/8 ballads replete with the longings of teenage hearts, amply fulfilling Gribin and Schiff's prescription for doo-wop composition in that "both the words and melodies … touch the emotions while leaving the intellect unscathed."[31] It was perhaps this lack of versatility that meant that both groups failed to have a lasting impact on the charts, but their collective success encouraged other groups to form. In the end, the real breakthrough for the teen girl singer came in late 1960, just over two years after the arrival of Bobbettes and the Chantels, when the Shirelles became the first of the new girl groups to top the mainstream charts with "Will You Love Me Tomorrow." Various reasons have been proposed for the record's success: the immediacy and relevance of the lyrics; the novelty of the arrangement; or simply the happy combination of the right song, singer, and producer. Above all, however, it seems the directness of Shirley Owens's vocal performance made the record speak to a waiting audience of young girls, unlike any other before it. Where the Bobbettes had been precocious and Arlene Smith had been prodigious, Owens's teen voice could be heard for what it was: developing, vulnerable, sweet, real.

Teen singing in the 1960s

Before "Will You Love Me Tomorrow" was released, Doris Coley had been the Shirelles' usual lead singer. Coley's vocal approach frequently emulated Arlene Smith's, and many of the group's arrangements were influenced by the Chantels' girlie doo-wop. However, the result was not always wholly successful: Coley had a lower natural instrument than Smith, for certain, but she also hadn't her technical or stylistic confidence. The group's third single on Scepter, "I Saw A Tear," recorded in 1960, demonstrates the mismatch between the demands of the genre and the ability of the singer. Where doo-wop technique "constructs" the vulnerability of the voice through stylistic tricks, Coley's vocals were genuinely susceptible to the problems of trying to rein in (or free up) a developing teen voice. In the verse of "I Saw A Tear" we hear the irresistible force meeting the immoveable object at the

---

[31]   Gribin and Schiff, p. 20.

top of the chest range, and at the very beginning and at the bridge, an unfocused and tentative head voice that contrasts sharply with the brassiness of the lower register. The rigidity of her vocal equipment and the pressure it is under make intonation and enunciation all the more difficult, and she falls significantly behind the beat on the pairs of upbeat eighth-notes (Example 1.3).

Example 1.3 "I Saw A Tear" (Stan Green and Shirley Reeves): The Shirelles [Scepter 1207, 1960], excerpt

"I Saw A Tear" is not a particularly easy song, either for the listener or for the poor singer; it is very demanding, melodically and textually, with all those leaps and difficult-to-spit-out lyrics. "Will You Love Me Tomorrow" is an altogether different proposition. Although its overall melodic shape is similar to "I Saw A Tear," the verse doesn't stretch the top of Shirley Owens's lower range, so she is not obliged to switch completely into head voice for the bridge. Furthermore, the song itself implies no stylistic imperative; it is not a doo-wop ballad or a blues shout but a neutral carrier for whatever is brought to it in performance.[32] With no obligation to incorporate any kind of technical display, Owens could simply sing without any complicated ornamentation or vocal tricks. The pop styling of the arrangement and, more importantly, the mix (or the "balance" as they would have called it) allow her lighter double-tracked vocal to take prominence over the instrument and backing vocal tracks without straining. Throughout the verse, the backing vocals provide a rhythmic pulse above the main vocal, but at the bridge,

---

[32] Written by Carole King and Gerry Goffin, the song originally had a country and western feel; Alan Betrock, *Girl Groups: The Story of a Sound* (London and New York, 1982), p. 14. The Shirelles were not instantly taken with the song, either, thinking it "too white" (perhaps a comment relating to its lack of stylistic markers); Greig, p. 35.

Owens is on her own. The plaintive quality of her edged-up throat resonance accurately dates her voice without exposing it too cruelly, but the comfortable, lower-pitched hook on the song's title phrase allows the memory to retain the pleasanter sound of her relaxed chest voice.

The way this record exploited Owens's teenage vocal vulnerability to its best advantage, rather than disguising it or avoiding problem areas, appears to have been something of a revelation. Using the bridge of a song as the showcase for the emotionally-charged and brittle upper chest voice, double-tracked to take the edge off the fragility and the insecure intonation, rapidly became a teen girl trademark. The Angels' first top-twenty hit, "'Till," recorded in 1961, provides an early example of the phenomenon; in addition, the lead singer Linda Jankowski incorporates a few of the hypervocalizing gestures of doo-wop, lending the vocals a slightly histrionic, theatrical tone. Each occurrence of the word "'till" is hit with a forceful enunciation of the initial consonant, a technique that delays the pitch-carrying vowel and starts the word with a petulant-sounding hiccup. At the bridge, the melody starts up the octave on the word "you." Jankowski punches the beginning of the note from underneath, the resulting word sounding much more like "hee-oo"; rhythmically she slightly anticipates the first beat of the bar, but the vowel sound is not fully resolved until nearly the second beat, and she never quite makes it up to the correct pitch. The second line of the bridge, beginning with the word "all," gets a similar treatment, though the effect is not nearly as severe because the note is much shorter. The recording conditions for this vocal may, of course, not have been ideal. Mixing desks were not universally equipped with the means to return a realistic ambience to the performer during recording, and if she were performing without sophisticated foldback, she may have felt it necessary to hit the high notes even harder.

"Will You Love Me Tomorrow" is written along the lines of a 32-bar AABA Tin Pan Alley standard, with the lower-pitch hook at the end of each A phrase; "'Till" is a variant of the same form. Songs with a verse–chorus–verse–chorus structure, in which the whole chorus (and hence, the memorable hook) could go up the octave, intensified the dramatic effect of the range shift. A mature voice could handle the break smoothly and elegantly; think, for instance, of Doris Day's "Que Sera, Sera," which first charted in 1956. But in 1962, smooth and elegant were not within the teen girl's natural constituency; much more relevant and exciting was the way Darlene Love hit the chorus of the Crystals/Blossoms "He's a Rebel," a song which shamelessly displays her impressive range. Not only is there a clear octave difference between the verse and the hook chorus (with an added semitone rise just to tweak expectations), if you listen all the way through, you also get Love shouting up to $c\sharp^2$ at the end; you even hear her tucking in a head-voice $f\sharp^2$ in the fade-out. And of course, the song features the teen trademark of the bungled word-stresses—"*I* bet he's al*ways* the one ... "—which Love takes in her stride.

At the time of recording, Darlene Love was no longer in her teens but an experienced professional singer who had the sustained power of a gospel soloist; however, the subject material and the technical construction of the song situated the record squarely in the teen arena. The song format of "He's a Rebel" was a winner, topping the pop charts and just missing the same place on the R&B charts in October 1962. After its release both the high hook chorus (which occurred many more times in a song than a bridge passage) and to a lesser extent the wailing fadeout, whilst not always guaranteeing success, became regular features of teen vocals. Up-tempo numbers now also reached into the high chest range, brisk declamation enhancing the brittleness of the vocal quality. While some teen singers were up to the challenge (notably the Angels' new lead singer Peggy Santiglia), others were not. Insecure intonation at the top almost seems to have become a virtue; and whereas double-tracking could be used to mask approximate intonation on the occasional note and to fill out the vocal, it also had the potential to make every note sound slightly out of tune, as pitches on the two tracks beat and phase against each other. A stirling example is provided by Little Peggy March's recording of "I Will Follow Him," one of the biggest hits of 1963. Little Peggy's tight and tense performance of the chorus ("I *love* him, I *love* him, I *love* him, and where he goes I'll *fo*llow, I'll *fo*llow, I'll *fo*llow") is exaggerated by the backing vocals that double her line an octave up—all the way to high c^3. Yet on this record, as with the vast majority of girl group records, even though the screech factor is introduced almost from the very beginning, the contrast with the mellower conversational range in the verse is still very important.

Younger, less technically able singers may have idolized Darlene Love in the same way that Doris Coley had modeled herself off of Arlene Smith, but the difference between 1962 and 1959 was that the fragile teen sound had been established as a viable commercial quality. Yet despite the initial success of many teen artistes, long-, or even medium-, term careers eluded them, a large proportion consigned to the "one hit wonder" category, others managing only a handful of follow-up singles at the most. There is an abundance of explanations for why so many girl groups suffered a quick demise—no real talent, no support, lawsuits, the Beatles, the pop world is "just like that"—but certainly one contributing factor could have been that their voices simply did not hold out. The extreme pressure one hears on these girls' vocal folds eventually would have caused them to develop nodules, to coarsen or just to give way. In order to survive vocally, a girl may have had to change her technique, and therefore her style of singing and vocal sound, but this might not have always been practical—executives were typically less worried about maintaining the artists' careers than maintaining a string of hits for the company.

The exigencies of live and television appearances also may have played a role in shaping the sound of the teen girl groups—"good" singing technique does not take into account how the body looks in performance. In the days in which she was still an aspiring star, Aretha Franklin is known to have complained about being told to use her stomach muscles to draw in her waist to appear as slim as possible on television, rather than keeping them relaxed and flexible to support her voice. The result was that she had to sing from her throat, and she felt that this jeopardized her performance (and her voice).[33] Franklin was a contemporary of the first girl groups—a year younger than Arlene Smith, and making her first record a year earlier in 1956—but, more experienced and clearly keenly aware of her vocal technique, she was perhaps less malleable than other teenagers in her position. Furthermore, she was not part of the girl group ethos: her early material—gospel, jazz and Tin Pan Alley standards—did not share the themes of teen pop, nor were her audience ever encouraged to hear her as a girl. Instead, she was being groomed by her record company, Columbia, for a long-term career as a genuine vocal talent and an all-round entertainer—her first two albums for the company were called *The Electrifying Aretha Franklin* and *The Tender, The Moving, The Swinging Aretha ...* (both 1962). If the importance of physical appearance could outweigh good technical judgment in even her case, given that the management had a vested interest in keeping her in optimal vocal health, how much less value might have been placed on the delicate instruments of more expendable teen singers?

When Pavletich refers to the "dumb" sound of the 1960s' girl singer, she primarily defines it in terms of (bad) vocal technique, encouraged and enriched by the lyrical material of the songs, their subject matter and their occasionally bizarre rhythmic cadences. The 1960s' teen singers rarely tackled repertoire written outside their own sphere but when they did, it could be performed in a way that transformed it into their own. The 1963 Christmas covers on the album *A Christmas Gift for You from Phil Spector* show how Tin Pan Alley could be adapted and translated into Brill Building teen-song. The arrangements may have further trivialized the already trivial ("ringa-linga-linga-ding-dong-ding"), and the Spector production values may have already been virtually synonymous with girl group pop, but the differences between the vocal approaches of Darlene Love on "White Christmas" and Ronnie Bennett on the Ronettes' "Frosty the Snowman" illustrate how "teen" had become an aural and technical construct. Love's voice is gospely, full, open-throated and well supported, and her delivery is also curiously peppered with Bing Crosby's signature mordent, making the whole track a more mature take on Spector's basic sound. On the other hand, Bennett's doo-wop swoops and glottal catches, her strong Upper West Side accent, her wayward intonation and the casual syncopation that destabilizes her lyrics' original accents ("Fros*ty* the snow*man*") give the children's song a teen credibility beyond that created by the backing track. The melody stretches her upwards into the brittle high-larynx range, yet the swoops allow her to reach the highest notes, if not in complete comfort at least with relative accuracy. By contrast, Bennett's performance of "Sleigh Ride," which is pitched to exploit her alto range, is styled much more closely to Love's "White Christmas," complete with a lower larynx, a neutral accent and "adult" mordents that hearken back to a crooner aesthetic. Bennett was clearly a more technically accomplished singer than the performance on "Frosty" would suggest; one assumes then that the vocal styling of "Frosty" was deliberately intended by Spector to create a younger pop sound. And by the same token, although the effect

---

[33]   O'Brien, p. 89.

is less pronounced, Love is made to sound more teen on "Winter Wonderland" through the use of double-tracking.

Spector's Christmas album provides evidence that by the end of 1963 at least one producer consciously elicited from his singers a teen sound that was, even within the narrow confines of his own production values, differentiated from an adult sound through both physical and musical techniques. Nevertheless, the deliberate reliance on "bad" vocal technique to project a teen sensibility onto female voices must have reached its apogee in the Shangri-Las' three 1964 hits: "Remember," "Leader Of The Pack," and "Give Him a Great Big Kiss." The Ganser and Weiss sisters—Marge and Mary Ann, Betty and Mary—made no pretence of being good singers, but they expressed themselves in a way that was immediately recognized and owned by their audience. When faced with a technical challenge, they did what came naturally, with their broad and unaltered Queens accents creating a very forward and nasal placement—what Pavletich calls "the 'nyaah' sound."[34] The arrangement of "Give Him a Great Big Kiss" stretched their abilities at both ends of the range. Marge, Mary Ann and Betty struggle to reach the low notes (g and $f\sharp$) in an accompaniment figure, and have to place the sound very forward and nasal to get any volume at all, yet when they are required to sing a higher figure, they don't even attempt to raise the larynx, but sing instead in their light and slightly hooty head voices, almost coincidentally creating a feature of the altered vocal tone. Lead singer Mary Weiss struggles to reach the top of the melody (e^2) in her edged-up chest voice, resolutely keeping her larynx high and the breath pressure full on, regardless of the effect on her intonation.

The Shangri-Las sang as if with no knowledge of or regard for any technique, as if they were speaking (or whining, or shrieking, or sobbing, or yelling) to approximate pitches, substituting "real" emotive vocal disruption for the technical affectations of doo-wop. This apparent vocal honesty had two quite important effects. First, the out-and-out rejection of the standard southern-inflected accent adopted by most popular singers gave their voices an even more untutored and, by implication, rebellious teen sound (compare Mary's performances to Peggy Santiglia's accomplished drawl on "My Boyfriend's Back").[35] To listeners not from New York, who may not have been able to distinguish West Side from Queens, it

---

[34] Pavletich, p. 83.

[35] The southern accent, once a clear marker for blackness, had long been the standard accent of popular singers; for a discussion, see my "White Face, Black Voice: Race, Gender and Region in the Music of the Boswell Sisters," *Journal of the Society for American Music* 1/2 (2007): 207–55. The Boswell Sisters were consistently mistaken for black singers because of their strong New Orleans accents, which they retained when singing. Curiously, Mary Weiss claims that James Brown booked the Shangri-Las for a tour in 1964, soon after the release of "Remember (Walkin' in the Sand)," without realizing that they were white girls; Miriam Linna and Billy Miller, "Mary Weiss of the Shangri-Las," http://www.nortonrecords.com/maryweiss/index.html, accessed 7 April 2008. This may be an indication of how the voice is racialized differently in different eras.

would have connected them with the Ronettes, who also made a feature of their natural accents—one might also note that both groups eventually cultivated a "bad girl" image. Second, it made Mary's voice instantly recognizable, so that she was identifiable to the listener as a personality, rather than just a singing voice. Moreover, her speaking voice was as prominent on their records as her singing, giving her aural identity even more precision and reliability. Yet Pavletich claims (implying that her source was Jeff Barry himself) that the songwriter "directed" the girls' performances, standing opposite the microphones and mouthing the words at them, extracting from Mary the emotionality that was her trademark.[36] Barry's co-writer Ellie Greenwich described the Shangri-Las' first two singles as "little soap-operas."[37] Pavletich concurs, calling them "the last stand of radio drama on the airwaves."[38] The lack of sophistication in their voices, at least in terms of conforming to "good" vocal technique, if not in the melodramatic delivery, made their performances worthy companions of *As The World Turns*.[39] Furthermore, although Weiss's voice was frequently double-tracked or subjected to delay effects, the spoken word and the sound effects (seagulls, motorbikes) grounded the songs in a "real" setting, as if they had been recorded as the events they described were taking place.

Virtually every writer who has discussed girl group music has focused on the issue of identification between its target audience (teen girls) and the music, particularly its lyrics. But the popularity of the girl group sound was no doubt bolstered and sustained by the ease with which its target audience, teen girls, could not just relate to it, but also reproduce it, singing into their hairbrushes and dancing in front of the mirror. As a fan turned artiste, Greenwich suggested as much: "We, girls, would live vicariously through these groups and lots of us formed our very own ... performing at school functions and parties or wherever they'd allow."[40] Yet even those not motivated enough to perform in public could share in the owning of the sound—what one now might call the embodiment of the teen voice. Susan Douglas writes lovingly about the experience of singing along to the records, and how this intensified both the loss and the discovery of the teenage self, the identification process whereby "superimposing our own dramas, from our own lives, onto each song, each of us could assume an active role in shaping the song's meaning."[41] With the best will in the world, few girls could sing like Doris Day or Judy Garland, but almost all could get very close to the sound of Mary Weiss.

---

[36] Pavletich, p. 83.

[37] Betrock, p. 102.

[38] Pavletich, p. 83.

[39] *As the World Turns* is a television soap opera that began in 1956, released by Procter & Gamble Productions Ltd. on the CBS network. Its final show is scheduled to air in September 2010; http://news.bbc.co.uk/1/hi/entertainment/8403036.stm (accessed March 1, 2010).

[40] Clemente, p. 5.

[41] Douglas, *Where the Girls Are*, p. 87.

Where have all the young girls gone? The teen voice after girl groups

The Shangri-Las flourished at the twilight of the girl groups' domination of the charts. Authors and pundits variously blame conflict within groups, a tailing-off of ambition, and most frequently the withdrawal of support from male industry moguls after the British Invasion, the implication being that even if they didn't self-destruct in career terms, without their "creators," the girls had little to offer the business or the public.[42] Motown may have nominally kept the girl group flag flying with Martha Reeves and the Vandellas, and especially through the leadership of the Supremes, but it was clear that a different agenda was being followed. Diana, Flo and Mary were not meant to be seen as teen: From the time of their first hit, they were young *ladies*; they were made to dress, and act, like women.[43] As Douglas noted, the Supremes were perhaps too glamorous, too "Vegas" for American teenagers to feel totally identified with them.[44] As folk, rock and soul eased the girl groups off center stage, singers with techniques more suited to long-term vocal stability—Aretha Franklin, Dionne Warwick, Dusty Springfield, Joni Mitchell—became popular, each a virtuoso in her own genre. But the vocal technique with which teen singers established a link with their young audience did not disappear: it can be heard in the voices of later 60s stars such as Cher. It can even be heard infiltrating male vocals of sub-Beatles guitar bands—think of any Freddie and the Dreamers or Herman's Hermits single you like—and the bubble-gum pop of, for instance, "Sugar, Sugar" by The Archies, another Jeff Barry production from 1969. Significantly, once Motown and Atlantic soul claimed a new strong, separate vocal identity for the black female pop singer—one based on gospel, blues and jazz vocalizing—it became rare for black girls to adopt the teen

---

[42] A typical apologia runs thus: "While the music of girl groups had flourished, many imaginative producers—from Phil Spector to Shadow Morton—had used the form to realise their musical visions, aided by a group of supremely gifted songwriters … . But with the British invasion, led by the Beatles, producers and writers turned their attention away from the girls; as the economic incentives of girl groups dwindled, intense creative competition died away. Without quality producers and writers behind them many of the artists found it impossible to continue; few of the great singers of girl group rock—Arlene Smith, Darlene Love, Shirley Alston—found success once their original musical creators had deserted them;" Greg Shaw, "Leaders of the Pack: Teen Dreams and Tragedy in Girl Group Rock," *History of Rock* 29 (1982), p. 568.

[43] Mary Wilson describes the vocal, physical and social "polishing" undertaken by Motown's artists through the guidance of its Artist Development program, although in the case of the Supremes she saw it as a natural development of their "own unique and very sophisticated style"; Wilson, *Dreamgirl and Supreme Faith: My Life as a Supreme* (New York, 1999), pp. 148–58.

[44] Douglas, *Where the Girls Are*, p. 96.

sound in which they had such a vital development role; vocally, "teen" gradually became synonymous with "white teen."[45]

In the 1970s the teen sound retreated even further as far as women artists were concerned, surfacing only occasionally in disco acts such as the Nolan Sisters and Tina Charles, although teen male singers like David Cassidy and Donny Osmond (Mary Weiss's natural histrionic successor: "Someone help me! Help me! Help me, *plee-heease*!") kept the torch burning for the high larynx and the closed throat. But in the 1980s the advent of MTV and the rise and rise of the new song-writing mega-producers such as Stock, Aitken and Waterman brought the expendable teen singer back to the industry's heart. The teen sound returned to chart-topping glory, and doors were re-opened for short-lived wonders such as Tiffany, who—like her 1960s' forbears—sang about the anxieties of adolescent love ("I think we're alone now").[46] When white teen babes re-emerged as a major force in pop, they had their vocal role models in girls that had made their mothers twist and shout. Individual voices like Cyndi Lauper and Belinda Carlisle or less individual voices like Madonna, Kylie Minogue and Debbie Gibson; and indeed all those that flowed from them—the Spice Girls, even Britney Spears and Kelly Clarkson—owe a fundamental debt to those 1960s girl singers who made it OK, even virtuous, to sound and to sing like a teenager.

---

[45]   There is an argument that the Supremes' sound, which was decidedly *not* based on black-identified performance styles, is anomalous in this respect, which would appear to be supported by Wilson's claim that "Motown knew the Supremes weren't really accepted by blacks"; Wilson, *Dreamgirl and Supreme Faith*, p. 222.

[46]   Darwisch, Tiffany, "I Think We're Alone Now," (MCA 53167, 1987).

Chapter 2
Vocal Decorum: Voice, Body, and Knowledge in the Prodigious Singer, Brenda Lee[1]

Robynn J. Stilwell

That explains why Brenda Lee was so successful. She was not a threat, and she was one of them. With Brenda Lee, you have somebody who was so titanically vocally gifted at such an incredibly young age that that was a blank slate that was waiting to be written on.

—Robert Oermann[2]

This purity, this harmlessness [of the child] is presented as complete vacancy; the absence of harmfulness amounts, in fact, to nothing at all, a blank image waiting to be formed.

—James F. Kincaid[3]

In the documentary *The Women of Rockabilly: Welcome to the Club*, country music historian Robert Oermann's almost clichéd comment about the most successful of these female singers of the 1950s has a disconcerting effect. The familiarity of the tropes entrained about Brenda Lee practically renders her invisible and mute at the very point where her exceptionality is most marked. But that erasure indirectly reveals much about the marketing of popular music, assumptions about gender, race, class, age, and sexuality, and our anxieties about the precociously gifted, reminding us that "prodigy" still carries with it the echoes of its archaic meanings as portentous, ominous, even monstrous.

Oermann's vision of Lee is of an empty vessel. She is "not a threat" to the girls who are presumed and assumed to be, and may genuinely in large part have been,

---

[1] * My thanks to my collaborators in this volume, as well as Lisa Rhodes and Mitchell Morris, for many fruitful discussions.

[2] *The Women of Rockabilly: Welcome to the Club* (Beth Harrington, 2004). This is an hour-long documentary, aired on many PBS stations in America, which combines recent interviews and archival footage of four female rockabilly singers.

[3] James R. Kincaid, *Child-loving :The Erotic Child and Victorian Culture* (New York, 1992), p. 13.

the primary consumers of pop records.[4] But this is not a strictly musical argument, of course; it is one based on a series of displaced virtual mating rituals in which music is part of an erotic exchange. This slippage of gendered encounters is based on a heterosexual economy of competition (among females) for the attention of the desired male. While this is normally configured with the male as the musical artist who woos his fans with his mating call, the placing of a female artist in the soliciting position is historically and culturally problematic, almost always an echo of the siren luring men into danger. When the female is prepubescent, the problematic becomes a minefield.

Too much emphasis on the overt sexual politics of popular music, however, can be distracting from the more subtle and complex workings of perception, reception, and performance revolving around the child prodigy. Brenda Lee's placement at a transitional point in musical and cultural history, her recognizability as a novelty figure, and her subsequent long, successful career that nonetheless operates outside the mainstream—in country music and cabaret—makes her a fruitful figure for examination.

The gravitational swing point of Lee's career trajectory coincides with the rise of rock and roll. She had been singing in public since she was three years old, on radio and television by the age of six, and was the main breadwinner of her family by nine. Her recording career started with Decca Records and legendary Nashville producer Owen Bradley at age eleven in 1956.

This period is simultaneously one of the most recognized turning points in twentieth-century American culture and still one of the most under-understood. The rise of the music industry as a rival to the movies as a cultural determinant, the emergence of musical styles that had been regionally (strongly) and racially (much more weakly) isolated through expanded media reach, the beginnings of the Civil Rights movement and the subsequent foregrounding of racial issues that interacted with both musical style and industrial practice in particularly volatile fashion, and the first stirrings of both the adolescent and the female as challenge to the status quo are all key elements. Their interaction is somewhat more complicated than the broad strokes we are normally given, however; and the roots reach much further back than 1954, the date usually cited as the beginning of the "rock era."

Rock and roll emerged as an umbrella term for a number of southern regional styles—including jump blues, New Orleans rhythm and blues, Texas Swing, even the Cajun two-step—but the music that is perhaps now most strongly associated with this moment tends to be rockabilly, a short-lived style that is itself rife with

---

[4]   In her autobiography, Lee does say that the vast majority of her fan mail was from girls: "The girls loved me, because I was someone they could talk to. The boys liked me— not as a girlfriend—but as someone they could confide in about the girl they did like. I hated that." Brenda Lee, with Robert K. Oermann and Julie Clay, *Little Miss Dynamite: The Life and Times of Brenda Lee* (New York, 2002), pp. 103–04.

contradictions, much like punk twenty years later.[5] Rockabilly was both "infantile" and highly sexualized, and these qualities were mapped onto prevailing patterns of racial thinking (largely ignoring other elements such as regionality, class, and age), particularly by those from outside the American South. Rockabilly was a southern, mostly rural, blues-based music that was considered "black" in style, but was almost exclusively "white" in appearance; the musicians made the marginal class of "white trash" audible and visible—and desirable—in mainstream American culture for the first time.

Although the contributions of female performers are now, belatedly, getting attention, rockabilly has long been associated with iconic male performers such as Elvis Presley, Jerry Lee Lewis, Carl Perkins, Johnny Cash, Gene Vincent, and Buddy Holly. Yet the androgyny of rockabilly performance—both in the musicians' appearance and, more importantly, vocal style—is a volatile point, one made more so by reconsidering the place of female performers, and further complicated when those performers are adolescents. Rockabilly is a fascinating laboratory for the examination of how "race makes and is made by relations of sex and sexuality, class, and culture"[6] as it mobilizes all these terms and to some extent makes them interchangeable (one could turn the equation around and argue, for instance, that "culture makes and is made by sex and sexuality, class, and race"). Unstated, but implicated in sex and sexuality, is puberty and adolescence, that broad twilight zone between child and adult that was in flux in the 1950s.[7]

One of the obvious functions of *Welcome to the Club*, was to spotlight four artists—the "women" of rockabilly, even though they were all girls in their mid-teens or younger at the time—who had had some impact at the time but had subsequently been forgotten, or erased, from the narrative of rock history. Adding the female voice, figuratively and literally, is one of the first maneuvers of many feminist strategies, to remind us that girls were, for a while at least, tolerated in

---

[5]   Indeed, punk was based on a "back-to-basics" approach that aspired to the lean qualities of 1950s rockabilly and spawned a brief resurgence of the style in acts like the Stray Cats and Robert Gordon. For more on the complexity of the early rock and roll style, see Robynn J. Stilwell, "Music of the Youth Revolution: Rock through the 1960s," in Nicholas Cook and Anthony Pople (eds), *The Cambridge History of Twentieth-Century Music* (Cambridge, 2004), pp. 418–52.

[6]   Ruth Frankenberg, "Introduction: Local Whitenesses, Localizing Whiteness," in Ruth Frankenberg (ed.), *Displacing Whiteness: Essays in Social and Cultural Criticism* (Durham, NC, 1997), p. 28.

[7]   France Winddance Twine has observed how puberty was a key turning point in racial awareness and definition, by themselves and others, for "brown-skinned white girls," or middle-class American girls of mixed African and European descent who went through adolescence in the 1980s. See "Brown-Skinned White Girls: Class, Culture, and the Construction of White Identity in Suburban Communities," in Ruth Frankenberg (ed.), *Displacing Whiteness: Essays in Social and Cultural Criticism* (Durham, NC, 1997), pp. 215–43.

60   *SHE'S SO FINE*

the boys' club before they were kicked out.[8] As such, it is informative and not only may awaken interest in these artists, but can be quite revealing in the ways in which the discourse is framed.

Among the four women discussed—Janis Martin, Wanda Jackson, Lorrie Collins, and Brenda Lee, with a nod toward Rose Maddox—Lee was both the youngest and most successful, the one most likely to be recognized by a modern audience. However, this memory is filtered through the persistence of her seasonal novelty hit, "Rockin' Around the Christmas Tree" and the more mainstream pop hits that came later in her career. Her child prodigy status is a chronological and marketing point, but rarely a musical one, a curiosity to be marveled at but held in a glass case, untouched, unexamined. Her voice was big for her size, her style was old for her age, but what is the effect beyond wonder, and perhaps, fear?

Brenda Lee was a child star who grew through adolescence to young adulthood during this period of musical and cultural transition, in a style heavily marked by sexuality, race, class, and regionality—in a diverse country being drawn together by technology, media, and even the external threat of Godless Communism, into a fantasy of an ideal (white) America. Lee's development exposes a number of issues surrounding concepts of the child, maturity, knowledge, and performance.

The child star

The child star is a figure well developed by the mid-twentieth century, refined by generations of vaudeville acts and film stars: precocious, charming, and occasionally alarming. While the attraction to cute children is undoubtedly in part biological, fostering a protective instinct, the *performing* child presents particular problems of both subjectivity and objectivity. There is a "to-be-looked-at-ness" (in Laura Mulvey's awkward but apt terminology) that is in constant tension with sexual spectacularization, and with the agency of the children themselves as skilled performers, who may grow as artists from cute (failed) mimicry to skilled technical performance out of step with their physical, intellectual, and psychological/emotional/social development as human beings.[9] The relationship between the performer/performance and the actual child can, and usually does, cause cognitive dissonance in the spectator/auditor.

The question of the child as a focus of inquiry (because in itself it replicates this focus of gaze) is a charged one, rarely approached or considered. James F. Kincaid, in his work on the construction of the child in Victorian literature and its ramifications in twentieth-century popular culture, is one of the few to confront the

---

[8] See, for instance, Rozsika Parker and Griselda Pollock, *Old Mistresses: Women, Art, and Ideology* (London, 1981); David F. Noble, *A World Without Women: The Christian Clerical Culture of Western Science* (New York, 1992); and Mary A. Bufwack and Robert K. Oermann, *Finding Her Voice: Women in Country Music, 1800–2000* (Nashville, TN, 2003).

[9] Laura Mulvey, "Visual Pleasure and Narrative Cinema," *Screen* 16/3 (1975): 6–18.

issue head-on—or at least to try to, because even Kincaid is constantly aware of the sensitive ground on which he treads, the way in which white, Anglo-American middle-class culture evades and resists, deflects and isolates questions of childhood purity, innocence, knowledge, love, affection, and sexuality. From a more empirical point of view and working at about the same time, sociologist Valerie Walkerdine's work on girlhood comes to some strikingly similar conclusions about what this hegemonic culture prizes in the child, corroborating Kincaid's possibly controversial proposals and their persistence in modern society.[10]

The crucial qualities can be encapsulated in Kincaid's triumvirate of emptiness, androgyny, and whiteness. Although there is, as we shall see, a way in which all of these factors collapse into the first, "emptiness," there is much to be illuminated by separating these strands and examining some of their constituent elements and the way that they weave together in the persona, presentation, and musical style of a white child prodigy in a genre—rockabilly—normally defined by overt displays of sexuality and the interplay of racial difference.[11]

The plenitude of emptiness

The most comprehensive and yet the slipperiest of Kincaid's categories is that of "emptiness." As Kincaid notes, emptiness is not so much the attribute of an actual child as it is a construct that post-Industrial Revolution Anglo-American bourgeois culture has created to project onto the "child," who is not defined so much by chronological age (although obviously that is a contingent element) but by lack or absence.

Emptiness is usually cast as such positive attributes as innocence or purity, for example; but these are qualities more easily defined by what they do not contain than by what they do. Purity is a lack of flaws, innocence a lack of guilt or of evil, but also of knowledge and capability. The ideal child is a passive, empty construction without initiative or intentionality. But of course, in modern society, innocence also has an unshakable connotation of sexuality, even if it is sexuality denied:

> [T]he division between adult and child … has been at least for the past two hundred years heavily eroticized: the child is that species which is free of sexual feeling or response; the adult is that species which has crossed over into sexuality. The definitional base is erotic: our discourse insists on it by loudly denying its importance. Of course other binaries are involved too, those

---

[10] See especially Valerie Walkerdine, *Daddy's Girl: Young Girls and Popular Culture* (Cambridge, MA, 1997).

[11] Genre and style are used with loose interchangeability in most popular music discourse; I will make a subtle distinction between "style" (a set of musical markers) and "genre," which includes modes of dress, speech, performance, lifestyle, and other extramusical elements that cluster around a musical style.

involving innocence and experience, ignorance and knowledge, incapacity and competence, empty and full, low and high, weak and powerful. All of these divisions are very wobbly, requiring massive bolstering by this discourse.[12]

Kincaid's "of course" is an important one. Although it is often used as if it were an unambiguous and monolithic term that can be safely used as a singular rather than a collective, sexuality is something that is expressed in a variety of arenas, perhaps the simplest of which is biological reproductive maturity; however, even that border is a hazy one. None of them come suddenly, they are traversed over a period of time and experience and may occur at different rates. Physical and emotional maturation, the acquisition of knowledge and understanding—not necessarily the same thing—are among the chief transformations one undergoes in moving from child to adult; these transformations, as Kincaid suggests, are not ones that are perceived as from one positive state to another, but from a kind of nothingness into being. Any number of nuances of behavior signal (quite often deceptively) the level one has achieved. These behaviors are not innate and fixed, but cultural, and as such are performances that individuals rehearse, first through mimicry and with gradual assumption of authority and ownership of the implications of those gestures and expressions.

It is in this liminal space that the precocious child is disruptive, no longer entirely empty or blank, but able to mimic adult behavior, perhaps with such a degree of proficiency that he or she actually seems to *know* in ways that one presumes a child should not know. Knowingness is a dangerous fullness, whether or not it is genuinely held or merely "performed" (or at any point along the learning curve between the two end points), and it may be useful to make part of our distinction between the precocious child, who is proficient in mimicry but only in a superficial or technical manner; and the prodigious child, whose mimicry is suffused with knowingness, who is more difficult to be caught "acting." It is almost never possible to tell if the prodigy actually "knows," but she can give the rattling impression that she does.[13]

The perfectly "empty" child occupies a position noticeably similar to the objectified female position posited in Laura Mulvey's seminal "Visual Pleasure and Narrative Cinema," this parallelism marking the essentially eroticized position of the child who is being observed.[14] However, the precocious or prodigious child

---

[12] Kincaid, pp. 6–7.

[13] Although acting is certainly a skill as much as singing or dancing, a prodigy like Margaret O'Brien might be instructive here. O'Brien was rarely sexualized to the extent of Shirley Temple or even of Judy Garland, but her skill amazed contemporary audiences with her seemingly transparent, or "natural," ability to project emotions. She was a real child who was unnerving in her ability to portray a real child. She was not an empty child at all.

[14] The slippage between objectification/spectacularization and sexualization can also be seen in the way a male star is often thrust into a gender- or sexuality-ambiguous position when he is the object of the camera's gaze/appreciation, whether in stereotypically

frequently turns this passive position into one that is active, even if in a passive-aggressive fashion; Kincaid, for instance, speaks about the role of the naughty child who generates the plot of various Buster Brown-type comic strips by provoking a spanking.

Kincaid, particularly with Buster Brown, but also with boy stars like Freddie Bartholomew, Ricky Schroeder, and Macaulay Culkin, argues for their androgyny, but this is a culturally tenuous line: androgyny is not so much defined by a presence of traits for both genders as it is by a lack of masculinity. Even the tomboy is less a "boyish girl" in some respects, than she is a "pretty boy"—while not as common as the girly girl or pretty little boy, she is present as Frankie in *The Member of the Wedding* (played by Julie Harris at the age of 26 in the movie) or Scout in *To Kill a Mockingbird* (played by Mary Badham in the movie). It is noticeable that these girls are much more frequently from the American South, a place where the harder/faster rules of gender and sexuality (and race) found in Britain or the urban Northeast of the US are more complex and fluid.[15]

More modern examples might be Midwesterners kd lang,[16] Melissa Etheridge, and Hilary Swank, with Swank in particular having begun as a child star literally taking over for a boy (Ralph Macchio) in *The Next Karate Kid III* (1994) even before her Oscar-winning turns as a girl who "passed" as a boy (*Boys Don't Cry*, 1999) and as a boxer (*Million Dollar Baby*, 2004). These women, particularly lang and Swank, have retained the lanky look of an adolescent boy into their thirties and forties; the truly "butch" girl has been erased from cultural currency.[17] But her

---

"feminized" action such as dancing or dressing (the extended scene of Tony Manero not just dressing but "primping" in *Saturday Night Fever* (John Badham, 1977)), but also in sports action or violence. For more discussion, see Steve Neale, "Masculinity as Spectacle," *Screen* 24/6 (1983): 2–16; Steven Cohan, "'Feminizing' the Song-and-Dance Man: Fred Astaire and the Spectacle of Masculinity in the Hollywood Musical, " Chapter 7 in *Hollywood Musicals: The Film Reader* (New York, 2002), pp. 97–101; and Susan Jeffords, *Hard Bodies: Hollywood Masculinity in the Reagan Era* (New Brunswick, NJ, 1994).

[15] Their stories are also shot through with issues of race and class, hinging on plot points of sexuality, whether it is Scout coming to a more nuanced understanding of her father through his defense of a black man accused of raping a white woman, or the simpler rite of passage of Frankie's brother's wedding and her assumption of an adult role in that ritual, guided by the maternal figure of the family's black housekeeper.

[16] lang is Canadian, but she is from Alberta, the "Midwest" of Canada.

[17] Gender in punk music of the 1970s is a complicated construct in that it embraced more women than any previous genre, at times in a consciously (or semi-consciously) transgressive fashion, and the aggressive, confrontational stance tended to read as masculine: both Patti Smith, who emerged in the 1970s, and Skin (of the group Skunk Anansie), who emerged in the 1990s, have the lean, rangy body type of the pretty boys, but dress either in masculine drag (Smith in a suit and tie), or the more unisex-but-still-butch jeans and tee-shirts or Skin's militaristic camouflage and khaki. Toyah Willcox was in her late teens when she memorably appeared in Derek Jarman's 1977 film *Jubilee* as a butch girl with cropped hair and khakis, but she was quickly remodeled into a more glamorous New Wave image

pretty-boy counterpart has become the classic look of rockabilly, of Elvis Presley, Eddie Cochran, Gene Vincent, and Jerry Lee Lewis, refined and reinscribed by Robert Gordon and Bryan Setzer in the punkabilly revival of the late 1970s and early 1980s.

Not surprisingly, both Kincaid and Walkerdine spend a great deal of time analyzing the 1930s images of Shirley Temple and Little Orphan Annie; the two are not dissimilar in appearance, and Temple's cinematic roles certainly often mimicked the basic narrative of Little Orphan Annie, in which the blond-curled, blue-eyed—or empty eyed!—working-class or poor little girl eventually "seduces" the upper-middle-class or wealthy mature male into forming a family unit. An adult female may be adjunct to this family formation, but it is the dyad of the man and the little girl that forms the primary relationship, rather than the adult-to-adult link.

Temple is a fascinating figure because, as a real little girl rather than simply an empty vessel or plot device, she grew and developed. We can see her learning and assimilating the behaviors that we mark as adult by virtue of their sexual implication or their demands on physical dexterity—although the separation between those two may be one that is more abstract than exists in reality. In the Jack Hays-produced Baby Burlesk short *Glad Rags to Riches* (1932), three-and-a-half-year-old Temple is cast in the stereotypical role of the actress betrayed by her two-timing boyfriend. Clearly, part of the amusement in these short subjects was exactly the lack of understanding that the children had in what they were doing, and also the immaturity of their ability to express this.

She sings, she dances, she emotes backstage, and those acting scenes most strongly point out the gap between her physical and verbal (and possibly cognitive) development. She is able to mimic the seductive moves of the stage actress and the melodramatic gestures of the backstage tragedian, though still retaining the traces of awkwardness that betray motor skills not adequately entrained; her line readings, however, are mechanical, and sometimes her toddler mouth can simply not form the words. There is a lack of integration between voice, body, and knowingness.[18] Toddler Shirley knows the beats to hit, but her physicality fails her. She doesn't invest real feeling in the words because she clearly doesn't understand them, but

---

on her way to sweet-faced, mainstream girl-next-door, even taking on the lead role in the musical *Calamity Jane*, once played by the ultimate girl-next-door Doris Day. As interest in the early 1980s turned to revisioning earlier forms of glamour, from the Edwardians to 1940s Hollywood and even 1960s Motown, Annie Lennox's New Wave masculine drag reflects both Smith's punkish look and the alluring transgression of 1930s Marlene Dietrich. Hers is perhaps a more even mix of the masculine and feminine, is more physically mature and can still seem more shocking and disruptive, quite possibly because gender fluidity is more expected and tolerated in the child/adolescent.

[18]   The quite evident lack of knowingness may allow these early films to border on child pornography, as in *War Babies* (also 1932), a parody of *Carmen* in which kisses are traded for lollipops, which are established as currency with the use of a special cash register and in which one suitor tops another's flaunting of "Charmaine's" flower by picking his teeth with the giant diaper pin last seen holding on her diaper.

she can begin to sing their melody with the inflections of an adult; and we know that her mother would practice line readings with her in just this way.

Only a couple of years later, her gross and fine motor skills are the equal of any adolescent as she tap-dances on a piano top and engages in a romance with leading man John Boles in *Curly Top* (1935). The facial expressions exchanged by the two are not those of father and daughter, but of sweethearts. By *Poor Little Rich Girl* (1936), Temple can outdance adults Alice Faye and Jack Haley, and her vocal skills, while still behind her physical coordination, are now at least that of a typical teenager twice her age. Perhaps not coincidentally, the blatant sexuality of the Baby Burlesks—some of which strike modern viewers as child pornography—and even the coquettishness of *Curly Top* are muted in some of her later films. This could be in response to the Hays Code (implemented in 1934) and restrictions on what could and could not be portrayed in movies, bringing with it a period of greater restraint as well as more subtlety and symbolism. It could also be that in some ways, the flirtatious, physically capable eight-year-old is somehow more disturbing than the awkward, obviously mimicking toddler. The knowingness is more convincingly performed, and the possibility of real knowledge is offered, a knowledge that society would like to deny to the child.

The perfectly empty child would, necessarily, not create noise, figuratively if not literally.[19] The voice brings with it all sorts of trouble, disrupting the emptiness with agency and individuality and the body. As with dancing, singing uses the possibilities of the body to express emotional "truth" in ways that range from the abstract and formalized to the apparently unmediated and "transparent."[20] In reality, of course, these are all learned gestures, but some seem more "natural" than others: gospel shouting is being "taken by the spirit," whereas the Queen of the Night's aria from Mozart's *The Magic Flute* can be seen as possessed by evil because of its precise and even "mechanical" nature. One's ability to transmit these gestures effectively certainly signal one's talent and skill, but they can also appear to signal knowledge and experience, that "knowingness" that can rupture the emptiness so worryingly.

---

[19] Perhaps tellingly, one of the most frightening images in recent popular culture has been that of an "empty child" from the 2005 BBC series of *Doctor Who*, a dead child in a gas mask whose touch transforms all into his empty image and who has the ability to "om-com"—make any speaker grill resonate. He plaintively asks of all, "Are you my mummy?" He is both empty and noisy, the ur-orphan, who briefly reconstitutes a family comprised of his child-mother Nancy and the war-orphaned alpha male Doctor. When he is repaired (refilled) and unmasked, however, he is shown to be a perfectly adorable blonde, blue-eyed child who doesn't make a sound.

[20] Coming at this dichotomy of innocence and knowingness from another direction is the persistence of comic characters such as Fanny Brice's "Baby Snooks," Red Skelton's "Mean Wittle Kid," Lily Tomlin's "Edith Ann" and even Bruce Willis's voicing of the infant "Mikey" in the *Look Who's Talking* movies—where the innocent "shell" of a child is filled with the wit and observations from an adult perspective, creating a different kind of (strangely more acceptable) cognitive dissonance.

Framing the discourse: White/girls

The whiteness of the ideal eroticized child is obviously inherent in the racial aspects of blonde hair and blue eyes, but in the Victorian literature and English working class of Kincaid and Walkerdine, it is an essentially "empty" or "null" category in and of itself.[21] When we move into American culture, with its racial and ethnic mix, we encounter not only the "classic" erotic children that Kincaid talks about, but other, more problematic ones, usually marked by deviance along one of these major fault lines. The parade of cute African American boys from Sammy Davis, Jr. through Michael Jackson to Emmanuel Lewis and Gary Coleman can be seen to mirror the procession of little blonde white girls from Shirley Temple to the Olsen twins.

But there also exists in American culture a category that blurs race and class, "white trash." This term has been used disparagingly by both middle- and upper-class whites and by African Americans as an expression of difference—and abjection—creating that overlap of class and race. It is, however, a cultural space that been re-claimed since the late 1980s, notably by entertainers like Roseanne Barr (and to a softer extent by Dolly Parton and Jeff Foxworthy), in much the same way feminists reclaimed the term "bitch." Even though academic theorization has moved toward rendering whiteness less transparent, more visible, white trash remains a sticky category. As with many terms derived to "other" a group, familiar connotations such as lazy, dirty, untrustworthy, and sexually promiscuous cluster around the designation; but also as many marginalized cultures have produced distinctive aesthetics—whether gay camp or numerous African American iterations from jazz to hip-hop—so has white trash produced "trashy."

Higher white social strata might use "trashy" in its understood meaning of something that is to be discarded: waste, excess; and perhaps the most singularly undeniable trait of trashiness is its excess—as humorist Florence King puts it, "the definition of trashy is trashy."[22] Rather like pornography, trashy (whether from the insider or outsider position) is something you know when you see it.[23] However, it matters who is determining the threshold of excess. Dolly Parton has

---

[21]   Obviously, since 1950, British society has become much more ethnically and racially diverse, but it still is less assimilated than American society, which has been absorbing, if not wholly assimilating, diverse populations over nearly 500 years, and the past 200 quite intensively. Different "waves" of immigration produce layers of assimilation and "whitening," explored in such books as Noel Ignatiev's *How the Irish Became White* (New York, 1995) and Karen Brodkin's *How the Jews Became White Folks and What That Says About Race in America* (New Brunswick, NJ, 1998), and even obliquely in one of the seminal musical theatre pieces of the twentieth century, Leonard Bernstein's *West Side Story*.

[22]   Florence King, *Southern Ladies and Gentlemen* (New York, 1975), p. 13.

[23]   Gael Sweeney reiterates this corollary to King's definition in "The King of White Trash Culture: Elvis Presley and the Aesthetics of Excess," in Matt Wray and Annalee Newitz (eds), *White Trash: Race and Class in America* (New York, 1997), p. 249.

frequently said of her famously excessive appearance that she modeled herself on a woman she saw in town when she was a girl. It didn't matter to her that the woman was considered "easy" ("a Jezebel") by the townfolk, young Dolly thought she was beautiful. Those who display "trash" do not necessarily place upon it the same values as those who are in higher positions of power to influence how wider society understands it.[24]

Gael Sweeney rhapsodizes:

> White Trash defines the self by display: it is not afraid to wear its philosophy on a tee-shirt or needlepoint it across a big pillow or proclaim it across the bumper of a pick-up, or tattoo it on an arm ... . White Trash has religion and is not afraid to push belief to the ultimate ... . White Trash has heroes and is not afraid to iconize them. White Trash knows what it likes and it likes big, bright, excessive. The construction of White Trash in popular culture is of total consumer and non-producer: White Trash is separated from the working class by their lack of connection with work or production, hence "lazy" and "shiftless" as common descriptive adjectives (compare to stereotypes of Blacks). The split between the producing man and the consuming female canonized in middle-class culture collapses in White Trash: both women and men love to shop, buy, dress, and display.[25]

Sweeney threatens to get swept up in glorifying the trash aesthetic—not least because "white trash" is not a monolithic group, and many who would be categorized as such from outside struggle mightily to show to themselves and others that they are *not* trashy, hence the aspiration for many to display restraint in behavior and dress. However, the key point here is that the glamorous excess of trashiness, like Dolly's wigs or Elvis's jumpsuits, while marked as sexual display, is not limited by gender.

Ostentatious display in dress is, particularly in American culture, often deeply gendered (as feminine) and racialized (as other, and darker—usually black or Latin). One particularly virulent example of the latter comes in *Saturday Night Fever*; as Tony Manero (John Travolta) primps in a car mirror—in a look not far removed from a 1950s rockabilly, with brightly colored clothing and a pompadour—his Italian-American friends taunt him that if he looks any sharper, he'll look like a "nigger or a spic." Rockabilly is a place where the gender- and race-unstable

---

[24] The (apparent) dichotomy of the innocent southern sexpot like Daisy Mae in the *L'il Abner* comic strip is also implicated in this. But the performance of sexuality and experiential—even theoretical—knowledge are not wholly dependent upon one another. When the teenage Britney Spears maintained her virginity despite highly sexualized dress and stage display, most scoffed; as a fellow southerner, however, I did not find the idea of a virgin with her provocative image dissonant. There is no evidence that her persona in any way changed because of the physical fact of having had sex.

[25] Sweeney, p. 250.

display of sexuality overflows in excess, whether in gold lamé, eyeliner, and big hair, or in hip-swiveling and come-hither looks under the eyelashes—and that's just the boys. The stakes are always higher for girls, particularly those already in the marginal position of poor, white, and southern, because the consequences are so steep. Trashy is as trashy does, therefore performing in a style as vividly but unstably marked is like walking a tightrope.

Welcome to the Club is fascinating for the way in which it places the young women of rockabilly, other than Brenda Lee, into certain comfortable, middle-class narratives of girlhood and burgeoning sexuality. Even their "noise" is channeled into tropes that lessen the apparent dissonance, but that also call into question whether those tropes are retroactively imposed—a discursive trick that threatens to collapse when touched.

Janis Martin, the tomboyish girl-next-door with the blonde ponytail and jeans, recounts the names she was called: "The Female Elvis, The Girl with the Golden Voice, Little Miss Elvis, Queen of Rockabilly, Little Miss Hillbilly, uh … Bitch." She is a Queen, a Girl, even a Little Miss, defined both as a female adjunct and a female-child adjunct of a male star, Elvis Presley. But the Martin of 2004 seems to relish most the final designation, Bitch, which she delivers after a dramatic pause and follows with a broad grin. In the images we are shown, and even in the tough-but-innocent styling of the teen voice that we hear, there is nothing that suggests "bitch" in its more common connotations of intentionally catty, devious, manipulative, and (usually) conventionally feminine, and even ultrafeminine. She appears more to be the "broad"—hard-drinking, tough-talking, able to deal with men on their level—but she's more than willing to embrace the strength that comes with the term "bitch."

Wanda Jackson and Lorrie Collins (who performed as part of "The Collins Kids" with her brother Larry) are presented as variations on a theme, that of the good girl who is just naturally sexy, but innocent of her attractions. This is a common southern stereotype with many variations, but Jackson and Collins fall on either side of the "trashy" divide. Jackson is the sultry gypsy type, with her long dark hair, exotic eye make-up, and dangling earrings, who dresses up because it makes her feel pretty:

> It really was not outrageous, by any means; but my dress was different, and I was singin' these songs which … was dirty music for them. And I think I was known [as] kind of a rebel. The cutest thing a guy wrote about me in the press. He said, she … he named all the songs I did, "Mean Mean Man," "Fujiyama Mama," "Hot Dog, That Made Me Mad," he said, "But really, when you meet Wanda, she's really a sweet lady with a nasty voice."

Jackson, like Martin, embraces a possibly negative designation—nasty—but stresses that deep down, she really is a sweet *lady*. She talks in great detail about her dresses, and recalls an incident in which a dress she and her mother had made was considered too risqué for the Grand Ol' Opry. She agreed to wear a jacket over it for respectability, although the incident upset her. Both the presence of her mother—as a presumably willing accomplice—and Jackson's distress at being considered "inappropriate" hint not at a kind of sexual flaunting but at a clash of expectations, a culture clash between, perhaps, rural and urban, middle and lower class. The irony is that, in many cases, rural approaches to sexuality in the South have historically been less repressive than "citified" ways, negatively reinforcing the "white trash" stereotype that is imposed from the higher classes.

Lorrie Collins, with her more conservative hair style and dress, classic features, and more youthful appearance was closer to the homecoming queen type—but not the bitchy, cheerleader homecoming queen, more the baton twirler, a more lithe, less outgoing girl—the type who was a good student, popular but not stuck up, and taught Sunday school, but who also was beginning to feel the power of her sexuality. As we see her from a late 1950s television broadcast, singing a seductive "Waiting Just For You" with almost no body movement and restrained, but extremely expressive facial expressions (including a distinctly "come hither" raised eyebrow), 2004 Lorrie says:

> Be maybe a little sexy, and it was like [hides mouth with hand like a child telling a secret] … . Women weren't supposed to be that way, but I didn't know any better. You know, I didn't know how I was supposed to be. [laughs] So I just was the way that I wanted to be, and I did catch a lot of flak. I remember that when we went back to Oklahoma, we always started singing in church, when we went back to our church, and there were some whispers about "There she is, you know. She sings those songs about *men*."

Note that in both cases, Jackson and Collins use the words of others to describe themselves. To some extent, their sense of self is determined by what others think of them, yet they also assert a paradoxical innocent sexiness. They were just "doing what came naturally." Wanda Jackson especially is reminiscent of Dolly Parton in her overt sexuality and enjoyment of it. Robert Oermann's comments about the Collins Kids, however, tend to rob Lorrie of her agency, making her safely childlike and demure, particularly alongside the active male counterpart of her brother: "The Collins Kids were a very physical act, particularly Larry, he was like a little flea jumping all over the stage. He was just hilarious. And she was cute, too. They were *adorable*."

Conceptions of childhood, puberty, and adolescence were in flux in the post-Second World War period. With the emergence of the teenager, adolescence became more protracted and more transitional—not merely a biological stage but a social and even commercial one. Different strands of development, previously compressed into a relatively short period around puberty, suddenly had more room in which to unpack. Physical, intellectual and psychological, social, and—of concern here—artistic maturity could have proceeded at very different rates.

The post-war decade, 1945–55, which saw the emergence of rock and roll, was also a period of some striking extremes in terms of female sexuality. The most popular sex symbols of the day included Marilyn Monroe and Jayne Mansfield, women with lushly mature female bodies but high, breathy voices that lacked "body." They were sex *kittens*—an immature designation—and their speech mimicked baby talk, a style of diction that we also find in rockabilly. Mansfield negotiates her role in the early rock and roll movie *The Girl Can't Help It* (1956) by making a distinction between the sex kitten Jerri Jordan who speaks/squeaks in a high voice and can't sing, and the real woman Georgianna who wants to marry and have children, whose voice is a rich, musical alto. Despite physical adulthood, the childlike voice is seen as sexually alluring.

As the voice production of Monroe and Mansfield attest, the voice of a "girl" was predominantly a head voice, one that did not engage the resonance of the body. A couple of decades later, Carol Gilligan's research on adolescent girls' psychological development also observed the phenomenon of girls "losing their voices" around puberty; not only did they lose a sense of self, or become fearful of expressing themselves, Gilligan also observed that the voice migrated up from the chest to the head.[26] This is the opposite of the physical development of the lengthening vocal tract, though it may have its roots in the vocal break, but it suggests a cultural weight put on that aural marker of puberty, much in the same way as the boy's breaking voice.[27] The head voice literally "vacates" the body, removing agency, creating emptiness, leaving it a blank slate to be written upon.

At the other end of the spectrum, Vladimir Nabokov's explosive *Lolita* was published in 1955, although it had been knocking around for several years before finding a publisher. The eponymous character is physically a girl on the brink of puberty (and when played in the movies, both Stanley Kubrick's 1962 version and Adrian Lyne's 1997 version, an actress in her mid-teens was employed), but Lolita is sexually active and knowing to the point of being blasé, despite her physical and behavioral immaturity.

Women had entered the workforce in unusual numbers because of the war, and many stayed either through necessity or because they liked working. Even if the housewife was still the default expectation for women, other options were beginning to become socially acceptable. More girls were going to college— admittedly, many looking for that all-important Mrs. degree—extending childhood/adolescence into the early twenties. With the emergence of the teenager as a marketing category, a chronological wedge was driven between childhood and adulthood, although maturity in its many guises (physical, sexual, emotional, psychological) might occur at any point along this broadened timeline. Yet the median age of first marriage for women in the twentieth century hit its lowest in 1956, at 20.1 years.[28]

---

[26] Carol Gilligan, *In a Different Voice: Psychological Theory and Women's Development* (Cambridge, MA, 1982).

[27] See Chapter 1 in this volume.

[28] United States Census Report: Estimated Median Age at First Marriage, http://marriage.about.com/od/statistics/a/medianage.htm (accessed August 8, 2006).

Even though later rock critics would shape popularity with a female audience as a negative, in the new youth market for popular music, girls were the biggest target demographic, more likely to purchase records. As Oermann says, Brenda was "one of them," the girls, which is true enough. But then he continues that she was not a *threat*. To whom? For what? Obviously, the implication is to other girls, in competition for boys, but it is also an implication that she's not projecting an erotic image. This is consonant with one of the two extremes of thinking about Brenda Lee (such as has been done)—that she was an innocent child, who, as she grew up and the sexual became more of a possibility, was shepherded toward "good music" by her management and record company;[29] but it clashes mightily with, say, Sheila Whiteley's recent, heavily sexualized reading of Brenda Lee as a Lolita figure.

This dichotomy would seem irreconcilable, but for the fact that neither view takes into consideration that children grow up, at different rates from others and even within themselves. One of the main difficulties with analyses like Whiteley's is that, for her, thirteen-year-old Brenda Lee is the same as the eleven-year-old or fifteen-year-old version, and that is demonstrably problematic, even in terms of musical style. The child can be eroticized at any age (sadly, statistics on pedophilia prove that, as predators tend to "hunt" in specific age groups), and it is the ever-shifting relationship between body, mind, and performance that I want to explore.

Rockabilly dichotomies

Although most people today tend to think of "rockabilly" and 1950s rock and roll as synonymous, it was only one of a number of emergent styles. The term "rock and roll" itself is a sort of sexualized "emptiness." The phrase was a long-standing euphemism for sex and had been around in music for at least a couple of decades by the 1950s, but as diverse styles were lumped together, was this a way of reducing the impact, of rendering safe the influx of debased black and underclass white southern music, or was it merely lack of nuance in listening? There is probably truth in these, and other, readings.

Rockabilly was a high-energy form of white country blues that had been developing from Jimmie Rodgers in the 1930s through Hank Williams in the 1940s. Even a cursory listen to Williams's 1947 hit "Move It On Over" demonstrates that the transformation from country blues to rockabilly was largely a matter of instrumentation (drums and electric instruments) and recording style (the Sun Records slapback reverb in particular), adding a dash of rhythmic urgency.

---

[29] See, for instance, Dave Sanjek, "Can a Fujiyama Mama Be the Female Elvis? The Wild, Wild Women of Rockabilly," in Sheila Whiteley (ed.), *Sexing the Groove: Popular Music and Gender* (New York, 1997), pp. 137–67.

72   *SHE'S SO FINE*

The early rockabilly artists—Elvis Presley, Johnny Cash, Billy Lee Riley, Jerry Lee Lewis, Roy Orbison, Gene Vincent, Eddie Cochran, John Scott—were all of the lanky pretty-boy type (some rougher than others), mostly from the Deep South, deploying the excesses of gender-troubling, sexually charged display that are associated with their "white trash" upbringing. Boys with the devil in 'em, but boys who you knew would show up for church on Sunday. The sinful and the sanctified are enshrined in the Saturday night/Sunday morning dichotomy familiar to both country and rhythm and blues, black and white, and the many cross-currents between the extremes. This affinity between country music and gospel, as counterintuitive as it might have seemed then (or even now) to those from outside the South, is fundamental to southern culture.

The physical and vocal characteristics of rockabilly performance have as much to do with getting the spirit and speaking in tongues as they do with sexuality; the two are, for many observers, too close for comfort. The tension between controlling oneself and losing oneself in the moment results in twitches of head and limbs, contractions of the torso, exaggerated vibrato in the voice (further exaggerated by reverb), slides, howls, growls and purrs, breaks and hiccups that fragment the lyrics into babble. And here, the slippery gendering of rockabilly is exposed, in the display of the body and the verbal regression into baby-talk—the very sounds made by Monroe and Mansfield and the like—and there they are received as key symbols of submissive sexuality. Baby-talk is double-speak, both mother-to-child and lover-to-lover. Like speaking in tongues, it makes the body both a site of inarticulate but deeply meaningful sound and a spectacle. It is a subjective, embodied experience but also an object to be observed—much like female sexuality is constructed, especially at that time. Perhaps the masculinity of rockabilly is so ferociously asserted so as not to reveal how close to traditionally configured "femininity" it skates.

Rockabilly is androgynous, infantile and sexualized, sinful and sanctified. Rather than being the strangest place for the emergence of a girl-child prodigy, it could be seen as the perfect space in its extremity.

Vocal decorum and the girl singer

However transgressive the male singers of rockabilly were, they were, of course, male and that has its privileges. In the big-band era, a female singer—even a physically mature woman with a rich alto voice like Alice Faye or Rosemary Clooney—was still a "girl singer," and there were certain expectations of decorum, physical and vocal. The voice would be smooth and in tune. The body—usually clad in a semi-formal or formal dress—would be predominantly still, perhaps presented three-quarters to the audience to maximize the contrast of breasts and hips with a small waist in the ideal hourglass figure. The singer would often be photographed or filmed from slightly above, the head tilted back to give the illusion of addressing someone taller—like a man. This is also a fairly submissive pose. The sultrier, more overtly sexual singers, like Julie London or Peggy Lee, might pose more flirtatiously, head tipped down and gazing up through the lashes, a come-hither look, with the hands clasped behind the back to emphasize the breasts—particularly if wearing a strapless gown.

These women were all white, of course, and that does make a difference. African American women, whether blues or gospel singers like Brenda Lee's idol Mahalia Jackson, tended to move more with the emphatic exertions of their singing style, moving their heads, hands, arms, even the entire body to add emphasis. The voices themselves broke through the appropriate containment of "polite" female expression, including breaks, shouts, and growls that symbolize the overtaking of emotion.

Such a lack of vocal decorum seems almost unknown among white singing stars, but Judy Garland formed a kind of middle ground. Garland, herself a child prodigy, seemed to burst onto the scene a fully-formed adult performer, despite her youth. That said, she was on the brink of puberty when she first emerged, and her vocal tremulousness suggests a barely contained emotionality, with her sometimes erratic hand/arm and body movements underlining a struggle for control.[30] She knew how to behave, she had had the appropriate social conditioning, but sometimes her hormones got the best of her. Garland's voice was centered in the chest, and her larynx position was low and mobile. Although possessed of a distinctly personal style, her swoops and slides and moans were colored with the abstracted codes of sexuality in performance that comes from the black and blackface tradition of vaudeville and torch singers. The little gulps and breaks in her voice were vocal signifiers of emotion that overcame articulation.[31]

Garland was an anomaly, a child prodigy in the performance of Tin Pan Alley songs. Prodigy is less rare in other styles, even operatic ones (Deanna Durbin, Jane Powell, Charlotte Church), and country music seems to throw up girl prodigies every twenty years or so—Lee in the 1950s, Tanya Tucker in the 1970s, LeAnn Rimes in the 1990s. There does seem to be something about southern culture that fosters—or perhaps does not restrain—this childhood sensuality.[32] Florence King insightfully remarks:

---

[30] Lee describes recognizing some of Garland's performance mannerisms as those Dick Barstow coached in Lee's own performances in nightclubs and cabaret in the early 1960s, after having worked with Garland, including on the "Born in a Trunk" number in *A Star Is Born* (George Cukor, 1954). Lee particularly notes the tensing of the hand gesture at the endings of songs; Lee et al., p. 126.

[31] See Laurie Stras, "White Face, Black Voice: Race, Gender and Region in the Music of the Boswell Sisters," *Journal of the Society for American Music* 1/2 (2007), p. 215.

[32] This is not entirely separate from the phenomenon of the child beauty pageant, which is fairly common in the South, and was brought to attention outside the region through the documentary *Painted Babies* (dir. Jane Treays, 1995) and more infamously the murder of JonBenét Ramsey. I am not arguing that the child beauty pageant is without its contradictory elements—Kincaid would argue that no such attention paid to a child could be without such crosscurrents—but it seems to me that there is a certain amount of culture

> Finally, the Southern woman's sensual talents can be traced to her relationship with her father. Southern fathers behave very seductively around their daughters. Southerners in general tend to be physically affectionate, and in addition, the Southern father is obsessed with sexual differentiation. He wants his sons to be manly and his daughters to be womanly, with no shades of gray in between. Subconsciously he begins, early in her life, to ensure her proper development by training her to respond to men. His modus operandi includes a great deal of hugging, kissing, and lap-sitting, which launches a little girl onto the path of sexual response. She grows to like the way men smell, the feel of whiskers and hard muscles, and connects these things with the security of father's love. *Provided this love affair does not go too far*, the Southern daughter emerges from it as a very fortunate young woman. [emphasis in original][33]

And southern culture also fosters more musical performance, particularly centered around the church, which gives children an advantage in learning how to become performers at a younger age.

While Tucker and Rimes sang in well-established styles, Lee was at the leading edge of rockabilly. Although her career model was Judy Garland, Lee's main musical influences were Hank Williams and Mahalia Jackson, and she blended those quite disparate styles into a third, distinct style that is unlike the more belting, bluesy style of the other rockabilly girls. Just as an aside, she sounds like no one so much as Buddy Holly, but Holly actually starts his recording career a bit later than Lee. Either they have some as-yet-unrecovered common influence, or they developed independently, or even, just maybe, contrary to the way that these stories get told, but in line with Jacqueline Warwick's work on the influence of the girl groups on the Beatles, Brenda Lee had an influence on Buddy Holly.[34]

---

clash involved in the subsequent media circus. JonBenét's mother, who was the driving force in getting her child involved in these pageants, was a southerner, displaced to a different type of conservative culture in Colorado; and the mainstream American culture created by the media continues to be rooted in the urban centers New York and Los Angeles (it is still common to find portrayals of white rural southerners that would be considered unthinkably offensive if of any other racial, ethnic, or religious group; ironically, the television comedy *My Name Is Earl* (2005–), which at first seems to be playing into those stereotypes, may in fact be one of the few positive portrayals in mainstream American media). While the tragic, and in this case lurid, circumstances of a murdered child are undoubtedly responsible for at least part of the media obsession with the case, one must suspect that the constant stream of photographs and videoclips of little JonBenét dolled up for the pageants were a large part of what kept the case in the spotlight. The dead child was a perfectly empty vessel for the wild speculation surrounding her death. Similarly, the short videotape of blonde, blue-eyed Elizabeth Smart playing (of all things) the harp, in addition to the intimations of sexual slavery in her abduction, was obsessively replayed.

[33]   King, p. 43.

[34]   Jacqueline Warwick, "You're Going To Lose That Girl. The Beatles and the Girl Groups," in Yrjö Heinonen, Markus Heuger, Sheila Whiteley, Terhi Nurmesjärvi and Jouni

Lee's collaboration with Owen Bradley may lead one to suspect that Lee was coached to develop her style, but that easy, Svengali theory robs Lee of her agency as an artist. She herself asserts that because of her family's strapped financial status and her own busy schedule of performing, she had little opportunity to be influenced by other singers and developed her own style—the hiccupping was just "there."[35] Bradley himself said:

> I know it sounds incredible, because she was only a child, but she really did know what she was doing musically. I always let her make decisions. Red Foley called her a little girl with grown-up reactions … . Red thought it was fascinating to watch her sit alone in a corner and make changes in both words and music to suit her own style.[36]

Hardly an empty child, then. But the backstage reality is only one aspect of studying performance.

Performing Brenda Lee

When we look at eleven-year-old Brenda Lee singing her first single "Bigelow 6-200," we see a Shirley Temple-esque child in a party dress with full petticoats and patent leather Mary Janes, singing a song that expresses emotions inappropriately advanced for a child who was actually, and convincingly, billed as nine. But that is in fact a great deal of the appeal, and has been for a long time, as we have seen: the frisson of wonder as a child performs to such an extraordinary technical level.

"Bigelow 6-200" reveals a confident singer in control of her style. Like her idol Judy Garland before her, hers is a fully embodied voice, but it simply comes from a different part of the body. Her vocal production is almost diametrically opposed to Garland's; the larynx position is tighter and higher, and there are almost no sliding/swooping gestures. She tends to vary not through pitch manipulation but through timbre and attack, with growls and hiccups and pushing the voice to a rough, raw position at the top of the throat. She is, at this stage, a bit of a "Lena," to use Laurie Stras's term from Chapter 1 of this book. The tightness is a way to control her voice, and also to gain volume. What she lacks in lung power, she can make up for in nasality and penetration.

The delivery is mature, even though the voice is clearly that of a child. But does she *know*? This seems to be predominantly a musical performance, in much the same way toddler Shirley Temple's line readings are musical, learned responses. Some words are punched harder, creating a kind of emphasis, but this could be just

---

Koskimäki (eds), *Beatlestudies 3. Proceedings of the Beatles 2000 conference* (Jyväskylä, 2001), pp. 161–67.

[35]   Lee et al., pp. 30–31.

[36]   Ibid., p. 38.

because of where they fall in the scansion of the lyrics—although it must be said that the lyrics and melodic phrasing are so cleverly fitted that these are the key words in any case: "phone," "wait," "ring," "fight," "please," etc. This combination of skillful music/lyric integration and secure vocal production gives the impression of knowingness; Lee, at eleven, may even have a basic understanding of the situation in the lyrics. But the performance still has a tendency to impress because of the musical skill involved rather than any precocious emotional maturity.

This dissociation between knowing and performing is even more evident when we see the brief clip of her performing this song on *The Steve Allen Show* in 1957, included in *Welcome to the Club*. At first, her body does not seem engaged in the performance (almost note-for-note like the record), nor does even her gaze, which tends to wander into the distance after she's turned from one camera to another. She only seems to remember to snap her fingers toward the end of the first phrase. This disengagement could well be sheer stage fright, performing on national live television. But that is only at the more obvious, emotive level at which we are accustomed to reading performance. A closer look at this clip, and stills from this period, show something more subtle, and indeed how very engaged her body was with performance.

On the television stage and in most photographs before she is about twelve, she keeps her arms close to her sides and does little more than rock her shoulders slightly to the beat of the music, tap her foot, and snap her fingers. She seems to be behaving with appropriate decorum. But the tension in her body is remarkable, the way in which the rhythm of the music is embodied by the tightness of her muscles, the pops of her fingers, and the flexing movement of her feet (Figure 2.1).

Upon seeing Lee perform for the first time, country music legend Red Foley commented: "I still get cold chills every time I think about the first time I heard that voice. About midway through the show we put her on, and she reared back and let go. One foot started patting rhythm like she was putting out a prairie fire, and not another fiber of her little body moved."[37]

Combined with the percussive effect of the hiccupping, this rhythmic stress demonstrates that her entire body is focused toward producing the musical performance. So at this point, it seems that her first single is a remarkable technical achievement that allows our child star to be prodigiously talented musically but apparently unworryingly innocent of adult knowledge of the romantic or sexual longing in the lyrics.

Lee's cover of her idol Hank Williams's "Your Cheatin' Heart," recorded in that same debut session (30 July 1956), shows even more evidence of musical fluency, because it is Lee's own interpretation, with some changes of melody that we do not hear in either Williams's or Frankie Laine's better-known versions. While the

---

[37] Ibid., p. 26. A review of her first Las Vegas engagement also commented positively on Lee's stillness (proper decorum), while missing the tension obvious to Foley: "As for being cool, calm and collected, the Lee lass makes Perry Como look like a jittery jumper in comparison" (p. 35).

Figure 2.1   Brenda Lee performing as a child in a party dress

persistent tendency to rock on upper neighbor tones to repeated notes might seem somewhat mechanical in this performance, it may also be a technical adaptation to the eleven-year-old's relatively tight vocal tract. We do not hear large scoops or slides in her singing at this stage of her development, and perhaps the most subtle ornamentation in this performance are the tiny breaks on the word "cry." We can, however, hear her making a decision that is musically interesting, but not necessarily one predicated on understanding the meaning of the lyrics. Whereas Williams, and most performers of this song, sing the opening melodic phrase as a smooth arch, with a slight scoop up to the long note of "heart" (Example 2.1(a)) Lee sings up to a peak on "cheat" and drops to a lower note (in a cambiata-like figure) on the unemphasized "-in'" suffix, before rising and striking a long, clear "heart" (Example 2.1(b)).

Even if this is product of a tight larynx, it is also a distinctive melodic interpretation, both rooted in the original performance and an individual decision that takes a set sequence of notes and revalues their rhythm and emphasis. While on the initial title phrase, this can also sound like a convulsive gulp—a valid emotional interpretation of the lyrics—Lee repeats this gesture every time the musical phrase recurs, regardless of lyrical content. This can, like the rocking on

Example 2.1(a) "Your Cheatin' Heart" (Hank Williams): title phrase, as sung 1
by Hank Williams (MGM 11416)

Example 2.1(b) "Your Cheatin' Heart" (Hank Williams): title phrase, as sung 1
by Brenda Lee (Decca MCL 1792)

repeated and focused listening, strike one as a rather mechanical but nonetheless musical response. Lee seems to have developed a technical maturity, albeit one informed by the more improvisatory conventions of stylistic performance, before intellectual, emotional, or even physical maturity.

It is a tricky assumption to make, however, given that we are—at this historical juncture—working from recordings. Even those recordings can be telling a deceptive story of maturation. Provocatively included in the Bear Family's box set[38] is an alternate take of "Bigelow 6-200," superficially identical in almost every regard to the single release. If the two performances were transcribed and put side by side, there would be little to no apparent discrepancy. However, there are subtle differences in performance and recording level. The electric lead guitar is more forward, as is Lee, with those two voices somewhat more isolated from the accompaniment; both also have more energy and snap (an informal poll among friends and conference attendees usually results in a "win" for the alternate take—except, interestingly enough, among people who know the original). There are no obvious flaws in the recording (a very tiny patch of slight sharpness in Lee's voice after the first bridge, but only for a couple of beats after the first leap up), and her performance is even punchier. Accents are hit with more diaphragmatic push; an interesting bit of rhythmic tension creates almost a triplet effect on her second plea of "What's the matter," making both a musical variation and a semantic intensifier, as does the increased rhythmic snap of "no more at all"; in the bridge, her emphatic "please" at the top of the melodic line has more sting rhythmically and a tinge of roughness in the timbre at the beginning of the vowel. It is not only a musically more engaging performance, it tilts the performance from one of mere technical skill to one with more emotional competency.

---

[38] *Little Miss Dynamite* (Bear Family B0000282SY, 1995).

Why was the single version the one that was chosen? A little decorum, perhaps? Intriguingly, Brenda Lee's cover of Hank Williams's "Jambalaya" recorded in the same session includes more growling and aggressive singing, and it is possible that this song, not being overtly a love song, was allowed to be a little more raucous. Oermann was right in one thing—the audience/target matters. But who is actually listening? And who is constructed in the performance itself as the "target"?

In a love song, a romantic/sexual lover is usually the target, placing the audience in the constructed position of the narratee, the object of the direct address. If the market for pop music was seen as primarily teenage girls, then this construction only makes sense if the singer is male. However, if the singer is another teenage girl, that could create bumps in the identification process. Playing into the marketer's concept of Lee as "not a threat," she recorded "One Teenager To Another" nine months (April 12, 1957) after her first session. The rather witty advice lyrics cast Lee as a confidante, even an older sister. Her position is one of knowing how both boys and girls act in romantic situations (girls make small talk/boys make big talk). Although still only twelve years old, Lee can "pass" in this case, because she sounds older, both timbrally and gesturally. She sounds like she knows what she is talking about.

The backing track struts in a slow tempo, with a sultry sax riff. Her vocal tract has lengthened and the larynx has dropped, creating a richer sound and more relaxed delivery, particularly in the bridge. She still sounds like a teenager, as she should, and the delivery still has elements of the somewhat mechanical musical choices. Each "a"[39] phrase, regardless of the lyrical content, has basically the same ornamental pattern, with unaccented lower neighbor notes on the repeated note and staccato phrase endings, and the title phrase (the refrain "b" at the end of each A section) is punctuated with "bouncy" glottal hiccups.

"Dynamite," from the same session, however, was the most overtly sexual song Lee had recorded to date, and one of the most blatant in her catalogue. From this song, Lee got her "Little Miss Dynamite" nickname, and it is this song on which Whiteley focuses her "Lolita" argument. Lee's performance is explosive (no pun intended). In some ways, her voice quality seems younger than in "One Teenager to Another"—perhaps because "Dynamite" is pitched higher —but what strikes me as musically more mature is the line reading—the ornamentations are less schematic than in earlier recordings. Certainly, the most prominent and striking vocal device in the recording are the growls on not only the hook word "dynamite!" but its rhymes "*love* me right" and "*hold* me tight," all of which are syncopated at the top of the melodic phrase after a suggestive gap in the vocal line. But Lee also puts softer purrs on the anacrusis "I (just explode)" of the last line of the first A section and other unaccented words that nonetheless further the sexual intensity of the lyrics. She also pushes and pulls some of the even notes

---

[39]   The song is a highly repetitive variation on the AABA song form (AABAAABA), with each larger section (four bars at the overarching slow "stroll" tempo) composed of an internal a+a+a+b (b=refrain "One teenager to another") structure.

in a subtle syncopation that adds intensity to the driving beat. This is a much more nuanced performance that not only pays more attention to the lyrics but is more varied and musically provocative. "Rock the Bop," recorded seven months later (November 29, 1957), shows even more flexibility. The larynx seems much more mobile, with more swoops and variation in dynamic, and a developing lower register as she drops down for the pick-ups of some phrases. Subtle yodel-yelps squeak off the end of some syllables, and for the first time, none of her ornamentation seems predictable as she swears she's "old enough to 'Rock the Bop'" at almost thirteen.

"Let's Jump the Broomstick" was recorded a year later (October 19, 1958, the same day as "Rockin' Around the Christmas Tree") and the influence of her other major idol, Mahalia Jackson, is evident from her opening "We-e-ell". The laryngeal flexibility and stylistic variation of "Rock the Bop" and "Dynamite" are here complemented by a richer, deeper voice quality as she matures physically. From the photographic evidence of the period, this is clearly not just in terms of biological maturity; even in heels and a party dress, she puts a great deal of "body English" into her singing, as radical in her postures as Elvis Presley or Jerry Lee Lewis (Figure 2.2).

Figure 2.2   Brenda Lee performing in her early teens

At fourteen, Lee recorded one of her most suggestive songs, "Sweet Nothings," her first real chart success. The track's little opening dialogue with backing singer Louis Nunley sounds far in advance of expected knowledge for her years; perhaps Lee is just mimicking the "music" of adult, or at least teen, sexuality in her delivery, but like Temple, she is very good at it.

Does she really *know*? Or has she developed to a point of musical competency that makes it impossible to tell?

Lee herself comments that she listens to this number and today, she can hear that she at least sounded like she knew what she was talking about, even though at the time she did not. It is worth noting that around the same time as recording "Sweet Nothings," Lee was learning dirty jokes from musicians around her and retelling them with great success, even though she hadn't a clue what they meant.[40] This isn't surprising: the keys to delivering a joke are musical, inflection and rhythm, both of which Lee had clearly mastered.

So it is possible—and this is probably the definition of "innocence," particularly eroticized innocence—that physical and artistic maturity is reached without an intellectual processing or physical experience. This is not Lolita, who has physical experience and knowledge, but not what we might call artistic competence. John Sloboda, in a recent paper on Mozart, pointed out that according to recent empirical studies of composers and musicians, it takes roughly an average of ten years of intense daily practice, efficiently guided by a parent or teacher, to achieve a high level of artistic competence and recognition.[41] The age at onset, if under the age of ten, was not significant. Considering that she started performing publicly at three and was essentially a jobbing professional (if not always paid) by six—spurred on by her own enjoyment of singing and guided by a mother motivated by the survival of a young family—Brenda Lee was right on track for her first hit single, and maybe slightly ahead of the curve for recognition among her peers.

There is some dissonance—highly erotically charged—in the marketing of Lee about this period. Early publicity photos, of course, emphasized her as a child, highlighting her baby face and tiny stature, often surrounded by adult men who tower over her. When publicity photos of Lee were sent to Paris for a 1959 tour, more recent shots were requested; when assured that this was, indeed, Brenda Lee of 1959, a story circulated that she was really a midget posing as a child prodigy— as Lee says, great publicity.[42]

Lee's manager, Dub Albritten, was highly resistant to her shaving her legs or wearing make-up, but after a while, the strain was beginning to show: "We never know how to dress her. She looks nine, is 14, and sings like 30 ... if we dress her to fit the way she sings, people say we're pushing her. If we dress her according

---

[40] Lee et al., p. 73.

[41] John Sloboda, "Mozart in Psychology," paper read at *Mozart 2006: Classical Music and the Modern World*, British Library (London), January 28, 2006.

[42] Lee et al., p. 58. Comparisons to both Temple and Garland were made in the French press.

to her age, people say we're trying to make her look like a child. We can do no right."[43] Lee herself was frustrated but realized there was a gap between image and internal maturity: "There wasn't much point in promoting me as a sexpot. I was too young looking for that."[44] But that "on the verge" quality is captured in a publicity photograph of her as a schoolgirl in a sweater-girl pose (Figure 2.3(a)). This is in some ways a classic example of the eroticized adolescent, physically "blooming"—just barely—in a recognizably sexualized pose, but with touches of innocence: the schoolbooks, the rolled-over position of her foot in saddle shoes. Just how iconic this pose was is demonstrated by its use in a contemporary lingerie ad (Figure 2.3(b)).

Figure 2.3(a) "Sweater girl" pose for schoolgirl Brenda Lee

By her mid-teens, however, Lee dressed and sounded like an adult. It is not that she did not sound like a woman already—it is that she sounded *more* like a woman by comparison. She had a well-developed and distinctive personal style of performance that we can hear most prominently, perhaps, in covers.

She recorded "Jambalaya" in that first recording session, and she recorded it again at fifteen (March 28, 1960).[45] We can hear the shape of the performance

---

[43] From the *Minneapolis Morning Tribune*, quoted in Ibid., p. 85.
[44] Ibid., p. 104.
[45] "Jambalaya (On the Bayou)," © 1952 Sony/ATV Music Publishing LLC. All rights administered by Sony/ATV Music Publishing LLC, 8 Music Square West, Nashville,

Figure 2.3(b)   An early 1950s ad, which demonstrates the iconicity of the pose

is somewhat set. The point can be made by comparing two basic, typical kinds of ornamentation: a hiccup in a syllable (represented by boldface) and a growl (represented by italics) (see next page).

Lee clearly knew from early on which musical beats she wanted to hit. In the 1956 version, her tight laryngeal position makes hiccupping much easier and more controlled than growling; the lower, looser position in 1960 allows not only more extended growling but also nuance and difference within that technique. But there are significant differences in what we may term knowingness. In the 1956 version, she sings the melody almost exactly as written, and the ornamentations in the first version are somewhat mechanical. She knows in a musical sense what she wants to do, which phrases she wants to highlight, but there is little variance from verse to verse, chorus to chorus. The second performance shows more sensitivity to nuance, the ornamentations are at times slightly shifted to highlight not only a point in the musical structure, but important lyrical moments. The most obvious example would be the difference in the lyrics "Kinfolks come": in the 1956 version, she growls through both, as she seems to control the sound best at the beginnings of phrases, after taking a breath; in 1960, she not only holds off the growl until the more crucial verb, she scoops within the growl. In the later version, she can also carry off more extensive hiccupping in the liquescent line, "Tonight I'm a-gonna

---

TN 37203. All rights reserved. Used by permission.

1956

Good-bye, Joe, me gotta go, me oh my oh
Me gotta go pole the pirogue **down** the bayou.
My Yvonne, the sweetest one, me oh my oh
Son of a gun, we'll **have** big **fun** on the bayou.

*Jam*balaya, crawfish pie and **filé** gumbo
′Cause tonight **I'm gonna see my ma
     chère amie-o**
Pick guit**ar**, fill fruit **jar,** and be
     gay-o
Son of a gun, we'll **have** big **fun** on
     the bayou.

Thibod**aux**, Fontaine**aux**, the place is buzzin'
Kinfolks come to see Yvonne **by** the
     dozen
Dressed in style, go hog wild, **me** oh
     my oh
Son of a gun, we'll **have** big **fun** on the
     bayou.

*Jam*balaya, crawfish pie and **filé** gumbo
′Cause tonight **I'm gonna see my ma
     chère amie-o**
Pick guit**ar**, fill fruit jar and be gay-o
Son of a gun, we'll **have** big **fun** on
     the bayou.

Settle **down** far from **town**, get me a pirogue
And I'll catch [scoop] **all** the fish **in** the bayou
Spend my mon to get Yvonne **what** she
     need-o
Son of a gun, we'll **have** big **fun** on the
     bayou.

*Jam*balaya and crawfish pie and **filé**
     gumbo
′Cause tonight **I'm gonna see my ma
     chère amie-o**
Pick guit**ar**, fill fruit jar and be gay-o
Son of a gun, we'll **have** big **fun** on the
     bayou.

1960

Well good-bye, Joe, me gotta go, me oh my oh
Me gotta go pole the pirogue *down* the bayou.
*My Y*vonne, the sweetest one, me oh my oh
Son of a gun, **we'll have big fun** on the bayou.

Well Jambalaya, crawfish pie, and filé gumbo
′Cause tonight **I'm gonna see my ma
     chère amie-o**
I'm gonna pick guit**ar**, fill fruit **jar,** and be
     gay-o
Well, son of a gun, we'll **have big fun** on
     the bayou.

Thibodaux, Fontaineaux, the place is buzzin'
Kinfolks *come* [scoop] to see Yvonne by the
     dozen
Yeah, dressed in style, go hog wild, me oh
     my oh
Son of a gun, we'll **have big fun** on the
     bayou.

Well Jambalaya, crawfish pie, and-a filé gumbo
′Cause tonight **I'm gonna see my ma
     chère amie-o**
Pick guit**ar**, fill fruit **jar,** and be gay-o
Well, son of a gun, we'll **have big fun** on
     the bayou.
                    [modulation up]
Settle **down** far from town, get me a pirogue
Gonna catch **all** the fish in the bayou
Gonna spend my mon to get Yvonne [very tense]
     what she need-o
Son of a gun, we'll **have big fun** on the
     bayou.

*Yeah Jambalaya and-a crawfish pie and-a filé
     gumbo* [higher]
′Cause tonight **I'm gonna see my ma
     chère amie-o**
Gonna pick guitar, yes, fill fruit jar, and be gay-o
Son of a gun, we'll **have big fun** on the
     bayou.

see my ma chère amie-o." The 1960 version also has a faster tempo (saxophonist Boots Randolph is practically in dialogue with Lee, interpolating "Yakety-Sax"-ish choruses between each verse-chorus pair), and a modulation up a step in the final section. Lee tightens her voice significantly, expanding the growling over entire lines, and the little liberties she has taken with the melody up until that point are exaggerated, until she is singing the first line of the last chorus almost as if in upper harmony to the understood melody.

The skill in the 1960 version of "Jambalaya" almost suggests a new kind of dissonance between age and maturity. The faster tempo that skims over the melody somewhat indistinctly, the smoothing out of melodic lines into almost conversational gestures, and the slightly dropped ends of syllables remind me of late Frank Sinatra, a kind of familiarity and control that borders on the jaded.

Similarly, Lee's 1961 recording of Gerry Goffin and Carole King's "Will You Love Me Tomorrow" has little of the youthful vulnerability of the Shirelles' version. The tempo is slower, more languid, less urgent. She sings in a slightly tremulous chest voice with a husky edge, with emphatic drops at the ends of phrases like full stops rather than commas. The second verse is slightly more hesitant, with a particularly quick, almost breathy delivery on "magic" that seems to set the word off as if in glitterpaint. Even in the plaintive bridge where Shirley Owens's voice so affectively pushed that vulnerable register of her voice up into her nasal passages, Lee is in control, belting at the top of her chest. Lee sings individual words and phrases more thoughtfully than Owens. But she sounds like she already knows that answer is "no."

She was just barely sixteen.

Brenda growing up

As Brenda Lee matured physically, her producer, Owen Bradley, moved her toward so-called "good music," or Tin Pan Alley tunes. As a young adult, she now had to fulfill the role of "good girl." Her vocal lines smoothed and she was more often placed in the victim position of other teen girls like Connie Francis or Annette Funicello. This wasn't an entirely smooth transition, as "I'm Sorry" was considered too mature for a fifteen-year-old by the record company.[46] Giving a little tweak to the binaries of race and gender, it is notable that Carla Thomas's "Gee Whiz" dates from within a year of Lee's "Break It to Me Gently." If anything, Thomas's recording, made at Stax in Memphis, sounds more "country" than Lee's Nashville recording, and Thomas did record other tracks in Nashville. Of course, her father Rufus Thomas was one of many African-American musicians who have expressed a great fondness and affection for country music, making the Grand Ol' Opry a part of his weekly schedule.

---

[46]   Lee et al., p. 75.

Lee's whiteness, however, gave her a visibility that Carla Thomas could not have. She could occupy that fascinating "child star" position by virtue of her race and class, though her positioning was not inherently stable. Unlike middle-class, Californian Shirley Temple, Lee was from poor, rural Georgia, prone to identification as "white trash," particularly given her musical style. Even after the success of "I'm Sorry," Brenda was so humiliated by her family living in a trailer that she would walk down the street to catch the school bus. She had to go to court in order to access her trust fund so that her family could buy a house.[47] Shirley Temple might have played poor southern children, but it was usually as an impoverished relative of a plantation family. Her class standing, unlike her sexuality, was rarely troubled.

Lee was, like most of the rockabilly girls in one way or another, at an unstable nexus of gender, sexuality, and race/class. Unlike Shirley Temple, audiences *saw* Lee only briefly, in contexts both unstructured by narrative and rigidly structured by staging—photographs and performances. We are more reliant on less studied, more ambiguous markers of race, class, sexuality, and age. At eleven, the sheer physical fact of her small size embodied a high, childlike voice, but she had remarkably clear technical control of a style that is marked by vocal excess, itself often a marker of sexuality. That her vocal virtuosity is more evident in *less* overtly sexual songs suggests that a sense of propriety influenced at least some of the choices of material, as such concern was taken in her appearance. As she matured, so did her voice, but she remained noticeably a child for several years; and as she reached puberty, in some senses her material "youthened" to adolescence, though she still assumed a position older and wiser than her years.

But as she passed this early teen stage, into her pop phase, she became physically integrated with a musical maturity and at least an intellectual, if not experiential, knowledge of what she was doing. The more "excessive" elements were smoothed out as voice and persona converge. She was presented as a young woman—and in an era when many of her age group married in their late teens (Brenda herself did), she *was*.

This career trajectory from rock and roll to pop to country, where Lee has been successful since the 1960s, was one that several artists of the period traversed—Ray Charles and Bobby Darin are other examples. But the effects of those stylistic shifts on their careers were radically different: Charles gained audiences and respect with each new style; Darin had to fight to win and re-win audiences, and undoubtedly the difference was based on perceptions of race and class. But it is a mistake to think that those styles were as clearly differentiated at the time as they seem now in retrospect. People in New York and Los Angeles may have been surprised when Ray Charles moved from rhythm and blues to country, but the styles have so much in common at their roots in the American South that the "transition" was not as radical as it may have seemed. Darin's shift from "Splish Splash" to "Mack the Knife" in nine months was certainly a shock, but his turn to folk and country

---

[47]   Ibid., p. 76.

a few years later was perhaps more surprising because his Northeastern Italian heritage mitigated so heavily against it. Lee, as a rural white southerner from a working-class, literally cotton-picking background, was, like Charles, moving within familiar ground the entire time—it was mainstream musical culture that was missing the historical connections.

Two dominant but contrasting readings of Brenda Lee persist: she was a "good girl" and her career was thus shepherded; or she was a Lolita figure. The difficulty with both readings is not that they're necessarily wrong, but that they are partial. To take the simpler idea, that Lee was guided toward a more pop style of singing as she matured, since that was more appropriate for a young lady, this argument is implicitly bracketed from a larger musical shift toward the pop end of the spectrum and doesn't take into consideration that those songs were also seen as more likely hits.[48] Songs recorded in this period such as "Be My Love Again" are swaddled in strings and the Anita Kerr Singers, but could easily have been recorded in a bouncier, more stripped down rockabilly style. So while it makes a smooth narrative to say that there was nervousness about displays of musical conventions of sexuality by a blossoming young woman, one should also acknowledge a certain amount of business sense in the move.

But this also rebounds on the earlier end of her career, implying somehow that it was "okay" for a prepubescent child to be singing these sexually charged songs. Robert Oermann's extraordinary claim of Lee's "blankness" probably unintentionally echoes James F. Kincaid's potent trinity of elements that have, since the early Victorian period, gone into the eroticization of the child. Kincaid finds that again and again, the three commonalities of the eroticized child are whiteness, androgyny, and emptiness—all of which are reducible to emptiness, lack, blankness—the better to fill you up with projections, my dear. When dealing with literary characters, such as Kincaid does, or even the paintings that Whiteley cites, we are not dealing with "real" children as such (although we must consider any real models). But when dealing with a performer, a young human being, this emptiness is itself a projection onto a real child. And therein lies the tension.

---

[48]   Some of the songs she sang in this period, like "I'm Sorry," or "I Want to Be Wanted," would not have been out of place in the repertoire of, say, Connie Francis, although "Break It To Me Gently," is definitely more typical of Patsy Cline—and both Francis and Cline were friends of Lee's.

Chapter 3
"He Hit Me, and I was Glad": Violence, Masochism, and Anger in Girl Group Music

Jacqueline Warwick

On the morning of September 4, 1957, a fifteen-year-old girl in Little Rock, Arkansas, prepared for her first day of high school. Before bed the previous night, she had carefully ironed the black and white shirtwaist dress her mother had made, and that morning she put on her best shoes, combed her hair, and donned sunglasses to complete her sophisticated high school girl look. Elizabeth Eckford's meticulous preening and jitters about the first day of school were more heavily weighted than the rituals of most other girls preparing for the same rite of passage, however: Eckford was one of nine black adolescents—six girls and three boys—selected to integrate Little Rock's all white Central High School. Her experiences that day were a milestone in the history of the southern Civil Rights movement, documented by the photographs of Will Counts as well as television news cameras and print journalists. Rarely has a girl's coming of age been accorded this kind of political significance.

As is well-known, Eckford went to her new school alone; the other members of the Little Rock Nine had decided in a series of phone calls the night before that they would travel to school together, escorted by NAACP leader Daisy Bates and two police cars. Because the Eckford family had no phone, Elizabeth was not contacted, and she was unprepared for the angry crowd and armed militia determined to block her entrance to the school. Indeed, so accustomed was this dutiful girl to relying on authority figures to direct and protect her that she assumed the soldiers of the Arkansas National Guard were there to help her enter the building as she had been instructed. It was only when the white soldiers raised their bayonets against her while members of the crowd shouted "Lynch her!" and "No nigger bitch is going to get in our school!" that she realized her mistake.[1] Denied protection from the soldiers, and taunted by angry voices calling to "drag her over to the tree [and hang her]," Eckford turned back to the street, obliged to move through the mob to seek refuge on a bus stop bench. There she at last found

---

[1] Vicki Lebeau, "The Unwelcome Child: Elizabeth Eckford and Hannah Arendt," *Journal of Visual Culture* 3/1 (2004), p. 52.

support, as white New York journalist Benjamin Fine stood beside her, raised her chin with his hand and warned "don't let them see you cry."[2]

For my purposes in this discussion, the most significant feature of Eckford's horrific experiences is the composure she maintained throughout her ordeal. The extensive documentary evidence reveals that, even before Fine admonished her to keep her chin up, Eckford presented an impeccably demure demeanor as she walked the gauntlet up and then back down the school steps. How was it possible for a solitary teenage girl to appear calm and collected in the face of seething rage and hatred? Feelings of terror and outrage would have been natural to anyone in her situation; why did she control these emotions behind a still and impassive face?

Such is the experience of girls, especially middle-class girls and aspiring middle-class girls who have been trained to swallow their undecorous feelings and conform to the ideal of the "nice girl." In the case of Elizabeth Eckford, the responsibilities of being a good girl were compounded by the obligation to be a credit to her race, and to maintain proper comportment and polite behavior when greeted with obstinate and ignorant racism. In a famous article "Reflections on Little Rock" of 1959, Hannah Arendt expressed outrage that a child like Eckford had been abandoned by her parents and elders to confront the dangerous mob. Responding to her criticisms, Ralph Ellison chided Arendt for failing to grasp "the everyday 'terrors of social life' for black men, women and children" and explained that in the case of a black child "the best form of protection may well be pain; 'the child is expected to face the terror and contain his fear and anger precisely because he is a Negro American ... It is a harsh requirement, but if he fails this basic test, his life will be even harsher.'"[3]

It is striking that Ellison adopts the standard male, assumed neutral, gender even in a discussion focused on the ordeal of a teenage girl. Recalling her frightening childhood walk through a predominantly white neighborhood to reach her grandmother's house, bell hooks reports that "I learned as a child that to be 'safe' it was important to recognize the power of whiteness, even to fear it, and to avoid encountering it."[4] The project of containing fear and anger within acceptably decorous behavior is a central feature of the experience of girls and women, particularly girls and women of the middle class or those with middle-class aspirations.

Anger and girlhood

Ellison's and hooks's perceptive remarks about the socialization of black children in the 1950s bear a strong resemblance to contemporary analyses of the social education of teenage girls of various racial groups. In their 1992 ethnographic

---

[2]   Juan Williams and the *Eyes on the Prize* Production Team, *Eyes on the Prize: America's Civil Rights Years, 1954–1965* (New York, 1987), p. 102.

[3]   Cited in Lebeau, p. 56.

[4]   bell hooks, "Representing Whiteness in the Black Imagination," in Ruth Frankenberg (ed.), *Displacing Whiteness: Essays in Social and Cultural Criticism* (Durham, NC: 1997).

study of schoolgirls, *Meeting at the Crossroads*, Lyn Mikel Brown and Carol Gilligan observe:

> Like her other classmates, Jessie shows an emerging propensity to separate what she knows and loves from what she believes she ought to do in order to be seen as cooperative, kind, and good—the kind of girl others, she thinks, want to be with. If she stays with what she wants and says what she thinks, she fears she may be the cause of social chaos, abandoned by others in her undesirable feelings, her messiness. ... The terrifying or terrorizing nature of [the idea of the perfect girl] lies in its power to encourage Jessie to give over the reality of her astute observations of herself and the human world around her—or at least to modulate her voice and not speak about what she sees and hears, feels and thinks, and therefore knows.[5]

Other scholars of girl culture, such as Michelle Fine and Valerie Walkerdine, consider that middle- and working-class girls are socialized to consider anger and aggression dangerous and unsuitable feelings. Walkerdine's analysis of comics aimed at pre-teen middle and working-class girls in 1980s Britain reveals that:

> girls are presented with heroines who never get angry. Their victory is in their very passivity ... anger signifies as wholly negative, and is therefore never used in any positive way: it is never justified, nor is rebellion ever sanctioned. This leads to the suppression of certain qualities as bad and therefore not to be displayed ... passivity is thus *actively* produced as the result of an internal struggle.[6]

Elizabeth Eckford's passivity in 1957 guaranteed her survival, and Benjamin Fine's championing of her on that first dreadful day of high school has faint echoes of fairy tale narratives in which a good and long-suffering heroine is rescued by a handsome prince.

The phenomenon of masking rage with grace is particularly acute for girls of the black middle class (and for working-class girls of any ethnicity who aspire to upward mobility), for whom the risks of "uncivilized" behavior carry harsher penalties than for their white peers. In her book about vaudeville performers the Whitman Sisters, for example, Nadine George-Graves argues that African American women are especially pressured to be respectable in order to counteract assumptions that they are all morally incontinent.[7] Furthermore, Lyn Mikel Brown

---

[5] Lyn Mikel Brown and Carol Gilligan, *Meeting at the Crossroads: Women's Psychology and Girls' Development* (Cambridge, MA, 1992), pp. 60–61.

[6] Valerie Walkerdine, "Someday My Prince Will Come," in Angela McRobbie and Mica Nava (eds), *Gender and Generation* (London, 1984), p. 96.

[7] Nadine George-Graves, *The Royalty of Negro Vaudeville: The Whitman Sisters and the Negotiation of Race, Gender and Class in African American Theater 1900–1940* (London, 2000).

argues that idealized femininity centers around representations of white, middle-class values. She notes that "conventionally ideal girls, perfect girls … look, speak and act in particular ways; they are white and well off, nice and kind, self-effacing, empathic, diligent, serious, generous, and compliant."[8] Elizabeth Eckford knew this well, and the burden of respectable behavior was also imposed on the other members of the Little Rock Nine, who had been carefully screened by the Little Rock school board "because they were trying to get 'good' Negroes, and none of the 'radicals.'"[9] It is surely no coincidence that two-thirds of the group was female.[10]

Indeed, the story of fellow Little Rock Niner Minniejean Brown illustrates the importance of maintaining ladylike demeanor: a few months into the school year, when the black students had become more or less accustomed to being subjected to verbal and physical assault at every opportunity, Brown's "good girl" mask slipped. Standing in line at the cafeteria, Brown endured the repeated chant of "nigger, nigger, nigger" from the boy behind her for several minutes, but then suddenly she "turned around and took [her bowl of] chili and dumped it on the dude's head."[11] Brown's burst of fury garnered applause from the black cafeteria workers, but it led to her suspension from school, and she was expelled a few months later for transgressing the codes of conduct required for an ambitious black girl. In the end, only three of the Little Rock Nine were able to persevere at Central High until graduation, and only one of these was female.[12] The double burden of representing race and gender in a hostile environment proved onerous indeed for the girls of the Little Rock Nine.

In this chapter, I want to address depictions of girls negotiating conflict in girl group music, a style that achieved popularity in the years immediately following the crisis of the Little Rock Nine, and alongside the emerging notion of adolescence

---

[8]   Lyn Mikel Brown, *Raising their Voices: The Politics of Girls' Anger* (Cambridge, MA 1998), p. 148.

[9]   Williams, p. 97.

[10]   For an introduction to theories of whiteness and femininity, see (among others): Wini Breines, *Young, White and Miserable: Growing Up Female in the Fifties* (Boston, 1992); Ruth Frankenberg, *White Women, Race Matters: The Social Construction of Whiteness* (Minneapolis, 1993), and Frankenberg (ed.), *Displacing Whiteness: Essays in Social and Cultural Criticism* (Durham, NC, 1997), especially France Winddance Twine's essay "Brown-Skinned White Girls: Class, Culture, and the Construction of White Identity in Suburban Communities" (pp. 214–43) and bell hooks's "Representing Whiteness in the Black Imagination" (pp. 165–79).

[11]   Ernest Green, cited in Williams, p. 117.

[12]   Green, the eldest of the group, graduated in 1958, at the end of that first year of desegregation. In the fall of 1959, following a year in which all public schools in Little Rock were closed in a desperate last bid to stop integration, three of the Nine—all girls, including Elizabeth Eckford—began to attend Hall High School, in an upper-middle-class white area of the city, without meeting violent opposition. Carlotta Walls and Jefferson Thomas returned to Central High and graduated in 1960. See *The Little Rock Nine*, http://www.centralhigh57.org/The_Little_Rock_Nine.html (accessed December 16, 2004).

as a fixed subject position. With the mainstream success of girl groups such as the Shirelles, the Crystals, the Ronettes and the Shangri-Las, North American popular culture was for the first time focused on girls and their experiences. What is more, the professional system that produced the American girl group genre involved black and white musicians working together, a highly successful example of the integrationist policies espoused by figures such as Martin Luther King, and one that turned many non-white singers into models of girlhood for audiences of all racial backgrounds. Just as girls like Elizabeth Eckford were socialized to conceal their anger, girl group songs are not normally thought of as "angry music," but themes of conflict, rage and even violence run through this repertoire if we know how to look for them.

Girl group music

The girl group genre was at the forefront of popular music during the early 1960s, an unprecedented instance of teenage girls occupying centre stage of mainstream commercial culture. The genre is generally understood to involve groups of teenage girl singers backed by studio musicians, performing songs written by professional songwriters and dealing with themes of interest to young girls grappling with the approach of adulthood: songs about boys, the strictness of parents, and the behavior of other girls dominate the repertoire. Some of the best-known songs and groups include the Shirelles' pivotal 1960 "Will You Love Me Tomorrow?", the Ronettes magnificent 1963 "Be My Baby" and the Crystals' "Then He Kissed Me" of 1962. Solo artists such as Little Eva of "Locomotion" fame and Lesley Gore with "It's My Party" are also connected to the genre by virtue of the themes of their songs and shared musical characteristics with the girl group style: untutored lead vocals by young singers, dialogue with female backup singers, and pop instrumentation over rock and roll grooves. Most of these songs also present narratives urging passive behavior as the key to winning a boy's love ("Then He Kissed Me") and the necessity of swallowing anger and maintaining composure as the right way to restore the proper order of things ("It's My Party" and its follow up hit, "Judy's Turn to Cry"). Indeed, a song like Skeeter Davis's 1963 hit "I Can't Stay Mad at You" presents a girl whose refusal to feel anger verges on passive aggressive control; though the boy in the song appears to be doing everything in his power to upset her and thus possibly extricate himself from the relationship (lying, and betraying her with other girls), Davis sweetly insists that she can neither stay angry nor leave, and she is supported by an upbeat groove and perky backing voices.[13]

---

[13]   Although Skeeter Davis fits best into the category of country music, with her interpretations of ballads like Chet Atkins's "The End of the World," "I Can't Stay Mad at You" aligns her with girl groups. The song was written by Carole King and Gerry Goffin, its narrative emphasizes teen relationships, and it features a chorus of backing singers

I think it is crucial, in the context of this discussion, to emphasize that even solo artists connected to the girl group genre sound like groups of girls, because of the backing voices on their records. In her study of anger in contemporary girls' culture, Rachel Simmons suggests that one of the easiest ways—if not the only way—for girls to accept angry feelings is to be part of a group of peers and not take sole responsibility for the uncomfortable emotions. Adolescent friendships involve Byzantine rules of alliance building among girls, who can cruelly exclude one another by conspicuously fostering friendships with others. Adolescent and pre-adolescent girls often find anger so frightening that they are unable to express these feelings to their friends; a girl who is outraged by another girl's actions may feel incapable of confronting her friend. Instead, she will simply withdraw her friendship and complain about the offensive behavior to other girls, often leaving the perpetrator confused and panicky because she does not know what she has done wrong. Simmons describes this process:

> alliance building forces the victim to face not only the potential loss of the relationship with her opponent, but with many of her friends. It goes like this: Spotting a conflict on the horizon, a girl will begin a scrupulous underground campaign to best her opponent. Like a skilled politician, she will methodically build a coalition of other girls willing to throw their support behind her. Friends who have "endorsed" her will ignore the target, lobby others for support, or confront the target directly until she is partly or completely isolated.[14]

This kind of scenario is presented musically in the Cookies' 1963 "Don't Say Nothin' Bad About My Baby" (written by Gerry Goffin and Carole King), in which a group of girls confronts another girl about her criticism of one of their boyfriends. In this song, backing vocalists initiate dialogue with a girl who does not speak, and lead singer Earl-Jean McCrea enters with soft, light singing only when the terms of the conversation have been established by her friends. Thus, the injured party whose boyfriend has been maligned does not have to express rage herself, because her gang does it for her. The lead singer's ladylike persona remains intact, and the other girls are able to feel self-righteous and noble about their indignation because it is on another's behalf.

Strategies of this sort have been attractive to girls because they do not require them to disrupt decorum by confronting injustice and expressing outrage for themselves. If we consider that girl group songs (and other pop songs) present their listeners with opportunities to rehearse the experiences and emotions performed, it is highly significant that the few songs dealing with girls' anger are overwhelmingly presented as coming from a group. Indeed, the only significant

---

(actually overdubs of Davis herself) singing a doo-wop inspired "dooby dooby dooby doo down down."

[14] Rachel Simmons, *Odd Girl Out: The Hidden Culture of Aggression in Girls* (New York, 2002), pp. 79–80.

(in terms of major chart success) exception to this trend would be Lesley Gore's unprecedented "You Don't Own Me" of 1964.

Discipline and control

Girl groups in the 1960s were famous for their appearance, with wigs and matching dresses signifying the height of teenage glamour, and choreographed dance moves to accompany their singing. Indeed, the Supremes' famous "Stop in the Name of Love" hand gesture often serves as a kind of shorthand to represent the whole genre. The costume and specific kinds of posture of the girl groups can be understood as ways in which the young singers were compelled into repressive versions of young female identity. The physical attributes of feminine appearance have always required degrees of bodily constraint, ranging from the cruel historical custom of footbinding among upper-class Chinese women (a form of crippling abandoned more for its class associations than for its misogyny) to the removal of body hair in contemporary Western society. In their social contexts, these practices are generally accepted as normal responsibilities of femininity, and they are readily taken on by girls and women who wish to appear presentable and attractive, but they should nonetheless be considered forms of repressing and violating the female body. Rosemarie Garland-Thomson considers the meaning of mutilation in her analysis of physical disability and femininity:

> Not only has the female body been labeled deviant, but historically the practices of femininity have configured female bodies similarly to disability. Foot binding, scarification, clitoridectomy, and corseting were (and are) socially accepted, encouraged, even compulsory cultural forms of female disablement that, ironically, are socially enabling, increasing a woman's value and status at a given moment in a particular society.[15]

In this analysis, extreme physical restraints of female bodies are directly linked to conforming to a society's preferred view of girls and women, thus actually affording better social opportunities to compliant females. Girls and women who resist these painful, punishing regimens cannot expect to earn social approbation.[16]

---

[15]   Rosemarie Garland-Thomson, *Extraordinary Bodies: Figuring Physical Disability in American Culture and Literature* (New York, 1997), p. 27.

[16]   A vivid example of this comes from Jung Chang's account of her grandmother's childhood in pre-revolutionary China, which included footbinding at the age of two by her mother. Drawing on her grandmother's recollections, Chang describes how the toddler's foot was crushed with a stone and bound tightly in cloth, beginning a process that would last for several excruciating years. Chang explains that, "In those days, when a woman was married, the first thing the bridegroom's family did was to examine her feet. Large feet, meaning normal feet, were considered to bring shame on the husband's household

96 SHE'S SO FINE

Singing and performing choreographed dance moves was not a painful experience for members of girl groups (though it often was at least arduous and exhausting), but to accept these physical constraints was to be complicit in regulating the bodies of other young females. When singers displayed themselves for spectators through stage and television performances and publicity shots, they communicated particular ways of being girls to their audience members, who could copy their stances and train their own bodies in turn. Susan Bordo notes that

> With the advent of movies and television, the rules for femininity have come to be culturally transmitted more and more through standardized visual images … . We are no longer given verbal descriptions or exemplars of what a lady is or of what femininity consists. Rather, we learn the rules directly through bodily discourse: through images that tell us what clothes, body shape, facial expression, movements and behaviour are required.[17]

The stylized and coerced performances of girlness involved in girl group songs had far-reaching consequences, and they effectively wrote an embodied gender script for the girls who watched them.

This kind of strictness with the body is perhaps an inevitable part of human experience in the industrial capitalist sphere, and males as well as females tend to accept it willingly for the purpose of social betterment. Aspiring to the middle-class ideal, girls in Western society are invariably instructed to "sit like a lady" with knees together and ankles crossed in order to shield the genitals, and this mermaid-like posture contrasts with the more aggressive pose of knees apart and feet firmly on the floor that is customary for men. Most males and females rarely consider the ways in which they sit or move to be learned postures, however, and assume that their bodies are natural entities rather than culturally formed constructions. Training the body into an age-appropriate version of femininity is an ongoing experience for girls and women; indeed, the cultivation of "proper" femininity is a never-ending project, demanding tireless vigilance and self-policing.

Let us consider a television performance of Martha and the Vandellas performing their 1963 hit "Nowhere to Run" on ABC's *Shindig!* (readily available online at video archive sites). I find this performance striking for a number of reasons, not least because of the dramatic contrast in dress and comportment between the group members and the *Shindig!* dancers. Martha and the Vandellas are poised up on pedestals—literally with nowhere to run—and wearing tight

---

… sometimes a mother would take pity on her daughter and remove the binding cloth; but when the child grew up and had to endure the contempt of her husband's family and the disapproval of society, she would blame her mother for having been too weak;" Jung Chang, *Wild Swans: Three Daughters of China* (New York, 1991), pp. 31–32.

[17] Susan Bordo, "The Body and the Reproduction of Femininity," in Katie Conboy, Nadia Medina, and Sarah Stanbury (eds), *Writing on the Body: Female Embodiment and Feminist Theory* (New York, 1997), p. 94.

sheath dresses and pointy-toed, high-heeled shoes that are the height of elegant discomfort, while the television show's regular dancers romp about in knee socks, sweaters and skirts. What is more, the group's song is about the phenomenon of feeling trapped and helpless, miserable because of a powerful obsessive love: "It's not love I'm running from/It's the heartache I know will come / 'Cause I know you're no good for me / But you've become a part of me / Everywhere I go, your face I see / Every step I take, you take with me".[18]

This kind of theme is common to the girl group repertoire, and, of course, to popular music in general. In this treatment, the narrator finds herself unable to escape a relationship that she knows is damaging, and the song's musical language corresponds to her situation. Backing vocalists and instruments perform a descending ostinato figure outlining G major; the looping repetitions of an ostinato signify, in this context, the very nature of obsession. Lead singer Martha Reeves's melody, however, begins with an aberrant B♭, which functions like a blue note in this harmony; this note proves central to her melody, and she keeps returning to it in her efforts to resist the obsession represented by the G major tonality. Throughout, the song's percussive register is dominated by the metallic slither famously created in the Motown studio by rattling the snow chains taken from someone's car—chains binding the narrator to her destructive relationship, a theme also explored in another girl group classic, the Cookies' 1962 "Chains."

The notion of imprisonment through love is hardly exclusive to girl group music, of course, but the importance of restraint and punishment—both self- and other-imposed—in girls' experience makes a song like this different from a piece such as Fabian's "Turn Me Loose" (1959). "Nowhere to Run" describes how the punishing love object has become "a part of me," taking every step with the narrator, and seeming to observe her when she looks in the mirror to comb her hair; these lyrics are particularly poignant to a listener who has worn stiletto heels that make every step agonizing, or subjected herself to close scrutiny and painstaking self-improvement in the bathroom mirror.

This kind of attention to monitoring the self was an explicit and important part of Motown's regimen for artists; the Detroit record company's famous Artist Development program sought to mould urban black teenagers into models of sophistication and deportment. Berry Gordy's vision was to groom his artists to perform in such upscale venues as New York's CopaCabana and Las Vegas, and male as well as female performers were expected to attend "finishing school," where Maxine Powell coached them on posture, table manners and elocution. Artist Development at Motown also encompassed vocal coaching with Maurice King and choreography with Cholly Atkins, who worked hard to create dance routines for singers that would reinforce their sophistication. Motown singers often worked at their lessons eight hours a day, and it is clear that the female artists in particular embraced this training as a means of upward mobility and ladylikeness. The stiff elegance of Martha and the Vandellas' matching dresses

---

[18] Lyrics credited to Lamont Dozier, Brian Holland and Edward Holland Jr.

98   *SHE'S SO FINE*

in this television appearance marks the group as refined, adult, in contrast to the vulgar frills and girlish bows prohibited by middle-class tastes. As Carolyn Kay Steedman recalls in her study of femininity and class in post-war Britain, "the material stepping stones of our escape [from the working class] were clothes, shoes, make-up."[19] Thus, appropriate dress and comportment are essential to the enterprise of becoming an "ideal" girl and woman, and tastes must be cultivated just as discomfort must be endured. What is more, proper dress and comportment can actually mask a working-class body, enabling admission to higher-class groups for girls and women.

Michel Foucault has theorized the creation of this kind of docile body in relation to the rise of institutions of the body politic, including schools, armies and prisons, for whom discipline and control over bodies becomes an end in itself—bodies are tamed and taught to be self-regulating merely for the sake of discipline and order.[20] Sandra Lee Bartky adds:

> The disciplinary project of femininity is a "set-up": it requires such radical and extensive measures of bodily transformation that virtually every woman who gives herself to it is destined in some degree to fail. Thus, a measure of shame is added to a woman's sense that the body she inhabits is deficient … .[21]

Bartky also itemizes specific ways in which female bodies are rendered docile, reporting that the correct posture for women and girls involves pulling the stomach and buttocks in and protruding the chest to "display her bosom to maximum advantage," and that an appropriately feminine walk involves a gentle rolling of the hips (although to overdo this is to disrupt decorum and invite censure). She summarizes women's magazine advice on:

> the proper way of getting in and out of cars … a woman must not allow her arms and legs to flail about in all directions; she must try to manage her movements with the appearance of grace—no small feat when one is climbing out of the back seat of a Fiat—and she is well advised to use the opportunity for a certain display of leg.[22]

Describing her tutelage under the formidable Maxine Powell at Motown's finishing school, Mary Wilson of the Supremes recalls being taught how to climb in and out of a car exactly as Bartky describes. Wilson reports that lessons like these became

---

[19]   Carolyn Kay Steedman, *Landscape for a Good Woman: A Story of Two Lives* (Boston, 1987) p. 15.

[20]   Michel Foucault, *Discipline and Punish: The Birth of the Prison* (London, 1995).

[21]   Sandra Lee Bartky, "Foucault, Femininity and Patriarchal Power," in Katie Conboy, Nadia Medina, and Sarah Stanbury (eds), *Writing on the Body: Female Embodiment and Feminist Theory* (New York, 1997), pp. 132, 139.

[22]   Ibid., p. 136.

ingrained into her habitual way of moving and thinking about her body: "I can remember feeling [Mrs. Powell's] eyes upon me as I walked around ... . Were my shoulders straight? Was my posture good?"[23]

This kind of self-monitoring and fixation with appearance is grotesquely twisted in self-mutilating disorders that are disproportionately female: the self-starvation that characterizes the illness anorexia, and trichotillomania, the practice of tearing out hair, eyebrows or eyelashes, are two examples of "ordinary" grooming practices taken to dangerous extremes. Arguably, shaving one's legs is different from ripping out one's eyelashes only in degree, not in kind. Self-mutilation is often understood as an expression of rage against others directed against the self—the girl who cuts herself experiences rage, but believes that she can only feel anger towards herself, never towards others. Feminist theorists such as Bartky and Carol Gilligan have argued for an understanding of these kinds of disorders as expressions of rage, a symbolic acting-out of the larger culture's mistreatment of women that affects girls on the cusp of adulthood. Lyn Mikel Brown notes that "early adolescence ... disposes girls to see the cultural framework, and girls' and women's subordinate place in it, for the first time. That their reaction to this awakening would be shock, sadness, anger and a sense of betrayal is not surprising."[24]

Rage and violence

Explicit references to physical restraint and even violence are a recurring topic in several important girl group songs. Claudine Clark's 1962 "Party Lights," for example, articulates the frustration of being held against her will at home when other teens are free to attend a party, and the singer's throaty growls and whining vocal quality indicate her strong feelings of dissatisfaction: "I see the lights, I see the party lights / They're red and blue and green / Everybody in the crowd is there / But you won't let me make the scene."[25]

Like Rapunzel in her impregnable tower, the protagonist of this song is confined to her bedroom, with her mother serving the dual role of witch and doorkeeper. The girl's frustration is heightened by the fact that she can see and hear the party she longs to attend, and we too hear it; during the instrumental break of the song, a tenor saxophone solo provides a jaunty obbligato to casual chatter and laughter. No information is given as to why the girl has been kept at home when all her friends are across the street at a party—in a girl's eye view of the situation, the specifics of her offence are irrelevant. The near universality of her experience (being denied access to an exciting social event by an unreasonable and immovable mother) is made clear by the fact that a chorus of backing vocalists begins the song, with

---

[23]   Mary Wilson, *Dreamgirl and Supreme Faith: My Life as a Supreme* (New York, 1999), p. 151.

[24]   Brown, p. 16.

[25]   Lyrics credited to Claudine Clark.

Clark's distinctive, oddly child-like voice entering only once the melody and groove are well established.

It is important to note, however, that the song's musical language is buoyant and danceable, and that the singer unfailingly calls her mother "dear" in spite of her declared anger and resentment. The prominent snare drum, tenor saxophone, rollicking repeated chords in the piano and chorus of hearty backup singers create a cheerful backdrop to the protagonist's pleadings and reproaches. This represents, of course, the noise of the party, but it also seems to suggest that the girl's expressions of rage are merely playful and that her confinement is as festive and enjoyable as the party she is missing. The potential for understanding this girl's anger as a force to be reckoned with is undermined by a musical setting that insists it's all in good fun. "Party Lights," then, presents a complicated view of a girl's fury that is clearly audible in her full-throated, bluesy growls, explicit in the lyrics, and yet trivialized and neutralized by a light, appealing setting. It is reminiscent of a kitten puffing itself up and hissing with rage; because there is no real threat, the anger is adorable.

The song is something of a rarity in the girl group repertoire in that the performer, Claudine Clark, also wrote the song; the twenty-one-year-old Philadelphia native had studied music composition formally at Coombs College. It is perhaps no surprise to find that this nuanced representation of a struggle to express anger while maintaining the posture of a cheerful, good girl was actually written by a young woman barely out of her teens. While Clark worked to present a version of girl's rage that did not disrupt her sense of herself as a nice girl, however, other singers and songwriters explored male anger towards girls in songs such as "Johnny Get Angry," a Top Ten hit for Joanie Summers in 1962. The song was written by Brill Building lyricist Hal David (best-known for his collaborations with Burt Bacharach) and composer Sherman Edwards in the same year that both men contributed to the soundtrack of Elvis Presley's film *Kid Galahad* (Phil Karlson, 1962). The film recounts the story of a young ex-soldier who demonstrates his courage and integrity with his fists; a turning point early in the plot sees him successfully fending off hired thugs who attack a woman.

In "Johnny Get Angry," the girl narrator implores her boyfriend to prove his love by behaving more like Kid Galahad, and to demonstrate his manhood by taking charge of her and other boys' access to her: "Oh, Johnny get angry, Johnny get mad / Give me the biggest lecture I ever had / I want a brave man, I want a cave man / Johnny, show me that you care, really care for me."[26]

Since the impact of second-wave feminism, the lyrics of this song have been provocative to many feminist thinkers. Outspoken activist kd lang has performed "Johnny Get Angry" in such a way as to make clear the connection between these kinds of gender behaviors and domestic violence; Lori Burns has analysed lang's

---

[26]   Lyrics credited to Hal David and Sherman Edwards, 1962.

version of the song as a feminist revision.[27] Certainly, lang's 1985 performance (which involves hitting herself and collapsing on the stage as though beaten into submission) brings to the foreground the dangers of stereotypes that insist on male strength and female weakness, but I would suggest that much of the tension and ambivalence highlighted by lang is already present in the original 1962 recording.

The song features a distinctive chromatic riff in the bass that slides between D and B♭, undergirding the two main harmonic centers of the song (D major and B♭ minor). Twenty-year-old Summers's voice, with its warm, full-voiced sound and petulant quality (familiar to listeners in 1962 from Pepsi Cola jingles that she recorded throughout the 1960s) sounds at once womanly and girlish. Her voice is entirely appropriate for a song about a girl seeking to understand the appropriate roles in a heterosexual romantic relationship; she cajoles and berates "Johnny" by turns, signalling her frustration when he won't behave the way she thinks a boyfriend ought to. At the same time that we hear her pouting and whining, however, she demonstrates such a full, controlled vocal sound that we may wonder who, in fact, is in charge of this relationship.

While Summers is pleading for boorish, domineering and possessive behavior from her boyfriend, Johnny appears to refuse this kind of controlling role. Is he, perhaps, a new kind of boyfriend interested in equality and mutual trust in a relationship, creating confusion for a girlfriend invested in more patriarchal behaviors? Since normative conventions insist that he be the powerful one in this relationship while she remain passive and subservient, the song's very questioning of Johnny's masculinity might be read as a critique of repressive gender roles.

Some aspects of the instrumentation in "Johnny Get Angry" support this interpretation, most notably the kazoos heard during the instrumental break, a section of the song usually given over to electric guitar in a rock and roll song or to saxophone in a rhythm and blues context. The kazoo's sound is distinctive, created with a membrane in a metal tube that adds a buzz to vocal sounds when it is hummed into; the kazoo is perhaps more accurately understood as a vocal distortion device than an instrument. Kazoos termed as such are a uniquely American phenomenon, patented in 1923, but part of a larger instrument family of mirlitons. Mirlitons made of horn and egg membrane are believed to have been used in African tribal ceremonies to mask the voices of participants in centuries past, and these horn-mirlitons became known in North America as a result of the slave trade.[28] If we consider the kazoo's function of masking voices, we may understand its presence in this song as revealing that all the characters are actually in masquerade. Certainly, in contemporary culture, the sound of the kazoo is understood as irreverent, teasing, and possibly disruptive. The startling kazoo solo

---

[27]   Lori Burns, "'Joanie' Get Angry: kd lang's Feminist Revision," in John Covach and Graeme Boone (eds), *Understanding Rock: Essays in Music Analysis* (Oxford, 1997), pp. 93–112.

[28]   See *Kazoobie Kazoos*, http://www.kazoos.com/historye.htm (accessed February 24, 2005).

102   *SHE'S SO FINE*

in "Johnny Get Angry" must be heard as cheeky and mocking, almost literally giving the raspberry to the ideas presented through the lyrics.

The Crystals' 1963 "He Hit Me (and It Felt Like a Kiss)," however, cannot be interpreted as gently sassing patriarchal relationships; it describes being a girl in love as physically punishing in a very straightforward way. The Crystals are among the most famous and successful girl groups, well known for songs like "Da Doo Ron Ron" and "Then He Kissed Me," but also notorious for this song, though it made no chart impact at all: "He hit me and it felt like a kiss / He hit me and I knew he loved me / If he didn't care for me / I could have never made him mad / But he hit me and I was glad."[29]

Gillian Gaar reports that twenty-year-old Carole King and her husband Gerry Goffin based the song on Little Eva's explanation of a black eye bestowed by her boyfriend, thus gesturing towards an understanding of it as "authentic," and Alan Betrock wonders whether the song's producer, Phil Spector, was deliberately seeking to release a flop in order to get out of an unsatisfying business partnership with Lester Sill (Philles Records).[30] The theory that the song was a throwaway is undermined somewhat by its inclusion in the box set *Back to Mono 1958—1969* (Phil Spector Records Inc., 1991), one of only sixty songs intended to showcase the best of Phil Spector's entire oeuvre as a record producer during an eleven-year period, and recent events in Spector's life do little to challenge our understanding of him as a violent misogynist.[31]

Barbara Alston, a former member of the Crystals who sang lead on "He Hit Me," has complained:

> we didn't like that one. After we cut it, we absolutely hated it. Still do. Phil was so particular about the arrangement and sound that we had a terrible session. What made it worse was that after a few weeks had gone by and the record was issued and started selling, the kids at school started singing it and their teachers heard them. They didn't like the title and the lyrics, so the P.T.A. got it banned.[32]

Alston seems reluctant to address the source of the teachers' outrage, and skirts around the song's message that seems to condone and even celebrate male violence against women in ostensibly loving relationships. Her distaste for "He Hit Me" stems from the fact that it was not a pretty song and that it came about through

---

[29]   Lyrics by Gerry Goffin and Carole King.

[30]   Gillian Gaar, *She's a Rebel: The History of Women in Rock and Roll* (Seattle, 1992), p. 44, and Alan Betrock, *Girl Groups: The Story of a Sound* (New York, 1982), p. 35. Betrock's theory is reiterated in Charlotte Grieg, *Will You Still Love Me Tomorrow?: Girl Groups from the 50s On ...* (London, 1989).

[31]   At the time of writing, Spector is preparing to stand trial for the shooting murder of a Hollywood waitress/actress in his Alhambra mansion in the spring of 2002.

[32]   Cited in Betrock, p. 35.

an arduous recording session. She does not speak of her feelings about enacting this kind of dutiful acceptance of abuse, or for promoting an understanding of beatings as loving. Similarly, lyricist Gerry Goffin admits ruefully that "the song's blatant masochism was 'a little radical for those times'," but he does not appear to consider its message to be a dangerous courtship model.[33]

The song begins with a solo ostinato figure in the double bass that outlines a G-major triad, accompanied only by a single triangle chime on the downbeats. When the voice enters after four measures with the words "he hit me," percussive forces expand to include a grating, scraping sound on the fourth beat of every bar, a creepy effect that might be rendered by a guiro. Although G major has tried to establish itself as the tonal centre, lead singer Barbara Alston's melody is unmistakably in B minor, and the rest of the song enacts an uneasy struggle between these keys. Thus, Alston's C♯ on the word "hit" is an uncomfortable tritone away from the root note of the bass foundation we have accepted, and it creates an ugly dissonance that is every bit as troubling as the words, which are foregrounded in the mix in a production style that is unusual for Phil Spector. Furthermore, the voices of the Crystals have a wooden quality on this recording that is entirely unlike their passionate performances on songs such as their first hit, 1961's "There's No Other Like my Baby" or their 1963 triumphs, "Da Doo Ron Ron" and "Then He Kissed Me"—here, they sound almost robotic as they plod through the stiff, awkward melody.[34]

The vocal melody insists on B minor, repeating a stepwise descent to its tonic, over a relentless G-major bass line that is soon bolstered by other instruments doubling it. The instrumental forces build inexorably through a process of accretion, with first guitar, then organ and finally strings adding to the lugubrious figure initiated in the bass. Percussive sounds also expand to include a bass drum that sounds like a painful heart thumping. At the second chorus, a high, nagging rattle enters with incessant sixteenth notes, and backing vocals are also in an eerily high tessitura.

Over the course of the song, the backup singers and the strings enact a dialogue with the lead voice, at first echoing either her line or the bass line and then departing into melodic figures of increasing complexity. The sound of the string orchestra, long understood as a syrupy soundtrack to fairytale romance, is complicit in helping the song's protagonist accept physical abuse as a testament of love. The quasi-operatic gestures of the backup singers—standing in for a community of supportive female friends—also confirm the rightness of the damaging relationship by moving ever

---

[33] Cited in Gaar, p. 45. I have been unable to locate a comment from Goffin's co-songwriter, his then-wife Carole King.

[34] Three different voices provided leads on records by the Crystals: Barbara Alston was the soloist on their first recordings, "There's No Other Like My Baby," "Uptown," and "He Hit Me," Darlene Love (who was never actually a member of the group) sang lead on "He's a Rebel" and "He's Sure the Boy I Love," and Dolores "Lala" Brooks was the lead singer on the group's remaining releases.

upward to a climactic f♯″. I understand the string section and backup singers to represent cultural forces that can pressure women into accepting dysfunctional relationships as normal. The conventions of romance ideology tend to valorize passionate intensity that can explode into violence, and many victims of domestic abuse are encouraged to stay by female friends promoting the oppressive notion that love will redeem suffering.

The harmonic language also works to bring about resolution; as the first verse draws to a close, the singer's B minor and the bass line's G major collude together to resolve on a shimmering B-major chord. This shift is a relief after the dissonant struggles of the song, and it undergirds the final word of the lyrics "if he didn't care for me, I could have never made him mad, so when he hit me, I was glad." The two irreconcilable keys of the song achieve B major through movement that sidesteps the conventions of pop music's harmonic writing—the happy climax, welcome as it is, is not based on rational thinking. In my analysis, the musical language of the song enacts a virtuosic rationalization of wife- or girlfriend-battering, as disparate tonal centers come together in a transcendent moment. "He Hit Me (and It Felt Like a Kiss)" can perhaps be understood as an articulation of the thought processes of denial and rationalization that enable women to endure beatings from their partners. Thus, a song that appears at the level of lyrics to be a straightforward celebration of physical violence as a loving corrective might also be read as an attempt to speak from the position of a girl in this kind of situation, a compassionate performance of the unhealthy logic that makes abuse tolerable.

In a climate where violence against women is at last discussed openly in public discourse, it is impossible to respond to "He Hit Me" as we might have in 1962. The twisted connections between romance, obsession, and violence were not yet of general psychological interest to a society that laughed when Ralph Kramden alluded to hitting his wife in the 1950s television series *The Honeymooners*. Even so, the song was advertised in *Billboard* magazine at the time as "a serious ballad with a telling message," suggesting that my analysis of the song resembles at least some contemporary readings.[35]

The record was condemned early on for its lyrics and Spector was compelled to pull it out of circulation, so the song never entered the realm of stage or television performances that would have required rehearsed dance steps from the singers. This presents a tantalizing though appalling line of thought: how might such a song have been choreographed? A literal pantomime that acted out the events described would of course be impossible, out of the question on conservative prime time television variety shows such as *Shindig!* or *Hullabaloo*—sites where the Crystals and most other girl groups performed regularly. But a more stylized vocal choreography, along the lines of Cholly Atkins's work with Motown artists such as Martha and the Vandellas, would surely strike viewers as an equally outrageous violation of a song that is so blunt in the presentation of its subject matter.

---

[35] Cited in Jay Warner, *American Singing Groups: A History 1940–1990* (New York, 1992), p. 352.

Ultimately, the song could never be danced to by performers or listeners— its stark lyrics and dirge-like musical language do not inspire that kind of bodily response. In this important way, "He Hit Me" is entirely unlike other, more acceptable pop songs that present images of violence and are nonetheless enjoyed by mainstream audiences. The harsh, unappealing musical language of "He Hit Me," and its goal as I understand it, are markedly different from "Nowhere to Run," "Party Lights" or "Johnny Get Angry."

Angry girls after the 60s

The song's function in girls' and women's culture is complicated and deepened because of its appearance in the work of Courtney Love and her alternative rock band Hole in the mid-1990s: my reading of "He Hit Me" is enhanced by a consideration of this revival of a song that was then thirty-two years old.[36] Hole performed "He Hit Me" during their 1995 appearance on the television show *MTV Unplugged*, a programme that featured rock bands playing acoustic instruments in an intimate setting with a small live audience; the show participated in the mid-90s "unplugged" craze inspired largely by Eric Clapton's 1992 album featuring mellow, contemplative versions of his youthful hits such as 1970's searing, electric guitar-driven "Layla." By 1995, the programme had spotlighted acts such as Nirvana, the iconic band of Courtney Love's tragic husband Kurt Cobain. Hole's appearance on *MTV Unplugged* followed the success of their prophetically-named album *Live Through This* (Geffen Records Inc.) in 1994, released only a week after Cobain's suicide and shortly after the deadly heroin overdose of Hole's bassist Kristen Pfaff.

Both Hole and Nirvana were part of the "alternative" rock moment of the mid-90s that emerged largely from Seattle, Washington, and Love was also presented in the media as a participant in Olympia, Washington's "Riot Grrrl" movement. The Riot Grrrl movement of the 1990s has interesting parallels with the girl group moment of thirty years before (though Riot Grrrl music never attained the mainstream appeal or commercial success of 60s girl groups). Here again we witnessed depictions of the lives and concerns of young girls in a landscape dominated by representations of adolescent and post-adolescent masculinity. Riot Grrrl's musical version of girlhood used distorted electric guitars and a punk-inspired anti-virtuosity, thus (arguably) drawing on a language associated with men and boys, just as early girl groups had (arguably) done in borrowing from the musical vocabulary of doo-wop

---

[36]   The performance from *MTV Unplugged* was later included in Hole's 1997 album *My Body the Hand Grenade* (Geffen Records Inc.). The band never made a studio recording of "He Hit Me," but the song can be understood as a companion piece to their original composition "(He) Hit So Hard" from 1998's *Celebrity Skin* (Geffen Records Inc.).

in the late 1950s.[37] Riot Grrrl songs celebrated girlhood and female strength, and angrily criticized violence against girls and women in the forms of incest, rape, and eating disorders brought on by unhealthy ideals of thinness and compliance. As the name of the movement itself suggests, Riot Grrrl was far more confrontational and politically savvy than any other girl-driven cultural phenomenon; most participants in the scene were college-educated white girls and women who read feminist criticism and actively sought to reform their audience's behavior through circulating underground magazines, building national and international support networks for rape and incest victims, and banning men and boys to the back rows of their concerts.[38] While the extent of Love's involvement in this movement has been disputed (not least by Love herself), study of her work from the mid-1990s reveals a similar preoccupation with drawing attention to misogynist practices and with giving voice to girls' anger.

Given that so many of Love's compositions (solo and collaborative) explore themes that expose the dark, ugly side of girlhood and adult femininity, Hole's television performance of "He Hit Me" is apt. Love introduces the performance by saying "this is a sick song—one of those Phil Spector songs. This one was written by Carole King, which really makes you think." By identifying the song as "sick," and naming King as its author (omitting to mention the participation of Gerry Goffin), Love signals to her audience in the television studio and to viewers elsewhere that they are about to hear something disturbing, unexpected and disappointing from a woman known for comforting, empowering songs such as "You've Got a Friend." Although Hole's performance uses only acoustic instruments and thus lacks the raw power of electric guitars, it adheres to a rock aesthetic and involves a significant amount of vocal distortion from Love. Significantly, the band takes liberties with the song, adapting the contours of the vocal melody, flattening the

---

[37]   See my discussion of the origins of the girl group sound in girl groups in Jacqueline Warwick, *Girl Groups, Girl Culture: Popular Music and Identity in the 1960s* (New York, 2007), pp. 13–32.

[38]   Marion Leonard, "'Rebel Girl, You are the Queen of My World': Feminism, 'Subculture' and Grrrl Power," in Sheila Whiteley (ed.), *Sexing the Groove: Popular Music and Gender* (New York, 1997), p. 230–56. I want to acknowledge that the Riot Grrrl movement was not solely about young women's anger, although media interest in the scene focused almost exclusively on this theme. Songs like Bikini Kill's "Rebel Girl" celebrate friendship between very young girls with lyrics such as "she's got the coolest trike in town," and Gayle Wald reminds us that Riot Grrrl's insistence on tropes of cuteness and girlish innocence alongside their aggressive musical language "signifies ironically within the context of punk youth music subcultures, where 'youth' is more likely to be associated with aggression, violence, and crisis, and where youth and youthfulness are frequently conflated with boyhood ... in the context of Riot Grrrl performance these images of playful and happy girlhood are attempts at self-consciously idealizing representation;" Gayle Wald, "Just a Girl? Rock Music, Feminism, and the Cultural Construction of Female Youth," in Roger Beebe, Denise Fulbrook, and Ben Saunders (eds), *Rock Over the Edge:Transformations in Popular Music Culture* (Durham, NC, 2002), p. 200.

ostinato figure into a guitar riff of repeated notes, changing lyrics from "and when he *kissed* me, he made me his" to "when he *hit* me, he made me his," and adding a concluding section where Love moans "baby, won't you stay" repeatedly, implying a collusion between abuser and abused. Throughout, Love's growling and vocal sneering bring anger and pain to the forefront in an unmistakeable way.

At the time of the performance, Love was hardly a naive girl seeking to make sense of the uncharted world of teenage relationships, but rather a world-weary and often bitter woman; a widow, a mother, and a self-confessed heroin user whose struggles with personal demons had been minutely scrutinized by the press for several years. Her performance of "He Hit Me" fairly drips with rage, self-loathing and the desire to shock. In many ways, though, Hole's rendition of "He Hit Me" is actually less unsettling than the Crystals', partly because the band was already infamous for its brooding, provocative music—the line "he hit me and I was glad" becomes less outrageous when performed by the author of "I'm Miss World, somebody kill me." Also, the listener can plainly hear anger in this performance, in contrast to the numb bewilderment of the original recording. It is tempting to celebrate this audible anger as a welcome sign of the times, an indication that girls in the mid-90s were able to express the rage that was forbidden to them thirty years before, that anger is at last an acceptable and empowering emotion for females, and that the dark, masochistic rationalizations performed by the Crystals are no longer useful to adolescent listeners.

While it is true that the emotional palette of girls as they are represented in mainstream culture has broadened in recent years, numerous self-help and other psychology books on the subject indicate that negotiating feelings of anger is still perilous for girls and women.[39] In her analysis of girls' anger in the popular television series *Buffy the Vampire Slayer*, furthermore, Elyce Rae Helford concludes that the only acceptable form of anger for a teenage girl in the early years of the twenty-first century must still adhere to white, middle-class standards of "ladylike" identity; the show's heroine is slim, blonde and fashionable, and she makes witty repartees to diffuse her rage as she fights and kills the vampires and demons intent on destroying the world, while two vampire slayers presenting different versions of girlhood are punished.[40] The violent temper of a young woman like Courtney Love remains highly unorthodox, and Love's ambition, self-interest and sharp tongue have made her one of the most hated women in rock

---

[39]   Here we might include such works as Harriet Lerner, *The Dance of Anger: A Woman's Guide to Changing the Pattern of Intimate Relationships* (New York, 2005); Mary Pipher, *Reviving Ophelia: Saving the Selves of Adolescent Girls* (New York, 1995); and Rosalind Wiseman, *Queen Bees and Wannabes: Helping your Daughter Survive Cliques, Gossip, Boyfriends and Other Realities of Adolescence* (New York, 1995), which inspired the 2004 Hollywood film *Mean Girls,* starring teen idol Lindsay Lohan.

[40]   Elyce Helford, "'My Emotions Give Me Power': The Containment of Girls' Anger in Buffy the Vampire Slayer," in Rhonda V. Wilcox and David Lavery (eds) *Fighting the Forces: What's at Stake in Buffy the Vampire Slayer* (Lanham, MD, 2002), pp.18–34.

and roll history (second perhaps only to Yoko Ono, another rock wife who dared to pursue her own career in music, and who was reviled for loving her genius husband insufficiently and for having the temerity to survive him).

It is hard not to notice, however, the proliferation of teenage girl singers in contemporary pop culture who perform anger on their second or third albums. Following an unremarkable career as a perky pop singer, and after the main activities of the underground Riot Grrrl movement, Alanis Morissette released *Jagged Little Pill* in 1995 (Maverick Records Inc.). The first single "You Oughta Know" addressed a former lover who has moved on, and it fairly bristled with a rage that was shocking from a twenty-year old former child star. Other former child stars Britney Spears, Christina Aguilera, and even Kelly Clarkson, winner of 2001's *American Idol* competition, have all followed suit with songs like "Stronger," "Fighter" and "Miss Independent" on their sophomore albums. Aguilera in particular has developed the persona of a crusader for justice for girls, a gritty pop/punk princess who sings about the need for girls and women to resist sexist double standards, celebrate their inner beauty and speak out against domestic violence. On her 2002 *Stripped* album (BMG Records Inc.), Aguilera's soulful virtuosity, the use of distorted guitar sounds, and her outspoken lyrics (naming her father as an abuser, for starters) are a far cry from her first hit, the dance pop styled "Genie in a Bottle," to say nothing of the material she performed as a member of Disney's *New Mickey Mouse Club*.

Other contemporary teen pop divas such as Avril Lavigne, Pink and Gwen Stefani mine similar territory, so that the "angry young woman" stance has become, perhaps, just one more contrivance for girls and women. The hackneyed positions available to pop entertainers can solidify with depressing speed into controlling stereotypes. All of these young artists work within the confines of the mainstream record industry; collaborating with professional songwriters and producers, performing on major music television events such as awards shows, and promoting themselves in the popular press. Can we believe their rage is sincere? Cynics need look no farther than the example of Ashlee Simpson, the younger sister of blonde pop princess Jessica Simpson. In an early phase of her career, Ashlee Simpson was marketed as an edgy, defiant brunette with punk leanings, a sort of brooding anti-Jessica (one of her first hits was "Shadow," an apparently autobiographical account of being an overlooked younger sister). Once her position in the pop firmament had been established, Ashlee underwent a transformation, with surgically altered features, blonde hair, toothy smile, and a more sunny, ladylike demeanour.

I want to resist the idea, however, that these two incarnations of Ashlee Simpson are incompatible, and that her present, cheerful persona gives the lie to her earlier, angrier self. Rather, I would like to celebrate the example of a successful teenage pop star who performs emotional complexity and demonstrates that happy, pretty girls can also experience anger and sadness. Even in her new public presentation, Simpson continues to perform her darker, brooding songs, and by performing anger, she complicates the "good girl" stereotype without adopting wholesale the burden of the "angry young woman" role. To insist that a defiant, angry stance must be maintained at all times is to perpetuate reductive and damaging dualities of good, nice girls vs. bad, defiant ones as the only two possible versions of girlhood. As Sharon Lamb and Lyn Mikel Brown note in their recent study of stereotypes of girlhood used in contemporary marketing (echoing the conclusions of Valerie Walkerdine cited above), the insistent association of anger and related emotions with bad girls ultimately teaches girls that anger itself is always bad, and incompatible with being a happy and well-liked girl.[41]

It is easy to disparage the anger of a compliant, "cute" pop singer as contrived, and to wish that girls could draw strength instead from the powerful anger of more plausible, adult women. Learning to shout back alongside someone like Courtney Love is certainly healthier than swallowing one's rage as unladylike; still, I think it would be a mistake to dismiss pop-friendly versions of girls' anger as having no disruptive force. In this important way, then, the token "angry girl" songs performed by perky pop stars are valuable, precisely because the poses do not dislodge our understanding of them as bubbly, happy girls. Ashlee Simpson's enactments of rage, schooled and calculated though they may be, may well prove essential in providing a vocabulary for "nice" girls to express their anger in a socially sanctioned way.

---

[41] Sharon Lamb and Lyn Mikel Brown, *Packaging Girlhood: Rescuing Our Daughters from Marketers' Schemes* (New York, 2007).

PART II
"Everything's Coming Up Roses": British Girls in the Mid-60s

Chapter 4
Dusty's Hair

Annie J. Randall[1]

By the time Dusty Springfield died in 1999 she had already been anointed by the music press and music industry as an icon of the swinging 60s, if not *the* fab icon among Britpop solo singers of the era. Rising phoenix-like from the ashes of bygone pop celebrity, Dusty's late 80s revival seemed to ameliorate the bitterness associated with the public relations debacles that had plagued her for the preceding twenty years.[2] Indeed, her aptly named hit of 1989, "Nothing Has Been Proved," neutralized the singer's unmarketable sexual ambiguities and rebranded her as a commercially viable "survivor":[3] one who had triumphed over press incursions into her personal life regarding "drink, drugs, and lesbian sex" and had claimed a place in pop's pantheon of stars.[4] While the hit-induced lovefest between Dusty

---

[1]   Material from this chapter first appeared in *Dusty! Queen of the Postmods* by Annie J. Randall (2009), pp. 13–33. Reprinted by permission of Oxford University Press, Inc.

I am deeply indebted to Paul Howes, Carole Gibson, John Harding, Peter Walmsley, Edward James, Myra Brent, and Mary Donohue for sharing their expert knowledge of Dusty Springfield's life and music with me. I am grateful also to those of Dusty's associates— Madeline Bell, Norma Tanega, Pat Rhodes, Simon Bell, and Derek Wadsworth—who generously granted interviews, thus providing me with valuable insights into the singer's musical process. Participants in both the Women's Studies Colloquium at McMaster University (Hamilton, Canada) and the graduate musicology seminar at New York University responded to early versions of this work in 2004–05 with astute comments and suggestions, all of which have enriched this essay.

[2]   These debacles ranged from cat and mouse games with the press concerning her sexual orientation to periodic articles on the consequences, both personal and professional, of the singer's politics and "difficult" personality. See Lucy O'Brien's *Dusty: A Biography of Dusty Springfield* (London, 2000), *passim.*

[3]   This recording followed Dusty's earlier breakthrough collaboration with the Pet Shop Boys, "What Have I Done to Deserve This?" of 1987, which reached the number 2 position on top 10 charts in the UK and US and remained in the charts for nine and eighteen weeks respectively. Chart information taken from Paul Howes, *The Complete Dusty Springfield*, revised and expanded edition (London, 2001).

[4]   Predictably, all of the unmentionable topics resurfaced in the years following the singer's death as evidenced in dozens of potboiler headlines such as "Dusty, Troubled Diva: Hollywood to film soul legend's life of drink, drugs, and lesbian sex," *Sunday Express* (London), May 1, 2005. The most sensational treatment of Springfield's sexuality, alcoholism, and drug abuse appeared just one year after Dusty's death: *Dancing With*

and the press ran its course through the 90s, the only "safe" interview topics seemed to be Dusty's over-the-top 60s look—the trademark hairstyles and dark eye makeup—and her often-repeated love of "black music." Rarely treated with depth, these topics were mined instead for jokes and nostalgia—a consequence of the press's usual avoidance of complexity (unless, of course, it involves scandal, in which case no detail is too small to report) and the singer's own apparent decision to stay firmly on neutral ground.[5] Yet, the interviews and newspaper articles of Dusty's final years hint at a much larger and more interesting story than journalistic fixations on hair, makeup, and Motown would suggest.[6] It is a story in which the singer's unique sound and look participated integrally in at least three important cultural phenomena: a "mod revolution" among teenagers, especially girls; a distinctly camp sensibility in pop culture; and a participation in black American culture among European music fans that had, heretofore, been the near-exclusive preserve of jazz aficionados. Indeed, Dusty seemed to embody the postwar generation's experience of profoundly changing gender roles and race relations and to give voice to its emerging new perspectives.

While I suggest here that Dusty's look and sound must be considered in tandem, I also want to emphasize at the outset that her sound—both the characteristic "grain" of her voice and the rare musical imagination behind it—was and is the more significant of the two.[7] Her music's enduring connections to fans' emotions,

---

Demons: The Authorized Biography of Dusty Springfield (New York, 2000) written by a journalist who had followed Springfield's career since the 1960s, Penny Valentine, and Vicki Wickham, Springfield's longtime personal friend and, later, manager. It is important to note that the term "authorized" (implying the cooperation of the subject) is misleading: the text was not authorized by Dusty but by the executors of Dusty's estate.

[5] Television interviews from the period 1989 to 1991 (on UK "chat shows" such as *Sunday, Sunday*, *Night Network*, and *Aspel* with interviewers Gloria Hunniford, Annabel Giles, and Michael Aspel, respectively) share these characteristics. Dusty was promoting her comeback album, *Reputation*, at this time (released by Parlophone in June 1990).

[6] A small number of serious studies have appeared since then and have explored the more complicated aspects of the singer's life and career. These include Lucy O'Brien's biography *Dusty*, and Patricia Juliana Smith's essay, "'You Don't Have to Say You Love Me': The Camp Masquerades of Dusty Springfield," in Patricia Juliana Smith (ed.) *The Queer Sixties* (New York and London, 1999), pp. 105–26. O'Brien, a respected pop music journalist, takes a traditional biographical approach while Smith considers the singer's appearance and musical identity from a queer perspective. Adele Patrick challenges Smith's and others' interpretations in "Defiantly Dusty: A (Re)Figuring of 'Feminine Excess'," *Feminist Media Studies* 1/3 (2001): 361–78. Paul Howes's *The Complete Dusty Springfield* (2001 and 2007), containing annotated entries on all of Springfield's recordings, live performances, and radio and television appearances in the UK and US, is unsurpassed as a comprehensive sourcebook for Springfield's career.

[7] This now-familiar concept was first articulated in the influential 1972 essay by Roland Barthes, "The Grain of the Voice," in Simon Frith and Andrew Goodwin (eds), *On Record: Rock, Pop and the Written Word* (London and New York, 1990), pp. 293–300.

memories, and identity formation contain infinitely more layers of meaning than Dusty's overanalyzed layers of makeup.[8] Nevertheless, it must be affirmed that the look enabled the voice to be heard, and that her sound and image are forever linked through this material bond. Had the singer not transformed herself from Mary O'Brien (see Figure 4.1) into the glamorous Dusty Springfield (see Figure 4.2) it is doubtful that record producers would have offered her a contract or promoted her as a solo singer. Given the popular music industry's innate conservatism, it is possible that Dusty's compelling sound, had it not been wrapped in a pretty package to ensure sales, may never have reached a broad public. So, as much as one might want to enter directly into a discussion of Dusty's sound, it is necessary first to consider her look and its reception among fans during the singer's rise to fame in the mid-1960s.

Figure 4.1   Dusty Springfield as a teenager, aka Mary O'Brien

Figure 4.2   Publicity photo of Dusty Springfield, 1964

[8] I drew this conclusion after interviewing a number of UK and US fans. While all of them had fond memories of Dusty's unique appearance in the 60s, it was clear that the deep emotional connection they felt with the singer derived overwhelmingly from her music (interviews with the author, July 2004.) Tia DeNora's concept that music acts as a "technology of self" seems especially pertinent here, given these fans' close, decades-long relationship with Dusty's music; see DeNora's *Music in Everyday Life* (Cambridge, 2000).

Mod icon

Thanks to the large number of posthumous tributes and TV biographies, it is now well known that Mary O'Brien was Dusty Springfield's given name, that she was born a redhead to Irish, middle-class parents, and grew up in Ealing, London. For her countless British fans in the 1960s, many of them holdovers from her days with ersatz folk group, the Springfields, Dusty, the suburban accountant's daughter, was a model of self-transformation; and no better symbol could be invented to represent her ugly-duckling-to-swan story than her beacon-like wigs. In the post-2000 era of "makeover" television shows and routine plastic surgery it is perhaps hard to recall a time when dramatic alteration of one's looks was the exclusive domain of movie stars and the very wealthy. Ordinary girls in the 1960s (and it is almost always girls and women who seek drastic change to their faces, bodies, and hair) had to settle for ordinary makeup and padded bras to satisfy their *trompe l'oeil* desires. The story of Dusty's physical transformation—one the press seemed never to tire of telling—demonstrated that even "plain" girls could become glamorous and mod. Hence, legions of female fans copied Dusty's look; they replaced their bookish glasses with false eyelashes, blackened their eyelids, and purchased blonde wigs and "false pieces" to augment their own hair—now dyed blonde like Dusty's— and held fastidiously in place with vast quantities of hairspray. The appeal of self-transformation was powerful, in part, because it seemed so easy and fun; the labor and discomfort, both physical and psychological, behind Dusty's look was largely concealed from public view while her fun-loving, down-to-earth qualities were accentuated. Her heavily reported transfiguration from an "overweight blob" to an attractive, stylish woman seemed within the grasp of nearly everyone, and, as a result, Dusty developed an extraordinarily loyal fan base among girls and boys who identified themselves as "mods."[9] Journalist Ray Coleman noted the phenomenon in a *Melody Maker* article of 1964: "Her gay, dashing image clicked with thousands. And girl hit parade fans, notoriously apathetic towards girl singers until now, accepted her as the symbol of a new 'mod revolution.'"[10]

Dusty borrowed elements of her look from blonde glamour queens of the 1950s and 1960s—Brigitte Bardot, Kim Novak, Monica Vitti, Catherine Deneuve—and pasted them together according to her own taste. The result was unlike that envisioned by record producer Svengalis such as Berry Gordy and Phil Spector who were largely responsible for the uniform appearance and projection of wholesome femininity of American girl groups; rather, it was a camp version of feminine display that drew attention to its artificiality and communicated with delicious theatricality its own obvious fakeness.[11] Tapping into the emerging camp

---

[9]   O'Brien, p. 17.

[10]   Ray Coleman, "Dusty: Pop Probe," *Melody Maker*, November 21, 1964.

[11]   Martha Reeves's memoir of Motown in the 1960s documents Berry Gordy's efforts to transform the Detroit girl groups into "ladies" via extensive etiquette training in addition to careful supervision of the groups' choreography, makeup, hair, and attire, both on and off

wellspring of the early 1960s British arts scene, and indeed helping to create it, Dusty was able to participate in pop music's dance of teenage sexual attraction while at the same time parodying it. Too brazen for some (mothers, for instance, who refused to allow their daughters to leave the house if they did not wash off their Dusty-clone makeup) and intoxicatingly liberating for others (the first wielders of "girl power" according to Lulu), Dusty's *outré* look seems now, in retrospect, to have been a stroke of genius that served at least two purposes: it satisfied the record company's demands for sex appeal, but also allowed the singer to express her own ambivalent relationship to such calculated allure.[12] Dusty herself later acknowledged that her look was a form of drag, and like drag queens, she accentuated its extreme contrivance and telegraphed its unnaturalness through public self-referential remarks.[13]

If camp is defined as "the lie that tells the truth" then Dusty's highly artificial look speaks volumes about the material, constructed, and highly constricted nature of mid-60s white, middle-class femininity.[14] Creating this look required the kind of leisure and disposable income that had not been known among teenagers in Britain for generations; many fans recall spending a week's wages on a pair of fashionable shoes, a dress, or other items of the female mod uniform. A "how-to book" such as *Your Hairdo* was but one of hundreds of items aimed at young girls that encouraged them to spend their time and money on a particularly elaborate and costly style of personal grooming that was peddled as essential for their social success (see Figure 4.3).[15] Once such commercialized trappings of femininity were cast in the harsh light of "false consciousness" by writers such as Betty Friedan and Germaine Greer, the ubiquitous blonde beehive, "dolly frocks," and makeup were replaced by the "natural" look of the late 1960s and early 1970s.[16] One need only compare cover photographs of Dusty Springfield and Carole King on their respective albums, *Ev'rything's Coming Up Dusty* (Philips, 1965) and Carole King's million-selling *Tapestry* (A&M, 1971), for evidence of this. The photo of King, showing the singer without shoes or makeup, with "hippy" hair and jeans, contrasts sharply with Dusty's bewigged, peroxided, and mascara'd persona and underscores its camp artifice.

---

stage. Reeves credits Maxine Powell, Cholly Atkins, and Maurice King for shaping these aspects of the Vandellas' image; see Martha Reeves and Mark Bego, *Dancing in the Street: Confessions of a Motown Diva* (New York, 1994), pp. 109–11.

[12]   Lulu is quoted in the video documentary, *Full Circle* (Taragon, 1997).

[13]   Dusty stated, "if the truth were known, I think I'm basically a drag queen myself!" "Going Back," interview with Kris Kirk in *Gay Times,* September 1985.

[14]   Philip Core, quoted in Andrew Ross, "Uses of Camp," in Fabio Cleto (ed.), *Camp: Queer Aesthetics and the Performing Self—A Reader* (Edinburgh, 1999), p. 317.

[15]   See Elaine Budd, *Your Hairdo* (New York, 1966).

[16]   Betty Friedan, *The Feminine Mystique* (New York, 1963); Germaine Greer, *The Female Eunuch* (New York, 1971).

Figure 4.3   Cover of how-to book for girls, *Your Hairdo*, 1966

Just as this hyperfeminine look played on the unnaturalness of traditional gender roles, the stiff hyperblondeness of Dusty's wigs (especially when viewed alongside the Ronettes' or Vandellas' equally over-the-top black beehives) seemed also to demonstrate the constructed nature of racial difference by "sending up" one of its chief signifiers: hair. Its campy, gross exaggeration of hair color and texture ridiculed notions of "natural" racial superiority that had, just two decades before, been used as justification for anti-Semitic policies in Europe and were still being used in the US and South Africa to justify racial segregation. What more deliciously camp mockery could there be of Aryan "superiority," ethnic authenticity, or racial essentialism than an Irish redhead wearing an überblond, mile high, beehive wig while singing cover versions of black American music?[17]

There was, clearly, no pretense of authenticity attached to Dusty's look, as numerous newspaper articles from the period attest (see Figure 4.4). Her real

---

[17]   A musical analogue to this send-up of Aryan self-importance is Dusty's outrageously camp "Don't Speak of Love" (with text by Vicki Wickham and Simon Napier-Bell), sung to the tune of Richard Wagner's "Pilgrim's Chorus" from the opera *Tannhäuser*. Though first recorded in 1968 "Don't Speak of Love" was not released until 1996 at which time it was included on the compilation CD *Something Special* (Mercury 528 818-2); Howes, p. 89.

name, along with images and testimonies of her pre-Dusty appearance had always been staples of articles and interviews. Yet, the "real Dusty" was, nevertheless, thought to emit from the elaborately prepared mask in the form of her "soul" sound. Discourses of authenticity were reserved for Dusty's voice even though, as was perfectly obvious to fans across the globe, its characteristic features originated in cultural and historical traditions far removed from her own.[18] While this seemingly glaring contradiction was blithely perceived as but another colorful strand in the fabric of swinging London, it was just one of a veritable pileup of disjunctures that came together in the figure of Dusty Springfield. Fans took in stride the apparent contradictions between Mary and Dusty, Britpop and US pop, a blonde singer with a black sound, colonial privilege and black Americans' commensurate lack of

Figure 4.4   Newspaper article on Dusty's wigs (from a fan's scrapbook)

---

[18]   Dusty's longtime friend and musical associate, Madeline Bell, put it this way: "Britain suddenly had a soul singer. ... when you say "soul singer," you don't mean that the person is black, you just mean that the person sings from there [the heart]. That's what a soul singer is; soul singers don't really have a color." Quoted in *Full Circle*.

120   *SHE'S SO FINE*

privilege, Dusty's "bent" sexuality and her songs' straight lyrics.[19] The spectacular collision of these elements at the intersection of gender, race, nation, and sexuality and their complex manifestation in Dusty's music makes Springfield one of the most fascinating pop singers of her era. In the following section I discuss Dusty's signature sound within the context of this intersection at the time of the release of her first albums in the UK and the US in 1964–65.

White Queen of Soul

When Dusty decided to pursue a solo career in 1963, the break with her musical past was dramatic. Not only did she adopt the striking new look of a blonde movie star, but also a compelling new repertoire as well. As her albums of 1964 and 1965 show, this new music was unmistakably American urban pop and was influenced most strongly by the vocal and instrumental sounds of black American artists. As a result of this strong identification with the US she became known as the "White Queen of Soul."[20] Of the eight songs that appeared on both Dusty's UK and US albums of 1964 (see bulleted items in Table 4.1) six were originally recorded by black American singers: "Mama Said" and "Will You Love Me Tomorrow" by the Shirelles, "When the Lovelight Starts Shining Through His Eyes," by the Supremes, "Mockingbird," by Charlie and Inez Foxx, "Anyone Who Had A Heart" and "Wishin' and Hopin'" by Dionne Warwick.

Dusty's second album, *Ev'rything's Coming Up Dusty* (see Table 4.2) was also dominated by cover versions of songs originally recorded by African American singers; of the thirteen songs released in the UK the only exceptions were: "Who Can I Turn To?" recorded by Tony Bennett, "If It Don't Work Out," composed for Dusty by Rod Argent, and "I've Been Wrong Before," recorded by Cilla Black. As Paul Howes has written, such concentration on American songs "was unheard of for a British artist in 1964 and an extraordinary coup for Dusty merely to get her record company [Philips] to agree."[21] Already viewed as a "generational leader," largely because of her wildly popular radio and television appearances on British

---

[19]   Dusty used the word "bent" during an interview with Ray Connelly (*London Evening Standard*, 5 September 1970) to characterize the rumors that were then circulating about her sexual orientation. It was during this interview that Dusty effectively "outed" herself as bisexual. O'Brien gives a full account of the interview in *Dusty*, p. 138.

[20]   The origin of this term is unknown although a similar term used to describe Dusty in the 1960s, "The White Negress," is credited to British pop singer Cliff Richard; see O'Brien, p. 61. Richard's source may have been Norman Mailer's article, "The White Negro: Superficial Reflections on the Hipster," *Dissent* 4 (Summer 1957): 276–93.

[21]   Howes, p. 265. Though these artists' names are widely known in the UK today, they were virtually unknown in the UK in the early 1960s.

DUSTY'S HAIR

121

Table 4.1   *A Girl Called Dusty* (UK release, April 1964, Philips BL7594)

- • Mama Said (Shirelles, 1961)
- • You Don't Own Me (Lesley Gore 1964)
-   Do Re Mi (Lee Dorsey 1962)
- • When the Lovelight Starts Shining Through His Eyes (Supremes 1963)
-   My Colouring Book (Kitty Kallen, 1963, Sandy Stewart 1963)
- • Mockingbird (Charlie and Inez Foxx 1963)
- • Twenty-Four Hours from Tulsa (Gene Pitney 1963)
-   Nothing (Marie Knight 1961)
- • Anyone Who Had a Heart (Dionne Warwick 1964)
- • Will You Love Me Tomorrow (Shirelles 1961)
- • Wishin' and Hopin' (Dionne Warwick 1963)
-   Don't You Know (Ray Charles 1953)

Note: Original artists listed in parentheses.

● = Cover versions that appeared on both UK and US releases.

Table 4.2   *Ev'rything's Coming Up Dusty* (UK release, October 1965, Philips BL1002)

- • Won't Be Long (Aretha Franklin 1960)
- • Oh No! Not My Baby (Maxine Brown 1965)
- • Long After Tonight is All Over (Jimmy Radcliffe 1964)
- • La Bamba (Ritchie Valens 1958)
- • Who Can I Turn To? (Tony Bennett 1964)
-   Doodlin'(Baby Washington 1963)
- * If It Don't Work Out
-   That's How Heartaches Are Made (Baby Washington 1958)
- • It Was Easier to Hurt Him (Garnett Mimms 1965)
- • I've Been Wrong Before (Cilla Black 1965)
- • I Can't Hear You (Betty Everett 1964)
- • I Had a Talk with My Man (Mitty Collier 1964)
-   Packin' Up (Margie Hendrix 1965)

Note: Original artists listed in parentheses.

● = Cover versions that appeared on both UK and US releases.

* = First recordings of these songs were by Dusty Springfield.

programs such as *Saturday Club*, *Top of the Pops*, and *Ready, Steady, Go!*, Dusty's fans followed her enthusiastically into this new musical terrain.[22]

While the notion of covering the hits of African American artists on such a scale was unheard of in Britain c. 1964, it was common practice in the US; the early careers of Elvis Presley, Bill Haley, and Pat Boone, for example, were built upon covers such as Big Mama Thornton's "Hound Dog," Joe Turner's "Shake, Rattle, and Roll," and the El Dorados' "At My Front Door," respectively. In one sense, then, Dusty was following a well-worn path in her choice of material, and evidence was abundant that such covers could generate enormous sales.[23] No doubt, such pragmatism was part of her thinking; yet, this fearless leap into black American music during such segregated times by a British, middle-class, female singer suggests that far more was at work than careerism or sheer daring.

Dusty's affinity for the musical products of African American culture—blues, jazz, and gospel—originated in her childhood and can be seen within the longer historical context of British fascination for the music of black Americans, starting with the Fisk Jubilee Singers' tour through England, Ireland, Wales, and Scotland, c. 1870.[24] Many of the terms that Dusty used to describe the qualities she admired in such music (its "strength" or "power") were similar to those used by nineteenth-century journalists reporting on the Fisk singers' renditions of spirituals or, later, in twentieth-century reviews of black blues and jazz musicians' recordings. A sense of the exotic, mysterious, and alluring black Other comes through vividly in the use of such terms as does the colonial reflex to capture and appropriate the Other's unique cultural products. It was through these recordings and the discourse of the exotic Other surrounding them that Dusty gained her first exposure to the distinctive sounds of African American culture and, as a result, declared her intention to become "a blues singer" at the age of eleven.[25]

Introduced to this repertoire through the activities of her father, a jazz record collector and amateur classical musician who listened with his children to radio broadcasts of American music on the BBC, Dusty modeled her own singing style largely on those of the singers she heard on these recordings and broadcasts, which, most likely, would have included Bessie Smith's generation of blues artists.[26]

---

[22] Simon Bell, Dusty's longtime friend, backing singer and musical associate, commented that young fans in the 60s like himself regarded Dusty as a "leader of a gang that you were part of" (interview with the author, July 2004).

[23] Dusty's contemporaries, the Beatles, also covered such songs; their first US album (*Introducing ... the Beatles*, Vee-Jay, 1964), for example, included a Shirelles cover, "Baby It's You," and a cover of the Cookies' hit, "Chains."

[24] Andrew Ward, *Dark Midnight When I Rise* (New York, 2000), 201–44.

[25] O'Brien, p. 15–16.

[26] Valentine and Wickham shed tantalizing light on Dusty's access to her father's eclectic music collection in *Dancing With Demons*, p. 25. The singer herself also describes her father's influence in the video documentary, *Full Circle*. I am indebted to Christina Baade for sharing her extensive research on jazz reception in Britain from c. 1920 to c. 1950

As her own first recordings attest (made on an amateur recording device) she had, by her early teens, already developed a feeling for syncopation along with a mature-sounding voice that could reach high notes at full volume without shifting into the lighter, head voice sound (often called "belting" or "shouting").[27] Indeed, Dusty's ability to dwell an octave above middle C in her chest voice is a key feature of her 60s sound, as heard most thrillingly in her number 1 hit of 1966 "You Don't Have To Say You Love Me."[28] Notably, on these early tapes she invests the words with meaning through deft vocal inflection in the manner of good blues singers—unlike the delivery one might expect from a teenager imitating a foreign style.[29] Further evidence of Dusty's precocious affinity for a "black sound" includes schoolgirl accounts of her convincing performance of Bessie Smith's "St. Louis Blues" at a convent school talent show and similar testimonies to her gift for singing in the American style.[30]

Though Dusty's early professional career took her away from her early love of black American music and into the repertoires of British pop (the Lana Sisters) and folk music (the Springfields) she returned to it with almost religious fervor from the moment she heard the Exciters' hit, "Tell Him," blaring from a record shop window in Manhattan in 1963.[31] This epiphany, as she tells it, was the moment of conversion that determined her break with the Springfields and set her on a course toward a solo career built on a foundation of covers of US songs mainly by African American singers. Along with "Tell Him" were two other recordings that Dusty said "changed my life": Dionne Warwick's "Don't Make Me Over" (1962) and, later, Lorraine Ellison's "Stay With Me" (1966). Needless to say, these three records are musically compelling for their groundbreaking sounds, chief among them Warwick and Ellison's singular vocal styles and the Exciters' "power,

---

(especially on *Radio Rhythm Club* broadcasts and the music newspaper *Melody Maker*, both favorites of jazz fans such as Dusty's father). Baade's work was especially useful in helping to imagine what sorts of music circulated in the O'Brien household during Dusty's youth and how it may have been received.

[27]   Valentine and Wickham discuss Dusty's first recordings (early Tin Pan Alley classics "I Love a Piano," "Pretty Baby," and "When the Midnight Choo Choo Leaves for Alabam'") in *Dancing with Demons*, p. 25. These recordings, made in Dusty's early teens, have been transferred to CD and appear on *Simply Dusty* (Mercury 546 730-2).

[28]   Another stunning example of this vocal feature is found on Dusty's less well-known recording of "Di Fronte all'Amore" [In the Face of Love]. Recorded in 1965 it was first released in Italy, Argentina, and Australia. The song achieved international distribution only in 1996 when it appeared on the compilation CD *Something Special* (Mercury 528 818-2).

[29]   See n. 27 above.

[30]   O'Brien, pp. 15–16.

[31]   This visit to the US was among Dusty's last tours with the popular folk group the Springfields. Their song "Silver Threads and Golden Needles" was a top 10 hit on both sides of the Atlantic in 1962 and was the centerpiece of their 1963 American tour.

precision, and ballsiness."[32] One could simply conclude that Dusty, as an excellent musician herself, gravitated naturally toward good music and wanted to perform it. Certainly, the quality of the music is inarguable; yet, its quality alone does not explain adequately Dusty's lifelong, close personal identification with these sounds and the cultural history they represented, or her less passionate identification with white European music traditions. Attraction to "the music itself" does not explain Dusty's determination to break through the heavily policed gender borders that prevented white female pop singers from jumping racialized musical boundaries as had Elvis, et al., in the mid-1950s, nor her internalization of the "inner secrets and ethnic rules" of the black American tradition and her application of the "soulful" sound to *all* of her repertoire, not just the American covers.[33]

The consistency of Dusty's vocal interpretations of US covers throughout her forty-year career demonstrate that the singer was not selectively mimicking musical devices nor engaging in what might be called "vocal blackface," but had embraced wholeheartedly African American musical traditions. In countless interviews on radio, television, and print media, Dusty acknowledged the many black American singers who had influenced her sound and to whom she was profoundly indebted; indeed, as has been often quoted, she said that singing with Martha and the Vandellas at the Brooklyn Fox in 1964 was "the biggest thrill of my life." Her Brooklyn performance with the Vandellas and other Motown acts, including Smokey Robinson and the Miracles, the Temptations, and the Supremes, inspired Dusty to initiate (with producer Vicki Wickham) the historic television special, *Sounds of Motown*, a 1965 program that was as important to the Motown artists' careers in Europe as the Beatles' *Ed Sullivan Show* appearance had been in the US in 1964 (see Figure 4.5). Unlike many of her British predecessors in the jazz field who appropriated elements of jazz without attribution and with little affinity for the culture from which it came, Dusty was scrupulous throughout her career, often to the point of self-effacement, in attributing the source of her sound to African American musical traditions. The internationally televised *Sounds of Motown* made clear to her fans both this connection and the importance Dusty placed on acknowledging it. Martha Reeves has said that Dusty "introduced the Motown sound to England. I think she can take credit for that.... There were other ladies who embraced our music and did cover versions: there was Cilla Black, Petula Clark, there was Lulu... however, Dusty was the one who got into the music and actually did cover versions and glorified the music; she was in awe of us and we were in awe of her."[34]

---

[32] Dusty made these comments and used this expression during the radio program *My Top Ten*, BBC Radio 1, August 5, 1989.

[33] Paul Gilroy states that outsiders can participate in musical blackness via the "inner secrets and ethnic rules" of African American music that "can be taught and learned"; see *The Black Atlantic: Modernity and Double Consciousness* (London and New York, 1993), p. 109.

[34] Quoted in *Full Circle*.

Figure 4.5   Martha Reeves and Dusty Springfield

Signifyin(g)

The musical devices and strategies of the African American tradition that Dusty had initially learned from records, and later honed during her close association with gospel-trained Madeline Bell and Doris Troy, can be placed in critical context through the rhetorical concept of "signifyin(g)" as defined by Henry Louis Gates and applied to music by Samuel Floyd.[35] The work of Eileen Southern, Portia Maultsby, Guthrie Ramsey, and George Lewis are also centrally important in tracing the genealogy of sounds and musical practices that are commonly referred to, simply, as "black," thus allowing us to speak with long overdue precision about "black music" and its transmission among diverse communities both within and

---

[35] See Henry Louis Gates's seminal definition of the black rhetorical practice of "signifyin(g)" in *Figures in Black: Words, Signs, and the "Racial" Self* (New York and Oxford, 1989), p. 49. Samuel L. Floyd applies Gates's ideas to music in *The Power of Black Music: Interpreting Its History from Africa to the United States* (New York, 1995), pp. 6–7.

outside the African American diaspora.[36] Central features of vocal music that are given a distinct cultural and historical identity when operating within the larger sphere of signifying involve: the soloist's individual relationship to the beat; newly invented passages of text and music added to pre-existing songs; individualistic, improvised ornamentation; call and response between soloist and backing singers; head voice and chest voice used for specific expressive purposes; use of "vocal noise"; and the transgression of traditional male and female vocal ranges, thus making the tenor–baritone ranges available to women, and the alto–soprano ranges available to men.

These devices, deployed according to musical strategies that George Lewis identifies as "Afrological," developed along the circuitous, geographically far-flung routes of diasporic migration[37]—from south to north, rural to urban, plantation to farm to factory, from sacred bowers to churches, from juke joints to jazz clubs, from radios to boom boxes, along the minstrelsy and chitlin' circuits, from steamboats to underground railroads to "pimped rides"—yet retain their signifying character via distinctly African American troping processes.[38] As Gates and Floyd argue, this sophisticated, constantly hybridizing troping process is the living product of African American communities' social and historical relationship to the dominant culture; it enacts and preserves group identity while resisting cooptation and assimilation. In addition, the singer expresses his or her own identity against that of the group. This confluence of historical and musical factors unfolding over centuries on US soil accounts for the richness, complexity, and, to some, impenetrability, or even ineffability of "black" music. The notion of an essential blackness in music is demolished by this historically and culturally constructive argument. Gilroy echoes and maintains that constructed blackness in music, "whose inner secrets and ethnic rules can be taught and learned," proves the very constructedness of race itself, a position shared by Ignatiev, Roediger, and Frankenberg who extend this critique of racial essentialism in their own deconstructions of whiteness.[39]

---

[36] Eileen Southern, *The Music of Black Americans: A History* (New York, 1997); Mellonee V. Burnim and Portia Maultsby (eds), *African American Music: An Introduction* (New York, 2004); George Lewis, "Improvised Music After 1950: Afrological and Eurological Perspectives," in Daniel Fischlin (ed.), *The Other Side of Nowhere: Jazz, Improvisation, and Communities in Dialogue* (Middletown, CT, 2004), pp. 131–62; Guthrie Ramsey, *Race Music: Black Cultures from Bebop to Hip-Hop* (Berkeley, CA, 2004).

[37] Lewis, "Improvised Music after 1950."

[38] In the age of digital music, the troping continues wherever "beats" are generated; Joseph Schloss, *Making Beats: The Art of Sample-Based Hip-Hop* (Middletown, CT, 2004).

[39] Gilroy, p. 109; David Roediger, *Working Toward Whiteness: How America's Immigrants Became White* (New York, 2005); Noel Ignatiev, *How the Irish Became White* (New York, 1995); Ruth Frankenberg, *White Women, Race Matters: The Social Construction of Whiteness* (Minneapolis, 1993).

Indeed, Ignatiev's work would seem to shed light on Dusty's unusually close identification with African American culture in the racially segregated 1960s, an identification that was conveyed to her audiences through newspaper interviews in which she stated, "I have a real bond with the music of coloured artists in the States. I feel more at ease with them than I do with many white people. We talk the same language … . I wish I'd been born coloured. When it comes to singing and feeling, I just want to be one of them and not me."[40] Ignatiev, in *How the Irish Became White,* traces the historic origins of whiteness and the long exclusion of the Irish from its privileged aegis because of the centuries-long colonial relationship of Northern Ireland and England. Dusty, as an English woman of Irish descent, cannot have been impervious to the persistent second-class status of the Irish in the UK and the many parallels between their treatment there and that of African Americans in the US—the most obvious being the Northern Irish struggle for civil rights of the 1960s and the US civil rights movement of the 1950s and 1960s.[41] Although her middle-class background insulated her from the anti-Irish hostility that was typically aimed at Irish laborers, the notion of "double consciousness" would have resonated with her and many other Irish or Irish descendants living in England during the 1960s. Coined to describe the two identities that blacks were, by necessity, forced to adopt as members of two non-integrated social groups, W. E. B. DuBois wrote, "One ever feels his two-ness—an American, a Negro; two souls, two thoughts, two unreconciled strivings; two warring ideals in one dark body, whose dogged strength alone keeps it from being torn asunder."[42] The concept, if not the exact term "double consciousness," has been used by Irish writers such as W. B. Yeats to describe similar conflict between their own warring Irish and English identities.[43]

Another point of connection between Dusty and African American culture was her affinity for the self-defined, highly individualistic personae projected by such blues singers as Bessie Smith, Big Mama Thornton, Ruth Brown, and jazz singers such as Billie Holiday, Ella Fitzgerald, Nina Simone, and Abby Lincoln. Peggy Lee, a singer who Dusty mentioned often as an influence and who also crossed racial boundaries to participate in black musical traditions, also belongs in this group; likewise, Tina Turner, a quintessentially powerful female stage presence, who was cited by Dusty as her "favorite performer." To use Farah Jasmine

---

[40] From Coleman's *Melody Maker* article.

[41] Many of the two movements' objectives were the same: to secure "one man, one vote" voting rights, to prevent discrimination in education and public housing, and to address police brutality.

[42] W.E.B. DuBois, *The Souls of Black Folk* (1903), ed. Henry Louis Gates (New York, 1989), p. 3.

[43] George Bornstein, "Afro-Celtic Connections: From Frederick Douglass to *The Commitments*," in Tracy Mishkin (ed.) *Literary Influence and African-American Writers* (New York, 1996), pp. 171–88. I am grateful to Linden Lewis, Glyne Griffith, and John Rickard for their insights on this topic.

Griffin's succinct description of Billie Holiday, these women were "take no shit hip chicks" who were perceived to be in control of their musical and sexual lives; and while Dusty made frequent public defenses of her femininity, she projected similar independence and agency both professionally and personally.[44] Dusty eschewed the suffocating image of the "good girl" that, whether accurate or not, was projected publicly by most British female solo singers of the period, and was branded "a troublemaker" and "hell raiser" for her transgressions of behavioral gender norms.[45] These transgressions ranged from speaking out against apartheid in South Africa or ruminations on why she chose not to marry or have children, to public disclosures of her own promiscuity and bisexuality (see Figure 4.6).[46]

Figure 4.6   *Record Mirror*'s report of Dusty's forced departure from South Africa, 1964 (from a fan's scrapbook)

---

[44]   Farah Jasmine Griffin, *If You Can't Be Free, Be a Mystery* (New York, 2002), p. 49.

[45]   In a 1983 interview, Dusty recalled that Max Bygraves and Derek Nimmo, well-known British variety performers, "publicly criticized me as a troublemaker" after her 1964 expulsion from South Africa for refusing to sing in front of segregated audiences; interview with Kirk, *Gay Times*.

[46]   Coleman.

African American musical traditions allowed Dusty to express herself in ways that white European musical traditions did not and her early affinity for this mode of self-expression also explains her relative lack of identification with the conventions and devices of musical whiteness. The African American expressive traits that seemed to magnetize Dusty—principally, signifyin(g)'s emphasis on individualistic and stylized troping, and playing "against," "around," "behind," or "in front of" the beat—are all frowned upon or outright forbidden in traditional European school music or in private "classical" lessons. Having established her musical tastes and aural mode of learning at an unusually early age, she perceived an extreme dissonance between the tradition she had heard on records and the one she was being taught in school; hence, given her preference for the former, it is unsurprising that she resisted the central tool of European instruction, note reading, as a foundation of her musicality.[47] The social, even political, authoritarianism embedded in note reading practices—especially its externally determined "right way" to execute the melody, harmony, rhythm of a given piece—was antithetical to the signifying sensibilities Dusty had developed in her youth.[48] She seemed to dismiss it summarily with the statement, "I never got into Beethoven," despite her father's love of the composer's music.[49] Dusty's signifying and simultaneous rejection of note reading proved to be flashpoints in the singer's professional career, representing a clash of black and white, old and new musical cultures. When confronted with conventionally trained British session musicians' strict adherence to the printed score, Dusty found it difficult to communicate the individualistic sound she wanted from the drummer, the bassist, or the guitarist—sounds that would have required them to diverge from the printed score or adopt nonstandard playing techniques. As Derek Wadsworth (trombonist and arranger for Dusty's band, the Echoes) observed, the musicians often pretended not to know what she was talking about or claimed that the sounds she wanted were either impossible to produce or not worth the effort it would take to produce them.[50] Despite such resistance in the recording studio, Dusty was determined to capture, for example, something of the exhilarating sound of Motown's Funk Brothers or James Brown's backing band, the Famous Flames; to this end, she paid for her band members' tickets to see Brown in concert in London so that they could study the Flames' playing techniques and instrumental arrangements. Dusty's suggestions to Wadsworth were so detailed and astute that he altered his academic

---

[47] See O'Brien, p. 46; and Valentine and Wickham, p. 109.

[48] Grant Olwage, "Discipline and Choralism: The Birth of Musical Colonialism," in Annie Randall (ed.), *Music, Power, and Politics* (New York: 2005), pp. 29–65.

[49] Quoted in *Full Circle*.

[50] These innovations included seemingly small, though musically significant, techniques such as: plucking the electric bass with bare thumb or fingers instead of a plectrum; playing a simple upstroke afterbeat on rhythm guitar; or extending the range of percussion sounds to include accents like the clinking of a lightbulb, etc. Dusty probably first heard these sounds in the Funk Brothers' instrumental backing on Motown records.

style of arranging to conform to her tastes. He said, unequivocally, "I learned the art of arranging from Dusty."[51] Wadsworth also reports that Dusty fought with her record label, Philips, to get backing singers with vocal qualities similar to those she had heard on American records of girl groups such as the Shirelles, the Velvelettes, the Chantels, et al., regardless of whether or not they could sight-read their arrangements. Dusty preferred that her favorite singers, Madeline Bell, Doris Troy, and Leslie Duncan, improvise their harmonies in the recording studio in order to produce a quality of spontaneity and individualism, a process that was more time-consuming and, consequently, more costly for the studio. Dusty's mid-60s popularity with the British public guaranteed her records' profitability and, thus, allowed her to extract from Philips the expensive extra studio hours she needed in order to produce the instrumental and vocal sounds she wanted; given this liberty, she was notorious for taking several weeks to record tracks for her albums, whereas her contemporaries, Tom Jones and Lulu, by contrast, would take a single day. The superior sound quality, arrangements, instrumental/vocal balance, and overall production values of Dusty's records, when compared to those of her contemporaries, was noted at the time and is still palpable today.[52] Though John Franz is listed as the producer on virtually all of Dusty's hit records in the 1960s, Dusty herself was, for all intents and purposes, the actual producer and was responsible for their sound. She said in an interview of 1973: "All the hit records I had in England were found, produced and almost promoted by me. I never took any credit ... . But I did the whole bloody lot myself."[53] Thus, production credit was informally (rather than legally) claimed by Dusty, and has been heartily confirmed by participants such as Derek Wadsworth. Certainly, for Dusty to have seized such authority in the highly sexist and very white world of London recording studios in the 1960s required the determination of a "take no shit hip chick," one whose musical imagination challenged the raced and gendered boundaries of popular music in the mid-1960s.

Dustifyin(g)

The albums of 1964 and 1965 offer a wealth of examples of Dusty's fertile musical imagination and demonstrate her voice's distinctive "grain," her signature control

---

[51]   I am grateful to Derek Wadsworth for this information (interview with the author, July 2004).

[52]   From London music producer Mike Ross-Trevor, I learned that young sound engineers and producers in the 60s (including Ross himself) studied Dusty's records and tried to emulate their unusually polished, multilayered sound—the creation of which was no small feat considering the limitations of the era's four-track magnetic tape recording equipment (interview with the author, July 2004).

[53]   As quoted in Adam Sweeting's "The Invention of Dusty Springfield," *The Independent*, March 26, 2006.

of a wide range of vocal devices, and the overall means by which she crafted a singular musical identity. Comparison of Dusty's interpretations of selected songs with their originals reveals the singer's individuality and also her close knowledge of the stylized tropes characteristic of 60s African American pop. In these songs we hear clearly both Dusty's adherence to a well-defined tradition with long historical roots and her specific contributions to it; hence, the term, "Dustifyin(g)." Because all of the songs' original versions were still very much within the public's memory at the time of Dusty's releases, the cover versions functioned as what might be called "transatlantic commentaries" and stimulated discourse among fans—still lively today—as to the relative merits of each. Often with academic precision, fans will dissect elements and levels of "Dustification" in particular songs or perceived style periods in the singer's career. In that spirit and with the limited purpose of highlighting signature features of Dusty's vocal style, here follows my own observations of some of her tropes in selected songs from 1964–65.

On her recording of Charlie and Inez Foxx's duet, "Mockingbird," Dusty sings both the upper and lower vocal parts, thus demonstrating a wide range, consistent quality throughout the vocal registers, and an ability to generate volume in the low register (which often sounds quite breathy in women) as well as in the high. In other words, her reach into male vocal territory sounds effortless, and, in fact, she sounds more comfortable there than Douggie Reece, with whom she sang the song in live performances.[54] Dusty's command of pop-gospel melodic embellishment is evident here; and though some of the florid upper line is cribbed verbatim from Inez Foxx, other passages and inflections are original.

Again subverting gender roles, though this time via a change in text rather than vocal parts, Dusty's cover of Garnett Mimms's "It Was Easier to Hurt Him" presents a response to the original's implied power dynamic between the song's disaffected lovers. The male upper hand is decisively slapped down as Dusty cuts out the opening lines, "Give her some hard times, treat her mean; that's what all the guys say. It'll only make her love you more, but it just don't go down that way," and proceeds to sing the song from the perspective of a woman who, after mistreating her boyfriend, now regrets his departure. Needless to add, in popular songs from this era, it was atypical for the girlfriend to actively dole out abuse (think of "Johnny Get Angry" or "He Hit Me (and It Felt Like a Kiss)"), yet here Dusty sings, "The way I cheated him and mistreated him / How could I forget?" Just as Dusty takes over male vocal territory in "Mockingbird," here she usurps male prerogative in love relationships by taking over Mimms's song. However, there is no analogue in Dusty's version for the universalized male position as stated by Mimms with lines such as, "that's what all the guys say," and "that's what I thought was being a man." By contrast, Dusty's substitution, "that's what I thought was being so smart," personalizes the situation and thus avoids the

---

[54]   One need only compare the recording with Reece (as performed live on BBC radio, 5 July 1965, now available on *Dusty: The BBC Sessions*, Zone Records, Zone X002) and the recording that appeared on the 1964 album *A Girl Called Dusty* to hear this.

unpleasant suggestion that *all* women might be inclined to behave nastily toward their lovers.

The notion that Dusty herself is the protagonist of her songs, gender-switching or otherwise, is a recurring theme in reviews of Dusty's music. The affect projected by Dusty's covers of two girl group songs, the Supremes' "When The Lovelight Starts Shining Through His Eyes," and the Shirelles' "Will You Love Me Tomorrow" would seem to feed this notion. In the latter, Dusty's vocal "attack" (analogous to her gutsy public persona) is reinforced throughout the song by a booming bass drum and militaristic snare figure that are absent in the original. While Dusty was a fan of Phil Spector's "wall of sound" aesthetic, the extra bombast seems misplaced here as accompaniment to the shy question, "will you still love me tomorrow?" Indeed, the vaguely martial tone places a sense of threat behind the words that, while musically exhilarating, gives the innocent teenage plea the tone of a more mature woman's ultimatum, as if the boyfriend will be given his marching orders summarily should his reply to the question be anything other than an ardent "yes."

Dusty's sense of vocal attack is also on display in her Supremes' cover and is reinforced by a number of elements in the accompaniment: livelier horns, accentuated bass drum, and replacement of handclaps with tambourine. These elements, in conjunction with a solo vocal track that is notably more foregrounded than Diana Ross's, contribute to the intense forward motion of Dusty's version. The good-natured group "grunt" by the Motown band, which adds a schoolyard flavor to the middle of the Supremes' song, is absent from Dusty's and its deletion eliminates distraction from the vocal track and focuses more attention on its robust affect. Perhaps for these reasons, the producers of a commemorative box set of Holland–Dozier–Holland's Motown hits seem to have preferred Dusty's version as they chose to include it rather than the Supremes' version on the CDs. Paul Howes comments:

> it sounds every bit as powerful as the Motown tracks alongside it. ... It just doesn't sound out of place at all, which has to be a testament to Dusty's skill and determination in attempting to reproduce the Motown sound in a London studio ... [It] somehow embraces her into the Motown family.[55]

Howes's comment reminds us that Dusty was indeed responsible for the overall sound of her records: the choice of songs, details of the instrumental and vocal arrangements, and recording/mixing decisions. In other words, it was most likely her decision to foreground the solo vocal track and to eliminate the aforementioned background elements that would have detracted from it; this was *her* sound, *her* desired affect, *her* commentary on the original.

Dusty's personal imprint, both as vocal interpreter and producer are also clearly evident in her cover version of Dionne Warwick's "Anyone Who Had a Heart."

---

[55]   *Dusty Springfield Bulletin* 57 (2005): p. 4.

The differences between the original and cover leap out at the listener within the first few seconds of each song. Warwick's interpretation might be characterized as a true whisper, the exhausted utterance of a depressed woman who is actually alone with her thoughts. Dusty's is, by contrast, a "stage whisper," full of theatrical gestures; she too is a woman alone, but on stage in front of thousands of onlookers. Most indicative of this difference is Dusty's gradual increase in volume building to a sudden withdrawal of intensity at the climax on the words, "what am I to do?" Such theatricality is underscored by the foregrounded vocal track, sharp violin accents, spooky guitar reverb, and crashing timpani at the end, none of which is present (nor needed) in Warwick's decidedly less histrionic original version. Both songs are saturated with drama thanks to the operatic recitative effect of Burt Bacharach's music and Hal David's text, but it is a very different type of drama in each and the two recordings' musical choices reflect two different tellings of the same story.

While the discussion of Dustifyin(g) has concentrated so far on Dusty's solo voice, no assessment of her 60s sound would be complete without reference to her voice in concert with other voices, specifically, when engaged in call and response with her backing singers. Two songs from this period are illustrative of Dusty's handling of this fundamental feature of signifying: "Needle in a Haystack" (a cover version of the Velvelettes 1964 Motown hit), and "Go Ahead On" (composed by Madeline Bell and Dusty, recorded in 1966). Dusty's cover of "Needle in a Haystack" is faithful to the original in all important respects and is most notable for copying the close interaction between solo and backing singers; in both versions the frequent "doo lang" interjections, "oooo" backup passages, and collective handclaps create a lively conversational quality, as if one were overhearing candid girl talk between teenagers with boy trouble. At certain points in the song the backing singers share the lead line with Dusty ("those guys are sly, slick and shy") or finish her sentence ("finding a good man, girl, is like finding a needle in a haystack") as girlfriends in conversation might do spontaneously. Likewise, the rhetorical "what did I say, girl?"—taken straight out of black American vernacular—might also occur in spoken conversation and is woven into the refrain naturalistically.

These various modes of call and response between lead and backing singers are also all used in "Go Ahead On."[56] In contrast to many girl group songs of the era in which an "alpha female" lead vocalist musically dominates her subordinates, "Go Ahead On" conveys equal status among the singers. As this brief excerpt from the song shows, the backing singers (in bold type) are either starting or finishing the lead's sentences, suggesting that the participants are of one mind or that there are no hierarchical boundaries between them: "You never call me on the phone, **make me so sad**/Sittin' all alone, **feelin' bad/Tired of being your fool** 'cause you told

---

[56] "Go Ahead On" is included in the 1998 compilation CD *Simply Dusty* (Mercury 546 730-2).

me lies/**I can't take no more** of your alibis/Go 'head on, **go 'head on**/Go 'head on, **go 'head on."**

While the hierarchical boundaries were blurred musically in songs like this, they were, however, fully evident visually; in live performance on Dusty's television shows the backing singers were dressed uniformly and very simply in contrast to Dusty's glittering gowns.[57] This, in addition to the fact that the singers were almost always off-camera, reinforced Dusty's status as a solo star but it also masked the importance of her regular backing singers—Bell, Duncan, Troy and, later, Kay Garner—who provided the response to her call on the recordings that forged her mid-60s sound identity.

One further example of call and response (in this case, a response that was *seen* as well as heard) is worthy of mention and displays another of Dusty's approaches to this device: "Gonna Build a Mountain" a gospel-influenced song by British composers Leslie Bricusse and Anthony Newley.[58] As can be seen on a video recording of her September 1966 performance on her first BBC series, Dusty and backing singers Madeline Bell, Leslie Duncan, and Maggie Stredder are engaged in an improvised passage of call and response on the words "higher and higher" when Dusty suddenly substitutes the words "lower and lower" as if to see if the backing singers would continue their echoing response faithfully. They do not take the bait and continue their decrescendo on the words "higher and higher" (even though Dusty's "lower and lower" would seem a better match for the song's dwindling volume), which then proceeds to a vigorous crescendo and hand-clapping, foot-stomping climax. This brief group shot of soloist and backing singers seems intended to demonstrate Dusty's soul "authenticity" by placing her in close musical and physical proximity to Madeline Bell who was known as an accomplished gospel singer in her own right.[59] Dusty's affinity for call and response is evident throughout her career and most of her albums contain more than one song featuring some sort of interaction with backing singers. Dusty switched roles occasionally and sang backing vocals for others: Madeline Bell in the mid-1960s, Anne Murray and Elton John in the 1970s, to name but a few.[60]

Though she was sought after as a backing singer, especially in the so-called "lost years" of the mid-1970s when her career had lost momentum, Dusty had the

---

[57]   See, for instance, the performance of "Gonna Build a Mountain" on the DVD *Dusty at the BBC* (Universal, 2007).

[58]   Like "Needle in a Haystack" and "Go Ahead On," this song was not included in the albums of 1964 and 1965, although it was in Dusty's mid-60s repertoire for TV and live performances of that period.

[59]   Madeline Bell, a native of Newark, New Jersey, and veteran of Professor Alex Bradford's gospel choir, made her singing debut in London as a member of the hit musical, *Black Nativity,* in 1963. She maintains an active performing career in Europe, now appearing mainly as a soloist.

[60]   She adopted the pseudonym Gladys Thong for these forays into non-solo singing; see the complete discography for Gladys Thong in Howes, pp. 486–88.

voice and center-stage personality of a diva soloist. The sound of her voice and its ability to express a broad range of meanings and emotions are worthy of a chapter in themselves; yet, one trait can be isolated as the most important, the one carrying the greatest sense of individuality, the "grain."[61] While the term "grain" is used to describe the individualistic "fingerprint" of a voice and implies that we all possess a uniquely grained voice, Dusty's stands out for its singularity and recognizability. It would be difficult to find another recorded voice that sounds exactly like Dusty's; she is instantly recognizable in the way that Billie Holiday, Judy Garland, Ella Fitzgerald, or Peggy Lee are. Each of these singers matches a singular vocal timbre with an equally singular musical imagination; the rare combination results in an intensely expressive blend of tone and text that transfixes fans and even inspires cult followings among them. While these qualities are on display in all of Dusty's work, some songs exhibit a particularly serendipitous union of song and singer in which the qualities are most evident; of the songs on Dusty's albums of 1964 and 1965, "I've Been Wrong Before" stands out as such a union.

Composer Randy Newman seems to have constructed this song's deceptively simple accompaniment to foreground the dramatic text as much as possible.[62] Dusty's close microphone creates intimacy and allows us to hear the inner workings of the voice; it is almost uncomfortably intimate, not unlike an invasive film close-up. As a result, we can hear the slight rasp in Dusty's voice, a quality that vocal specialists refer to as "vocal noise" and that fans often cite as the aspect of Dusty's voice that they find most touching and saturated with feeling. Dusty places this sound consistently on the first word of the phrase "I've been wrong before" thus attaching its sense of damage directly to the singer herself, the "I" of the song.[63] While Dusty expresses the protagonist's personal devastation clearly through consistent use of this device, she uses vibrato just as carefully to convey extreme despair. Dusty appears to have mapped her vibrato according to the song's structure which divides into roughly equal thirds: in the first she uses a slow vibrato at the ends of melodically descending phrases; in the second she employs a fast vibrato to accompany this section's rising phrases and increased volume; in the third she returns to a slow vibrato. Both singer and listener are wrung out at the end of this song, as if having experienced the emotional trajectory of a three-act drama condensed into less than three minutes.

Dusty's voice, described variously as "rich," "smoldering," "like a reed instrument," "breathy," "dusky," "husky," cannot be characterized by one set of descriptors because it changed over the course of her career, taking on different hues in the 1970s (when she used her head voice more frequently, sang higher

---

[61] Barthes.

[62] Cilla Black's recording of this song was released just months before Dusty's in 1965. The accompaniment is nearly identical on both. Howes, pp. 149–50.

[63] For further analysis of the significance of vocal damage see Laurie Stras, "The Organ of the Soul: Voice, Damage, and Affect," in Neil Lerner and Joseph Straus (eds), *Sounding Off: Theorizing Music and Disability* (New York, 2006), pp. 173–84.

generally, and developed a breathy quality) and the 1980s and 1990s (by which time years of smoking and drinking had dried out her voice and diminished her breath support, consequently limiting her ability to create long phrases or execute dynamics as she had in the past). Nevertheless, Dusty retained her compelling stage presence to the end of her career and, despite its changes, her voice remained a highly expressive instrument. As Elvis Costello has said, "her voice is one of the greatest voices in pop music, without a doubt."[64] One cannot argue with this nor the rest of his statement, the sense of which is at the heart of this essay's first section: "I don't think she's ever really got credit for that because people concentrate on the icon aspect of it—the hair, the eyelashes, and the hand movements." Yet, as much as one might want to separate the voice from the "icon aspect" and treat it in its abstracted, disembodied form, it must be acknowledged that voices do not operate independently of the bodies that contain them, the values we attach to them, nor, indeed, of the things we say and feel about them.[65]

---

[64]   Quoted in *Full Circle.*

[65]   For fuller treatment of the topics raised in this essay see my book, *Dusty! Queen of the Postmods* (New York and London, 2008).

Chapter 5
Brit Girls: Sandie Shaw and the Women of the British Invasion

Patricia Juliana Smith

From late 1963 until the end of decade, popular music witnessed an unprecedented phenomenon, the sudden and sweeping appearance of a seemingly endless parade of British singers and musicians on the international stage who would, for a brief time, not only reconfigure but also dominate that peculiarly American genre called rock and roll. Forty years after the "British Invasion," its significance is evinced by an ongoing critical and commercial interest in the period; yet most critical histories and analyses of 1960s popular culture would still lead one to believe that this amazing achievement was, for all intents and purposes, a boys-only event.

One popular myth about "Swinging London" still in circulation is that anyone who wanted to be a star could go there and be one, talent (or lack thereof) notwithstanding. By the end of the 1960s, this concept was both immortalized and parodied in the film *Smashing Time* (1967), a satire on every trendy excess of the times." In one memorable scene, Yvonne (Lynn Redgrave), one of a pair of provincial girls seeking fame and fortune in the world capital of groovy-ness, wins a television contest and uses her winnings to "buy" a career as a rock star. In the studio, her pathetic limitations as a vocalist are apparent, and the studio surroundings are far from glamorous, with seedy hired musicians, playing everything from bassoons to sitars, and grey-haired, bespectacled women back-up singers chanting "Ba-ba-ba-ba" at given intervals. Every musical cliché and gimmick known to British pop is thrown into the mix along with lyrics that begin with the all-too-true line, "I can't sing but I'm young."[1] It is all unthinkably awful, but the cynical producer manipulates a few mixing-board controls and the result is a highly polished recording, with a sound that is painfully familiar, an eerie mixture of virtually any song by Sandie Shaw, Cilla Black, Lulu, or, more particularly, Petula Clark. Within a few days, Yvonne is a household name, even in such households as Buckingham Palace.

If the notion that youthful exuberance and extroversion made talent irrelevant was, in fact, already in spin during the 1960s, it is no doubt the result of a plethora of such performers who flourished, however briefly, in the middle years of that decade. Mediocre male performers surely outnumbered their female counterparts, yet popular music history has been particularly unkind to most of the women of

---

[1]   *Smashing Time*, dir. Desmond Davis (Paramount Pictures, 1967).

the British Invasion, and the tendency is to disparage the lot of them as if they were indistinguishable from one another—if they are acknowledged at all. Even the pioneering feminist critics have given them short shrift; Gillian G. Gaar, for example, grants them, as a whole, a brief honorable mention, while Charlotte Greig dismisses the lot of them, aside from Dusty Springfield, as decidedly inferior performers noteworthy for little more than the attitude they embodied.[2] Lucy O'Brien, however, offers a dissenting opinion, suggesting the existence of a female "Fab Four" among the British girls—Dusty Springfield, Cilla Black, Sandie Shaw, and Lulu.[3]

While there is some sense in this paradigm and certainly many parallels to be drawn among these four singers, it is nonetheless more fanciful than factual. They never worked together as a unit as did *the* Fab Four, nor were they ever seriously in competition with the Beatles. It would be equally wrong to suggest artistic equality among them or to suggest that Cilla, Sandie, and Lulu were Dusty's "rivals"—for Springfield was, beyond a doubt, without peer. But to dismiss the other three as mere "dolly birds" or "pop tarts" is not only to ignore the role they played in the British Invasion but also to fail to comprehend the elements that led to their popularity and their continuing influence on artists of subsequent generations. Indeed, Cilla Black, Sandie Shaw, and Lulu, as well as Dusty Springfield, were pivotal figures in a transition of female pop stars from girls to women. As Gaar observes, they presented "a more sophisticated image ... grown-up, yet hip, giving the impression of independence, unlike the 'little girl' dependence of the girl groups."[4] In doing so, they anticipated the desire for sexual equality and freedom that would emerge more fully in the 1970s and 1980s.

That the singers who most closely exemplified this tradition were British is perhaps not so accidental as it might seem. Until the 1960s, rock and pop music in America was dominated by homegrown performers; only a few "foreign" recordings managed to enter the charts, and even then they were usually regarded as one-off novelties.[5] Though the "Brit Girls" of the 60s were heavily influenced by American pop, particularly the girl groups, Lucy O'Brien suggests they were also part of another, even older continuum:

> The tradition of the British female singer with the reassuring 'girl next door' image had been set during the Second World War when a bouffanted Vera Lynn

---

[2]   Gillian G. Gaar, *She's a Rebel: The History of Women in Rock and Roll* (Seattle, 1992), pp. 56–57; Charlotte Greig, *Will You Still Love Me Tomorrow? Girl Groups From The 50s On ...* (London, 1989), pp. 92–97.

[3]   Lucy O'Brien, *She-Bop II: The Definitive History of Women in Rock, Pop and Soul* (London, 2002), p. 94.

[4]   Gaar, pp. 56–57.

[5]   It is interesting to note that "Silver Threads and Golden Needles," a recording featuring Dusty Springfield as the lead singer of the Springfields, managed to break into the US charts in 1962, a year and a half prior to the advent of the Beatles.

became the Forces' Sweetheart. Her optimistic delivery and lush orchestrations were followed by the crooning ballads and novelty pop of the '50s, with singers such as Ruby Murray, Alma Cogan and the young Petula Clark continuing the trend for British girls to sing light and sweet, or saucy, like the Beverley Sisters.[6]

O'Brien's placement of Petula Clark at the end of this wholesome and peculiarly British line of female singers is apt. Although frequently grouped among the 60s Brit Girls, her association with the British Invasion is, to a great extent, coincidental; "Downtown," her first truly global hit, was released in late 1964, mere months after the Beatles had made their American debut. Evoking the glorious exhilaration of urban life, where "you can forget all your troubles, forget all your cares," the song became a virtual anthem-*qua*-advertisement for "Swinging London," despite the fact that no particular metropolis is identified in the lyrics, and the image of Clark attired in the trendiest Mod outfits suggested she was very much part of the *zeitgeist*. But Clark was seven years older than Springfield and at least a decade older than Black, Shaw, and Lulu. She had had a long career in show business before 1964. She was thirty-two, married to a Frenchman older than she, and the mother of two small children, and thus she seemed a bit matronly in comparison with her supposed competition.

Clark's 1960s career was, in fact, only one of many phases in her long career. She had been a performer before any of the other 60s female pop stars were born. As a child star she entertained British troops during the Second World War and had appeared in numerous films in the 1940s and 1950s. By her twenties she had begun a string of pop hits, including "Sailor," which topped the British charts in 1961. Her career underwent a dramatic change at the beginning of the 1960s, when she married French publicist Claude Woolf and settled in her husband's country. There she began making youth-oriented "beat" recordings in French and, until "Downtown," enjoyed greater popularity in France than her native country, with such hits such as "Ya Ya Twist," based on Lee Dorsey's "Ya-Ya," and "Chariot," which, in English translation, subsequently became Little Peggy March's "I Will Follow Him." Thus Clark was hardly a newcomer on the scene in 1964.

Clark, then, was a bit too "grown-up" and too commercially slick to play any authentic or influential role among British Invasion performers. Even Dusty Springfield, who might encourage listeners to "just do it" in "Wishin' and Hopin'" or beg to be taken "up to heaven all the way to Cloud Eleven" in "I Want Your Love Tonight," would never think of uttering lyrics so frank—yet so domestic—as Clark singing "Take off your clothes, my love, and close the door" in "Don't Sleep in the Subway." Clark represented "Swinging London" primarily to older listeners wanting to be "hip" but uncomfortable with more youthful or eccentric acts and their music. In this regard she certainly succeeded; she sold more recordings than all the other British girls of the 1960s put together and continued to record long

---

[6]   O'Brien, pp. 90–91.

140   *SHE'S SO FINE*

after the others stopped. All the same, she was hardly in the same league as her younger contemporaries, whether musically, aesthetically, or even culturally.

An unfortunate assumption has long held that Cilla Black, Lulu, and Sandie Shaw—who are generally mentioned by critics as a triad when mentioned at all— were no more than fluff, disposable entities from a subculture based on ephemerality. Lacking the extraordinary and extravagant artistry of Dusty Springfield, the show-business savvy of Petula Clark, or the self-destructive penchant for notoriety exhibited by their other contemporary, Marianne Faithfull, they seemed quite ordinary by comparison. Each had undeniable limitations, yet it is their seeming lack of any extraordinary quality, I would argue, that comprises the very essence of their appeal and their success. They were, for all intents and purposes, girls like any other girl, save for their seemingly fairytale-like transformations into pop icons, and because they were ordinary girls who succeeded in spite of it all, Cilla Black, Sandie Shaw, and Lulu were in many ways the archetypal Brit Girls of the 1960s and the foremothers of the "Girl Power" the Spice Girls would later claim as their own invention.

If Cilla, Sandie, and Lulu are often clumped together as group, it is most likely the result of certain parallels and coincidences. As O'Brien notes, "each of the four major [British record] companies had their token girl star, groomed for acceptable family pop entertainment: Dusty Springfield on Philips; Cilla Black ... on EMI; Sandie Shaw on Pye, and Lulu on Decca."[7] Each released her first solo recordings between September 1963 and September 1964, and each had finished her run of major hits in 1969.[8] They seemed to have risen from virtually nowhere to the heights of stardom in weeks rather than years, and they were young, fashionable, and fun, each exhibiting defined personalities—whether cheeky, eccentric, outrageous, insouciant, or even at times pensive—the likes of which were relatively unknown

---

[7]   O'Brien, p. 90. Pye also had Petula Clark, and Decca had Marianne Faithfull. Neither Clark nor Faithfull, however, completely corresponded to the "girl star" model of the other singers under discussion. In the end, neither did Dusty Springfield. For further discussions of the careers of Faithfull and Springfield, see, respectively, the essays by Norma Coates and Annie Randall in this volume; see also my "'You Don't Have to Say You Love Me': The Camp Masquerades of Dusty Springfield," in Patricia Juliana Smith (ed.) *The Queer Sixties*, (New York and London, 1999) pp. 105–26.

[8]   Cilla Black's first single, "The Love of the Loved," was released in September 1963; although she continued to record throughout the 1970s, her last significant hit single, "Conversations," was issued in June 1969. Lulu's debut disc "Shout" was released in April 1964; "Oh Me, Oh My (I'm a Fool for You Baby)," her final major hit, excluding her various comebacks in subsequent decades, came out in October 1969. Sandie Shaw's "Always Something There to Remind Me" was released in September 1964 and reached number one on the British charts within a month; "Monsieur Dupont," in 1969, was her last hit until her 1980s comeback. Although Dusty Springfield was already an experienced recording artist as a member of the Springfields, a similar pattern can be seen in her 1960s chart history as a solo artist, beginning with "I Only Want to Be with You" in November 1963, and ending in 1969 with "Brand New Me."

among American female teen singers. Indeed, personality seemed central to their appeal, with musical talent sometimes an afterthought. Even so, one figure—Sandie Shaw—stands apart as the archetypal British girl singer of the 1960s, and warrants greater attention than has heretofore been her lot.

Shaw was not a singer on a par with Dusty Springfield, who, by 1964, was already a seasoned professional. Shaw herself recalls that Springfield "seemed so much older and more sophisticated than me ... . Her voice was wonderful and her songs were great. She spent much more time and money on her productions in the studio than I could afford."[9] But because Shaw's first hit, "Always Something There to Remind Me," was a relatively sophisticated Burt Bacharach–Hal David composition with a lush orchestral arrangement, the type of material usually associated with Springfield and Dionne Warwick, it is easy to forget that she recorded it as a seventeen-year-old with very little performing experience behind her. Hers was not a typical seventeen-year-old voice; its timbre was darker and her diction more clipped than anything heard in contemporary American girl-group recordings. It hinted at womanliness, yet its occasional unsteadiness—upon which her critics have readily pounced—also betrayed a certain immaturity and vulnerability. It would be several years into her career before her voice matured, and two decades before she would reveal it as the fine instrument it had become. But if Shaw were to suffer by comparison with Springfield, she nonetheless possessed a far greater musical aptitude than her two closest competitors.

Cilla and Lulu

Cilla Black and Lulu not only lacked Shaw's complexity but her intensity as well. In retrospect, they seem to have been girls from the provinces—much like the protagonists of *Smashing Time*—for whom a musical career was a lark, something that happened almost by accident, much like the experiences of the characters in the film. They were veritable *tabulae rasae*, naive girls who sang whatever material was given them and charmed audiences through a cheerful candidness based largely on an absence of sophistication. Cilla Black's appeal depended largely on two factors, her personality and her connection to the Beatles. In 1964, she was actually the best-selling female recording artist in Britain, with two back-to-back number one records on the British charts, "Anyone Who Had a Heart," a cover version of Dionne Warwick's American hit, and "You're My World," an Italian ballad in English translation that became her signature song. These two early successes were followed by string of others: "I've Been Wrong Before," "Love's Just a Broken Heart," "Alfie," "Step Inside Love," "Surround Yourself with Sorrow," and "Conversations." Her repertory lacked any clear focus, at best a potpourri of contemporary trends—cover versions of American pop hits, translations of romantic Italian ballads, Broadway show tunes, and, every now

---

[9] Sandie Shaw, *The World at My Feet: A Personal Adventure* (London, 1991).

and then, Lennon–McCartney compositions. She would as readily sing "Old Man River" as Martha and the Vandellas' "Heatwave," and the results were as mixed as her material.

She had virtually no vocal training or technique—her recordings belie an immense break between her upper and lower registers with little in between, and her leaps from one to another often give the impression of two altogether separate voices, one capable of a certain amount of lyricism if not quite sweetness, the other strident and metallic. Her relatively slight vocal range was strained at the top, and her means of reaching for high notes included sudden downward transpositions, drastic increases in volume, the occasional bizarre falsetto, and laryngeal contortions that no trained singer would attempt.[10] Beatles' producer George Martin, who would eventually oversee all her major recordings, initially regarded her as hopeless, yet eventually managed, as he did with certain other Brian Epstein discoveries of limited vocal means, to work around her deficiencies. One of his frequent solutions was simply to overwhelm a problematic vocal by increasing the decibels of the instrumental arrangement.[11] Even so, Martin's productions could not conceal all of her shortcomings; she was well beyond her capabilities in the big, melodramatic ballads that, it would seem, were mandatory for all female singers of the time. While many British fans actually admired her "interesting" voice, the appeal was not universal. She is remembered outside of Britain as a one-hit wonder for "You're My World," a recording that painfully showcases the range of her shortcomings.

This is not to say her musical output was uniformly dreadful. As an Epstein protégé, she had access to Lennon–McCartney songs written specifically for her. "The Love of the Loved" is a perky, charming piece of well-crafted pop that sets her voice to its best advantage. "It's For You," a work that is unlike anything else in the Lennon–McCartney catalogue, is possibly her finest work. It is a sophisticated song with complex jazz phrasing, edgy key changes and shifting tempi, and it demonstrates her ability to manoeuvre around her limitations and use her "break" for dramatic contrast. It would seem likely that the Beatles' tunesmiths understood what Black could and could not accomplish, as they provided her with songs that flattered her vocal qualities. In truth, Black hardly lacked fine material; rather, she mingled it quite indiscriminately with wildly unsuitable selections.

But the girl who was born Priscilla Maria Veronica White never aspired or claimed to be a great singer. A product of one of Liverpool's poorest and most dangerous Irish Catholic neighborhoods, her greatest ambition was simply to be

---

[10] I am grateful to Laurie Stras for her explanations of the vocal problems of young and untrained female singers in their attempts to access their upper registers.

[11] Such was also the case with Billy J. Kramer, an Epstein protégé noted more for his good looks than his artistry. Martin employed overdubbed vocals and an extremely loud piano to disguise the flaws in Kramer's "Do You Want to Know a Secret?" The public did not seem to notice the tricks, as the recording rapidly rose to number two in the British charts, the first major success for this artist.

a star, and in this she succeeded. In many ways a true amateur, she haunted the legendary Cavern Club, the main venue of the various Liverpool rock groups, and was always available when a female voice was required for a number. Through her friendships with the members of the Beatles, Black came to the attention of Brian Epstein, their manager, who decided that she would be the "girl singer" of the pop empire he was building. Given Epstein's closeted homosexuality and his thwarted desires to be a fashion designer, it is conceivable that Black gave him a chance to play Pygmalion. Having no particular style, either musically or sartorially, Cilla could easily be shaped into his vision of what a female star might be, one who possessed just the right amount of androgyny to keep her from being terribly alluring or sexually threatening. Years later, Sandie Shaw pointedly recalled that "Cilla was a bit of a frump when she first came down to London to Liverpool":[12]

> A Raphael and Leonard haircut and John Bates clothes gave her a miraculous transformation … . I have this image of her there on stage, lit by a solitary pin-spot, belting out heavy-duty ballads, her pale skinny arms stretching up and out from her sleeveless long frocks like branches from a tree. During the years of pantos and summer seasons this impassioned *chanteuse* gradually turned into the chummy comedienne we are more familiar with today. To envisage that change would have taken a huge leap of the imagination.[13]

Even so, the gradual change to which Shaw alludes was due in great part to the quality that attracted fans to Cilla Black in the first place: She was a personality. After decades if not centuries of derision and marginalization, Liverpool Scousers suddenly found themselves seen as charming and even desirable, thanks to the Beatles' popularity. In the 1960s, Cilla's charm was her combination of vivacity and cheekiness, along with a certain (and perhaps *faux*) naivety – traits she shared with the Beatles. She came across as an uncultured provincial girl, not always impressed by the right things or aware of the significance of the persons and things around her, even as Epstein strove to present her as a pop diva.

The personality traits that came across as disarming and cute in a twenty-ish Cilla Black eventually created a media monster who has, to a great extent, obviated the memory of the vivacious Liverpool girl. The abiding post-1960s image of Cilla Black at the forefront of British cultural consciousness, however, is that of the brash and often vulgar host of the game show *Blind Date*, someone "a little like a Saturday night, light entertainment Margaret Thatcher," according

---

[12] The "frumpiness" to which Shaw alludes would suggest that the parodic film *Smashing Time* only slightly exaggerated some of the foibles and excesses of "Swinging London," as its protagonists Yvonne and Brenda (played by Lynn Redgrave and Rita Tushingham, respectively) are provincial girls whose initial attempts to be hip after their arrival in London are anything but fashionable. It is worth noting that the film's writer, the notable critic and musician George Melly, was himself a Liverpudlian.

[13] Shaw, p. 211.

144   *SHE'S SO FINE*

to *Times* entertainment editor Caitlin Moran.[14] In the 1960s she came across as ordinary and likeable girl, modest yet effusive, seemingly without pretension and surprised by her own stardom. BBC critic Adam Webb aptly observes that Cilla "succeeded … just by being herself. …. The very imperfections that would be anathema today were the ones that drew the public's affection in the first place."[15] Perhaps unwittingly, she embodied the egalitarian and protofeminist spirit of the 1960s that suggested that success might be possible for any other ordinary girl who set her mind to it.

So, too, did Lulu. Born Marie MacDonald McLaughlin Lawrie, the daughter of a Glasgow butcher, she was, like Black, a Celtic outsider newly arrived on the London scene. But if Cilla Black managed to attract a following in spite of a certain frumpiness, Lulu's appeal was as compelling as it was problematic. At the age of twenty, Black was virtually an adult woman when she entered the charts in 1963; Lulu, on the other hand, was an underage fourteen when she was discovered singing in a Scottish club during the same year. The qualities that made Lulu an overnight sensation are evident in her earliest television appearances: a stunning ebullience, seemingly boundless energy and enthusiasm, and unforced cheer. But what truly intrigues—and disturbs—is the image of a diminutive figure embodying some liminal space between childhood and womanhood, sweet and innocent, yet simultaneously flirty and cheeky. These factors, combined with a booming, gritty—even raunchy—voice at odds with her appearance, are analogous to the those exhibited only a few years before by the American singer Brenda Lee, to whom Lulu was often compared.[16] The comparison with Lee, who maintained a substantial British following, would have been compelling from a publicist's point of view, considering that Lee was rapidly maturing by the time Lulu came on the scene. But while there was always an element of the eroticized child in Lee's presentation, Lulu took matters a bit further, even while appearing completely innocent; Lee might sing "Sweet Nothings" with a cute suggestiveness, but Lulu wiggled and bounced while performing cover versions of songs originally written for African American male performers. Sandie Shaw's recollection of Lulu is as exact as it is cutting:

> Lulu was always a cheeky bum-wiggler. A lot of come-on with no pay-off. Her miniskirt and flick-ups shook in suggestive unison …. Although her hips swayed, she never thrust her tits. She was the acceptable face of Sixties naughtiness … .

---

[14]   Caitlin Moran, "Cilla: My life's a lorra, lorra fun again." *TimesOnline*, December 16, 2004, http://entertainment.timesonline.co.uk/article/0,,14934-1405247_1,00.html (accessed May 7, 2005).

[15]   Adam Webb, "Cilla Black: *Beginnings,*" *BBC Easy Listening, Soundtracks and Musicals*, September 24, 2003: http://www.bbc.co.uk/music/reviews/rx54 (accessed May 10, 2005)

[16]   See Robynn Stilwell's observations on Lee in Chapter 2 of this volume.

> As she matured, any hint of sexiness was quickly diluted by her BBC TV series
> so as not to offend the family.[17]

By the end of the 1960s, Lulu was trapped in a sort of permanent adolescent image that undoubtedly interfered with her efforts to transform herself into the credible mature singer that, as her recorded output demonstrates, she could certainly have become.

Though lacking any extensive formal training, even at a remarkably young age Lulu demonstrated an ability to fit appropriate vocal coloration and emotional pitch to a given song, and to shift between high and low registers without resorting to obvious artifice. Her earliest influences were American soul singers, and her early stage shows were comprised of cover versions of their recordings. She observes, "People were amazed when they discovered my age. Some thought I sounded black, which I took to be a compliment."[18] Her stylistic spectrum ranged from rock/soul ("Shout"), mainstream pop ("The Boat That I Row"), folk/rock ("Morning Dew"), soul ("Leave a Little Love"), and big melodramatic power ballads ("Best of Both Worlds"). Her early recordings are among her most interesting, inasmuch as they seem devoid of a certain "femininity" that would be expected from a "cheeky bum-wiggler." She made relatively few covers of American girl group songs; indeed her personal style was driven by a seemingly unselfconscious assertiveness—if not aggressiveness—that would eschew the feminine. Instead, she was more inclined to cover songs done by American *male* singers, the lyrics of which, when switched for a female point of view, suggested a sense of determination and independence yet uncommon among women singers. A certain pragmatic diffidence towards unfaithful or uncertain lovers marks "Leave a Little Love" and "Best of Both Worlds," which, much like Lesley Gore's "You Don't Own Me," can be seen as early examples of pop "girl power," in which the girl expresses a certain autonomy in romantic matters, as opposed to the "wishing and hoping" of the desiring girl or the self-mortification of the rejected girl all too common in 1960s girl music. Overall, the lyrics of her songs, composed by an eclectic assortment of writers from Neil Diamond to David Bowie, run the gamut from the banal nonsense of "Boom Bang-A-Bang" to a vast array of emotional states in "Morning Dew."

As a recording artist, Lulu never stayed in any one place stylistically for an extended period, even in her peak years between 1964 and 1970. This could, of course, be attributed to the very early age at which she began recording, but her manager's decisions about her career directions and changes in record labels and producers—with whom Lulu was, at times, at odds—surely contributed to the shifts in her material and thus in her style. The tracks on her earliest album, *Something to Shout About* (1964) include some of her grittiest vocals, particularly in cover versions of songs originally performed by the Isley Brothers ("Shout"

---

[17]   Shaw, p. 211.

[18]   Lulu, *I Don't Want to Fight* (London, 2002), p. 62.

and "You'll Never Leave [Him]"), Marvin Gaye ("Can I Get a Witness"), and Jerry Butler ("[S]he Will Only Break Your Heart"), as well as an odd British quasi-soul number, the Rolling Stones' "Surprise Surprise."[19] Darlene Love and the Blossoms' "He's Sure the Boy I Love" is one of the few girl group covers among these early recordings, but in a sense it falls in line with the male-to-female sexual transpositions the other songs require.[20] When the sex of the vocalist changes but the lyrics, save for the gendered pronouns, remain the same, the result is inevitably some sense of displacement, particularly in a period where traditional gender roles are only starting to erode; in effect, one aurally perceives a woman (or, more precisely, a girl), but the attitudes towards love and sex are those generally restricted to male prerogative. Such usurpation of male privilege, though, is arguably already present in Love's version of "He's Sure the Boy I Love," inasmuch as the female vocalist recites all the shortcomings of her love object—a departure from the uncritical adoration that he would traditionally require—and at the same time stakes a possessive claim on him, not out of a fear that no one else wants her, but rather with a sense of female bravado suggesting that she has sufficient confidence in her own worth to override whatever he lacks, yet without stridence or mockery. This is hardly typical girl group fare.[21]

In spite of these provocative forays into American soul music, "Shout" and "Leave a Little Love" were Lulu's only hits between 1964 and 1966. Her manager Marion Massey, feeling that certain drastic changes were necessary, dismissed her original Scottish backing band (the Luvvers) and negotiated a contract with Columbia Records that would link Lulu with Mickie Most, one of the most commercially successful British producers of 1960s. While Most produced some of Lulu's most successful recordings, the material he chose for his only significant female act was often ill-advised artistically. Among her recordings

---

[19]   Lulu claims in her biography that Mick Jagger and Keith Richards wrote "Surprise, Surprise" for her. Ibid., p. 71.

[20]   Lulu made five cover versions of songs that might be considered "girl group" material, including "He's Sure the Boy I Love," all recorded between 1964 and 1965. The others are "Heatwave" (Martha and the Vandellas), "Can't Hear You No More" (Betty Everett), What's Easy for Two is So Hard for One" (Mary Wells), and "The Trouble with Boys" (Little Eva). With the exception of the last-mentioned song, which assumes the resigned devotion to boys typical of girl group songs, the lyrics demonstrate the same sort of independence regarding relationships that is heard in "He's Sure the Boy I Love." For a discussion of "Heatwave" as a watershed recording in terms of expression of sexuality in girl group music, see my "'Ask Any Girl': Compulsory Heterosexuality and Girl Group Culture," in Kevin Dettmar and William Richey (eds) *Reading Rock and Roll: Authenticity, Appropriation, Aesthetics* (New York, 1999), pp. 93–124.

[21]   "He's Sure the Boy I Love," like "He's a Rebel," was released under the name of the Crystals, another Phil Spector-produced girl group, but actually recorded by Darlene Love and the Blossoms, a group who never received the credit due them. I attribute this recording to Love and her group as a matter of historical accuracy. For more observations on the lyrics of the Spector recording artists, see Smith, "'Ask Any Girl'," pp. 105–12.

from 1966 to 1969, pop gems such as "To Sir With Love," "The Boat That I Row," and "Morning Dew" (with its uncanny vibraphone and sinister guitar accompaniment) coexist with embarrassingly banal nonsense such as "I'm a Tiger" and the schlocky "Boom Bang-a-Bang." The latter, with its heavy-handed oom-pah-pah waltz metre, was, in its way, the perfect entry for the UK in the 1969 Eurovision song contest (in which it was one of four songs to tie for first place) and, ironically, Lulu's only UK number one. Many parallels can be drawn between Lulu's Eurovision experience and that of Sandie Shaw two years earlier, as I shall discuss subsequently. In both cases, the singers were coming of age and thus pushed into the "family entertainment" arena by managers who did not trust their ability to maintain success in an ephemeral pop market. Although seeming triumphs, their Eurovision victories cost both Lulu and Sandie Shaw credibility among their base audiences and consequently undermined their careers, almost irreparably in Shaw's case.[22]

Although Lulu was an adult by this time, such infantilizing material stood in the way of her achieving any sort of artistic maturity. None of this was lost on Lulu herself:

> My own recording career seemed to be stuck in a rut. Mickie Most had turned me into a pure pop singer and it wasn't the only sort of music I wanted to be credited with. Given the choice, I wanted to go back to my first love—the rhythm and blues songs of my childhood ... . 'I'm a Tiger' and 'Boom, Bang-a-Bang' were rinky-dink and lightweight. It drove me mad. I used to fight with Mickie, trying to convince him to do material that was more soulful and took advantage of the raw power of my voice.[23]

The opportunity to become a credible blue-eyed soul singer did, in fact, arise when Lulu's contract with Most expired, and it is tempting to imagine what Lulu might have become. A contract with the American soul label Atlantic, which had recently signed Dusty Springfield, resulted in two albums that demonstrated what Lulu could accomplish in this genre. The single "Oh Me Oh My (I'm a Fool For You Baby)" is a tour-de-force that bears generic similiarity to much of the *Dusty in Memphis* material; indeed, in showcasing Lulu as a mature soul singer, it suggests that Atlantic might have been grooming her as a successor of sorts to Dusty Springfield, whose personal problems were already taking a toll on her career. Unfortunately, although "Oh Me Oh My" came close to cracking the US top 20 as a single, neither album nor their singles were successes with her fan base in Britain. In the mid-1970s, she did some impressive studio work with David Bowie, but by then she had, like Cilla Black, embarked on a path to which female pop stars

---

[22] See Lulu, pp. 125–32, for her recollections and insights regarding the Eurovision Song Contest.

[23] Ibid., 134–35.

148   *SHE'S SO FINE*

seemed willingly and inevitably doomed—marriage, a gradual withdrawal from the pop scene, and subsequent enduring success in "light entertainment."

Sandie

If one were to rely on surfaces alone, Sandra Goodrich would seem just another ordinary girl with a fairytale success story. Prior to her ascension into pop stardom, she held a tedious job, entering data as a punch-card operator at the Ford Motors plant in Dagenham, her hometown. Like her contemporaries, her fame as Sandie Shaw, the barefoot Mod chanteuse, waned almost as quickly as it had begun, once the 60s ended.

Sandie Shaw was, nonetheless, atypical among the Brit Girls in a variety of significant ways, including ethnicity, class, regional background, religious inclinations, and upbringing, as well as personality and physical appearance. Although her background was neither affluent nor privileged, as a much-loved only child of a lower middle-class couple, she grew up without the grinding poverty and violence that marked the childhoods of Cilla Black and Lulu. She was allowed to engage an imagination that expressed itself in creative ways—writing as well as singing—and religious exploration, a tendency that still plays a significant role in her life. The shy and imaginative teenager had the ability and potential to become a university student—an option she deferred for a quarter of a century—but chose rather to work in an undemanding job as she prepared for a musical career. Although her publicity would stress all that was ordinary about her—save for her entry into the music business, which was actually similar to that of other female pop stars in its telling—Sandie Shaw nevertheless evinced a certain depth few of contemporaries possessed.

This depth was manifested primarily through the personality she displayed, one that would become, however unlikely, a template for the Mod girl ethos. She was neither a flamboyant stage presence like Dusty Springfield, nor was she effusive, bubbly, and cute like Cilla Black and Lulu. She seemed reserved, even aloof; indeed, what was most likely an aspect of shyness was perceived by the public as an expression of her being the epitome of coolness. As such, she was emulated by many young women longing to be trendy and popular—even if Shaw would later reflect that her public image made her seem more cold than cool, and thus off-putting to many whose companionship she sought most. Although only months older than her contemporary Lulu, Shaw seemed somehow more mature if nonetheless naive. Fashionable, hip, yet unpretentious and shy, she embodied a seeming contradiction: the nonchalance typical of the new freedom of women in Swinging London, and, simultaneously, the bewilderment and melancholia of innocence giving way to experience. To Morrissey, who was responsible for her 1980s resurrection as a pop icon, Shaw "sounded as if she'd just walked in off the street and begun to sing, and strolled back home and bought some chips."[24] While perhaps not an entirely accurate statement—her recordings surely convey a compelling level of complex emotionality—the charm of the quotidian is central to the appeal, even if the reality were nothing quite so simple.

Shaw's "coolness," whether in terms of personality or constructed attitude, could also be seen as a marker of her ethnic and regional difference among the Brit Girls. The putative norm set by Beatles centered on singers and musicians from the industrial and relatively impoverished north, rude and provincial in the eyes of many in the more affluent and metropolitan south. Like Cilla Black and Lulu, three of the four Beatles were Celtic by ancestry and, to a great extent, culture.[25] Shaw, by contrast, was a Londoner, albeit it one from Essex suburb of Dagenham. She was English and looked it—tall, angular, and thin, she had a physique similar to that represented in Anglo-Norman effigies. It would be difficult to describe her as "cute," an apt term for most of her other female contemporaries, yet her looks were nonetheless striking, even to the extent that she took up modeling ancillary to her singing career. Looks and self-presentation were not, moreover, the only elements that differentiated Shaw from her contemporaries; if Shaw's Celtic contemporaries readily embraced the influence of African American rhythm and blues artists, Shaw looked to some rather eclectic sources. Although her influences included Jackie DeShannon, Burt Bacharach, and Jacques Brel, even as she covered material ranging from rock, country, folk to jazz and show tunes, it would be incorrect to assume that black music made no impression on her. If her Celtic contemporaries from the north felt affinities with African American music, Shaw's recordings clearly reflect the influences of calypso, a genre that, since the 1950s, had carved its own niche in Afro-British music.[26] Though written by her collaborator Chris Andrews, her "Long Live Love" was arguably the last big calypso hit to top the British charts. Nor was it an isolated entity in her recorded output; Shaw experimented with a calypso-style delivery in her cover of Peter, Paul and Mary's "Lemon Tree," and she and Andrews continued to revisit Caribbean musical styles—albeit

---

[24]   Morrissey's statements were made on the British television program *Brit Girls*, broadcast December 13, 1997, Channel 4 (UK). See http://www.morrissey-solo.com/ articles/bg-sl1297.htm (accessed October 17, 2005).

[25]   John Lennon and George Harrison each had Irish-born grandparents, whereas Paul McCartney, Dusty Springfield and Cilla Black each had one Irish-born parent. While it is outside the range of this essay, it is worth noting the extensive contribution made to British popular music by singers of Irish or other Celtic ancestry, including, in addition to those already mentioned, Lulu (Scottish), Van Morrison (Irish), Mary Hopkin (Welsh), Tom Jones (Welsh), Kate Bush (Irish), Annie Lennox (Scottish), Morrissey (Irish), and Boy George [O'Dowd] (Irish), among others.

[26]   The significance of calypso in Britain—or, for that matter, the evolution of a distinctly Afro-British musical culture—has so far received relatively little critical attention. The 1998 CD anthology *From Calypso to Disco: The Roots of Black Britain* (Sequel Records NEMCD 974) and its booklet provide a useful historical overview of this phenomenon.

150   *SHE'S SO FINE*

with dubious results—with such "novelty" numbers as "Oh No He Don't" and "Push It To Make It Go." A certain Latin influence pervades many of Shaw's recordings as well; she made a substantial number of Spanish-language recordings and enjoyed significantly more popularity in Latin America than in the English-speaking countries to the north.[27] The result of her wide diversity of influences was a sound that was both uniquely her own and yet lacking any specific generic or stylistic classification.

Critics have been unkind to Shaw's reputation, excoriating her as a weak or untrained singer. Shaw had her limitations, though surely not as severe as Charlotte Greig maintains:

> True to the mod code, Sandie didn't actually do much. But she looked great. She was the epitome of the singing fashion plate, all big eyes, shiny hair and long, bony legs. In a gesture that preceded hippiedom, she went barefoot; so fascinated were people by this development in the whacky world of pop that whenever she appeared on TV, the camera seemed to be permanently on her feet … . It was not the extraordinary skill and talent of pop girls like … Sandie Shaw that fascinated the public; quite the opposite … . Sandie often sang out of tune.[28]

This quasi-parodic assessment is patently unfair and only partially accurate. A careful audial examination of her recordings gives little evidence that she frequently sang out of key, and her bare feet were hardly the main reason for her appeal. Grieg would seem to be addressing the stereotypes of *Smashing Time* rather than Sandie Shaw herself.[29] Nonetheless, the notion of male critics positing 1960s female singers as ineffectual and insignificant has become so deeply entrenched that even some female critics have accepted this perception.

Shaw's vocal timbre was not the problem; her warm contralto lower register was husky, even sexy at times; she did, though, fall victim at times to a lack of control over her slow vibrato on extended notes (some might call it a "wobble") and her upper range was often strained. It would probably fair to assess these difficulties as the product of her relative inexperience as a singer, as she had done very little performing before turning professional. Even so, one might argue that she used her shortcomings resourcefully and as a means of artistic expression. Her occasional nasality has struck some as irritating, yet it had dramatic effect. Many, if not most, of her early songs are informed by an intense *psychomachia*, an inner

---

[27] Her recordings for Spain and Latin America were collected and reissued on CD in 2004 as *Marionetas en la Cuerda: The Complete Spanish Recordings* (EMI International, 598835).

[28] Grieg, pp. 96–97.

[29] The mean-spiritedness evinced in Greig's assessment seems completely out of keeping with what is otherwise an intelligent and well-balanced study of women in 1960s pop music. Perhaps most troubling is the fact that Greig excoriates Shaw for presumed faults that might be attributed to the American girl groups that she apotheosizes.

conflict between girlhood and womanhood that plays a formidable role in female adolescence. Shaw's warm, dark voice, produced with a combination of head and throat placement, exudes maturity and confidence, that of a confident and knowing woman. This is the voice Shaw uses to sing lyrics that are relatively sophisticated, reassured, or simply unusual for a girl in her teens. In contrast, passages sung in her higher head or nasal voice are usually those with lyrics expressing the wildly raging emotions of insecure adolescence—romantic anxiety, disappointment, possessiveness, even fear. Shaw could switch back and forth between vocal colorations with some facility, making it difficult to attribute these supposed shortcomings to faulty technique alone. By the end of the 1960s, the less pleasant aspects of her singing had been minimized, perhaps by greater maturity and experience, and were entirely missing by the time of her 1980s recordings, which evince a dark, supple, and passionately charged voice under complete control.

Shaw's strange and varied career began in 1964, when she was, according to her publicity, "discovered" by Adam Faith, a British pre-Beatles pop idol, while performing as a supporting act on a bill he topped.[30] Faith introduced her to his manager, Eve Taylor, and, by the end of the year, she was at the top of the British charts with a cover version of Burt Bacharach and Hal David's "Always Something There to Remind Me," originally recorded by the obscure American singer Lou Johnson only months before.[31] Coming after a false start with "As Long as You're Happy," a catchy if clichéd pop tune featuring a strong stylistically unfocused vocal, the choice of material for her first hit was particularly savvy, considering the vogue its composers were then enjoying. Its arrangement, based on piano, bass, guitar, and Latin percussion backed by brass and strings, uncannily resembles those of recordings overseen by Bacharach himself, although he had no direct participation in its creation. If slightly unsteady at times, Shaw's vocal is still remarkably mature for a seventeen-year-old singer, only occasionally revealing adolescent angst.

Despite this auspicious beginning, Shaw entered the British pop scene too late to carry her success across the Atlantic. By the end of 1964, American musicians' unions, alarmed by the erosion of their hegemonic grip on the charts, issued a sweeping ban on live performances by British performers, and sought the protection of the American government to limit the number of work permits and entry visas issued to them. Thus Shaw, unable to book more than a handful of live engagements stateside, was never able to make any significant impression on American audiences. At home, however, she had the strongest performance on

---

[30]   As with most "overnight sensation" stories, the facts, obscured by time, are rarely as simple as they are presented and variations of the tale abound. See Shaw, pp. 51–54, for her version.

[31]   Although "Always Something There to Remind Me" reached the number one position in the UK charts, it was less successful in the US, where success always eluded her, peaking at number fifty-one. Johnson's version fared only slightly better, reaching number forty-nine on the American charts three months earlier.

the British charts of any female singer, British or otherwise. An unbroken string of fifteen hits between 1964 and 1968 included two more chart-topping singles, "Long Live Love" (1965) and "Puppet on a String" (1967), as well as "I'll Stop at Nothing" (1965), "Message Understood" (1965), "Tomorrow" (1966), "Nothing Comes Easy" (1966), "Tonight in Tokyo" (1967), "You've Not Changed" (1967), and "Today" (1968). Although her successes waned late in the decade, an additional single, "Monsieur Dupont" (1969), entered the Top 10 before her career came to a deadlock that, despite her artistically astute self-produced album *Reviewing the Situation* (1969), effectively kept her out of the public eye until her 1980s comeback. Her return to performance at the urging of Morrissey and Johnny Marr of the Smiths was one of the first of a series of 1980s comebacks of 1960s pop icons supported by much younger musicians, and presaged that of Dusty Springfield with the Pet Shop Boys. By 1990, though, Shaw was tired of the music business and stopped performing in order to pursue the education she had postponed years before.

Arguably, Shaw could have continued to perform with some success, as both Cilla Black and Lulu have done; certainly she made maintained an avid following. Her decision to retire, though, might be seen as being in keeping with those characteristics that set her apart from her peers. Perhaps Shaw's lasting appeal was built upon those elements that made her a singular—and uniquely *English*—singer. Although Shaw recorded a few American girl group covers as early album tracks, most of her recordings subsequent to "Always Something There to Remind Me" were British products, composed for her by songwriter Chris Andrews, who was able to set her voice to its best advantage. Though synthesizing various generic influences, these songs are nonetheless definitive and often well-crafted examples of 60s pop. Their distinction lies in their numerous departures from the subject matter and points of view common in 1960s feminine musical fare. Shaw's music did not bewail the treachery of the male sex or wallow in abject brokenheartedness; rather, her songs tended to show insight into the male perspective, to contemplate discarding unwanted boyfriends, or to subvert male–female relationships so as to overturn the traditional double standards. For example, her biggest US hit, "Girl Don't Come," empathizes with a boy who has been "stood-up" by a much-desired young woman, while "Stop Feeling Sorry for Yourself" advises a heart-broken young man to avoid depression by going out and socializing, uncannily (if only coincidentally) foreseeing Shaw's later career as a psychologist. If Shaw's songs seem quaint by today's standards, her inroads into female sexuality were bold in their time. A chorus of shrill female backing voices shouting "I won't stop!" and "Don't care what they say!" underscores an expression of an almost alarming level of female determination to "get the boy I love" in "I'll Stop at Nothing."[32]

---

[32]   One of the most discordant aspects of many of Shaw's recordings is the vocal backing, which often sounds disturbingly like middle-aged women imitating hysterical teenagers. The image this calls to mind is the grey-haired women singing "Ba-ba-ba-ba" while backing Lynn Redgrave's character Yvonne in the aforementioned scene in *Smashing*

While comparable with Springfield's "I'll Try Everything" ("I'll cheat and I'll lie and I'll try 'til I die"), the single-minded ferocity of Shaw's declamation and lyrics ("When he says 'no' I'll just smile") makes Dusty's proclamation seem cool and almost rational in comparison. In "You Can't Blame Him," the girl excuses her boyfriend's infidelity, but not in the long-suffering attitude of Lesley Gore's "Maybe I Know" or the grandiose misery of "You Don't Have to Say You Love Me." Instead, in this rougishly bouncy and bluesy number, the singer's persona laughs it off in a spirit of sexual equality—"You see, I'm the same," that is, she does the same to him. Along the same lines, "Tomorrow" is a contemplation of how best to dump a faithful but absent boyfriend for another one closer at hand. Ethical (or, at least, *almost* ethical) issues abound ("What else can I do? I don't love him no more ... . I respect him.") before she resolves, in an almost *manly* acceptance of responsibility, "That's the way it must be." Similarly, "Nothing Comes Easy" reverses traditional gender roles by presenting the dilemma of a girl for whom the quest is more interesting than the conquest, dumping a boy who, once she has him, becomes clinging and no longer interesting: "I had a hard time getting him / and I'm regretting it now."

Despite her musical ventures into a variety of protofeminist issues, over the decades Shaw has suffered the ignominy of being remembered for one dreadful recording that she was loathe to make, "Puppet on a String," which subsequently won the 1967 Eurovision song competition. In February 1967, the month of her twentieth birthday, Shaw had received an abundance of unwanted publicity when named as the co-respondent in a divorce scandal. Recently, in a 2004 interview with pop journalist Stephen Wright, Shaw has recalled the ugly atmosphere of the situation: she was "one of the first women the tabloid press set out to 'get,'" even though "a sexual history" would be "almost invariably an asset for a male pop star":

> I don't know if you understand what a truly awful time for me that was. I mean, I wasn't a hooker and I wasn't even putting it about; I was simply engaged to the wrong person. You know, I haven't a clue why it was such a surprise to anyone that I might actually be sexually active. When you look at pictures of me at the time, and it is quite obvious that I am, and you can tell from looking at me that I am obviously very knowing. The whole thing just seemed so stupid.

Time. As Pye, Shaw's recording company, was notoriously stingy with its recording budgets, even for such high-profile acts as the Kinks and the Searchers, one can only imagine that the session singers were not of the best caliber. Certain arrangements forced Shaw to sing in harmony with vocalists not in harmony with each other; "I'll Stop at Nothing" is the most painfully obvious example but hardly the only one. Conceivably, some of Shaw's reputation for lack of vocal control or singing out of tune is the fault of her quite dreadful backing vocalists.

154   *SHE'S SO FINE*

> I look as if butter wouldn't melt in my mouth, all sweet and young, but I didn't look naïve.[33]

Eve Taylor, seeking to "redeem" her supposedly fallen protégé, pushed both the moronic song and the artistically demeaning competition on Shaw, gambling that a victory would make her a national heroine and a "family entertainer," thus undoing the harm the scandal caused, and, presumably, to save her from being permanently banned from appearing on the BBC: "[The BBC] were the bastion—in some ways they still are—of correct, conservative behaviour. And obviously, they didn't think that I represented that. However, so it went, if I did Eurovision, that would change people's minds and kind of wipe it out."[34]

That Sandie Shaw's career should culminate in "Puppet on a String" is painfully ironic. After a string of hit songs that questioned or subverted the double standards that governed gendered behavior, she not was not only publicly humiliated by them but also, as a form of public penitence, saddled with a song that reinforced them. Not only did the song go against Shaw's sensibilities by suggesting that women should willingly become "puppets on strings" to dominating male lovers, but it also severely undercut whatever critical success she had attained, leaving the public to associate her primarily with a tacky piece of pop schlock. Subsequently, Shaw's anger became all too apparent whenever "Puppet on a String," was mentioned, even to the point of her walking out during a television interview. Only in recent years has she been willing or able to speak of the song with equanimity.

For all her intentions, Taylor effectively ended her protégé's career through this attempt to change her artistic direction. Shaw recorded and produced the adventurous *Reviewing the Situation*, with songs as diverse as its eponymous song by Lionel Bart from the musical *Oliver*, Bob Dylan's "Lay Lady Lay," Dr. John's "Mama Roux," the Bee Gees' "Sun in My Eyes," the Beatles' "Love Me Do," and, most amazingly, the Rolling Stones' "Sympathy for the Devil," without Taylor's knowledge. Upon the album's release, Taylor, incensed by Shaw's rock ambitions, quashed its promotion, and the album completely vanished from the public eye and ear until 2004, when Shaw herself oversaw its reissue. Though unfocused in its attempt to do too much at once, the album nonetheless gives Shaw the rock credibility critics have denied her and stands as a sad relic of what might have been had Shaw been left to her own devices.

It was not, in fact, until the 1980s that Sandie Shaw had the opportunity to demonstrate her talent fully. In 1983, Shaw, by then deeply involved in the Buddhist religion (to which she has reputedly made hundreds of converts) and pacifism, privately recorded *Choose Life*, a fund-raising album to promote the World Peace Exposition. Few copies were made and thus *Choose Life* made little impression. It is nonetheless an interesting recording that demonstrates Shaw's

---

[33]   Sandie Shaw, "December 04 Newsletter," http://www.sandieshaw.com/newsletters/news-04-12.php (accessed October 20, 2005).

[34]   Ibid.

ability to move beyond 60s pop. The songs, all of which Shaw co-wrote, possess an intense if at times child-like mysticism resembling that of Kate Bush's earlier work. The following year, a letter from two admirers, Morrissey and Johnny Marr of the Smiths, coaxed her out of "official" retirement, and her collaborations with them returned her to the British charts after an absence of more than a decade. Shaw's "comeback" resulted in three more chart hits, "Hand in Glove" (1984) on which she is backed by the Smiths, "Frederick" (1986), and "Are You Ready to Be Heartbroken" (1986).

Her album *Hello Angel* (1988) was the culmination of this second phase of her career and saw Shaw reunited with her 1960s collaborator Chris Andrews, with whom she co-wrote many of its songs. Yet the recording is neither nostalgic nor sentimental; it is instead firmly grounded in the moment, with sophisticated lyrics examining issues—lives frayed by experience, the failure of long-standing relationships, homosexuality and other alternative lifestyles, socio-economic issues under Thatcherism—from which most commercial youth-oriented music shirks. The album also reveals Shaw's strong, mature, and secure mezzo-soprano voice, audible but not fully developed in her 1960s recording, in full bloom, free of adolescent emotionality, yet flexible enough to express a wide range of moods. Indeed, her cover versions of the Smiths' songs give new insights into the lyrics that Morrissey's mannerisms often obscured. Shaw might well have been able to continue in this vein for years, had she not chosen to retire yet again.

What's it all about?

While the most popular and best-known British female performers of the 1960s were all white, it would be wrong to assume that there was no ethnic diversity among them, for "British" and "English" are not synonymous. The Celtic peoples of the British Isles have for centuries been marginalized by the dominant English and restricted to lives of manual labor and relative poverty. It is perhaps not surprising, then, that numerous Celts, like Cilla Black and Lulu, have gravitated towards African American music, as previously noted, or have found a certain parallel sensibility in it.[35] Angela Carter, perhaps the most astute observer of her own generation, notes this affinity among marginalized white British youth:

> One of the interesting things about the music boom ... was the way that young white kids from the most deprived parts of Britain, Liverpool, Newcastle, places not exactly slick with prosperity in those days ... these poor whites took to the

---

[35] This African American/Celtic affinity is explored in Irish author Roddy Doyle's novel *The Commitments* (London, 1988) and Alan Parker's 1991 film of the same title.

music of poor Blacks from the most wretchedly segregated and oppressed parts of the deep South of the U.S. like ducks to water.[36]

That ordinary girls from such less-than-privileged backgrounds, regardless of their respective British ethnicities, could become pop stars was, arguably, part of their lasting appeal; they were, in their way, akin to fairy-tale princesses who underwent fabulous transformations. Accordingly, they were perfect icons for a idealistic generation, the first, according to Carter, that "didn't define itself ... by what its parents had done for a living."[37]

In attempting to discern what set the select Brit Girls apart from the other female pop stars, one cannot escape noticing a pattern of parallels among them. Cilla Black, Marianne Faithfull, Sandie Shaw, and Lulu were all born within a five-year period during the 1940s, and were between the ages of fifteen and twenty when they gained their first fame. Along with Dusty Springfield, they all had their first hits within a ten-month period between late 1963 and autumn 1964; in the wake of the British Invasion, Petula Clark had an international hit with "Downtown" a few months later. All these women came to the end of their run of hits by 1970 or 1971, Faithfull much sooner than the rest. It is not insignificant that their glory years almost exactly parallel those of the Beatles, who entered the charts in late 1962 and disbanded in 1970. It would follow that they were part of a certain *zeitgeist*, whether called the "British Invasion" or "Swinging London," of which the Beatles were the life force; when the Beatles went away, they took the period with them.

To understand the peak years of their popularity in this regard is hardly to demean these women; indeed, if one examines the histories of the various British male groups or solo singers of the period, it becomes evident that Black, Shaw, and Lulu—as well as Springfield and Clark and, to a lesser extent, Faithfull—actually enjoyed greater commercial success and endured longer than the vast majority of their male peers, certain notable exceptions (e.g., the Rolling Stones, the Kinks, the Hollies, the Who) notwithstanding. Most of the Brit Girls, moreover, were able to revive their careers by the 1980s, many of them returning to the pop charts after an absence of nearly two decades. Even so, the popular concept remains that they were, for the most part, ephemeral attractions, while such male acts as the Searchers, the Yardbirds, or the short-lived Zombies, significant talents though they were, are more likely to be regarded as unfairly or tragically neglected. To call these women marginal figures in a greater movement called the British Invasion, then, is simply inaccurate—unless, of course, we forget that this is all too often the fate of women who outperform men in what is, for the most part, a men's enterprise.

---

[36] Angela Carter, "Truly, It Felt Like Year One," in Sara Maitland (ed.), *Very Heaven: Looking Back at the 1960s* (London, 1998), pp. 210, 212–13.

[37] Ibid., p. 210.

An artistic reputation, though, can never solely rely on the number of records one has sold, though without those numbers one cannot easily reach a substantial audience. Still, how that audience responds—and how long that audience responds—is a substantial indicator of artistic influence. Their 1980s comebacks were, as often as not, in collaboration with male artists a generation younger than they, such as the Pet Shop Boys and Morrissey, who had once been fans. One might argue, accordingly, that a significant facet of 1980s Britpop style was influenced by the peculiarly 1960s sensibility of the Brit Girls, namely the queerness and gender bending that were so much in evidence in the former. This claim is more logical than it might seem on the surface. The performing styles, visual appearances, attitudes, and songs of the Brit Girls often marked a departure from traditional girl group ideals of femininity and suggested a desire for liberation from traditional gender roles. That their comebacks and collaborations—including Lulu's 1970s work with David Bowie and her 1990s recording with the boy band Take That— have generally involved openly gay male performers or ones with significant gay followings, then, is perhaps not surprising, inasmuch as such performers also defied gender roles by assuming "feminine" poses or androgynous personae.[38] The Brit Girls were as likely to cover songs originally recorded by male (and frequently black) artists as the presumably normative female ones; thus they transgressed, albeit subtly in some instances, accepted gender codes; likewise, the queer or sexually ambiguous male performers who adopted them as icons looked to these female models as they "feminized" British pop and rock.[39] The Brit Girls' influence on the "boys," then, can be seen as an indirect result of the manner in which they reconfigured pop cultural perceptions of what a girl should be and do. And while the Brit Girls' renegotiations of femaleness opened new opportunities and a freer range of expressive possibilities for the women who came after them, their influence on subsequent Brit boys was conceivably stronger.

Charlotte Greig suggests that Cilla, Lulu, and Sandie, among others, represented a new and consequently iconic model for female singers:

---

[38] Lulu has returned to the charts at least once in every decade from the 1970s to the present. In 1973, David Bowie oversaw her first career revival by producing and playing on her recording of "The Man Who Sold the World" and its B-side, "Watch That Man," both of which are covers of Bowie's own recordings. Twenty years later, she returned to the top of the British charts performing with Take That on "Relight My Fire."

[39] This is not to say that 1980s queer or androgynous male performers were the first to "feminize" British pop and rock. Girl groups like the Shirelles undoubtedly exerted a significant influence on the British Invasion groups of the 1960s, including the Beatles, whom many regarded as androgynous or "effeminate" in their time. The male groups of the 1980s to whom I refer (e.g. the Pet Shop Boys, the Smiths, Culture Club, Soft Cell) unabashedly presented themselves as feminized men to an extent unthinkable in the 1960s. The most important influences fueling this trend, I would suggest, were David Bowie and the various female performers of the 1960s, all of whom had functioned as personal heroes/ heroines for a whole generation of British pop stars in the 1980s.

158 *SHE'S SO FINE*

> [I]n Britain a new image of young women arose which was much more sophisticated than the American girl teenagers who had squealed on [the American television show] Bandstand … .

> [T]he archetypal sixties' British dolly bird was older than the American teenage miss, probably in her early twenties; she was assumed to have a job of some kind, and to have left her childhood girlfriends behind. She was portrayed as more interested in going out with men than in girl talk, and as having a fairly blasé attitude towards sex; none of that 'wearing his ring' nonsense for her … . The new young women of British pop reflected this image to perfection.[40]

This argument is cogent up to a point; Springfield and Black were already in their twenties by the time they arrived on the Mod scene, but Lulu and Sandie Shaw were only in their mid-teens, the same age range as the average American girl group singer. Whether they really maintained a "fairly blasé attitude towards sex" is also questionable. Lulu insists that she remained a virgin until her marriage to Maurice Gibb, Cilla Black eventually married the only man ever in her life, and Dusty Springfield, despite her numerous lesbian affairs, was apparently more tormented than blasé about them. Only Sandie Shaw and Marianne Faithfull were unabashed about their sexual activities—and were duly attacked as a result. Yet whether or not they were personally more mature or more sexually knowing than their American contemporaries is ultimately beside the point; what matters is that they projected an image of greater sophistication than had previously been the norm through a combination of factors such as song lyrics, vocal presentation, and Mod fashion consciousness.

It is true, as Greig suggests, that the British girls rarely sang about "going steady," marriage, or "how guys are;" equally rare in their repertory are the "advice songs" addressed to other girls—even if Sandie Shaw was willing to dispense advice to lovelorn boys.[41] Romantic desperation, when it does appear, is of an overblown, obsessive "You Don't Have to Say You Love Me" variety—but Cilla, Lulu, and Sandie, unlike Dusty, generally avoided emotionally extreme lyrics. Perhaps the lack of "girl talk" in the British girls' songs derived in great part from their early practice of covering songs originally performed by male artists, inasmuch as they learned from the beginning of their careers to strike romantic poses that might be commonplace for young men but a bit surprising for young women. Greig also observes that a certain sort of androgyny was an essential ingredient comprising the female Mod:

> Despite her appearance of complete passivity and feminine quiescence, she was a complex being who in some ways defied accepted notions of how women

---

[40] Greig, pp. 87–88.

[41] On the "between girls" sorts of lyrics of American girl groups and solo singers of the late 1950s and early 1960s, see Smith, "Ask Any Girl," 93–124.

should look and behave. If she was blank, she was also inscrutable; if she was the epitome of delicate femininity, she was also curiously masculine.[42]

Such gender ambiguity is also at play in these singers' vocal performances. If even relatively young singers such as Lulu and Sandie Shaw *seemed* somehow older than their American contemporaries, one explanation might well be that they were, for the most part, altos with relatively dark timbres. Rarely did any of these young women even begin to approach a soprano range, and in the few instances in which they did, the high notes were often accomplished through a falsetto.[43] The association of character with vocal range and timbre has long been utilized in opera; the highest soprano parts are usually associated with innocence while mezzo-sopranos and contraltos occupy the roles of more worldly and experienced women.[44] These associations have long been in place, so much that audience perceptions of virginity and sexual experience are informed in much the same way in popular music as well. Compounding the impression of age and sophistication—even if not entirely accurate—among the British female singers of the 60s is their modes of vocal placement. While the high nasal voice figures largely in American girl group music, the Brit Girls have generally utilized head and throat placement and thus sound less "girlie-girlish," even when they do resort to nasality.

The Mod fashions for which these singers became virtual models were also a symbolic gesture towards breaking with the sort of femininity-as-usual visual image associated with American girl groups and singers of the previous decade. With the notable exception of Dusty Springfield, British female singers dispensed with back-brushed, heavily lacquered coiffures and evening gowns in favor of Vidal Sassoon's low-maintenance *garçon*-style haircuts and the mini-skirted styles of

---

[42] Grieg, p. 94.

[43] One might argue that the young Marianne Faithfull, much like Mary Hopkin, approximated a soprano range; surely Faithfull attempts this in several early recordings (e.g. "I Have a Love"), but in such recordings her voice sounds painfully strained. Her voice has, of course, long since darkened dramatically. Relatively few female singers use a falsetto voice effectively, but Dusty Springfield and Sandie Shaw were adept in using it for effect. Springfield sings "In the Land of Make Believe" on the *Dusty in Memphis* album almost entirely in falsetto; Shaw does likewise in her cover version of Donovan's "Oh Gosh" on her *Reviewing the Situation* album. Shaw's hit "Girl Don't Come" evinces her ability to switch from full voice to falsetto and back in a single line with the word "die" (streched over four notes) in the reprise of the line "You hurt inside, you want to die (oh-oh-whoa-oh)."

[44] The typical heroines of nineteenth-century Italian opera, for whom virginity and vulnerability are quintessential, are mostly sopranos. The most significant mezzo-soprano roles were those of worldly, sexually knowing, and often dangerous women, such as Amneris in *Aida*, Eboli in *Don Carlos*, Venus in *Tannhäuser*, Ortrud in *Lohengrin*, and Kundry in *Parsifal*, as well as the most sexually cunning women in opera, namely the eponymous protagonists of *Carmen* and *Samson et Dalila*.

Mary Quant and other Carnaby Street designers.[45] Although later feminists would cite the mini-skirt as a potent symbol of female sexual objectification, during the 1960s it was a daring sign of women's sexual liberation from traditional mores and the artificial "lady-like" strictures of previous decades. Indeed, both Sassoon and Quant believed that their easy-going styles freed women from time-consuming beauty routines and thus contributed to their liberation by giving them more time for the pursuit of pleasure. All in all, it was not very difficult to emulate the Brit Girls; potentially, at least, any girl with the right attitude and a modicum of talent could be one, even girls who weren't really British. For many young women (and possibly a few young men), being a Brit Girl remains as desirable today as it was four decades ago.

Epilogue

The Brit Girls have endured. Petula Clark has aged gracefully, settling into the role of elder diva and still performing, albeit much less frequently, even in her seventies. Dusty Springfield, sadly, passed away, but not before receiving the belated acclaim and respect she long deserved. Marianne Faithfull has successfully transformed herself as a highly acclaimed *chanteuse*. Cilla Black and Lulu carry on in their now-familiar show-business roles. Only Sandie Shaw has moved on to other endeavors.

In the 1990s, Shaw studied at Oxford and earned an MSc degree from Birkbeck College, University of London. She subsequently qualified as psychotherapist and set up the Arts Clinic, a Harley Street practice that specializes in the treatment of entertainers, as well a practice for the treatment of women with issue of low

---

[45] It is ironic that Springfield, who was in the vanguard of Mod fashion at the beginning of her career as a solo artist, became more "retro" over the course of the 1960s. Her extraordinary hairstyles were *au courant* in 1963, but by early 1965, Cilla Black and Lulu had abandoned the "big hair" look in favor of the simpler, more contemporary look, while both Sandie Shaw and Marianne Faithfull had a more casual, long-haired look from the outset. Strangely enough, Petula Clark, the least "trendy" British female vocalist, sported a Mod coiffure when she made her breakthrough recording "Downtown."

One can only speculate as to why, after 1964, Springfield became more extremely dressed, with bigger hair, more make-up, and more hidden behind long-evening gowns. Some have suggested that her consciousness about her looks lead her to conceal herself behind a "drag queen" façade. As I have suggested elsewhere, she possibly chose a hyperfeminine masquerade to conceal her lesbianism, which had gradually become a topic of much speculation during this period. See Annie Randall's essay on Dusty Springfield, Chapter 4 in this volume; see also Smith, "'You Don't Have to Say You Love Me'," pp. 105–26.

self-esteem and related problems.[46] On her website, Sandie Shaw reveals her motivation in founding a psychotherapy clinic for women:

> It has concerned me ... that so many women suffer from low self worth. It comes from a deep disrespect of our own femininity and leads to further disrespect of other women. Instead of supporting each other with the sharing of our knowledge we undermine each other's efforts to become happy and fulfilled. Women's lack of self-esteem straddles all classes, backgrounds and races. It is all the more surprising in seemingly confident professional women.[47]

As I have argued elsewhere, such issues run deeply in the lyrics of girl group music, which is hardly surprising as the music expresses the conditions under which most girls have been socialized.[48] It is apt, then, that Shaw, whose lyrics suggested alternatives to the old gender roles, would devote her later career to healing those whose crises might well be expressed in the words most girl groups sang.

Though quite ordinary in many ways, the Brit Girls of the 1960s were nonetheless extraordinary in having helped to reverse the concepts of passivity and submissiveness that informed so much of the "girl pop" that came before them, and, consequently, paving the way for the bolder, more independent young women who came after them. In this sense, despite often vast differences in vocal style, succeeding generations of female artists as diverse as Chrissie Hynde, Annie Lennox, Kate Bush, Alison Moyet, Madonna, Sinead O'Connor, the Spice Girls, All Saints, and Dido are deeply indebted to them. At Dusty Springfield's funeral in 1999, Lulu eulogized her great contemporary as a pioneer in creating a new sort of "girl," one who broke the old mold of feminine expectations and roles: "Dusty was the first person to demonstrate girl power, in my opinion .... She had tremendous courage because she bared her soul to the whole world. To sing with that passion takes tremendous courage .... She had such a great spirit that it will never die, she will always be around."[49] By creating new possibilities for female pop stars, the Brit Girls, each in her own way, contributed to the concept of girl power, and, perhaps for that very reason, they are still much beloved. The words of Sandie Shaw, now Sandra Goodrich, psychotherapist, are an apt summation: "Girl Power? ... This is Woman Power. And the best is yet to come."[50]

---

[46]   Shaw discusses her educational experiences and her subsequent career in psychotherapy in an "alumni news" article, "The World at Her Feet," in *BBK Magazine*, a periodical published by Birkbeck College, Issue 18, May 9, 2006.

[47]   See http://www.sandieshaw.com/womensclinic.php (accessed October 20, 2005).

[48]   See Smith, "Ask Any Girl."

[49]   Richard Duce, "Stars Mourn Dusty, First Girl-Power Icon," *The Times* (London), March 13 1999.

[50]   See http://www.sandieshaw.com/biography.php (accessed October 20, 2005).

Chapter 6
Mary Hopkin and the
Deep Throat of Culture

Sarah Hill

For all its reputation as a musical culture, the number of Welsh women pop stars can be counted charitably on two hands, with some fingers to spare. In the 1960s, when women's voices were the mainstays of Motown, the folk circuit and the Haight-Ashbury, in Wales only one woman really managed to cross over from Welsh-language folk to mainstream Anglo-American pop.[1] Mary Hopkin's career serves as a case study for the linguistic and musical border-crossings and the larger cultural issues that they reflect. More importantly, her career challenges the place of the female pop voice in Wales, and of the female Welsh pop voice in Anglo-America.

Welsh-language popular music has always been about by the possibility of community formation, without cultural hierarchy or any deference to "fame," local or national; it evolved for the benefit, and furtherance, of the Welsh-speaking community. The Welsh pop music "industry" is not driven by financial reward; critical acclaim and public exposure in Wales are fairly easy to come by, but the trappings of fame in the Anglo-American market are antithetical to the cultural and political purposes of Welsh popular music and are, therefore, not worth acknowledging. It is fair to say that a Welsh musician's place is in the home, and the home is Wales.

A Welsh musician's relationship with the dominant, Anglo-American culture is largely determined by the linguistic tradition from which he or she emerged. For monoglot Anglophone Welsh musicians, the drive to succeed in the larger, mainstream market is a given; for bilingual Welsh musicians, the drive to cross over is a compromise, linguistically and culturally. Though the process of domestication—the adoption of a "foreign" cultural product, Anglo-American popular music, into the vernacular language—is common to a multiplicity of cultures, the crossover more perilous to Welsh popular music entails the adoption

---

[1] For the purposes of concision, "Anglo-American" refers to "British and American" rather than a particular subset of American ethnicities. "Welsh popular music" refers to popular music sung in the Welsh language; "Anglophone Welsh popular music" refers specifically to popular music originating in Wales and sung in the English language. This is in no way to suggest that Anglophone Welsh popular music is not inherently "Welsh," or that "Welsh popular music" is by its nature only applicable to music sung in the Welsh language. The terms are much more easily delineated in the Welsh language itself, but for obvious reasons of linguistic access, these less satisfactory English equivalents are here preferred.

of the "foreign" language, English, which effectively reverses the domestication process. This linguistic crossover has always been seen as particularly damaging to the future of Welsh pop and, by inference, the Welsh community. A successful crossover meant that Welsh musicians would abandon their roots for recognition in Anglo-America, and that other bands would be similarly discouraged from enriching the Welsh language for what amounts to very little financial reward. While many bands protest that they maintain a sense of "home" culture—some essential "Welshness"—while singing in language many consider to be "foreign," this is a problematic idea and very difficult to sustain.

In his article, "A Theoretical Model for the Sociomusicological Analysis of Popular Musics," John Shepherd writes:

> when the social, political and economic environment is given, unchangeable and experienced by all in much the same way, there is no need to spell it out and explicitly discuss it. One simply reproduces it, and communicates personally and intuitively within it. The communication is from within the person, and is in continual tension with the superimposed abstract framework, whether social or musical.[2]

Though Shepherd was referring specifically to the blues, there are some important parallels to draw here with Welsh popular music and the idea of an essential "Welshness." For the majority of Wales's modern cultural history, the Nonconformist chapel was the focus of Welsh social life. The chapel was the spiritual and social home of the Welsh-speaking communities scattered throughout Wales, and as such it exerted a powerful influence over the modernization of Welsh cultural life. It was, to use Shepherd's words, given, unchangeable, and experienced by all Welsh speakers in much the same way. After the first Welsh "pop boom," circa 1966, the chapel was the primary sponsor of cultural production. It is therefore impossible to think of the development of Welsh-language popular music in the same chronological terms as its Anglophone counterpart. Of course, Anglophone popular music existed in Wales in the post-war years, but the process of creating a popular culture in the Welsh language was very slow, and ultimately influenced by a longer, culturally-specific musical tradition. This tradition had been nurtured in local, regional and national Eisteddfodau—cultural festivals in which poets and musicians compete in strictly ruled metrical and musical forms such as *cynghanedd*[3]

---

[2]   John Shepherd, "A Theoretical Model for the Sociomusicological Analysis of Popular Music." *Popular Music*, vol. 2: *Theory and Method* (1982): 145–77.

[3]   *Cynghanedd* is defined by the University of Wales Dictionary as "harmony, agreement, concordance," as well as "a system of consonance or alliteration in a line of Welsh poetry in strict metre with internal rhyme; the metrical craft or technique of Welsh poetic art in the strict metres."

and *cerdd dant*,[4] respectively—and in local and national organizations aimed at the preservation of the Welsh language, such as the omnipresent Nonconformist chapel and the Welsh League of Youth (*Urdd Gobaith Cymru*).[5] Within this cultural framework, original songs written in the Welsh language were, generally speaking, based on existing folk melodies (British, American or Welsh), and lyrical themes tended toward the patriotic, the pastoral, and the chaste.

When contemporary Welsh pop music began in earnest in the mid-1960s it was inextricably linked to a period of intense and sustained language activism. If musicians or bands wished to sing covers of popular Anglo-American songs they did so in the Welsh language, thus providing a "native" alternative to what was at that time the steadily encroaching Anglicization of a very fragile linguistic culture. This domestication was a political act and a powerful statement of community ethos. Musicians' membership in the Welsh Language Society (*Cymdeithas yr Iaith Gymraeg*) was safely assumed, from its founding in 1963, and most pop concerts from the late-1960s until very recently were organized by, and in order to promote, the *Cymdeithas*. But for those first few years there was no network of small venues for Welsh pop concerts, and most were therefore held in town halls or chapel vestries. Because of this latter patronage, as it evolved, Welsh pop lagged several decades behind its Anglophone parent. It was, until 1973, primarily acoustic, and remarkably innocent.

Against this background, a particular kind of vocal style emerged which was central to the Welsh pop-musical aesthetic:[6] unadorned, uninflected, much like the physical spaces—chapels, Eisteddfod fields—that gave rise to its practice. The reproduction of this central and learned aesthetic is a primary marker of membership in Welsh cultural life, and it is common across gender and genre boundaries. Following from Shepherd, I would like to suggest therefore that there is inscribed in the Welsh pop voice the connection to a cultural history that has been set, for the last several hundred years, in opposition to the dominant cultural paradigm of the larger geopolitical area: Anglophone, Anglican, Anglo-American. A departure from this inferred "Welsh vocal style" necessarily involves a kind of

---

[4]   *Cerdd* (poem), *tant* (string). Traditionally, impromptu singing with harp. The harpist begins by playing a traditional melody, and the singer improvises his or her own countermelody. The two musicians are meant to finish at the same time. The singer should sing clearly and illustrate the mood and meaning of the verses chosen; the countermelody should complement the natural rhythm of the verses, as well as the rhythm in the harp's melody.

[5]   The *Urdd* is Wales' largest youth organisation. It was founded in 1922 with membership open to children under the age of 18; today the *Urdd* has over 50,000 members.

[6]   Again, it needs to be stressed that "Welsh" in this instance refers specifically to "Welsh-language." The vocal style of contemporary Anglophone Welsh artists was decidedly different, and based upon a separate tradition. For more on the Anglophone Welsh pop voice, see Trevor Herbert and Peter Stead (eds), *Hymns and Arias: Great Welsh Voices* (Cardiff, 2001).

cultural compromise, and it goes back to what I suggested earlier, that there is a multi-step process involved in the domestication of Anglo-American popular musical style. And here is where I would like to problematize the female Welsh pop voice.

For Welsh women singers, there is often an additional step in the crossover process outlined above, that of adopting a "masculine," "rock" voice. This raises issues not only of cultural acceptance or rejection, but also, more simply, of image and (re-)interpretation. There are certainly examples of the female Welsh pop voice in the late-1960s, for example, in groups such as Perlau Tâf (Taff Pearls), Y Diliau (The Honeycombs) and Y Pelydrau (The Rays), and in the popular duet Tony ac Aloma. But "pop" in the Welsh sense is notoriously all-inclusive, and these early female Welsh pop voices were firmly rooted in the acoustic folk tradition—never utilized in a forceful, non-feminine, "rock" manner. I was reminded of this point while reading Sheila Whiteley's book *Women and Popular Music*, whose chapter, "Repressive Representations" ends: "Mary Hopkins [*sic*], the Welsh folk singer, was a Paul McCartney discovery. She was frequently described as the epitome of the passive feminine role—England's sweetheart."[7]

On the surface, this is a harmless remark, and it is basically accurate. Mary Hopkin was a Welsh folk singer; she developed a working relationship with Paul McCartney; she could be interpreted as epitomizing the passive feminine role, both in her physical appearance and in her vocal production. It is that term "England's sweetheart" that causes concern. Whiteley no doubt intended to group Mary Hopkin with other late-1960s British female pop singers such as Cilla Black, Lulu, and Sandie Shaw, whose music enjoyed success in the UK pop charts, whose hit singles were attributed to male songwriters, and who enjoyed fruitful business and personal associations with powerful male musicians. A suggestion of commonality between these singers is understandable. But there is a deeper significance here, one that Whiteley touched with her term "England's sweetheart," and it has to do with balance of power and cultural encoding.

Whatever stylistic or vocal similarities existed between Cilla Black, Lulu, Sandie Shaw, and Mary Hopkin, their place in British pop culture was determined by their "otherness"—that is, their gender, and their roots. If in the 1960s London were to be considered the center of British cultural production then the four singers just noted represent the margins of that culture: Cilla Black was born and raised in Liverpool, Lulu came from Glasgow, Sandie Shaw from Essex, and Mary Hopkin from Pontardawe in South Wales.[8] London could be interpreted as the

---

[7]   Sheila Whiteley, *Women and Popular Music: Sexuality, Identity, and Subjectivity* (London and New York, 2000), p. 41.

[8]   In the case of Cilla Black and Lulu, their position within "marginal" yet *urban* Britain is an important distinction to make here. Liverpool and Glasgow had their own popular music traditions; Lulu's recording of "Shout" (1964), for example, must be considered as a direct result of local exposure to early American soul music. This places her in somewhat different company from Mary Hopkin, whose potential early exposure to

metaphorical dominant, or "masculine" figure, and the four provinces, the four singers, the passive, or "feminine" presence: "England's sweethearts."[9] Taking this argument one step further, in Mary Hopkin's case, this generalization can be extended to a much larger political construct, whereby her presence is not only passively feminine, but, more specifically, passively Welsh.

In her article, "On Musical Performance of Gender and Sex," Suzanne Cusick writes:

> all voices, but especially singing voices, perform the borders of the body. They perform those borders' relationship both to the body's interior and to the exterior world, a relationship that in late twentieth-century culture can be gendered in terms of the borders' relative penetrability. ... [T]he act of singing a song is always an act that replicates acceptance of patterns that are intelligible to one's cohort in a culture. ... Most often taken as a sign of something like passionate, non-verbal, even mystical inner life, our ability to use our bodies to make this "music"—our ability to sing—also communicates to our cohort the depth to which we have allowed cultural norms to penetrate and discipline our bodies' interior spaces and interior actions.[10]

"Borders" are central to the understanding of the Welsh psyche. The geographical borders of Wales and England are notoriously wonky, and the linguistic borders between the two nations are similarly, and endlessly, problematic. On a list of certain passive stereotypes, Cusick's use of the term "penetrability" can be applied figuratively to the idea of linguistic borders, with Welshness in general, and Mary Hopkin in particular. The penetration of foreign cultural influence—the passive acceptance of a dominant foreign language—is a particularly violent metaphor,

---

American soul music is nonetheless imperceptible in her contemporary recordings. I am grateful to Edinburgher Dr. Ken Gloag for making this point.

[9] It could rightly be argued that the British Invasion, led by four young men from Liverpool, effectively shifted the balance of cultural power away from London and into the provinces, and that their popularity allowed other British artists, male and female alike, to succeed in the US charts. Two women in particular, Dusty Springfield and Petula Clark, broke through to the US market in the wake of the British Invasion in spite of their gender and in spite of their "otherness"—Dusty Springfield for her indeterminate sexuality, Petula Clark for the palpable vestiges of a classical training; yet their later careers did not follow the same trajectory as their contemporary male counterparts. It could also be argued here that the registral similarities between Dusty Springfield and Petula Clark—both women tended toward their comfortable, middle-range chest voice—were also markers of some sort of "otherness," or halfway point between the popular contemporary "folk" voice (high, pure) and the contemporary "rock" voice (low, masculine). Suggesting here that London was the center of cultural production is merely to establish a mainstream industrial locus.

[10] Suzanne G. Cusick, "On Musical Performances of Gender and Sex," in Elaine Barkin and Lydia Hamessley (eds), *Audible Traces: Gender, Identity and Music* (Zurich and Los Angeles, 1999), pp. 29, 32.

but by applying it here to the development of a female Anglophone Welsh pop voice that multi-layered crossover process becomes much more than a mere stylistic shift; it becomes a battle to retain linguistic cultural norms in an otherwise hostile environment. Furthermore, it suggests that regardless of crossover, traces of a "home" culture will still be evident to other members of that culture.

Cusick suggests that girls are taught at puberty not to adapt to changes in their physicality; that the continuation of vocal production in their prepubescent register is, in essence, a denial of change. That Mary Hopkin generally sang in her upper register is significant; it suggests that the tradition that shaped her early vocal production—chapel, Eisteddfod—remains somehow embedded in her voice. Taking this one step further, the high, sweet manner of Welsh folk singing based on the determinedly Welsh chapel and Eisteddfodic traditions is unsullied by linguistic impurities; it denotes, for want of a better description, cultural virginity. By contrast, an altered voice—a voice that has gone through a natural and audible change—is somehow transgressive, culturally despoiled. The masculine rock voice is therefore as far removed from the female Welsh folk voice as can be imagined.

Cusick suggests that:

> [o]ne's choices about participation in Song ... can be understood as choices about the relative openness of an orifice. Thinking of the throat as an orifice through which Culture might penetrate the body's borders (and occupy some of its most interior spaces, shaping its potentials for expressivity) illuminates the background cultural practice "women sing, men do not"... .[11]

If the body is a border, the kind of "extraterritorial penetration" Cusick mentions is, to return to an earlier metaphor, linguistic.[12] In attempting to cross over to Anglo-American culture, it was necessary for Mary Hopkin to allow the English language to penetrate her throat, as it were. By assuming a passive cultural position—Welsh deferring to the dominant English—Mary Hopkin was allowed a modicum of success in the Anglo-American market. And this brings us back to Sheila Whiteley, for Mary Hopkin's career was ultimately mediated by Paul McCartney, a dominant English musical presence. Mary Hopkin, sheltered by McCartney's worldly experience, becomes the passive Welsh feminine presence: England's sweetheart.

---

[11]   Ibid., p. 39.

[12]   This is a somewhat problematic construct for the consideration of male Welsh crossovers into the Anglo-American market. I would argue that the male Welsh voice has inscribed in it its own set of codes, and that the adoption of the foreign language is in its own way an act of submission; but I can think of no examples of the successful bilingual (male) Welsh band that does not maintain—and exploit—its 'otherness' within the Anglo-American culture. This, I believe, represents a shift in the balance of power, and it is an idea that I explore further in *"Blerwytirhwng?" The Place of Welsh Popular Music* (Aldershot, 2007).

Mary Hopkin was still in school when she released her first singles on the Cambrian label, many of which, in the spirit of domestication, were cover versions of familiar songs. Among these early singles was "Tro, Tro, Tro," a translation of "Turn! Turn! Turn!,"[13] the song that in 1968 introduced Mary Hopkin to the wider British public on the television show *Opportunity Knocks*.[14] Her first appearance on *Opportunity Knocks* brought her to the attention of Twiggy, who suggested to Paul McCartney that he sign Hopkin to the recently-founded Apple Records label, which he did almost immediately. McCartney suggested a number of songs for Mary Hopkin to record, among them "Those Were the Days," which became a worldwide hit, bumped "Hey Jude" off the number one spot in the UK charts, and helped make Mary Hopkin's first English album, *Post Card*, a commercial success.[15] Mary Hopkin was thus "discovered" in many senses of the word, and accepted by a national British audience: the first successful crossover of a Welsh-language singer.

With Cusick in mind, it should be possible to use Mary Hopkin's career as a blueprint for the development of successive feminine negotiations of Welshness. Given that Mary Hopkin's version of "Turn! Turn! Turn!" was so successful in its time—it was released as the B-side of "Those Were the Days"—it is useful to contrast it with her Welsh recording, if only to highlight the distinctions between the two traditions in which she was active.[16] There are a few important points to note about the Welsh version, originally recorded for Cambrian in 1967 and re-released on Sain in 1996. First of all, Mary Hopkin was seventeen when she made the recording. She had been gigging with a local band for some time, and recorded this song after the band had broken up. She was no doubt familiar with the Byrds' 1965 version of the song, and may perhaps have preferred to pitch her own version somewhat closer to the folk-rock than the folk. The style with which she did record the song bears some relation to the contemporary style of Welsh folk singing (Example 6.1). The parallel passage from 'Turn! Turn! Turn!' reveals a different approach (Example 6.2).

Though it is difficult to quantify such things, it is important to highlight a few basic distinctions between Mary Hopkin's performances in Welsh and English. First, she maintains a much stricter adherence to tempo in the Welsh version. The English version is much freer rhythmically, but I would argue that the Welsh version actually *swings*. It seems to move along much more fluidly, and much more quickly; the English version seems lumbered down by its own vowels. Granted,

---

[13] "Turn! Turn! Turn!" music by Pete Seeger, lyrics taken from the book of Ecclesiastes. Though many versions were recorded in the 1960s, it is perhaps best known by the Byrds' 1965 recording. Rereleased on Mary Hopkin, *The Early Recordings* (Sain SCD 2151E, 1996).

[14] *Opportunity Knocks* was an ITV television talent show hosted by Hughie Green, and could be considered the forerunner to current "instant fame" shows such as *Pop Idol*.

[15] Mary Hopkin, *Post Card* (Apple St-3351, 1969).

[16] I owe a debt of gratitude to Robert Burke for assuming the burden of transcription for me here.

Example 6.1 "Tro, Tro, Tro" (Pete Seeger): Mary Hopkin [Cambrian CEP414, 1967], opening phrase

Example 6.2 "Turn! Turn! Turn!" (Pete Seeger): Mary Hopkin [Apple 2, 1968], opening phrase

Welsh here holds a fundamental linguistic advantage over English: the word "tro," with the long "o," is much more conducive to the swing feeling than the more awkward English "turn." Even singing with a Welsh accent, that unforgiving "ur" rather puts a damper on the refrain. The differences in accompanying guitar patterns are also interesting to note. While neither departs from its initial arpeggiated pattern, the Welsh version maintains a straight-eighth pattern, providing a forward propulsion; the 3+3+2 pattern in the English version, while potentially lending the performance rhythmic interest, when paired with Hopkin's almost obscene *rubato*, causes it to lose all momentum.

But the more important distinctions to note here are performative. The listener would note immediately a distinction in production. First, the Welsh version sounds much more vibrant, more resonant with what one assumes is the chapel in which the performance was recorded; the English version is dampened by studio walls and filters.[17] Mary Hopkin's voice soars in the Welsh version with a kind of grace not captured on the English version, tempting one to infer that the home environment allowed her a type of vocal comfort, which the foreign environment did not. Second, the Welsh version retains something of a learned interpretation, and this is apparent in her voice. Welsh popular music was nurtured in the chapel, the chapel was one of the primary locations for the performance of early Welsh popular music, and the subject matter and instrumentation were limited by that location. The same is true of the method of singing. The Welsh chapel informed all manner of popular song, from the traditional, to folk, through skiffle, well into the 1970s.[18] Words were always paramount to personal inflection, and songs—of whatever kind—were generally unadorned, save for a rather fast and unassuming kind of vibrato. A very sweet type of vocal production, for lack of a better word, can therefore be interpreted as evolving from the chapel tradition, and regardless of musical genre—from folk to pop—that type of vocal production rarely altered. It was, in Cusick's words, the cultural norm intelligible to the cohort of Welsh speakers. When a singer—of either gender—moved from one genre to another within the framework of Welsh popular music, the application of that particular vocal quality was perfectly natural, perfectly understood, *within the culture*; when this genre shift happened in tandem with a shift into Anglophone culture, that otherness of style prevented the completely successful crossover *into the foreign, Anglo-American, culture*. That is, a singer such as Mary Hopkin may have succeeded in the Anglo-American market, but the musical tradition which had informed her manner of singing forever relegated her, in the ears of the wider Anglophone public, to the categories "folk," "sweet," and "Welsh." Sheila Whiteley's phrase "England's sweetheart" now has a particularly patronizing overtone to it.

Moving beyond the musical, in order to interpret Mary Hopkin's projected image it is informative to consider the iconography of early Welsh pop. The year

---

[17]   The state of the Welsh recording industry in the mid-1960s did not allow for advanced studio technology. Many, if not most, of the seminal recordings of the Welsh pop canon were recorded either in chapel vestries or town halls.

[18]   That is to say, all manner of popular song—traditional, folk, and skiffle—would have been performed in chapel vestries, though listening now to early recordings by close-harmony groups such as Hogia Llandegai and Hogia'r Wyddfa, their attempts at skiffle fall somewhat closer to the light entertainment mark than the alternative 50s rock and roll sound of their contemporary, Lonnie Donegan.

172   SHE'S SO FINE

1969 was saw a number of significant events in Wales: the investiture of Charles as Prince of Wales took place at Caernarfon Castle amid much local protest; the first independent Welsh record label, Sain, founded; and the first Welsh pop magazine began its initial run. That magazine, *Asbri*,[19] had on its first cover a picture of the singer and Sain founder, Dafydd Iwan; the second issue had on its cover a picture of Mary Hopkin (Figure 6.1). In this picture she is demure, looking away from the camera, dressed very conservatively, her hair pulled neatly into two ponytails. By way of contrast, a contemporary cover of *Rolling Stone* magazine shows Janis Joplin in a rather typical pose, the vision of late-60s hedonism.[20] It is important to contrast these two images, not to suggest any inherent inadequacies in Welsh pop, but to highlight the different criteria by which they were celebrated. Not only was 1969 the year of the founding of Sain, of the publication of *Asbri*, but it was also the year of Woodstock, of Altamont; it was two years after the Summer of Love, the first issue of *Rolling Stone* and the release of *Sgt. Pepper*; the Beatles were breaking up and heavy metal was around the corner. Why celebrate Mary Hopkin?

First of all, that picture of Mary Hopkin on the cover of *Asbri* is more complicated than it appears. It is an image of youthful innocence; it is an acknowledgment of her successful crossover from Welsh to English; and it is a territorial means by which the Welsh audience could contain Mary Hopkin in the wake of her growing fame, of keeping her Welsh, familiar, "in the home." It was a means of highlighting her innocent nature, of keeping her in her (cultural) place, of denying her pop star status. To emphasize this, the accompanying article in the second issue of *Asbri* is not an interview with Mary Hopkin herself, but rather a series of remembrances of Mary Hopkin, written by her childhood friend, Menna Elfyn, who subsequently became a noted poet. Whether in an effort to embarrass the poor pop star or just to keep her grounded in the world of Eisteddfodau and the Welsh League of Youth, the picture incorporated into the article shows Mary Hopkin *as the Welsh want her to be remembered* (Figure 6.2). This is no "local girl makes good," no "local girl hangs out with the Beatles"; this is "local girl used to dress up in national costume and win chapel singing competitions." Those were the days, indeed.

Volumes have been written about the Welsh national dress and the invention of tradition.[21] What is important here is the equation of the *image* of Welshness with the *sound* of Welshness. How Welsh was Mary Hopkin? According to the pictures in Asbri, for the Welsh audience, she was Welsh enough never to have submitted

---

[19]   Literally, "vivacity."

[20]   Mary Hopkin's dress and demeanor on the cover of *Asbri* calls to mind the character of Dorothy in *The Wizard of Oz*, but it is certainly a coincidence that the picture of Janis Joplin on the cover of *Rolling Stone* 29 (March 15, 1969) is accompanied by the strapline, "A Report on Janis Joplin: The Judy Garland of Rock?"

[21]   In particular, see Prys Morgan, "From a Death to a View: The Hunt for the Welsh Past in the Romantic Period," in Eric Hobsbawm and Terence Ranger (eds), *The Invention of Tradition* (Cambridge, 2000).

Figure 6.1   Mary Hopkin, cover girl (published in the second issue of *Asbri*, 1969)

Figure 6.2   "School Days": Mary Hopkin, second from right (published in the second issue of *Asbri*, 1969)

to the English language; her throat had not been penetrated; she was *essentially* Welsh. But beyond the borders of Wales, how was that Welshness received? In an era of ethereal soprano voices, what distinguished Mary Hopkin from other British singers in the 1960s? And how much control did she have over the way her voice was used?

It has been well documented that Mary Hopkin was not overly fond of some of the songs Paul McCartney suggested she record for *Post Card*, and that some of his choices were made in order to emphasize the particular quality of her voice that had been cultivated back in Wales.[22] This touches on the notion of being "passively Welsh." Perhaps because of her age, perhaps because of her nature, perhaps because of her relative lack of cultural capital, Mary Hopkin's early Anglophone career was controlled by someone whose musical taste was not always beyond reproach. Indeed, the direction in which Paul McCartney sent Mary Hopkin was as surprising as it was occasionally embarrassing. To take an obvious example, although "Those Were the Days" sold in its millions, in retrospect it is a song singularly unsuitable for a young woman of nineteen. The lyrics alone are telling: "Once upon a time there was a tavern / Where we used to raise a glass or two / Remember how we laughed away the hours / Think of all the great things we would do. / Those were the days my friend, we thought they'd never end / We'd sing and dance for ever and a day / We'd live the life we'd choose / we'd fight and never lose / For we were young and sure to have our way."[23]

Significantly, Sandie Shaw released her own version of the song at exactly the same time as Mary Hopkin. This might suggest that it was bound to be a hit for someone, but it seems an odd coincidence nonetheless. Two young women singing a song about lost time and lost hopes and, heaven forbid, going to taverns to drink—the kind of nostalgia pervading the song would seem to be for lost youth.[24] But both versions were released in 1969, the end of a momentous decade, the middle of a protracted and controversial military conflict, the cusp of a new musical era. To Paul McCartney's ears, and to the ears of millions of other people, Mary Hopkin's was a voice simply dripping with innocence, reminiscent of a simpler time, of old-fashioned music, just like the stuff they must sing over there in Wales. In her recording, she expresses all that regret, with a voice itself steeped in nostalgia—but a nostalgia born of uncounted years of subservience to the English

---

[22]   See in particular Mark Lewisohn's interview with Mary Hopkin in *Record Collector* 108 (August 1988).

[23]   "Those Were the Days," lyrics by Gene Raskin.

[24]   An important parallel to make here is Fairport Convention's recording of 'Who Knows Where the Time Goes?' from *Unhalfbricking* (Water Music Records, 1969; Island Records (CD) UICY-9320, 2003). When she wrote the song, singer Sandy Denny was not much older than Mary Hopkin, and the sense of lost youth, of regret and nostalgia, is just as powerful in that song. While it is tempting to interpret all such contemporary songs as reflecting the political and social uncertainties of the time, it is enough here to note the two singers' similarities of vocal range and affect, though shaped by different cultural influences.

state; a nostalgia for a different way of life; a nostalgia for a language on the verge of extinction. Nostalgia is purely subjective, of course, but given certain earlier metaphors, I feel it must be stated that the recording of Mary Hopkin singing "Those Were the Days" was undoubtedly heard differently in Wales than it was in England.

So here we have a young singer being groomed for success by one of the most successful songwriters in pop history; yet *Post Card* is really a missed opportunity. Paul McCartney could have written a song for the album, perhaps tried to move Mary Hopkin in the direction of contemporary folk-rock, if not a bit further; but he filled the album with show tunes and pop standards. With the exception of two tracks written for her by Donovan, the songs on *Post Card* were cover versions of songs McCartney knew and loved, with the token Welsh-language song added for a touch of the down-home. Despite its lack of stylistic continuity, *Post Card* was, surprisingly, reviewed favorably in *Rolling Stone*.[25] Though not entirely enamored of Mary Hopkin's voice—"Mary's voice, a smooth vanilla soprano, isn't going to win an MBE for its flexibility (she seems to lack the inclination or technique to express different feelings through different vocal nuances, and winds up sounding like a hybrid of mechanical Joan Baezes and Marianne Faithfull)"—reviewer John Mendelsohn nonetheless gives "imaginative producer" Paul McCartney full marks for creating an "ambitious exploration of the Pop medium." Mendelsohn appreciates Hopkin's suitability to the album's Donovan tracks, though the songs themselves tend to be "ponderous and over-long." Most problematically, however, Mendelsohn states that "[e]thnic balladry is represented by 'Y Blodyn Gwyn' (which is Welsh and sounds like a hymn)," and applauds McCartney's choice of "revived late-Forties-type numbers":

> "Those Were the Days" is, of course, a knock-out (particularly the banjo, little kids' chorus, and Mary's pose as a dowdy and discarded old pub lady), and what better ending could such a program have than Irving Berlin's "Show Business" ("there's no business like …")? Paul should win some sort of award for his choice of what Mary would sing and for what he has happening behind her singing.

As an indication of the cultural capital that the Beatles obviously had in 1969, Mendelsohn's review ends by practically ignoring the artist at hand: "An absolute must for Paul McCartney people, Mary Hopkin fans will also like it." In other words: Mary Hopkin, accessory.

Considering *Post Card* at a 35-year distance and from a purely aesthetic standpoint, it is anyone's guess what "Y Blodyn Gwyn" ("The White Flower") and "There's No Business Like Show Business" had in common. It certainly remains a mystery why Paul McCartney felt that Mary Hopkin could out-sing Ethel Merman on the latter. And no matter what people *think* Mary Hopkin listened to in her spare time, chances are that, as a young woman of nineteen newly relocated to London,

---

[25] John Mendelsohn, "Mary Hopkin: *Post Card*," *Rolling Stone*, May 17, 1969.

176   *SHE'S SO FINE*

it wasn't "Inch Worm." Nonetheless, the music needed to match the image, and the image was imposed by the industry: passively female, passively Welsh.[26]

By the time Mary Hopkin crossed over, one "other" Welsh female voice had already stated her sense of entitlement to the Anglo-American audience. Shirley Bassey's position in Welsh popular culture is problematic on a number of levels: she came from a large family on the rougher side of Cardiff; her father was a Nigerian seaman; she is unabashedly flash, the mark of the Anglo-American reward culture, the antithesis of the reserved and unassuming Welsh culture.[27] Her voice carries with it an openness of experience or, in Cusick's terminology, her throat has been penetrated: her vibrato is as wide as the Bristol Channel, all sense of subtlety hidden in its depths. She wears her Welshness proudly[28] and the Welsh audience embraces her; but, like Mary Hopkin, Shirley Bassey's otherness is acute. Not only is her voice forceful and deep, it is not a late-1960s pop voice. Shirley Bassey's voice would have been the more appropriate vehicle for some of the material Paul McCartney chose for *Post Card*: capable of cabaret numbers as well as Broadway standards, capable of inflecting world-weariness and irony into even the most trite of nostalgic lyrics, and capable of meeting the metaphorical gaze of

---

[26] There is another connection to be drawn here between Mary Hopkin and Sandy Denny of Fairport Convention. By some accounts the image Sandy Denny portrayed in the press was in some contrast to her actual nature: while she was often pictured wearing conservative, "feminine" clothes, her penchant for heavy drinking and her complicated personal life were perhaps not as well known to the folk-rock audience who may have imposed upon her an interior life more in keeping with the sweetness of her voice. Sandy Denny's effective duet with Robert Plant on "The Ballad of Evermore," from *Led Zeppelin IV* (Atlantic, 1971; Atlantic (CD) 7567826385, 2003), offers another dimension to her voice, perhaps more reflective of her actual life, and the distance between folk-rock and hard rock (or "cock rock") is lessened considerably as a result. Listening to "The Ballad of Evermore," in fact, one is reminded of Grace Slick from the Jefferson Airplane, whose similarly intriguing personal life contrasted sharply with her external feminine image. All this suggests that women in Anglo-American culture were better able to assert their individuality than their Welsh counterparts, and that the era of sexual liberation had not quite filtered through to the Welsh-speaking community, whether in Wales or elsewhere.

[27] Shirley Bassey recorded her debut single, "The Banana Boat Song," in 1957, when she was 20 years old. She had left school to work at a factory, but left for London to pursue fame. Early singles played on a kind of knowing sexuality: "Kiss Me, Honey, Kiss Me," "As I Love You," "As Long as He Needs Me"; but it was the release of the title track to the 1964 film *Goldfinger* that established her reputation on both sides of the Atlantic. A cursory listen to the opening verse alone is enough to hear the determination, grit and self-confidence that so contrasts with contemporary Welsh-language recordings in general, and Mary Hopkin in particular.

[28] Sometimes literally so. At the outdoor concert held in Cardiff Bay to celebrate devolution, Shirley Bassey appeared onstage wearing the Welsh flag, the red dragon adorned lavishly with sequins.

MARY HOPKIN AND THE DEEP THROAT OF CULTURE

the dominant English culture with defiance and sexual confidence. Capable of, in other words, definitively subverting the Welsh stereotype.

The Welsh stereotype was, of course, alive and well in the late 1960s British media, and Mary Hopkin was its embodiment. But the discomfort Mary Hopkin felt with her public—and musical—persona is palpable, and exploited, in a clip from the BBC television show *24 Hours*, broadcast on the eve of the 1970 Eurovision Song Contest.[29] Eighteen months after her success on *Opportunity Knocks*, Mary Hopkin was chosen to perform the British entry, "Knock, Knock, Who's There?", and was duly presented to the British television public, yet again, as "the shy Welsh girl." This item lasts about ten minutes, and only once is any mention made of the British Eurovision entry; the more interesting story seems to be how simple and unassuming Mary Hopkin is, how sweet and naive, and how many times a day she used to go to chapel. This was the image thrust upon Mary Hopkin; however true some elements of it might have been, however shy she may have been, it did not allow for her to express an opinion, or to develop musically; the passive stereotype. The *24 Hours* exposé exposed little more than unfortunate cultural sterotyping:

[In the background, "Turn! Turn! Turn!" We see Mary walking through London.]

Voiceover: *Mary Hopkin walked from school to stardom without changing pace, personality or hairstyle. She's Welsh, shy and protected by a cast-iron innocence that brought her childhood dolls from a council house to the London Palladium. She's prim as a Welsh Sunday, and as her grandmother Blodwen says, "show business can't change a good chapel upbringing." She sings more than she speaks. Show business lightning struck Mary Hopkin eighteen months ago, when Beatle Paul McCartney heard her sing, brought her to London and rapidly called a tune to the first of three hits. [...]*

[cut to clip from *Opportunity Knocks*, and interior, with Hughie Green]

Hughie Green, what is it about [Mary's] voice that had star quality and such appeal?

HG: Well I think one of the main things is it's a plaintive voice, and I think as far as Mary herself is concerned, she is recognizable as the girl next door with a lovely voice.

How much of a fluke was it in the first place that opportunity knocked for Mary Hopkin?

---

[29] *24 Hours* (BBC, March 20, 1970). Mary Hopkin ultimately came in second in the Eurovision Song Contest, behind the Irish singer, Dana. Amongst her fellow competitors was a surprisingly young and sweaty Julio Iglesias, who finished fourth.

HG: Well I … can tell you that on this very same tape here, David, we recorded two other girls who were on a par with Mary as far as talent was concerned. And to a certain extent we needed someone from Wales, and it was out of the three girls and we didn't know which one really was the best. And the other two boys and myself, we said, "ok, we'll take Mary." And of course then her next good piece of luck was Twiggy.

[Twiggy is interviewed about her postcard campaign for Mary Hopkin. The voiceover returns]

With the Beatles' Apple organization pulling the strings, Mary slipped into stardom easily and coolly. A girl simply starting a new job, she'd insist. It brought her up to £1000 a week. She bought herself a dog, called Barnabus. She couldn't think of much else to buy. She's made no concessions to the pop industry and its people, who know her as an isolated girl and hardly one of their own.

[cut to exterior shots of Pontardawe]

Mary was born and brought up in the Welsh-speaking town of Pontardawe near Swansea, where singing is a way of life. She's the daughter of the town's housing officer and has two elder sisters. Her parents still live in Pontardawe, where it's fashionable to claim to be Mary Hopkin's cousin, and where Mary first played her guitar at Eisteddfods—and never won a prize.

[cut to interior, flat. Mary Hopkin sitting on sofa facing the interviewer.]

Mary, it's a long, long way from that Welsh valley to this beautiful house in Maida Vale where you're now living. But could you start by telling me a little bit about your childhood in Wales. Tell me what of a typical Sunday. How did it go?

MH: Well usually I went to chapel about once every Sunday. It was the thing to do, you know. [exterior of chapel looming overhead] Um, a lot of my friends went three times every Sunday, so every Sunday is taken up with chapel.

What about Sundays now? Do you go to church here?

MH: Um, no, I'm even lazier now I think. I just laze around all day or go out. If it's a fine day I'll go for a walk or something.

Well do you think you've changed, if in Wales you went to chapel two, three times a day? And now you're in London—it's only eighteen months later, and you don't go at all. Is it you that's changed?

MH: Um, no. It might be because there's nobody here to tell me you ought to go to church. Because when you're that age you sort of have—you're sort of told you've got to go at that time, and then later on you just decide for yourself.

Well, you're in London now. You're nineteen. You've got fame, you've got fortune, full of what every nineteen-year-old girl dreams about. What's it like for you?

MH: It's nice to be famous, but I don't like sort of other people looking up to me, because there's no reason for that. It's lovely to hear from people, though, and have letters and things.

Mary Hopkin was by this point fully integrated into Anglo-American culture, yet it is clear from her Eurovision appearance that her voice was on the cusp of a real change. Having allowed English to assume the dominant role in her musical life, Mary Hopkin was poised to explore the possibilities of an Anglophone Welsh pop voice in the mainstream market. But following the release of her second album, *Earth Song/Ocean Song*, in 1971, Mary Hopkin left Apple Records and married American producer Tony Visconti. Her primary concern in the ensuing years was raising her family. She did, however, make an appearance on David Bowie's *Low*(1977), singing backing vocals on the track "Sound and Vision." While this might be considered "crossing over,"[30] it took a husband with influential contacts (and a production credit) to enable it to happen; and on an album notoriously light

---

[30]   This "crossing over" problem for female Welsh-language singers has been encountered more than once in the decades since Mary Hopkin released *Post Card*. In the mid-1970s Heather Jones attempted a similar transition from folk to rock, and Welsh light entertainment mainstay Caryl Parry Jones attempted different vocal styles to suit different genres—folk, rock, and even disco—all in the Welsh language. In contrast to Mary Hopkin, both of these women suffered from excessive prior exposure to the Welsh pop audience. For years they were known for a particular style of singing—acoustic folk—at a time when Welsh popular music was only beginning its halting steps toward amplification. When they attempted to change their musical image, to sing with predominantly male bands, they were generally kept in their place by the Welsh press. This could mean poor record reviews, but it also occasionally meant the public dissection of the singer's private life. In much the same way that in the 1970s Joni Mitchell's private life became more interesting to *Rolling Stone* than her recordings, the Welsh press perhaps felt threatened by a previously "harmless" folk singer asserting herself in a more masculine, newly rock context. It was not until the 1980s that the first "natural" female rock voice was cultivated in the Welsh language. By way of contrast, Rhiannon Tomos had not been a member of any earlier group—indeed, she had seemingly emerged from nowhere—and therefore had the benefit of not being associated with a particular sound or style of singing. She was viewed as a type of Welsh pop vanguard, although of course by that time the forceful female voice was a central and uncontested component of many notable Anglo-American pop groups. More particularly, because Rhiannon Tomos did not emerge from any obvious Welsh pop background, her own vocal delivery bore the distinct influence of earlier American singers such as Janis

180 *SHE'S SO FINE*

on lyrics, one would be forgiven for not recognizing Mary Hopkin in the mix.[31] In retrospect this did ultimately loosen the "shy Welsh girl" ties that bound her, and more importantly, it allowed Mary Hopkin's voice to be used without the burden of imposed cultural baggage.

Mary Hopkin's voice signifies a particular point in Welsh musical life, a referent embraced by subsequent generations of musicians, left determinedly unrecognized in mainstream Anglo-American culture. Her occasional comeback gestures—appearing on the Future Sound of London's *Dead Cities* (Virgin, 1996), in Sara Sugarman's 2000 film *Very Annie-Mary* and, perhaps most improbably, collaborating on Dolly Parton's 2006 EMI release, *Those Were the Days* (Sugar Hill Records 4007)—suggest a certain cultural currency, yet oddly returning her to her late-1960s incarnation. There is a particular place in Welsh culture reserved for Mary Hopkin, the local crossover success, but despite her many and varied experiences of these last forty years, she is still the unchanged girl on that *Asbri* cover, the local girl whose career—despite *Opportunity Knocks*, the Eurovision Song Contest, the Beatles, Donovan, Tony Visconti, David Bowie and Dolly Parton—remains *essentially* Welsh.

Joplin, thus allying her much more closely with the Anglo-American tradition than with the Welsh.

[31]   Mary Hopkin can be heard from 1:14–1:21; it should also be noted that she is credited on the *Low* liner notes as "Mary Visconti."

PART III
Girls on Top: Rock Chicks and Resistance at the End of the 60s

Chapter 7

Whose Tears Go By? Marianne Faithfull at the Dawn and Twilight of Rock Culture

Norma Coates

> It wasn't until Hazelden some fifteen years later when I first realized that during the time I was with Mick I had no history of my own. As part of the program, everyone tells her story. I was at a loss what to say and so I called my press agent and asked her to send down by post a copy of Spanish Tony's book, *Up and Down with the Rolling Stones*. I basically said to them, "You want my story? Read that." Because in those days I really didn't know I had a story of my own. I was just part of <u>their</u> story and I saw my own only through these books.[1]

Marianne Faithfull's account of the difficulty of telling her story during her first days in a 12-Step program while at the Hazelden Clinic in Minnesota in 1985 can be read as a metaphor for "women in rock" in the 1960s, at the actual time and in popular memory. What was a vibrant time for female pop artists, before, during, and even after the British Invasion is obscured by the masculine narratives that fuel what critic Philip Auslander calls "the rock imaginary" constructed in the late 1960s.[2] When the stories of female pop performers of the 60s are told, and until the past few years they have not been, their success or fame is frequently tied to the exertions of men: for example, the Ronettes and Phil Spector; the Supremes and Berry Gordy; the Shangri-Las and Shadow Morton; Cilla Black and Brian Epstein; Grace Slick and the other members of Jefferson Airplane, and Marianne Faithfull and the Rolling Stones, especially Mick Jagger.[3]

Over 40 years later, Faithfull and the Stones are still tied together, but now to the benefit of both. Improbably, given Faithfull's and Keith Richards's histories

---

[1]   Marianne Faithfull with David Dalton, *Faithfull: An Autobiography* (Boston, 1994), p. 268.

[2]   Philip Auslander, "Watch That Man. David Bowie: Hammersmith Odeon, London, July 3, 1973," in Ian Inglis (ed.), *Performance and Popular Music: History, Place and Time*, (Aldershot, 2006), p. 72.

[3]   There are exceptions to this statement, of course: Janis Joplin immediately springs to mind, as does Aretha Franklin. Even so, Joplin, given the circumstances of her untimely death, is often perceived as "poor Janis." Aretha Franklin is designated as a rock singer only when it suits the needs of the person writing about her. Her name is often coupled with that of Jerry Wexler, the Atlantic Records executive who "rescued" her from the middle-of-the-road mediocrity of her Columbia Records contract.

of drug abuse, and the impact of the passage of time in a genre associated, for better or worse, with youth, Faithfull and the Stones are two of the few 60s artists still recording and performing on a regular basis. The Stones are less overtly tied to Faithfull in press and television accounts of the supremely orchestrated, well-promoted, massively staged and wildly successful world tours that they embark upon every few years. Even so, the personae and rock authenticity of these aging multimillionaires is dependent upon their ability to conjure up their "lurid" and decadent past in the minds of fans and potential audiences. The specter of "fallen Marianne," constructed as the pop-singing beauty destroyed by trying to fly too close to the sun that was the Stones, combined with notable moments in the group's late 60s saga, including Altamont and the mysterious death of original Stone Brian Jones, invokes the mythological Rolling Stones, not the group of today who are, in the words of critic John Strausbaugh, more like a Stones cover band.[4]

Strausbaugh further locates the Stones' enduring appeal in the draw of "empty nostalgia" amongst the baby boom generation, a longing for the Stones of the past as well as their own past.[5] Strausbaugh does not address the group's appeal to generations born long after their heyday, but that, too, is a nostalgic longing to have "been there" at rock's creation myth and a connection to an era increasingly remote in sensibility as well as cultural history. The source of the Stones' appeal to younger fans is complicated; indeed the affective call of 60s rock to young people, especially young men, is worthy of a study unto itself, which I will not pursue here. Many young people grow up hearing and embracing, to an extent, their baby boomer parents' music. The chance to see a band from that era, possibly as a family event, likely accounts for some of their interest in the Stones.

The Stones' appeal, to youth as well as older audiences, may rely on an inflection of what media critic David Shumway calls "commodified nostalgia," a reference to the use of rock and roll music in certain films in order to encourage consumption as well as to create a sense of generational solidarity.[6] To existing audiences, the chance to consume the Stones in a myriad number of ways, including the purchase of commodities associated with them, is a chance to reconnect with their pasts, perhaps as an affective escape from their present.[7] For younger audiences, coming of age in an era of fragmentation, the opportunity to consume the Stones enables them also to consume the myths and the period of time that the group most represents, as well as an opportunity to "experience" a sense of generational

---

[4]   John Strausbaugh, *Rock 'Til You Drop: The Decline from Rebellion to Nostalgia* (London, 2001), p. 61.

[5]   Ibid., p. 78.

[6]   David R. Shumway, "Rock 'n' Roll Soundtracks and the Production of Nostalgia," *Cinema Journal* 38/2 (Winter 1999): pp. 36–51.

[7]   For example, the US promotion of the 2005–06 *A Bigger Bang* tour included, among other things: a sponsorship agreement with the National Football League; an appearance during the Superbowl half-time show; sponsorship agreements with Ameriquest Mortgages, Mercedes-Benz, and Sprint-Nextel.

solidarity that is no longer available. By denying or downplaying their advancing years, the Stones trade on nostalgia to re-inscribe their authenticity by encasing their 60s and early 70s selves, and the mythology about them, in amber. Their sound and attitude has changed little since the early 1970s; Jagger still prances around the stage like a man half his age, ignoring the fact that his act could collapse into parody at any moment.

Rare is the review or article about Marianne Faithfull that does not mention her connection to the Stones or her descent into drugs, addiction, and homelessness after she left their orbit. Even so, or because of this, Faithfull acquires more authenticity, as the term registers in rock culture, with every new release. Faithfull uses the 60s as much as the Stones do, but in an active way, as material. She mines her mystique and the era but her sound is not mired in it. Faithfull's 60s, and her subsequent story, enable her to play an evolving role that in some ways mirrors the relationship of women in general to rock music since that period. Over 60 years old, Faithfull is usually categorized as an "indie rocker" even though she frequently ventures out of the rock mode altogether, into Weimar cabaret, Kurt Weill, and, most recently, French pop of the 1960s. Two of her most recent recordings were collaborations with some of the leading lights of indie rock, primarily male with one notable exception, Polly Jean Harvey. Faithfull's work is reviewed and discussed on alternative hipster websites like *Pitchfork* (www.pitchforkmedia.com). She wears the mantle of authenticity despite her pop princess past, and her propensity to prefer interpreting the songs of others over writing her own (although she usually contributes a few songs to each new recording). Her link to the Stones and their conjoined pasts is made explicit in most articles about her, a practice that she claims to bother her but that she uses and indeed encourages.[8] It may be surmised that fans, especially younger fans, are initially attracted to her primarily because of her legend and—whether they know it or not—her connection to the Stones, and, secondarily, because of her younger collaborators. They stay because of her emotionally resonant and stylistically unique music that works as indie rock on a conceptual level if not always on a formal level.

Faithfull and the Stones remain relevant to current rock culture in other important ways. Arguably, "rock culture" is no longer what it used to be. Its referent, rock music, has fragmented into a vast number of genres and micro-genres. Rock music is no longer the default music of the young; that mantle would likely go to hip-hop, if it is to go anywhere at all. Even so, the idea of rock culture as it was defined by, and in, the 1960s remains important more as an ideal of what rock music did or more realistically, could, represent. Crucially, it also anchors rock mythologies as well as rock ideologies, especially those that construct rock and rock culture as white heterosexual male spaces. In turn, rock continues to signify in these ways in the larger realm of popular culture and commerce. The continued presence and reiteration of stories about Faithfull and the Stones

---

[8]   Approximately 200 pages of Faithfull's 295-page autobiography are devoted to her time in the Stones' inner circle.

in the 1960s signal rock, and its original Baby Boom audience, as an important cultural force even as the power of both wanes.

Rock culture and music, I argue, originally coalesced in the image of the Rolling Stones, especially Jagger. Stones biographer Steven Davis asserts that the Stones were writing and performing "proto-rock" songs as early as 1966.[9] That year also marks the emergence of rock journalism in the US, a foundational moment of rock culture. By this means, rock performers, not just their work, became objects of serious interest and discussion. Rock journalism was different than music trade journalism, in that it did more than report releases, change of management, and chart position. Early rock journals also opposed themselves to "teen idol" magazines, which were targeted to teenage girls and perceived as being filled with superficial and objectifying "information" about stars fed to the magazines by their publicists. Rock criticism purported to be more serious and probing in their coverage and creation of nascent rock culture.

At the same time, rock journalism helped to write contemporary norms for gender, race, and sexuality into rock culture and rock discourse. For example, historian Lisa Rhodes, in her recent study of women in rock culture in the late 1960s and early 1970s, attests that while she expected *Rolling Stone* magazine to reflect pre-Women's Liberation movement attitudes, she was surprised at the level of misogyny toward women expressed in the journal. She further observes that "the male writers at *Rolling Stone* wrote about women musicians much as their older generation, ideological 'enemies' at the "mainstream" magazines did."[10] *Rolling Stone*-style journalism may be discredited in academic circles, but it contributed greatly to the mainstream understanding of rock and rock culture of the late 1960s and early 1970s. Moreover, rock journalism, in large part because of normative ideologies that informed it, often mirrored the discourses about gender and sexuality in the mainstream press.

Magazines like *Rolling Stone*, by publishing in-depth interviews and articles about musicians, elevated them to role of spokesmen (gender intentional) for the counterculture. The rock star emerged, in part, out of this writing. Mick Jagger, because of the importance of the Stones to emerging rock culture, was arguably the first rock star and the prototype for those to follow. Jagger was charismatic, flamed the desires of both sexes, lived an increasingly flashy lifestyle, and dated the most beautiful woman on the pop scene, singer Marianne Faithfull. In Jagger's image, the rock star was a crucial part of the construction of rock as a "white, heterosexual male imaginary."[11] Indeed, the relationship with Faithfull defused his provocatively ambiguous public sexuality, moving the perception of it from the negatively-charged "deviant" to the more positive "decadent."

---

[9]   Stephan Davis, *Old Gods Almost Dead: The 40-Year Odyssey of the Rolling Stones* (New York, 2001), p. 160.

[10]   Lisa L. Rhodes, *Electric Ladyland: Women and Rock Culture* (Philadelphia, 2005), p. xiii.

[11]   Auslander, "Watch That Man," p. 72.

In the remainder of this essay, I discuss the interaction between Faithfull and the Stones in the late 1960s and the impact of their engagement on gender perceptions in rock culture. I employ the concept of the persona from performance studies to highlight the performative nature of gender in rock, arguing that the story of Marianne Faithfull assisted in "heterosexualizing" Jagger and the Stones, thus submerging the homosocial aspects of rock performance and reception. I conclude by considering how the stories about Faithfull and the Stones in the 1960s have helped them maintain their careers, suggesting that in Faithfull's case, they have enabled her and other "women in rock" to carve out a space for themselves within discourses of authenticity.

The link between Faithfull and the Stones was forged two years before Faithfull and Mick Jagger became a couple. In 1964, the seventeen-year-old Faithfull attended a party at the home of Stones' manager Andrew Loog Oldham with her boyfriend, later husband, John Dunbar. Oldham was a very young publicist whose genius lay in the creation and manipulation of image, pioneering what is now a common and necessary practice across the spectrum of popular culture. Oldham's oft-repeated line (especially by himself) about first setting eyes on Faithfull, "I saw an Angel with big tits and signed her," exemplifies his focus on image as well as his intuition about what type of female image was desirable—and saleable—in the pop world.[12] Another story from the first meeting is representative of normative gender relations of the era, even amongst the "hipeoisie," and the silencing of female voices, literally and figuratively, that would follow as pop turned into more serious "rock" later in the decade. As Faithfull recollects in her autobiography:

> I was sitting on the heater next to John [Dunbar] when I noticed this strange creature, all beaky and angular like some bird of prey, *lunge* toward me. He looked powerful and dangerous and very sure of himself. I was glad when, at the last minute, he spun around and with his back to me addressed John: Who *is* she? Can she *act*? What's 'er name? ... Andrew asked, almost as an afterthought, Can she *sing*? John: I think she can, why the hell not? You can sing, can't you, Marianne? And that was that.[13]

The next time Faithfull heard from Oldham was a week later when he phoned her and told her to come to Olympic Studios in London, where he'd booked time, presumably without hearing her sing, to record her first single. Apparently, Oldham did not care whether Faithfull had any true singing talent or not. What was important was that she was stunningly beautiful in a way that registered as particularly English, and that she fit the marketable image he'd designed for her. These things would haunt her, as she would not be recognized for her talent during her first career, but first for her beauty and second for her link to the Stones, specifically Jagger. Oldham's discovery, promotion, and crafted persona for

---

[12] Faithfull with Dalton, p. 21.

[13] Ibid.

Faithfull had nothing to do with her vocal talent and everything to do with her look, thus underscoring the hegemony of the male gaze in a medium in which the visual was important yet not necessarily the primary source of pleasure. Indeed, female performers were arguably judged more for their looks than for their music; the ample use of close-ups of white female performers on television programs of the period emphasized their looks, while full shots of male bands emphasized their literal performance, thus enacting the construction of the active male versus passive female binary that worked to marginalize women in pop and rock, or at least to keep them bounded in a specific area. White female performers were constructed as decorative singers; a direct contrast to active male musicians.[14] Moreover, female singers of the era primarily interpreted songs written by others, a practice at odds with the ideology of authenticity in rock that developed in the late 1960s.

At that initial session, motivated by the image he devised for her, Oldham first had Faithfull attempt a song by musical theater composer Lionel Bart (who would soon go on to compose the music for *Oliver*). Faithfull could not deliver the song, so Oldham had her try something else, "As Tears Go By," the first composition by the songwriting team of Mick Jagger and Keith Richards of his marquee band, the Rolling Stones. At this point in mid-1964, the Stones were still primarily performing covers of Chicago blues. Their great success with that repertoire, combined with his keen instincts, convinced Oldham to encourage Jagger and Richards to write their own songs, rights ownership being the most guaranteed way to make money in the record industry. Oldham allegedly gave his fledgling songwriting team these orders: "I want a song with brick walls all around it, and high windows and no sex."[15] Jagger and Richard followed these instructions perhaps too well, in Faithfull's analysis: "'As Tears Go By' was a marketable portrait of me and as such is an extremely ingenious creation, a commercial fantasy that pushes all the right buttons. It did such a good job of imprinting that it was to become an indelible part of my media-conjured self for the next fifteen years."[16]

Faithfull's observations are insightful. Oldham's image of Faithfull, reinforced in publicity photos and articles as well as the folk-pop songs he and later manager Tony Calder selected for her, became the persona "Marianne Faithfull." According to performance studies scholar Philip Auslander, the persona is neither a fictional character nor a "real" identity; rather, the persona is the performer's self-presentation.[17] Auslander also suggests that in the ideology of 60s rock,

---

[14] Certain African American performers, particularly Tina Turner, were afforded less restrictive movements on camera, the juxtaposition with white female performers thus invoking a different set of stereotypes.

[15] Faithfull with Dalton, p. 23.

[16] Ibid., p. 25.

[17] Philip Auslander, *Performing Glam Rock: Gender and Theatricality in Popular Music* (Ann Arbor, MI, 2006), p. 4, n. 3.

the musician's performing persona and real self were perceived as identical.[18] Faithfull's case proposes an amendment to that schema, as her persona was foisted upon her by outside forces, not only Oldham but by audience and critical discourses as well as gender expectations and norms of the era.

Oldham created for Faithfull the persona of an aristocratic, virginal, remote and smolderingly sexy yet untouchable princess. Her vocal style, a somewhat affectless and quavery soprano, fit this image well, as did Oldham's choice of repertoire for her, wispy folk-pop songs. Oldham emphasized Faithfull's upper-class lineage in his publicity for her. Faithfull's mother was an impoverished Austrian baroness and a grand-niece of Leopold von Sacher-Masoch, the author of *Venus in Furs* (1870) and namesake for the term masochism. Her father was a former British spy turned eccentric commune-founder. Her parents divorced when she was six. Faithfull did go to a convent school, but as a charity boarder. In her autobiography, Faithfull speaks of being so poor that she and her mother did not even have a telephone.[19] Nevertheless, Oldham foregrounded her aristocratic background, obscuring the fact that her noble lines were not British. With her milky skin, full lips and bosom, improbable but real name, and stunning looks, he cast her as the apotheosis of English womanhood, a symbol of racial purity during a period when the complexion of the British popular and the influences on the music popular amongst the young were getting darker. Popular music scholar Gayle Wald observes that "although white supremacy accords white women social privilege on the basis of race, such privilege is fundamentally self-divided, since it rests on white women's acquiescence to patriarchal and class oppression."[20] Issues of class resonated strongly and divisively in Great Britain in the mid-1960s. Faithfull, constructed as upper-class, would be punished for not acquiescing to either form of oppression.

Faithfull, Oldham, and the Stones were all instrumental figures in "Swingin' London" of the mid-1960s. As journalist Shawn Levy sees it, "in London for those few evanescent years it all came together: youth, pop, music, fashion, fine art, sexuality, scandal, theater, cinema, drugs, media: the whole mad modern stew."[21] The flowering of youth culture was unsettling enough, but another ingredient of the stew rankled the British status quo, an unprecedented mixing of classes. In Levy's account as well as contemporary chronicles, Swinging London represented a breaking down of barriers that was unprecedented, and unwelcome by some, in England. The sons and daughters of lords and earls openly cavorted and coupled with real or wannabe Cockney boys and the Kray Brothers, gangsters from the east side of London. By crafting "Marianne Faithfull" as the epitome of the white

---

[18]   Ibid., p. 66.

[19]   Faithfull with Dalton, p. 17.

[20]   Gayle Wald, "One of the Boys? Whiteness, Gender, and Popular Music Studies," in Mike Hill (ed.), *Whiteness: A Critical Reader* (New York, 1997), p. 155.

[21]   Shawn Levy, *Ready, Steady, Go! The Smashing Rise and Giddy Fall of Swinging London* (New York, 2003), p. 5.

English aristocratic female, Oldham inadvertently set a trap for Faithfull that would shortly ensnare her. As Faithfull sees it, "part of the rage toward me in the late sixties came, I'm sure, from this misconception that I was somehow the epitome of everything English. Whereas my mother was Austrian, my father of Welsh descent, and I was part Jewish and descended from a Moor turned Christian."[22] Faithfull was barely English, but looked the part, and in Oldham's image factory, appearances became the reality.

Faithfull's relationship with Jagger, which commenced in 1966, compromised Faithfull's upper-class and white persona. As fervently as he had turned the charity-boarder Faithfull into white nobility, Oldham turned the Rolling Stones, a collection of mainly middle-class boys from the suburbs, into lower-class thugs of a darker tint.[23] He deftly manipulated the press, trading on the "blackness" of the Stones' repertoire, and their studiously unkempt appearance, to ensure that any action of theirs deemed untoward by the mainstream press would be blown out of all proportion and thus generate more notoriety and publicity for the Stones while tapping into nascent post-war youth rebellion.[24] The Stones performed the "bad boy Stones" well in this period, misbehaving on respected television programs and urinating on garage walls, minor mischief that produced spasms of outrage. One of Oldham's publicity coups was getting the respected trade paper *Melody Maker* to run a headline inquiring, "Would you let your sister go with a Rolling Stone?", thereby constructing an aura of sexual menace around the Stones.[25] They were thugs who would encourage or even worse, force, sisters and possibly brothers to perform unspeakable sexual acts.

The menace was augmented by the behavior of audiences at Stones shows in the 1964–65 period. To spread the Stones and their R&B sound outside of London, upon becoming their manager in late 1963, Oldham sent the Stones out several times to tour the ballroom circuit. Keith Richards recalls that, "There was a period of six months in England where we couldn't play in ballrooms any more because we never got through more than three songs every night … . We'd walk into some of these places and it was like the Battle of the Crimea going on: people gasping, tits hanging out, chicks choking, nurses, ambulances."[26] Visual evidence from the period, preserved in documents such as Peter Whitehead's film *Charlie Is My*

---

[22] Faithfull with Dalton, p. 14.

[23] The Beatles, before Brian Epstein took control of them, were a better fit for the image designed by Oldham for the Stones. They were mainly from lower-class homes in Liverpool and had spent several years playing rough clubs in that city and the German port city of Hamburg.

[24] For example, the incident when they were fined for urinating on the wall of a gas station, which was reported as an act of hooliganism in the mainstream press, is a prime example of how Oldham's constructed image of the group was taken up, ultimately in the group's interest.

[25] Davis, *Old Gods Almost Dead*, p. 78.

[26] Ibid., p. 83.

Darling (unreleased documentary, 1966), a chronicle of their visit to Ireland, shows that the Stones' sexual threat was not confined just to the virtue of young girls. Jagger, thin, lithe, long-haired and thick-lipped, had an androgynous yet resolutely sexual appeal to both sexes. His stage performance exacerbated and exaggerated that appeal, using athletic leaps, smooth shuffle steps appropriated from African-American male and female performers, and a penetrating stare. Jagger also liked to face the drumkit and shake his backside at the audience. The sexual desire he aroused in the crowd, female and male, was often channeled into violence. Young men, faced with what was deemed an inappropriate object for their sexual desire would storm the stage, trying to punch each other and the musicians. Seats were ripped out and curtains torn to shreds.

Jagger's relationship with Faithfull "confirmed" his heterosexuality, stripping the danger from his omnisexual androgyny, at least in the eyes of fans and, shortly, rock critics. If Jagger could "win" the beautiful, virginal Faithfull, then his straight masculinity appeared solid, his "queerness" just a performance persona. If the relationship enhanced Jagger's persona, it sullied Faithfull's. Faithfull's white aristocratic persona did not mesh with Jagger's constructed black thuggishness. Downward class mobility is perceived as a personal failure while upward mobility is rewarded, or at least accepted. Indeed, Jagger was able to use his relationship with the "aristocratic" Faithfull to burnish his own reputation and signal his striving class aspirations.[27] Faithfull stopped recording for several years upon commencing her relationship with Jagger, in part because at that time she was not particularly interested in singing, and given gender norms, it was more or less expected of her to do so. The normative pull of gender convention, even in a countercultural inflection, was compounded by the submission and near-erasure of feminine pop music by that performed by groups of men in the wake of the Beatles' first great success in 1963. The entry of Faithfull into the Stones' scene, and into Jagger's life, was sufficient to confirm his, and subsequently, rock's heterosexuality at the time, at least among youthful audiences. The older members of the British establishment were more concerned about the overall impact of the new youth culture, particularly as represented by pop groups, on social mores and conventions and laws against sodomy were rescinded in Great Britain in 1967. Long-haired, "effeminate" young men may have been a thorn in the older generation's side, but that went hand in hand with generational antagonism in general. Instead, what was perceived as a growing use of psychoactive drugs amongst the pop-crazed youth became a target of adult concern and punitive action, culminating in a moral panic that linked increased drug use by English youth to pop music. Much was

---

[27]   Jagger achieved his goal in 2002, when Queen Elizabeth II made him a knight of the realm. Faithfull was widely quoted as saying that Jagger was a "tremendous snob" who "always wanted that [the knighthood] so much," further alleging that "Mick is bohemian—but not that bohemian." Quoted in Hugh Davies, "Mick is a tremendous snob, says Marianne," *The Daily Telegraph*, July 13, 2002, p. 3.

192   *SHE'S SO FINE*

made of this link in the mainstream press.[28] Pop stars fueled the panic themselves
with outrageous pronouncements in print and television interviews. For example,
Faithfull appeared on a television talk show in 1967, obviously stoned, extolling
the virtues of LSD animatedly asserting, "it opens the *doors* of perception."[29] With
the help of UK tabloid *News of the World* and, possibly, a frame-up, authorities
went after the pop group that represented the most flagrant threat to polite society,
the Rolling Stones.[30]

On February 13, 1967, Jagger, Faithfull, Keith Richards, and gallery owner
Robert Fraser were arrested during a drug raid on Richards's country house,
Redlands, in Sussex, where nine people were relaxing after a day of dropping acid
and driving around the countryside. Jagger, Richards, and Fraser were brought
to trial in late June 1967, an event that made front-page news for several days in
major newspapers, including the venerable *Times*, the UK paper of record, and
which spawned a protest by "400 young people massed around Eros in Piccadilly
Circus" at two o'clock in the morning.[31] Jagger was found guilty of possession
of four amphetamine tablets (purchased legally in Italy, by Faithfull) under the
Dangerous Drugs Act of 1965, sentenced to three months in jail, and fined.[32]
Richards was also convicted under the Dangerous Drugs Act of 1965 of letting
his premises be used for the smoking of "Indian Hemp" and sentenced to a year
in prison. Fraser was convicted of possession of twenty-four heroin tablets and

---

[28]   See, for example: "Youths and Girls on Drug Charges," *The Times*, January 26,
1965, p. 5; "More Young People Taking Drugs," *The Times*, March 30, 1965, p. 5; "Drugs
Preferred to Sex by Young?" *The Times*, April 12, 1965, p. 6; "Teen Trouble in Coffee
Clubs," *The Times*, May 12, 1965, p. 13; "Hazards of the Hallucinatory Drug," *The Times*,
August 22, 1966, p. 8; "Lord Chief Justice seeks control of entertainment clubs," *The Times*,
February 4, 1967, p. 13.

[29]   *Marianne Faithfull: Dreaming My Dreams* (DVD, Eagle Rock Entertainment, 2000).

[30]   In her autobiography, Faithfull alleges that the "Stones bust" was engineered by
the tabloid *News of the World*. Jagger had recently filed a libel suit against the paper for
erroneously naming him as the perpetrator of a night of drugging and sex at a club in
Kensington. Faithfull claims that the reporters mistook Brian Jones for Jagger. According
to Faithfull, the paper set up the bust with the West Sussex police and brought a man named
David Schneiderman in from California with a suitcase full of LSD in order to entrap
Jagger. In "Swingin' London" chronicler Shawn Levy's account, the fact that the police did
not make Schneiderman open his briefcase is more evidence of a frame-up. See Faithfull
with Dalton, pp. 98–105 and Levy, pp. 229–33.

[31]   Tim Jones and Christopher Warman, "'Stones'-protest at 2 am," *The Times*, July 1,
1967, p. 1.

[32]   The history recounted here is gleaned from several articles published in *The Times*
during the trial: Ronald Faux, "Mick Jagger to Face Sentence," *The Times*, June 27, 1967,
p. 2; "Mick Jagger is found guilty," *The Times*, June 28, 1967, p. 1; "Young woman 'wearing
only fur rug' at guitarist's party," *The Times*, June 29, 1967, p. 2; "Keith Richard says nude
girl came down from bath," *The Times*, June 30, 1967, p. 2; Ronald Faux, "Gaol sentences
on 2 Rolling Stones," *The Times*, June 30, 1967, p. 1.

sentenced to six months in jail. Jagger and Richards were released on bail pending appeal, and soon had their sentences overturned. In a surprise twist, public opinion, led by the editor of the *Times*, railed against the harsh sentencing of the two Stones for relatively minor drug violations. Several commentators, including *Times* editor William Rees-Mogg, asserted that the Stones were unduly punished because of their celebrity and unfairly used as scapegoats for a cultural shift that may have been inevitable.[33] Moreover, the panic over drugs was beginning to be seen in the press as just that. Just before the Stones' trial, the *Times* ran a two-part editorial advocating a more rational approach to the drugs issue and arguing for more distinction between classes of drugs, including alcohol.[34] The paper, in an earlier editorial, asserted that the world of pop music was a trouble spot, but also that much of the sensationalism about drugs was focused there, blaming the media for fanning the flames of panic.[35]

The public victory of the two Stones over what Richards called the "petty morals" of the older generation during his trial can, I suggest, be viewed as the true start of rock culture. Jagger, especially, was anointed spokesperson for the generation immediately upon his release from jail, when he was whisked away to a country house for a televised interview with several prominent members of the religious, political, and press establishment. This marked the start of, if not an open dialogue between the generations, then a bit of a truce, or at least an agreement to disagree on lifestyle issues among men.[36] Even so, the establishment could not totally acquiesce to the "new morality." Someone or something had to be punished for the flaunting of convention, and the line had to be held on some aspect of traditional morality, class, and gender relations. Gender norms, specifically femininity, would be the new battleground.

As Judith Butler asserts, gender "is a form of social power that produces the intelligible field of subjects, and an apparatus by which the gender binary is instituted.[37] To riff off another insight of Butler's, gender was troubled in the mid-1960s. Homosexual men were beginning their emergence from the closet and contributed to much of the excitement of "Swingin' London." Men were dressing and wearing their hair more effeminately. Women were asserting their sexuality more aggressively, egged on by fashions, such as the mini-skirt, created by new young designers. Pop music, especially, was inverting the male gaze by putting young men on display for the pleasure of other young men as well as women.

---

[33] William Rees-Mogg, "Who Breaks a Butterfly on a Wheel?," *The Times*, July 1, 1967, p. 11.

[34] Dr. David Stafford-Clark, "The Significance of Human Vulnerability," *The Times*, April 11, 1967, p. 11; "Disposing of the Myths and Half-Truths," *The Times*, April 12, 1967, p. 11.

[35] "A Dangerous Press Campaign," *The Times*, February 28, 1967, p. 11.

[36] Julian Critchley, "Jagger Meets Inquisitors," *The Times*, August 1, 1967, p. 6; Geoffrey Moore, "Generations Talking," *The Times*, August 4, 1967, p. 9.

[37] Judith Butler, *Undoing Gender* (New York: 2004), p. 48.

194 *SHE'S SO FINE*

Moreover, pop music was perceived as being the major site of class transgression, with young nobles consorting with the hoi polloi at clubs and parties, and possibly even worse, the presence of pop artists in the salons of nobility. The effort by the establishment to reinforce class and gender norms and conventions focused on young women, not young men. As I have argued elsewhere, rock journalism would do the same, quite effectively if not so directly.[38]

To these ends, a fourth person was put on trial in the Stones' drug case, this time in the court of public opinion. The day after Richard's trial, the headline in the *Times* was not about his sentence. Instead it screamed, "Young woman 'wearing only fur rug' at guitarist's party."[39] The article was primarily about Richard's testimony on the stand, but that was subsumed under the sensational headline. The photo accompanying the article was not one of Richards, but of Marianne Faithfull arriving at the courthouse. Thus the link was made between Faithfull and the notorious "girl in a fur rug."

Ostensibly, the "girl in the fur rug" was introduced as circumstantial evidence of the deleterious effects of marijuana on the inhibitions, particularly those of young women. From this moment on, the scene was transformed from a party at Richard's house consisting of eight men and one woman to an orgy orchestrated by an immoral young woman. Indeed the description of the purported orgy was titillating if not borderline pornographic; detailed accounts of a room redolent with the smell of incense, the woman letting her rug slip to expose her naked body, coupled with an implicitly racist comment about the presence of a Moroccan servant at the party in order to provide more evidence of "Miss X's" spurious morals, added to the "deviance" of the scene. This detail accelerated Faithfull's fall from the protection of her white privilege as well as that of her constructed class: to cavort sexually with a dark servant was a class and gender transgression of some magnitude.

With the entrance of the "girl in the fur rug" into the trial, it became less about drugs and more about proper femininity and the morals of those young women who stray from that path as well as an implicit warning about the perils of race and class transgression, given that the identity of "Miss X" was easily discerned. Blame for her plight shifted away from Jagger and Richards on to the girl herself, thus invoking a sexual double standard. The girl's reputation wasn't helped when Richard's lawyer asserted that an arresting officer's testimony had portrayed the girl in question as a drug-taking nymphomaniac.[40] She was implicitly blamed for her own predicament and dragged through the mud by innuendo. That the British establishment would work to reinforce class and gender norms is expected. What

---

[38] Norma Coates, "Teenyboppers, Groupies, and Other Grotesques: Girls and Women and Rock Culture in the 1960s and early 1970s," *Journal of Popular Music Studies* 15/1 (2003): 65–94.

[39] "Young woman 'wearing only fur rug' at guitarist's party," *The Times*, June 26, 1967, p. 2.

[40] Ibid.

WHOSE TEARS GO BY? 195

is less obvious is why, from the trial to the release of her unexpected masterpiece, *Broken English* (Island 422-84235502, 1990), in 1979, Marianne Faithfull became a rock culture punch-line. This lay, in part, to another by-product of the Stones' trial.

Jagger's triumph and elevation to the title of the first real rock star was completed by a rumor that spread after his trial. According to this rumor, upon entering Redlands at the start of the bust, police witnessed Jagger eating a Mars Bar out of Faithfull's vagina. Faithfull, Richards, and Jagger have always claimed this to be untrue, and there is no reason to doubt them. Faithfull tried to laugh the rumor off but asserts that, "my amusement began to wane when the damn story established itself as a set piece of British folklore."[41] Faithfull also characterizes the story as "a very effective piece of demonizing."[42] The Mars Bar tale never made it into the "polite" press, but has been giggled about in rock discourse for decades, and is still trotted out in articles about Faithfull.[43] Therefore, it may be deduced that she was demonized in the rock press and in other areas of rock culture.[44] The story also established itself as a part of rock mythology, crucial to rock culture as it was then emerging. Mick emerged from the Mars Bar story as the epitome of the decadent, hedonistic hyper-heterosexual, male rock star, free to do anything he wanted to, including eating candy out of an orifice of one of the world's most beautiful women, thus turning her into an object of his appetites and nothing more than a vessel for their fulfillment. This, of course, is as much a constructed persona as that of Faithfull, with the difference being that it has stuck to the Stones without it being held against them. Faithfull, on the other hand, became a symbol of the expected position of women in rock—objectified and in the service of the various appetites of the rock star. Her trivialization is indicative of the conservative double-standard of male and female sexuality in rock culture of the era, which still, albeit reduced in form, haunts rock discourse today.

As Faithfull observes in her autobiography, "in the end, the assault on the Stones backfired because it hugely empowered the Stones. The Rolling Stones

---

[41] Faithfull with Dalton, p. 113.

[42] Ibid.

[43] See for example: Mat Snow, "Marianne Faithfull: Venus & Mars," *Q*, December 1994; David Bowman, "Marianne Faithfull," *Salon*, January 9, 2001, http://www.rocksbackpages.com.proxy1.lib.uwo.ca:2048/article.html?ArticleID=3416 (accessed July 21, 2006); David Bowman, Horacio Silva and Zarah Crawford, "Jagger's Edge," *New York Times*, March 12, 2006, p. 6; Alexis Petridis, "Reviews: Pop: Rumours of Faithfull's ill health are greatly exaggerated," *The Guardian*, September 30, 2005, p. 38; Fiona Sturges, "Venus & Mars: Marianne Faithfull's 40-year career has been dogged by tales of sex," *The Independent,* October 16, 2004, p. 14. A Lexis-Nexis search of "General News" and "Major Papers" for the terms "Marianne Faithfull" and "Mars," performed on July 21, 2006, retrieved 30 entries.

[44] This is a personal anecdote, but it was a mark of rock "cool" to repeat and giggle about this rumor. I remember doing so myself, thus implicating myself in Faithfull's and— as a straight woman—my own abjection.

196   *SHE'S SO FINE*

and Her Majesty's government became powers of equal magnitude."[45] Jagger, especially, managed the trick of deriving great power from being cast in the role of the victim of government persecution, and from his ultimate triumph over it. Pop artist Richard Hamilton helped when he produced a famous series of prints, called "Swingeing London," from a photograph of Jagger manacled to Fraser as they sat in a car awaiting their transport to jail. The use of handcuffs on Jagger for so minor an offense had caused much comment in the press, usually in favor of the singer.[46]

The idea that Jagger was both victim and victor of the drugs trial was reinforced by a promotional film directed by Peter Whitehead for the Stones' first post-trial single, "We Love You." The proto-music video opens with a zoom-in on a front-page article describing the arrest of Brian Jones on drug charges, followed by a close-up of the chained feet and calves of a man walking through what is identifiable as a cellblock.[47] This scene ends with a shot and the sound of a cell door slamming. The next three shots are individual close-ups of Jagger, Richards, and a very stoned and bloated Jones, who had also been recently tried on drugs charges. Up to the bridge of the song, the video shows the group working in the studio. Once at the bridge, a shot dissolves into a close-up of a bewigged and spectacled Richards in the role of a judge in a Victorian courtroom. The next shot pans from a green carnation to a close-up of Jagger. The green carnation makes it clear that Richards and Jagger are restaging the trial of and linking themselves to Oscar Wilde, also persecuted for public behavior that went against the grain of prevailing norms of the day, who wore the flower to his trial. A third player is introduced, Marianne Faithfull, as Bosie, Wilde's male lover and catalyst for Wilde's ultimate downfall. Faithfull's hair is shorn into a boyish cut, and she appears to be under the influence of some drug or another, or at least achingly sad. She walks over to the Judge and lays a fur object, possibly a rug, on the table in front of him. She arranges it so that two long pieces protrude from it, as though she is offering herself up as a sacrificial lamb. The Judge lifts the rug up and the camera lingers on Faithfull's face as she vaguely shrugs. It is as if Faithfull/Bosie does not care about the morality she/he flaunted. A strange reversal happens next. The Judge orders Faithfull/Bosie to lift up the fur, which is now draped over a body. She does so, and up sits an apparently naked Jagger. The film ends with his defiant stare into the camera as he breaks into a sly grin. In this move, Jagger positions himself as the sacrificial lamb, the victim of the piece, but his stare and grin signal his ultimate triumph over it. Any notion that Faithfull was wronged in the entire process disappears, not literally, but in the sense that the idea of it no longer exists.[48]

---

[45]   Faithfull with Dalton, p. 118.

[46]   See, for example, Rees-Mogg.

[47]   Jones was not part of the Redlands bust but was arrested for drug possession several times during the same period.

[48]   The promotional film was a minor scandal in itself, as the producer of the BBC television program *Top of the Pops* rejected it, possibly because of the content, possibly

If rock culture demonized Faithfull, her fabricated persona had much to do with it. As a singer, she tried but could not break out of it. In late 1968, she recorded the instrumental tracks for a new single in LA, where the Stones were mixing *Let It Bleed* (ABKCO Records 719004, 1969), and finished the vocals in London. Some of the players on *Let It Bleed*, including Jagger, Charlie Watts, Jack Nitzsche, and Ry Cooder played on it. Faithfull's vocals were a departure from the angelic tones of three years earlier. Her voice was no longer sweet and its wistful vibrato was non-existent; instead, her voice was deeper, heading into the contralto range, and already scarred by smoke, whiskey and drugs. The song, "Sister Morphine," with lyrics by Faithfull and melody by Jagger, was released by Faithfull's label, Decca, in February 1969 and taken off the shelves two days later. According to Faithfull, Decca provided no explanation for their actions:

> The song must have come as a bit of a surprise to the old dears up at Decca. My previous album, *Love In A Mist*, three years earlier, had not signaled that much of a departure from my other records. I felt trapped; I wasn't going to be allowed to break out of my ridiculous image. I was being told that I would not be permitted to leave that wretched, tawdry doll behind.[49]

Unfortunately, since few heard Faithfull's version of "Sister Morphine," the public conception of her as a performer was still the "wretched, tawdry doll" that Faithfull describes. In her autobiography, Faithfull blames the "Sister Morphine" debacle for her precipitous decline into drugs and addiction shortly thereafter.[50] She also implies that the sexism inherent in the music business, and in rock, helped to drive her over the edge; she notes, correctly, that when the Stones recorded and released "Sister Morphine" on *Sticky Fingers* (Universal Distribution 001279902, 1971) two years later (credited to Jagger/Richards, not to Faithfull), no one batted an eye.

At this point, Faithfull became a crucial part of the Stones' growing legend. According to Faithfull, the English press, especially the tabloid press, savaged her as much as possible, reporting her every arrest and display of public intoxication, her messy divorce, and the suicide attempt that almost derailed Jagger's starring role in a feature film about Australian outlaw/hero Ned Kelly. According to Faithfull, her very public fall from rock as well as her constructed royalty, "gave license to every sadistic little creep in England to vent her vileness on me. Endless humiliating and shameful things."[51] While she was still with Jagger (they split up in 1970), she was increasingly perceived as a drag on his career. After they ended their relationship but when she was still part of the Stones' coterie, Atlantic Records mogul Ahmet Ertegun, who had just agreed to give the group their own record label and wanted

---

because of the images of an obviously drug-ravaged Jones. "TV producer bans Stones' film," *The Times*, August 24, 1967, p. 2.

[49]   Faithfull with Dalton, p. 167.

[50]   Ibid.

[51]   Ibid., p. 206.

to protect his $30,000,000 investment, allegedly urged Jagger to cut his ties with Faithfull, lest she drag him down with her.[52] Faithfull's constructed persona, which she didn't ask for, as well as her career as a folk-pop singer, augured her harsher treatment. Constructed as the exemplar of the best of English womanhood, her "descent" into drugs and depravity (not the more agreeable "decadence") was punished severely, even in rock culture. Shackled by traditional gender norms in order to expunge or at least submerge the homosocial implications of male rock fandom and performance, Faithfull and women perceived as being like her, such as groupies, became objects of scorn and off-color humor.

After her split with Jagger, Faithfull put herself at the mercy of her demons. She dived into heroin addiction and what she refers to in her autobiography as her years on the wall, spending time doing drugs, hanging out in a bombsite in Soho, and living with her mother, friends, or on the street. She lost custody of her son with Dunbar. She registered with the National Health Service as a heroin addict. Faithfull managed to make and release a couple of albums, *Rich Kid Blues* (reissue Diablo 861, 1998) and *Faithless* (reissue Essential Records 713, 1978) and even had a hit single in Ireland, "Dreaming My Dreams" during her years on the wall. During the 1970s, her name would continue to sell a few albums for her, now not because of her 1960s career, but because of what she represented and who she had been and had been with during that decade.

Following the drug bust and trial, the Stones and especially Jagger were the most powerful figures in nascent rock culture. Assisted by songs like "Sympathy for the Devil" and Jagger's appearance as the decadent rock star in the cult classic *Performance* (1970), the group acquired a new, demonic persona and made the most of it. The death of founder Brian Jones and the tragic events at the Altamont free concert reinforced the persona. After a string of classic albums, beginning with 1968's *Beggar's Banquet* (ABKCO Records 7539-2) and ending with *Exile on Main Street* in 1972 (Virgin 39524), the weight of their image and their expectations, along with Keith Richards's own descent into heroin addiction, took a toll on the group. In Faithfull's analysis, "all of the anarchy and hedonism which the Stones personified finally burnt out by the time they got to *Goat's Head Soup* [the 1973 album immediately following *Exile on Main Street*]."[53] By that time, the Stones had been a band for ten years and were all pushing thirty, thought to be old for a genre devoted (at that time) to youth. Rock was fragmenting as well, encompassing new sounds. Sixties bands were losing their relevancy in the face of stylistic and generational changes. Rather than retiring, the Stones cast their persona and their sound in amber. Sonically, they relied on Keith Richards's riffing and open-G tunings, Jagger's increasingly mannered vocals, their rock-solid rhythm section, and occasionally nasty lyrics to maintain their audience. They generally ignored new trends, or bent them to their formula. The group's one nod to the increasing plurality of rock and pop styles in the late 1970s, 1978's

---

[52]   Ibid., p. 196.
[53]   Ibid., p. 149.

Some Girls (Universal Distribution 91484), employed a "one of each" strategy, including for example a disco song ("Miss You") and a punk song ("Shattered"). By the turn of the decade they stopped trying to be current and settled into building their brand, the Rolling Stones, steeped in nostalgia for the receding 60s and dependent upon their 60s persona to maintain their decadent image in the face of encroaching age and immense wealth. They remain intertwined with Faithfull, more accurately with her 60s persona, as a way to activate nostalgia and reaffirm their authenticity. She may not be referenced in all, if any, articles about them, but the parallel discourse about Faithfull frequently mentions the Stones, thus encouraging the link. Moreover, the stories about Marianne Faithfull in the 60s and 70s are part of knowledge that constructs "the Stones" as a brand, a band, and a performative persona.

Faithfull's career benefits from the link as well, in tangible as well as more ineffable ways. The link with the Stones kept and keeps her in the public eye, for better or worse. While surviving in central London in the mid-1970s, Faithfull was exposed to and energized by the emerging punk scene, living with and eventually marrying a member of the Vibrators. She had several periods of being clean, and started to write music. She put a band together. Then, in 1979, she released *Broken English*, an album infused with punk energy and anger, if musically distinct from that genre, which surprised and shocked critics and the public alike. *Broken English* was immediately acknowledged as a masterpiece and introduced Faithfull to a new generation who could have written her off as one of the sadder and sillier casualties of the 60s.

Broken English, although much of it was written by others (the title song, inspired by the terrorist Baader-Meinhof gang, was Faithfull's), seemed to tell Faithfull's side of the story, lyrically and through her voice. Her angelic soprano was now a broken and cracked alto. Robert Palmer of the *New York Times* described Faithfull's voice on this album as "a croaking rasp."[54] Her "new" voice, an older and more damaged version of that recorded on "Sister Morphine" ten years previously, suited the words and music perfectly, especially on the album's most memorable and controversial song. "Why'd You Do It," with lyrics written by male poet Heathcote Williams, which came across as Faithfull's version of her life story. An outraged rant at a cheating lover peppered with four-letter words, the song seemed to be Faithfull's response to the abuse she had received over the years at the hands of Jagger, the press, rock culture, and the establishment. At the same time, it seemed to capture the feelings of many women in a sexist society and in rock culture. The punk spirit of the album showed through the most in this song. Punk opened a real space for women in rock as an expressive venue of their experience, in and out of rock culture. Faithfull was following in the footsteps of female punk artists such as Poly Styrene, the Raincoats, and others who were integrating a feminist voice and critique into their work and into rock music

---

[54] Robert Palmer, "Marianne Faithfull, Or the Power of Positive Singing?" *New York Times*, October 21, 1981, p. C25.

in general. Punk also helped to put aside the notion that "women in rock" were there to be decorative and pretty. That applied to vocals, as well. Faithfull's "ravaged" voice was a perfect expression of punk feminism and exquisitely well-suited to the messages of *Broken English*. Her voice contrasted dramatically with that of her 1960s recordings and, I suggest, can be read on its own as a feminist critique of the options available to female performers in that decade.

Faithfull has recorded and performed regularly since then, although she did not rid herself of her heroin addiction until 1985. She has used her story to craft public and performance personae of her own choosing. She claims that she has to "be Marianne Faithfull" every time she takes the stage, and that it is exhausting.[55] At the same time, though, it is a role she appears to enjoy. Even though "Marianne Faithfull" is a performance persona, it resonates as conveying the "truth" of the real person's experience. It enables her take her and her small but loyal cult of fans on some interesting musical excursions, including a stint as an interpreter of the songs of Kurt Weill. Through repetition of stories about her, and incorporation of them into her performance persona, she has become, in rock terms, authentic.

Faithfull is extremely canny about using the stories about her. Different facets of her story attract different types of audiences. Some come to her because of nostalgia for the 60s, whether they were alive during the period or not. Others are attracted by her feminist message of survival in the rock world, and her ability to now hold the title of rock royalty, still in part because of her association with the Stones but also because of her very presence, bearing, and intelligence. Two recent albums were collaborations with several well-known indie artists, including Beck, Billy Corgan, Polly Jean Harvey, Nick Cave, and Jarvis Cocker.

Beck, Corgan, and Harvey are major artists on the indie scene in the US, Cave and Cocker less so but still influential. Beck and Corgan, with his band Smashing Pumpkins, enjoyed radio success in the US in the mid-1990s on the heels of the grunge movement; both cultivated images as iconoclasts who focus more on following their own muses than on maintaining a flow of hit records. At least one critic has accused Faithfull's younger male collaborators as using Faithfull's distinctive, world-weary voice by proxy.[56] That Faithfull's voice, deep, whiskey-soaked, and cracked, provides young artists, male and female, with a link to the mythical 60s of their imaginations is evident. More interesting is that they choose a female voice to make this connection. In Faithfull's voice one accesses both the excesses and the collateral damage of the 1960s, especially to women in countercultural spaces such as the rock music of the era. As I have discussed, the dominant style of rock masculinity developed in the late 1960s, and the discursive treatment of Faithfull played a part in that. Faithfull's younger male collaborators may be using her voice as a proxy to refuse the straitjacket of rock masculinity.

---

[55] Hilton Als, "Talk of the Town: Faithfull," *The New Yorker* 78/28, September 23, 2002, p. 33.

[56] Simon Price, "Discs," *Independent on Sunday*, September 26, 2004, p. 24.

Faithfull's collaboration with Jarvis Cocker on *Kissin' Time* (EMI Music Distribution 811738, 2002) is especially compelling because Cocker and his band Pulp made a career of savaging Great Britain's class politics. In songs like "Common People" from 1996's *Different Class* (Island, 524165), Cocker's fictional character skewers an upper-class acquaintance for her attempts to understand how the "common people" live by having sex with them as nothing more than insulting condescension. Faithfull calls Cocker's contribution to the album, "Sliding Through Life on Charm" (a title that Faithfull gave him after finding it impossible to write the song herself), her story. Indeed, Cocker wrote it after reading her autobiography.[57] The occasionally profane song, musically very reminiscent of Pulp's sound on *Different Class*, cleverly invokes the aristocratic persona created for Faithfull in the 1960s to rip it apart. "Sliding through life on charm," in Cocker's words and Faithfull's delivery is a condemnation both of that persona and of upper-class codes of conduct that Faithfull was pilloried for violating. The last words that Cocker puts in Faithfull's mouth are most telling: "I wonder why the schools don't teach anything useful these days / Like how to fall from grace, and slide with elegance from a pedestal I never asked to be on in the first place."[58]

Faithfull seems more comfortable on her new pedestal, that of the "grande dame of rock'n'roll debauchery,"[59] or, more charitably, "the grand dame of Britrock aristocracy."[60] Both titles reflect her past persona, but Faithfull is now in control of it and uses it to her advantage and as she sees fit. Indeed, her past enables her to stay on the rock stage, even on the indie rock stage, well into her late middle-age. By all indications, she appears to revel in her new-found respectability amongst the rock set, especially its younger members. A more recent collaborator, Polly Jean Harvey, is one of a new generation of female artists whose very viability and visibility on the scene may not have been possible without the stories of Faithfull and other "women in rock" from the 1960s. As Faithfull found in punk a way through to her rage and her feminism, Harvey and others take from Faithfull the ability to use their constructed gender roles vis-à-vis rock to challenge it on its own terms.

In a 2002 promotional interview for *Kissin' Time*, Faithfull responded to a comparison with the late Nico, another beautiful blonde chanteuse from the 1960s who died a tragic death. Faithfull and Nico were friends and traveled in the same circles. When the interviewer asked Faithfull about her "tragic life," she responded:

---

[57] "Remaining Faithfull," *Toronto Star*, December 4, 2002, p. D01.

[58] Excerpt from "Sliding Through Life on Charm," Marianne Faithfull/Jarvis Cocker, EMI Music Pub Ltd. (c/o EMI Blackwood Music Inc. (BMI)/Universal—Polygram Int. Publ. Inc.).

[59] Andy Gill, "This Week's Album Releases," *The Independent*, March 1, 2002, p. 14.

[60] Garry Mulholland, "Kiss and Tell: The Time Out Interview Marianne Faithfull," *Time Out*, March 6, 2002, pp. 11–12.

I've never got the thing about my tragic life. Obviously I'd had some very hard times. But they were very much brought on by myself, to myself ... . The reason I wanted to write a homage to Nico is the frustration and fury you feel, as a talented woman, of not being recognized, understood, people not getting you. That's what we really do share.[61]

Faithfull's refusal to characterize herself as a victim or a survivor is admirable. Even so, she was trapped in a persona not of her own choosing, one that made her a convenient target for those in mainstream and countercultures who wanted to undermine the class, gender, and racial play of the 1960s and to restore norms to their "rightful" place. By facing her constructed persona straight-on and by using it while at the same time exposing it and the motivations behind it as the shams that they were, she helps to expose rock mythology for what it is, thereby creating a space for different articulations of gender and class in rock culture, and for re-thinking its past.

---

[61] Ibid.

Chapter 8
Bold Soul Trickster: The 60s Tina Signifies[1]

Susan Fast

In the Signifying Monkey we have a new trickster on the African-American landscape, cultivating a new language in order to help neutralize the forces of oppression and exploitation. For city dwellers, the Signifying Monkey is a key mythological figure in the African American's struggle for adjustment, dignity and equality: a trickster who will baffle, circumvent, and even subdue agents of oppression with the same wit, cunning and guile as tricksters past.[2]

The photograph reproduced in Figure 8.1 appears on the jacket of *Outta Season*, an album of blues and rhythm and blues covers made by the Ike and Tina Turner Revue in 1969. Their producer, Bob Krasnow, takes credit for the concept, explaining that "[i]t was a parody. All the white guys were doing blues records then, so I thought 'hey, the only way a black act can do the blues now would be to put 'em in whiteface, you know?'"[3] The complex image is worth considering in its particulars. In a carnivalesque reversal, Ike and Tina turn the racist legacy of blackface minstrelsy in on itself in a grotesque parody, while at the same time complicating the desire for the Other that the mask of traditional minstrelsy symbolized.[4] Instead of whites desiring blackness, as in traditional minstrelsy, we have blacks desiring whiteness that desires blackness. The image suggests that whites who appropriate black culture do so in superficial or stereotypical ways—by eating watermelon, the fruit so often used in racist caricatures of blacks,

---

[1]   I wish to thank Stan Hawkins, Kip Pegley and Annie Randall for reading through a draft of this essay and offering immensely helpful comments that have made my arguments considerably stronger; I am grateful to have such smart and dedicated colleagues. Thanks to Rob Bowman for talking through various points around the history of the Revue with me. I also wish to thank my research assistant Sean Luyk and the McMaster Arts Research Board for funding. Readers may wish to consult http://www.youtube.com for videos of the live performances mentioned in this chapter.

[2]   Samuel Floyd, *The Power of Black Music: Interpreting Its History from Africa to the United States* (New York, Oxford, 1995), p. 94. Floyd relies for this definition of the Signifying Monkey on the work of Henry Louis Gates, *The Signifyin(g) Monkey: A Theory of African-American Literary Criticism* (New York and Oxford, 1988).

[3]   Tina Turner with Kurt Loder, *I, Tina: My Life Story* (New York, 1986), p. 150.

[4]   For a discussion of black face minstrelsy and gender see Eric Lott, *Love and Theft, Black Face Minstrelsy and the American Working Class* (New York, 1993).

Figure 8.1 Album, Ike and Tina Turner, *Outta Season* (Blue Thumb LBS83241, 1969)

or by dabbling in black musics. But the prominence of the black hands—their foregrounding—belies Ike and Tina's racial identity, as do the knowing winks given by both; the real matrix of desire here includes not only white desire for blackness, but black desire for whiteness. It is about blacks reaping the benefits of whites who have reaped the benefits of appropriating black culture. It is a revision, a reversal, a "deform[ation] of the minstrel mask" (literally).[5] Ike and Tina confound, confuse, parody, and so reclaim the blues (which could here stand in for black music generally) by signifying on the minstrel mask and watermelon: note the bite taken out of each piece of the fruit, their eager, distorted mouths ready for more—this is about grotesque consumption, but is it theirs or does it belong to the white people they parody?[6] Joseph Roach has defined whiteface minstrelsy as "that which trades on stereotypical behaviors, such as white folks' sometimes comically obsessive habits of claiming for themselves ever more fanciful forms of property, ingenious entitlements under the law, and exclusivity in the use of public spaces and facilities."[7] Ike and Tina caricature the white fascination with black expressive culture in the late 1960s, suggesting that whites are so obsessed with it that they will even claim undesirable racial markers in the hope of appearing "authentic." Perhaps most remarkable about this image is Tina's participation: blackface minstrelsy was with few exceptions the domain of white men; that she dons the whiteface mask here alongside Ike speaks volumes about the ways in which her gendered, as well as racialized, practices of signifying were extraordinary in the 1960s and 1970s. The photograph can be taken as a metaphor for these practices and this essay an attempt to scrutinize them. I am interested here in Tina's performances throughout the 1960s, her embodied musical signifying practices: in the sound of her voice, her vocal gestures, her body on stage. I want to name the challenges she made to racialized and, especially, gendered expectations of black women musicians at this time, and to try to account for the ways in which she "de-colonized" normative practices.[8]

"Well ... there's somethin' on my mind"[9]

Because so little has been written about Tina, I want not only to provide some historical background for the reader before engaging in my analysis, but also to articulate some of the important general issues that arise with respect to this study.

---

[5] Floyd, p. 94.

[6] Thanks to Kip Pegley for this point.

[7] Joseph Roach, *Cities of the Dead: Circum-Atlantic Performance* (New York, 1996), p. 236.

[8] Stan Hawkins uses this term to discuss the ways in which Prince mixes musical styles and visual imagery from numerous artists and I think it is applicable to Tina as well. See *Settling the Pop Score: Pop Texts and Identity Politics* (London, 2002), p. 170.

[9] Opening lyric of "A Fool In Love," Ike and Tina Turner's first hit song.

206 *SHE'S SO FINE*

On my mind are fraught subjects such as popular music canons (who's in and who's out), the marginalization of live performance in favor of studio recordings, and whose voices we take seriously. But first a little context.

Ike Turner assembled his band, which he called the Kings of Rhythm, in 1951. Tina became part of this ensemble in 1957, and was inserted into the existing framework of the show: that is, she was not considered anything particularly special by Ike. After their first hit single, "A Fool in Love," was cut in 1960—a track, incidentally, that was supposed to be sung by *a guy* (gender is significant, see below) who didn't show up for the session—the owner of the independent Sue Records, Juggy Murray, suggested that Ike make Tina the star of the show.[10] In fact, according to Ike, Murray wanted to issue the record under Tina's name because he believed it was her voice that "made the track."[11] Not surprisingly, Ike was unwilling to relinquish control in this way, but from this point forward, as Kurt Loder has phrased it, "Ike began to look upon [Tina] as his possible ticket out of St. Louis," and indeed, this she certainly became.[12] In many respects, Ike's band was a second rate musical organization; it was Tina's voice and her stage presence that made it something special. In order to draw attention to her essential contribution, Ike decided to change the name of his band to the Ike and Tina Turner Revue in 1960 (extraordinary for many reasons which I will discuss below). But even though Tina's accomplishments in The Revue were remarkable, histories of popular and/or black music rarely do more than mention it, or Tina, and many leave both Ike and Tina out of their narratives altogether.[13] She appears mostly as a

---

[10]   This is the way the story is told in Turner with Loder, pp. 76–77. Ike does not contradict this in his own autobiography, *Takin' Back My Name: The Confessions of Ike Turner* (London, 1999). This is historically significant because it was not, in fact, Ike who recognized Tina's immense talent, at least not at first. Loder also indicates that Ike married Tina a little later on in order to keep her around: "Minus [Tina's] voice, most of this music would be of considerably less interest. Tina's continued presence, on record and in the Revue, was obviously imperative. Ike decided to marry her—a strategy that had always proved effective in the past whenever he required the prolonged services of a useful woman." Turner with Loder, p. 96.

[11]   Ibid., p. 77, but the fact that Murray wanted to issue the track under Tina's name is told by Ike in *Takin' Back My Name*, p. 74.

[12]   Turner with Loder, p. 63.

[13]   A range of survey-type books of popular music and, more specifically, black musics, were reviewed in order to determine how, or whether, Ike and Tina are taken up. No mention is made at all in: Norman Kelly (ed.), *R & B, Rhythm and Business: The Political Economy of Black Music* (New York, 2002), Frank Kofsky, *Black Nationalism and the Revolution in Music* (New York, 1970), Hildred Roach, *Black American Music: Past and Present*, Volume II (Malabar, FL, 1985), Guthrie Ramsey Jr, *Race Music: Black Cultures from Bebop to Hip Hop* (Berkeley, CA, 2003). Passing mention is made in Anthony DeCurtis, James Henke and Holly George-Warren (eds), *The Rolling Stone Illustrated History of Rock & Roll*, 3rd edn (New York, 1992), Brian Ward, *Just My Soul Responding: Rhythm and Blues, Black Consciousness, and Race Relations* (Berkeley, CA, 1998), David Nicholls (ed.), *The*

blip on the radar, and most often for her commercially successful comeback in the 1980s: as a woman over forty who moved from rags, via abuse at Ike's hands, to pop music riches (no small feat and certainly worth celebrating). The Ike and Tina Turner Revue of the 1960s and 1970s has been largely relegated to the dustbin of history—acknowledged as the wild and crazy precursor to Tina's solo triumph, the mythic institution through which she paid her dues, both in the form of grueling touring schedules on the chitlin' circuit and around the world, and through her physical and emotional torment at Ike's hand. There may be many reasons why Ike and Tina are second-rate members of the rock and roll canon: the original material was often wanting (with some notable exceptions); the production of the records could have been better; Ike made astonishingly questionable business decisions that kept the group in the "small times."[14] It is very likely that Tina was more raw and provocative a black and woman performer than American culture could really stomach at the time; she undoubtedly fit, for many other artists and audience members alike, into the "Jezebel" stereotype, one of several persistent images of black American women.[15] The Jezebel or whore stereotype is defined as "the

---

Cambridge History of American Music (New York, 1998), Maureen Mahon, *Right to Rock: The Black Rock Coalition and the Cultural Politics of Race* (Durham, NC, 2004), Reebee Garofalo, *Rockin' Out: Popular Music in the USA* (Upper Saddle River, NJ, 2002), David Szatmary, *Rockin' in Time: A Social History of Rock and Roll* 5th edn (Upper Saddle River, NJ, 2004), and Richard Crawford, *America's Musical Life: A History* (New York, 2001). Garofalo and DeCurtis et al. mention Tina's recording of "River Deep, Mountain High" only in relation to Phil Spector, who wrote and produced the track. Szatmary, at the time of this writing the best selling popular music textbook in North America, makes no mention of Tina outside of her relationship with Ike. The most substantial information appears in Nicholas Tawa, *Supremely American: Popular Song in the 20th Century: Styles and Singers and What They Said About America* (Lanham, MD, 2005). This source concedes that she made important personal contributions to the songs, whether or not she wrote them. Floyd, in *The Power of Black Music*, makes passing mention of Ike, but not Tina. This strikes me as particularly significant in a book that, in the end, offers more of less a survey of black music in the twentieth century; Floyd gives little mention to any black women musicians, however, and never uses their performances or recordings in his detailed analyses—these are reserved for male artists.

[14]   For more on this see Turner with Loder.

[15]   For discussions of these and other stereotyped images of black women see Leith Mullings, "Images, Ideology and Women of Color," in Maxine Baca Zinn and Bonnie Thornton Dill (eds.), *Women of Color in U.S. Society* (Philadelphia, 1994), pp. 265–89, and Patricia Hill Collins, *Black Feminist Thought: Knowledge, Consciousness and the Politics of Empowerment*, 2nd edn. (New York, 2000). Collins takes up current manifestations of, especially, the Jezebel image in her book *Black Sexual Politics: African Americans, Gender and the New Racism* (New York, 2004). Indeed, bell hooks places Tina squarely within this tradition of sexual stereotypes when she argues, "undesirable in the conventional sense, which defines beauty and sexuality as desirable only to the extent that it is idealized and unattainable, the black female body gains attention only when it is synonymous with accessibility, availability, when it is sexually deviant. Tina Turner's construction of a public

sexually aggressive, provocative woman governed entirely by libido," an image that is often opposed to another dominant stereotype of black women, the sexless Mammy, who is "the religious, loyal, motherly slave devoted to the care of the slaveowner's family."[16] These images developed during slavery but are stubbornly persistent, even to the present time.[17] Tina's skimpy costumes that emphasized her long legs and often exposed her belly, her frenetic dancing and her aggressive style of singing must have conjured up the Jezebel stereotype in many minds. Further, although Tina is fairly light-skinned, some of her facial features, such as her broad nose and thicker lips, moved her away from European beauty ideals, thus making her less marketable as an object of sexual desire in white culture, usually a key element for a woman to achieve success in the music industry. On some level, Tina must have known this, since she has increasingly shaped her appearance towards white standards of beauty since the 1980s.[18]

On the surface of it, then, Ike and Tina seem to have been everything that serious popular music posterity reviles: a commercially-driven enterprise, not too terribly innovative, not political in the way that some black performers of the 1960s were, with an intriguing but dangerously "other" woman fronting the organization. While she was hailed by, especially, white, British, blues-based rock artists of the late 1960s and 1970s as an important and influential singer, there has been very little analysis of Tina as an artist. Indeed, it is all but impossible to find commentaries that do not turn almost immediately to her raunchy, sexualized body in performance, relegating her voice, also described as little more than raunchy, to the background.

---

sexual persona most conforms to this idea of black female sexuality." See hooks, "Selling Hot Pussy: Representations of Black Female Sexuality in the Cultural Marketplace," Chapter 4 in *Black Looks: Race and Representation.* (Boston, 1992), pp. 65–66.

[16]   Mullings, "Images, Ideology and Women of Color," p. 267.

[17]   The Jezebel image in particular, which posits black women as having insatiable sexual appetites, and therefore as sexually aggressive, developed to rationalize white men's sexual assaults on black women. See Collins, *Black Feminist Thought*, p. 81. This image also developed, of course, in opposition to the (white, male) construction of white femininity, sometimes called "ideal" or "true" womanhood, in which white women "possessed four cardinal virtues: piety, purity, submissiveness, and domesticity" (p. 72). It is this persistent construction of "true" femininity that women such as Tina constantly struggle against.

[18]   For a discussion of ideals of beauty related to skin color, hair texture and facial features in black women see Collins, *Black Feminist Thought*, pp. 88–92. Tina's hair color has become increasingly blonde since the 1980s and she has admitted to having plastic surgery on her nose to make it smaller, although she claims that this was to repair damage done by Ike's constant beatings, during which her nose was repeatedly broken. bell hooks criticizes Tina for her increasing blondeness, arguing that "Blondeness ... serves as an endorsement of a racist aesthetic which sees blonde hair as the epitome of beauty"; hooks, p. 68. Thanks to Stan Hawkins for suggesting that the issue of Tina's light-skinned appearance is important to consider.

As if all of this might not be sufficient to render the group second rate, it must also be remembered that the Ike and Tina Turner Revue was, in its day, first and foremost celebrated for its live performances over its studio recordings, the latter of which rarely hit the mark squarely. The history of Western popular music has primarily been a history of commercial studio recordings that must demonstrate innovation, construed in very particular ways. The materiality and availability of the recordings allow us to create a shared and seemingly stable repertory of "music that matters." With few exceptions (think James Brown, *Live at the Apollo* [King Records, 1963], The Grateful Dead, *Live Dead* [Warner Bros, 1970], Kiss, *Alive* [Casablanca, 1975]), live performances have been considered less crucial, partly because they are simply less available for analysis (unless, as with the above examples, someone had the perspicuity to record the performances for posterity).[19] This is perhaps even more so when the artist in question could be dismissed as a glorified cover band—a lot of the songs Ike and Tina performed were covers—and when what matters about these performances is about the visual as well as the sound, and probably more about process than product. Some academics have begun to problematize this privileging of the studio recording, but it still holds considerable power in the imagination of those constructing popular music history.[20] This privileging of the studio recording, and of recording "original" material in the studio becomes particularly problematic for someone like Tina (and perhaps for other women as well), whose innovation lay, for the most part, elsewhere.

So how do we, then, "formulat[e] schemes for understanding those kinds of black music that do not easily fit into the familiar accounts of African American music," as Jeff Melnick has recently posed the question?[21] Tina was the only black, woman rock and roll singer—treading on territory that was, by this time, firmly established as white and male. Simultaneously, she ventured into the musical space occupied by the increasingly revered and singular James Brown, often covering his hit song "Please, Please, Please" in live shows, and in 1970 recording the song "Bold Soul Sister," an original Ike and Tina song in the style of Brown's new genre of funk music. She cultivated an image of the "tough girl" in an era when black women musicians were generally refining their sound and image to assimilate into

---

[19]   One corrective to this is the recent collection of essays entitled *Performance and Popular Music*, in which some key popular music performances are analyzed in depth. See Ian Inglis (ed.), *Performance and Popular Music* (London, 2006).

[20]   Jason Toynbee argues that recordings are only part of a "continuous process of performance and creation." Toynbee, *Making Popular Music: Musicians, Creativity and Institutions* (London, 2000), cited in Hawkins, p. 160. Hawkins follows this with the important observation that "for pop artists the structuring apparatus of performance does not end in the recording—performance is an ongoing process that is extended by its mediation through different contexts into different dialogues."

[21]   Jeff Melnick, "Story Untold: The Black Men and White Sounds of Doo-Wop," in Mike Hill (ed.), *Whiteness: A Critical Reader* (New York, 1997), pp. 139–40.

white culture, or were gaining respect through the cultivation of "serious" music derived from black gospel (i.e., Aretha Franklin). This last point is, of course, tied into issues of class as well as race: Tina's raw, tough girl image is rooted in the working class. And, finally, at the beginning of the 1970s, she appropriated white, male rock songs, covering material (like the Rolling Stones' "Honky Tonk Woman" and the Beatles' "Come Together") that was not only weird for a woman to take on, but decidedly inverted the normal trend of white rock artists covering black blues and R&B. That the true power of these accomplishments took place largely in live performances has not helped Tina find her place in the critical discourse of black music history; nor has her solo career, which veered her away from her R&B roots towards a more mainstream pop sound—a move that wrote her off in the minds of journalists and academics alike.[22] Further, as Ron Wynn, one of Tina's biographers has insightfully put it, "no matter how great [Tina] was as a member of Ike and Tina Turner's Revue, outside the Revue she was still not acknowledged, considered, or evaluated by the audience as someone with something important to say."[23] If Tina had been a solo artist during the 1960s, her reception might have been quite a bit different (witness Aretha, although the divergent images of the two women certainly need to be taken into account), but because she performed in a group, with her husband as band leader—with the added assumption that he was artistically in control—her singular contributions were received within a context that suggested she had little agency. It has not helped that Ike wishes to claim credit for all aspects of The Revue, down to the minute details of individual performances. In his autobiography, written long after Tina's massive success as a solo artist, and in such places as liner notes to recent re-issues of Ike and Tina recordings, Ike states that he was responsible for all the choreography performed by Tina and the Ikettes, that he coached Tina on her singing, that he decided what the girls would wear on stage, that, in fact, according to him "just as I controlled every note of the music, I controlled every step of the dancing."[24] In her autobiography, Tina concedes that Ike controlled the act in terms of what music was performed and recorded, and that he blamed Tina for commercial failures because she wouldn't

---

[22]   See, for example, the odd biography by Ron Wynn, *Tina: The Tina Turner Story* (New York, 1985), who has trouble admiring Tina even as he admires her! He criticizes her for wanting to be a "rock" artist and turning away from her R&B roots; he writes that one would never call Tina an innovator in the way that James Brown and Jackie Wilson are, and he dismisses most of her solo work. One gets the sense that Wynn, who confesses to seeing The Revue often during the 1960s and 1970s, is ultimately much more impressed with Ike than with Tina, but understands that Tina's name, not Ike's, will sell his book.

[23]   Ibid., p. 42.

[24]   Ike Turner, pp. 98–99. This point of view is also expressed by Rob Bowman in his liner notes to the DVD *Ike and Tina Turner Live in '71* (Reelin' in the Years Productions; Eagle Rock Entertainment, 2004), as well as in Neil Slaven's liner notes to *Ike & Tina Turner Revue with the Kings of Rhythm Orchestra Live!!!* (Kent CDKEND 102, 1993).

sing songs the way he wanted her to;[25] and he certainly controlled her with the constant threat of physical abuse. But Ike's claims of control go much further than this. Whether or not these claims are exaggerated—and there is reason to believe they are—the evidence we have on record and video performances of the Revue offer Tina and the Ikettes, both in their singing and dancing, as clearly responsible for the innovative sound and visual performances for which the Revue became acclaimed. Claiming increasingly more behind-the-scenes credit, while diminishing the role of embodied voices on stage or in the recording studio is a means through which Ike, and the writers who repeat and validate his stories, can continue to dilute the women's agency. Ike's claim of creative control over Tina and the Ikettes is a very familiar story. As Jacqueline Warwick has written, the majority of women who flourish in the music industry have to deal with the assumption that the men in their lives—lovers, brothers, fathers—were "the true architects of their successes."[26] In her analysis of the girl group artists produced by some of these men, Warwick takes what she calls a "Marxist feminist" position that allows her to place the bodies producing the music at the center instead of the periphery of the equation. Their performances, their vocal labor, she argues, are crucially important to the success or failure of the recording, and are in large part what an audience responds to and values in a song.[27] This is a useful view to keep in mind when considering Ike and Tina. While Ike wants to *say* that he invented her look, her movements, and her sound (and while there are certainly elements of his influence that are important to consider), it is Tina herself who *materialized* these extraordinary elements of her performances. It is her embodied voice, her physical presence on the stage, her costumed, moving body to which the eye, heart and soul are drawn. Perhaps that's exactly why, despite his desire to control the show, Ike was so profoundly frustrated with her.

Signifyin(g) for her black life

The theoretical lens of Signifyin(g), explicated most famously by Henry Louis Gates Jr,[28] and taken up by writers on music such as Samuel Floyd, David Brackett, Robert Walser and Ronald Radano, offers a useful way through which to address some of these issues.[29] To begin with, it focuses attention on the signifier, not

---

[25]   See, for example, Turner with Loder, p. 187.

[26]   Jacqueline Warwick, *Girl Groups, Girl Culture: Popular Music and Identity in the 1960s* (New York and London, 2007), p. 91.

[27]   Ibid.

[28]   For the remainder of this essay, I will dispense with the capitalization of this word and the parenthetical (g).

[29]   Floyd; David Brackett, *Interpreting Popular Music* (Berkeley, 2000); Robert Walser, "Out of Notes: Signification, Interpretation and the Problem of Miles Davis," *The*

the signified;[30] that is, what matters is the act, the performative moment, the body signifying; whatever may happen or have happened behind the scenes is of less importance; this neutralizes Ike's perceived control over the performance situation. Further, it frames and politicizes Tina's appropriations of various musical styles, helping to make sense of her choices.

Interestingly, although Gates engages in detailed analysis of two books by black women, he does not broach the subject of gender: for him, signifying is an African American tradition, and his aim is to explore "the relation of the black vernacular tradition to the Afro-American literary tradition,"[31] without taking into account differences other than race (broadly conceived in black/white terms). Similarly, the theoretical framework of signifying and its applications in music have been made by men working on music made by men: Samuel Floyd on various artists, Robert Walser on Miles Davis, and David Brackett on James Brown, to name three prominent examples (this is not intended as a negative critique of their excellent work, only offered as a fact). I would like to suggest that the political potential of signifying also lies in the ways in which it can negotiate issues around gender. Tina's signifying was politically radical not only because she was black, but precisely because she was a black woman. She signified not only on black musical traditions, but on those that had been developed by, and were associated with black men; she signified not only on black musical traditions, but on those black musical traditions that had been appropriated by white men.[32] Signifying was, for her, a means of survival: her ability to signify on black male musical models gave her credibility with Ike, indeed, was probably what kept her in the band, fulfilling his desires to emulate the styles of musicians he took seriously, although not enough to refrain from abusing her; signifying on rock and roll and eventually white rock music gave her credibility with white rock artists, whose support ultimately revived her career. Tina, the trickster, used what Floyd calls the African American musical trope of tropes, the Call–Response ("the dialogical, conversational character of black music"), in the service of "baffling" or "subduing" agents of oppression.[33] Further, one key aspect of signifying is the use of parody and this is, I think, a key element of Tina's appropriation of male-identified styles, whether black or white. In her book *She Bop II: The Definitive History of Women in Rock, Pop and Soul*, Lucy O'Brien characterizes Tina as a "pop cartoon character,"

Musical Quarterly 77/2 (Summer 1993): 343–65; Ronald Radano, *Lying Up a Nation: Race and Black Music* (Chicago, 2003), pp. 27–44.

[30]   Floyd, p. 95.

[31]   Gates, p. ix.

[32]   It needs to be said that the traditions I am identifying as "male" here are so considered only because women's contributions to them have generally been unrecorded or ignored. My thanks to Annie Randall for suggesting I include this clarification.

[33]   Floyd, p. 95.

a "rock chick parody."[34] She comments that Tina has always been in control of this parody, playing into assumptions and expectations in terms of her image and, I would argue, her vocal sound, around what a woman creating "rock" music should look and sound like. The element of parody is, then, key to understanding Tina's de-colonizing, destabilizing gendered and racialized practices.

Singing like a man, signifyin(g) on rock and roll

> Now, when I say I can sing, I know that I don't have a 'pretty' voice. My voice is not the voice of a woman, so to speak. That's why when I choose my music I think of men. I can relate to their delivery, I'm attracted to it. When I first started working with Ike, it was all men and just me, and I had to sort of keep up. So I had to take a lot of my training and my patterns of singing from the guys. I wasn't about girls and beauty and femininity. (Tina Turner)[35]

> I'd be writing songs with Little Richard in mind, but I didn't have no Little Richard to sing them, so Tina was my Little Richard singing in a female's voice ... so Tina concentrated on singing like a man. (Ike Turner)[36]

> Her voice was different for the type of music we were doing .... A woman doing that type of thing then was kind of no-no. She was like Bessie Smith and some of those other great singers; but they sang the down-home blues. What we were playing was more of a swinging-type thing. (Gene Washington, drummer for The Revue)[37]

> Larry King: You're in the Rock and Roll Hall of Fame. Do you consider yourself rock and roll?

> Tina Turner: Yes.

> King: That's your idiom?

> Turner: That's my style. I take great songs and turn them into rock and roll songs on stage. I don't really actually get rock and roll material because there's not that much good music out there. Because my performance is an energy on stage, I need that kind of music, so I just transform the music.[38]

---

[34]   Lucy O'Brien, *She Bop II: The Definitive History of Women in Rock, Pop and Soul* (London, 2002), p. 123.

[35]   Turner with Loder, p. 204.

[36]   Ike Turner, p. 87.

[37]   Turner with Loder, p. 65.

[38]   *Larry King Live*, CNN, February 21, 1997.

The gendered discourse around Tina's vocal style relies on stable and stereotypical notions about the voice, about masculinity, and about popular music styles. The one model that Ike claims for her is "male," although one can't escape the ways in which this is complicated by the fact that the male in question is Little Richard, whose voice and image decidedly queered early rock and roll. Tina herself never claims models, thereby emphasizing the uniqueness of her sound, her singularity, but she does want to claim that she "sings like a man," as do Ike and Revue drummer Gene Washington. Other than the quotations above, little else has been said about Tina's vocal style; I include the excerpt from Tina's appearance on CNN's *Larry King Live* show because it is interesting to rub this dialogue concerning genre up against the comments about gender: rock and roll is typically gendered as male (in fact, as a particular construction of masculinity that I discuss below) and so she once again aligns herself with this construction of maleness here. What is particularly interesting about this is that she separates her vocal sound out from any other stylistic feature (form, instrumentation, up-tempo song or ballad, timbre, groove, etc.), suggesting that her voice alone can transform a song into "rock and roll." This gives her enormous agency and control over her career (real or imagined), since no matter what material she is given to sing, no matter what musicians she works with, no matter who produces, it is the materiality of her voice that, in this paradigm, defines her work. Strikingly absent from this discourse is any overt mention of race, although race can easily be read into it: why did Ike claim Little Richard, a black artist, as a role model for Tina? Why does she insist on aligning herself with rock and roll, a genre largely defined by white performers?

Apart from the rhetoric, is there something "male" about the way she sings? Is it possible to enter into such a discussion without essentializing? And where *does* race come into the picture, if at all? "Even in our time," wrote Joke Dame some years ago, "the need to categorize a voice according to gender, to assign sex to the voice, has not ceased."[39] Although this is true, how voices are categorized according to gender is a complex matter. A significant sociological and psychological literature that attempts to account for vocal difference exists, some of it based on biology and some on the idea that vocal gender is socially constructed.[40] Still a very useful discussion of these issues, despite its age, is that by David Graddol and Joan Swan in their book *Gender Voices*.[41] Graddol and Swan argue that, "even if one accepts that many differences in voice quality between the sexes are consequent upon evolutionary history and anatomical make-up, it does not follow that the meanings which these voice qualities have acquired

---

[39] Joke Dame, "Unveiled Voices: Sexual Difference and the Castrato," in Philip Brett et al. (eds), *Queering the Pitch: The New Gay and Lesbian Musicology* (New York and London, 1994), p. 139.

[40] See, for example, Ann Weatherall, *Gender, Language and Discourse* (New York, 2002).

[41] David Graddol and Joan Swan, *Gender Voices* (Oxford, 1985).

are as biologically determined as the voice qualities themselves."[42] As with any other symbolic forms of communication, meanings are contingent and contested; nonetheless, certain vocal characteristics have been assigned gendered meanings: range, for example, but perhaps more importantly, according to several studies, timbre (harshness is associated with aggressive, authoritative characteristics and so, often, with masculinity; breathiness with sexual availability or arousal, or with submissiveness, for example, and so often with the feminine).[43] There is clear evidence that listeners readily distinguish between male and female voices, probably based on stereotypes that are socially learned early on, and that "individuals use their voice to accommodate towards perceived social norms of gendered identity."[44] Leslie Dunn and Nancy Jones argue that such conclusions perpetuate what they call, "myths of vocal gender" and that these "have served to reinforce patriarchal constructions of the feminine."[45] This is undoubtedly true, but it does not change the fact that the stereotypes—the "myths"—exist. Nor does it, as they also argue, prevent the "deconstruct[ion] [of] the traditional paradigms of the voice/body relationship ... in order to show that women can possess more assertive, less predictable forms of vocality."[46] Some important scholarship on such "deconstructions" has been carried out in studies of the castrato (by Dame and Wayne Kostenbaum, for example); in addition, there have been a few studies that examine heavy metal/hard rock singing and gender, and Ellie Hisama has made interesting observations concerning vocal range and gender in the music of Joan Armatrading. Even still, there is much yet to be explored in this area.[47]

---

[42]   Ibid., p. 35.

[43]   See studies cited in ibid., p. 34.

[44]   Weatherall, p. 52.

[45]   Leslie C. Dunn and Nancy A. Jones, Introduction, in Leslie C. Dunn and Nancy A. Jones (eds), *Embodied Voices: Representing Female Vocality in Western Culture* (Cambridge, 1994), p. 3. These characteristics of vocality cannot be singled out as defining gender alone. As Grant Olwage argues, in certain circumstances, such characteristics are also linked to race, and, especially, class. See his article "The Class and Colour of Tone: An Essay on the Social History of Vocal Timbre," *Ethnomusicology Forum* 13/2 (November 2004): 203–26. Weatherall also discusses cross-cultural speech norms, concluding, as have many others, that difference between accepted norms varies across cultures.

[46]   Dunn and Jones, p. 4.

[47]   For a discussion of vocal quality and gender see Robert Walser, *Running With the Devil: Power, Gender and Madness in Heavy Metal Music* (Hanover, NJ, 1993); Susan Fast, *In the Houses of the Holy: Led Zeppelin and the Power of Rock Music* (New York, 2001); Suzanne Cusick, "On Musical Performance of Sex and Gender," in Elaine Barkin and Lydia Hamessley (eds), *Audible Traces: Gender, Identity and Music* (Zürich, 1999), pp. 25–48; for a discussion of vocal range and gender see Ellie Hisama, "Voice, Race and Sexuality in the Music of Joan Armatrading," in the same volume, pp. 115–32; on the castrato voice see Dame, "Unveiled Voices," and Wayne Koestenbaum, *The Queen's Throat: Opera, Homosexuality and the Mystery of Desire* (New York, 1993).

Complicating the matter is the fact that there are generic conventions in popular music that must be taken into consideration in any discussion of gender and singing. Gene Washington notes that if Tina had been singing "down home blues," her style would have been acceptable for a woman, but because The Revue was doing "more of a swinging-type thing" it was not. But singers such as Bessie Smith, the "downhome" blues singer to whom Washington refers, do not sound like Tina, even if we imagine their voices transplanted into an up-tempo rhythm and blues song. Although such singers—and one could mention others here such as Memphis Minnie, or Tina's R&B contemporaries, such as Ruth Brown or Big Mama Thornton—had powerful voices, none of them so consistently emphasized full out belting, distortion, strain (singing in a high range that sounds as though it is pushing the upper limits of the range), clipped and choppy phrasing, with emotional excess that still manages to sound controlled. The women models for such singing come not from classic blues, but from gospel, which introduces much more of the emotional range employed by a singer such as Tina; especially close to Tina's vocal style are such gospel singers as Clara Ward, Sister Rosetta Tharpe, Marion Williams, and above all Mahalia Jackson, whose raw vocal sound, lower range, clipped phrasing, use of vibrato, distortion, power and strain closely match Tina's vocal qualities. Given that Tina's formative musical training took place in the black church, this influence is hardly surprising, yet she does not openly claim women gospel singers as influences. Interestingly, these gospel singers *have* been claimed by Little Richard as enormously influential to his singing style.[48] For Tina, then, certain vocal characteristics became gendered male through their association with early (and later and continuing) rock and roll, the sound of which was defined by men, and increasingly by white men, and her insistence on claiming a "male" way of singing, and rock and roll as her generic home. They have been interpreted in this context as markers of masculine power.

In her early 60s hits, Tina signifies on the rock and roll of the previous decade in particular ways and at particular moments of these songs; she calls forth established musical tropes from her male colleagues, engaging in a call and response that crosses from their songs to hers. In "A Fool in Love," one can hear echoes of Elvis and Buddy Holly in the opening "Well ...," ("Well bless my soul," "Wella, wella, wella," "Well I love you Peggy Sue"), heard in countless early rock and roll songs. Little Richard is invoked in the falsetto c^2-b^{b1} near the end of the last chorus that breaks out of the established vocal range of the song (think "tutti frutti, woooo"). The melody of the verses hovers around only a few pitches, with a concentration on the tonic G, like so many up-tempo rock and roll songs by Chuck Berry and Little Richard.

But it is perhaps the quality of Tina's voice that most aligns her with rock and roll. There is a particular bigness, directly from the opening "Well ..." and a distinctively hard edge: her voice is raw, assertive, aggressive, shouting, demanding

---

[48]   Andy Gill, "Ten Questions for Little Richard," in Kandia Crazy Horse (ed.), *Rip It Up: The Black Experience in Rock'n'Roll* (New York, 2004), p. 3.

and the melody is sometimes perched at the top of her range in a way that makes her sound strained and choked, much in the way Little Richard's was.[49] Perhaps the most extraordinary lick in this song—the lick that makes it so special—is Tina's rising growl that accompanies the chord change from I to IV in the chorus, capped off with her choked yelp. Other than her interjection "tell me one time," Tina sings no words in the chorus, she only vocalizes in this hard-hitting, forceful way. There is really no model for the grit of this gesture; it is singular. All and all, Tina's signifying takes on a particular mode: it is not only that she imitates; she *outdoes*. She does not repeat a trope; she repeats it with fervor. The repeated note melody of the verses, for example, is inflected in countless subtle ways—an increase in distortion here, a blue-note there—that are absent from early male rock and roll singers, who shout in a much more undifferentiated way. In her voice, the tropes become parody, they are caricatured. In the process is revealed a voice that can do better (with more inflection, more power) what has come before. In this lies Tina's power. As Grant Olwage has argued, while these characteristics come out of a particular socio-cultural milieu, or habitus, they can either be adopted or exchanged for others, that is, one can learn how to sing in different styles.[50] Tina, it must be remembered, chose to adopt these characteristics, chose to signify on black gospel and rock and roll and soul, despite her wanting to put this down to biology, that she had no choice because her voice just *is* a certain way.

The question is why. Why did she make these choices? Since she was part of a musical organization comprised entirely of men, with a band leader whose models were men (not only Little Richard, but perhaps even more blatantly, James Brown), it is not surprising that Tina would have wanted to fit—in fact, that she had to fit in or be dropped from the band—and perhaps claiming "maleness" as a way to define her singing was part of her strategy to do so. But claiming to be part of a "male" tradition was probably important to her in other ways as well. It set her apart, certainly, and gave her a dimension of toughness that has defined both her image and her singing (she can not only play with the boys, she can sound like them). Additionally, her claim may have had resonance for her life in another way, and that is that her experience as a woman (Ike's object) and her experience of seeing other women around her, including those she grew up with, may well have taught her that traditional femininity did not much pay off; that claiming the phallus—at least in the recording studio and on stage—was a way for her to be powerful and in control.

That Tina *could* cultivate such a singing style in the early 1960s in the US is certainly because she was a *black* woman. Given her ability to manipulate this vocal style and to claim rock and roll as her generic home, it is interesting

---

[49] A particularly good example of this is "I Idolize You," where the second part of each verse is pitched around c^2 and slightly higher. In "A Fool in Love," the melody is pitched around g^1', a comfortable range for Tina, but which she can make sound strained through her timbre.

[50] Olwage, p. 5.

to consider that later in her career Tina frequently commented on how much she disliked it and how her discourse became racialized (probably without her conscious knowledge). She came to think of the style of singing that she cultivated in the early days with Ike as "screaming and shouting ... because there wasn't really much to [his songs]. I'd always have to improvise and ad lib."[51] Tina makes this comment in relationship to her experience of recording "River Deep, Mountain High" with Phil Spector and others have repeated the sentiment: in the liner notes to the recording *The Ike and Tina Turner Revue Live with the Kings of Rhythm* Neil Slaven writes, "The first thing that Tina had to forget when she rehearsed [River Deep Mountain High] was all the cheap histrionics that Ike had taught her as stage craft. Here was a song with melody, not just a gospel-based vamp over which she could whip the house into hysteria."[52] These perceptions are linked to fact only tenuously. The opening melody for "River Deep" is a stepwise, diatonic arch that Tina phrases carefully, leaning into the rising line using her characteristic tight vibrato, but little distortion; by the time she hits the second part of the verse, however, she belts full out, with the same conviction, the same "histrionics," and over the same kind of single note melody that she frequently sang with Ike. The chorus and bridge offer other, contrasting melodies to that of the verses, however, so there is shape, contrast, and development in this song. And Phil Spector's arrangement and production make the piece spectacular, although Tina does not comment openly on these, only on the "melody." It must be conceded that some of Ike and Tina's early songs were well developed melodically as well: "I Idolize You" is a good example of a song with quite a wide melodic range and substantial melodic interest spread out over its sixteen-bar verse and eight-bar chorus/refrain. In Tina's mind, however, the seemingly more complex, worked out melody of "River Deep" became associated with life away from Ike, with the experience of working with Phil Spector, who believed in her as a singer, and so in a positive frame of reference for whiteness. She praises white rock music in a similar way, saying that "those groups were interpreting black music .... They touched on R and B, in a way, but it wasn't obvious. I mean, it wasn't the old thing."[53] How, exactly it wasn't the old thing is difficult to say, especially since the white rockers were trying their best to emulate the old thing. But this association of the development of black music into something new by white artists, and the association of melody, in particular, with white music is an important discursive formation for Tina. It resonates with an historical discourse that equates "black music" with rhythm, noise and "hotness" in opposition to the "refinement," much of which comes through melody, of European musics.[54] In her autobiography, Tina makes a similar connection of whiteness to refinement and civility (and, by extension, to upward mobility in terms of class) when she recounts two experiences from her childhood.

---

[51]   Turner with Loder, p. 119.

[52]   Slaven, liner notes.

[53]   Turner with Loder, p. 152.

[54]   For substantive documentation of this point of view see Radano, pp. 230–77.

"Being in love," she recalls, is "something that white people did, it seemed ... . I never saw that among black people in those days—which isn't to say it didn't happen; I just never saw it. Among the black people I did see, you were always aware that love was sexual, and there was something sneaky about it."[55] Tina's second experience with what she perceived to be white refinement occurred when she worked as a live-in domestic for a young white married couple. About this experience she writes, "I was learning about this other world—the white world, I guess—with magazines and books and culture ... . And it was from being around them that I started thinking about marriage and what it might be like. I had never thought about marriage before—not when I was living with my parents, with all their bickering and fighting. But the Hendersons' marriage was different. My Guy was the faithful type."[56] Tina's childhood, spent in extreme poverty and surrounded by loveless parents who gave her little attention, made her view the whiteness she experienced as redemption. Gayle Wald has written sympathetically about one facet of this, arguing that Tina's desire to sing white rock during her solo career was a result of her association of R&B and blues music with the poverty from which she came as well as all the years of abuse she suffered under Ike.[57] I would argue that this goes back much further, into her first, non-musical experiences with whiteness that she later mapped on to music in a variety of ways.

Running for covers

Signifying on a male-inflected vocal style was one way for Tina to reclaim power and agency and to problematize gendered notions of the voice and of the genre of rock and roll; covering music by men was another. Covers were a staple of Ike and Tina shows and of their studio recordings as well. From very early on in his career, Ike took pride in his facility in copying hit songs note for note; his thinking was that the ability to reproduce hit songs gave him insight into what the industry and the market were interested in, that it put his finger on the pulse. Three readily available live recordings include a considerable number of covers. The CD *Ike and Tina Turner Revue with the Kings of Rhythm Orchestra Live!!!* (Ace Reords, 1994[1964]) includes only five original songs out of eighteen tracks; *Live! The Ike and Tina Turner Show* from the same year includes a similar number. The DVD *Ike and Tina Turner Live in '71* (Eagle Rock Entertainment, 2004) includes only one Ike Turner song ("Ooo Poo Pah Doo") as well as Tina's/Phil Spector's "River Deep Mountain High"; the other nine tracks are covers. Many of Ike and

---

[55] Turner with Loder, p. 23.

[56] Ibid., p. 29.

[57] Gayle Wald, "One of the Boys? Whiteness, Gender and Popular Music Studies," in Mike Hill (ed), *Whiteness: A Critical Reader* (New York, 1997), p. 162. Wald does, however, comment that Tina's highly sexualized image points to the limited options for a woman trying to make it in the music industry.

Tina's covers were songs that were recent hits for other artists, and which were strongly identified with those other artists: "Please, Please, Please," for example, was James Brown's first R&B hit in 1956, but more importantly it appeared on his ground breaking *Live at the Apollo* album from 1963, the year before Ike and Tina's first recorded live version of it. *Live at the Apollo* was Brown's "biggest commercial breakthrough ... [selling] over one million copies, and remain[ing] in the LP charts for over a year, unprecedented achievements for a rhythm and blues album."[58] Sly and the Family Stone's hit, "I Want to Take You Higher," was recorded two years before we see it on the 1971 Ike and Tina DVD, but it may well have been a staple of Ike and Tina's show before that. The DVD also includes three covers of white rock music, The Beatles' "Come Together," The Rolling Stones' "Honky Tonk Woman" and Creedence Clearwater Revival's "Proud Mary."

In one of the only academic articles that tackles the subject, Deena Weinstein defines a cover song as an "itera[tion] (with more or fewer differences) [of] a prior recorded performance of a song by a particular artist, rather than simply the song itself as an entity separate from any performer or performance," and she argues that this practice is "peculiar to rock music."[59] Her examples range over fifty years, from the 1950s through the 1990s and all feature white artists covering either black or white records—not entirely surprising since she limits herself to "rock" music. But Ike and Tina, although not considered a "rock" act in the 1960s (at least not to anyone but themselves), engaged in this practice of covering, not, as Weinstein would have it in her examples of white artists covering well known black music in the 1960s, as a means of "validating their own authenticity as musicians," but in order to capitalize on the commercial success and familiarity of these songs. Covering a song is not only a means through which one "authenticates" oneself as an artist, not only a means of paying homage or respect, but if the song is well known, currently or recently on the charts, it is a way to bring the familiar into a live performance, which in the best of circumstances has the effect of electrifying a crowd. It also works to *associate* the performers with the artist who made the original recording in a range of ways that, I would argue, go beyond issues of authenticity. It aligns them with the commercial success of the song and by extension the artist, it functions to make the original artist "present" during the concert, it creates a dialogue between originating and covering artist. This last point is worth exploring a little further: part of what makes cover versions work, especially when the original is well known and/or by a particularly revered artist, is that the covering artist appropriates, to varying degrees, another musician's "grain" and this can be exhilarating for an audience to experience.

---

[58]   David Brackett, "Brown, James," *Grove Music Online*, L. Macy (ed), http://www. grovemusic.com.libaccess.lib.mcmaster.ca (accessed February 10, 2006).

[59]   Deena Weinstein, "The History of Rock's Pasts Through Rock Covers," in Thomas Swiss, John Sloop, and Andrew Herman (eds.), *Mapping the Beat: Popular Music and Contemporary Theory* (Oxford, 1998), p. 138.

For Ike and Tina, covering took a particular racialized and gendered trajectory throughout the 1960s and early 1970s. As previously noted, it was often a matter of covering what was currently, or recently, popular, but for them, for much of the 1960s, this meant what was popular in *black* music. Through much of the decade, The Revue allied itself with black R&B and soul music. Towards the end of the decade, they released two studio albums of blues covers. It was not until 1970 that they began to cover white rock music. I can find only one instance in which the music they covered was not associated with male artists ("Respect," by this time certainly Aretha Franklin's, appears on the 1971 DVD). Reflecting on these choices, one could argue that they follow those of other black artists in the 1960s—who among them was covering white music? While the explosion of rock and roll led young white musicians increasingly towards blues and R&B, were black artists covering rock and roll or white pop songs? Why did the exchange only go in one direction? Partly, it must have had to do with markets—what music did audiences, both black and white, want to hear black artists making? This must have been a concern for Ike, who was always interested in what music would sell and how his own outfit could copy hit records: if a black group *could* have sold records covering white music earlier in the 1960s, wouldn't he have tried it? But markets reflect larger social concerns and it strikes me that the decisions around what music Ike and Tina covered followed the progress of the civil rights movement in the 1960s: from a black act self-identifying as black, to them shifting into white rock music by the turn of the decade. In fact, we might dare to say that Tina's desire to cover white rock in the early 1970s (and, according to her, this was indeed her decision, not Ike's), was very bold and innovative. Musical genres are so bound up with (rigid) racialized and gendered identities that it is difficult indeed to break out of these molds.

The choice to cover music almost exclusively by male artists may have many reasons, among them the idea (perhaps Ike's, perhaps also Tina's) that male artists should be taken more seriously, that they have more clout (the better to be associated with), or that their music is heavier than that by women. But for Tina, it must certainly have also been another way to appropriate the power of these male artists, to, once again, demonstrate—this time not only through the abstractions of vocal technique, but through the direct invocation of a particular song—that she could do it as well as them.

Tina's covers of white rock music really constitute an entirely new chapter in her musical development, and they belong to the 1970s, so fall beyond the scope of this essay. Here, I want to concentrate on her musical relationship with James Brown over the course of the 1960s. Certainly the boldest example of Tina's live cover versions from the mid 1960s is James Brown's "Please, Please, Please." From the perspective of available musical models for a black R&B act at this time, James Brown makes considerable sense since he was arguably the most commercially successful black act after *Live at the Apollo* and commercial success was always at the heart of Ike's desires for the Revue. Nevertheless, it was bold indeed for Tina to take on James, since he is stylistically so unique (and again,

222   *SHE'S SO FINE*

was there anyone else covering James in the 1960s?) and because he presents a hypermasculine image. He is supremely in control: of his band, which had to play with impeccable precision or be fined by him, which he constantly directs and manipulates through his vocals; of his body, which he presented as tireless ("the hardest working man in show business"; the endless returns to the microphone after collapsing to his knees); a rags to riches black man who becomes a role model in his community; a womanizer, and woman abuser, with many well-publicized arrests for domestic violence. It is a hard, aggressive image that Tina took on. Were there any other women covering James? Not to my knowledge. There are some very intriguing questions yet to be explored about which artists are too "revered" and singular to be much covered, but James certainly would seem to fall into this category. As with the majority of Ike and Tina's cover versions, "Please, Please, Please," followed the original very closely (the exception to this was, of course, their version of "Proud Mary," which diverges significantly from the Creedence Clearwater Revival original and which, interestingly, became The Revue's biggest hit).

In *Live at the Apollo*, James uses "Please, Please, Please," as a frame for a medley of his other hits. It is, though, the musical context out of which "Please, Please, Please" emerges on *Live at the Apollo* that is perhaps more significant for my purposes here. James performs an emotionally wrenching version of "Lost Someone," in which he vamps on the theme of lost love for over ten minutes right before he launches into the opening of "Please, Please, Please"; James has connected with the audience during this performance, engaging in a call and response that has elicited ecstatic screams from them. Just when one thinks that this powerful exchange might go on forever, James launches into the opening of "Please, Please, Please," kicking up the emotional pitch when it seemed impossible to do so.

Three available live performances of "Please, Please, Please" by Tina indicate that she signified on James's *Apollo* performance of this song for at least the space of three years (between 1964 and 1967). Two appear on the album *Ike and Tina Turner Revue with the Kings of Rhythm Orchestra Live!!!* One of these is from 1964, the other from 1967. The third performance comes from the T.A.M.I./T.N.T. show from 1964 (this last is a video performance). Like James's live version, these take the song as a point of reference and use it as a framing device: the song's strong emotional pull is used as part of a process to bring the audience to increasingly higher emotional states. But instead of vamping on the theme of lost love as James does, Tina actually stops the music altogether and tells the audience a story of lost love as a spoken monologue, with the inflections and tone of a preacher in the black church. As the protagonist, James keeps himself at a distance by singing, instead of speaking, and by singing what amount to tropes about lost love, keeping the narrative at a depersonalized level: "If you leave me I'll go crazy," "I'll love you tomorrow, just like I love you today," "Come back home to me," "Everybody needs somebody," and so on. Tina, on the other hand, makes her story incredibly personal when she stops the music:

I'm going to stop the music for just a few minutes now, because I want to talk to you. I want to talk about love and hurt. Maybe there's some of you in the house this evening that's never been in love. Maybe there's some in the house this evening that's never been hurt. But just the same I want you to listen to me; because I've loved and I've been hurt. And sometimes I often wonder how I find myself? I wonder how many of you have ever been in love. How many of you have ever been hurt? Have you ever been in love with a man that didn't love you? Sometimes when you might have been in a dance like you are tonight, thinking about the man you love, and you look over in a corner somewhere and see him with another girl. Ladies and gentlemen the feeling that you get then is what I call hurt. But you know, it ain't nothing that you can do about it. Some of you might say, ah yeah Tina, there is something that I can do about it. But I'm gonna tell you something, because I know: if the man don't want you, you can't make him happy. You might as well try to forget about it. I'm gonna ask you something right now, if you feel like talkin' to me, I want you to sing along with me, if there's anybody in this house that's ever been hurt, I want you to sing:

(music begins): I, I, I

I'm gonna stop the music one more time. Cause I ain't through talking to you yet. First, I wanna say that I know that in the house this evening, we probably have some more respectable young ladies. But you know even the respectable ones have done some wrong once in their lives. If you haven't done wrong yet, you gotta do something wrong cause that's how life is. I said that for another reason 'cause folks, I still wanna know I'm not by myself. I wanna know how many of you have ever been in love with a married man? You know, I wanna know how many of you have ever been in love with your best girlfriend's old man? You know, when you're in love with a man that don't belong to you, you can't always have him when you want to, and you can't be with him when you really, really need him. Most of time you have to slip to see him. Well all of us know, young and old, when you start to slippin' doin' anything it gets out of hand sometimes. As a matter of fact it makes you start to wondering. Sometimes you say, I wonder, ha, I wonder if he hugs and kisses his old lady at home like he hugs and kisses me. All of us are grown ups and we can face the truth. But I got some young ladies in the house this evening that ain't talking to me. Maybe it's because you don't want to put your business in the streets. Or maybe the man that you're with this evening don't belong to you. Some of you think I may be hard what I'm saying because I'm saying it before so many people, but all of know that I'm telling the truth. But girls when I come upon one of those men that I can't have when I want him, whenever I think I want him, when I need him, you wanna know what I tell him?

In her narrative, Tina details worst-case relationship scenarios from a heterosexual woman's perspective: being in love with a man who doesn't love you in return,

224   *SHE'S SO FINE*

being in love with your girlfriend's man, being in love with a married man. In one of the other live performances of this song, the narrative revolves around "the only man I ever loved" getting married to someone else, with Tina herself sitting through the wedding, recounting each and every detail of the service. Tina signifies on the extreme emotional landscape that James creates in his live performance of "Please, Please, Please," pressing it into the service of a specific kind of gendered pain. The kind of detail into which Tina goes and the relative length of these narratives (nearly five minutes for the one transcribed above) signifies on James's use of musical repetition. As David Brackett has argued, "Please, Please, Please" established James's "stylistic trademark: insistent repetition of a single phrase (in this case, the song's title) resulting in a kind of ecstatic trance.[60] Does Tina make herself vulnerable in these narratives? Does she paint a pathetic figure? Does she elicit sympathy (apparently this was Ike's goal in deciding to include these monologues)?[61] Does she come across as strong, speaking her mind? Is she riffing on the genre of girl group music, engaging in a sister-to-sister confessional moment, albeit much longer and more detailed—and more "grown up"—than what occurs in girl group music? Or can we read her narrative as parodic, knocking out the power of James's extremely emotional performances by confessing scenarios that become more and more outrageous as the monologue progresses (a kind of "top that one" scenario). I think it is possible to read Tina's narrative in all of these ways and, in retrospect, perhaps it can also be viewed as a commentary on her own situation with Ike, who regularly slept with other women while he was married to Tina (in fact, he had a lover who lived in their house at one point), or on James's by now well-known history of domestic violence.[62]

Tina's vocals in these performances are taken from James almost note-for-note. The phrasing, the raspy, choked tone, the ad libs are all replicated with precision; yet

---

[60]   Brackett, "Brown, James."

[61]   In *Takin Back My Name*, Ike states that the idea for these spoken narratives came from him and that he included them in order "to make women like her … . In those songs I had Tina saying what women everywhere wanted to say to their men … . And boy, the women would stand up and be callin' me 'You dirty sonofabitch.' They believe her man. This shit ain't never happened, but they believe it, man," pp. 88–89. He then relates this to how Tina relaunched her career in the 1980s: "What she did in writing [her autobiography] … is the same thing on a bigger scale … . When she wrote that book she was trying to get sympathy from the public," p. 89. Ike's point is obviously to suggest that Tina's descriptions of his physical and emotional abuse in her autobiography are fiction, even as the song narratives were.

[62]   For descriptions of Ike's many lovers while he was with Tina, see Turner with Loder. Brown has been arrested several times for domestic violence. His most recent arrest in 2004 came on the heels of his being awarded the Kennedy Center for the Performing Arts Honor in 2003. Many protested against Brown receiving this award on the basis of his long history of domestic abuse. See Asjylyn Loder, "Godfather of Soul Accused of Spouse Abuse—Again," *Women's E News*. http://www.womensenews.org/article.cfm/dyn/aid/1706/ (accessed July 21, 2006).

this is repetition with a difference. James's voice—described as "one of the harshest in rhythm and blues,"[63] angular and clipped phrasing, his "hardest working man in show business" image, his development of funk music—a genre that until recently has belonged very much to black men—his reputation as an aggressive, demanding band leader, all work together as a particular construction of masculinity. Tina's replication of, at least, the musical elements of this construction, with precision, confound their association with masculinity and strip this gender construction of some of its power. Further, the spoken narrative signifies on another musical tradition that in this context rubs up against the presence of James's construction of masculinity: girl group music. Tina's narrative evokes those many girl group songs in which girls share their stories about boys with each other and through which they create a supportive community. The difference, however, is that Tina's narrative moves the conversation from adolescence to adulthood, where the stakes are quite different and perhaps more injurious. The boy has become a man; and sometimes he's married.

One could say that Tina continued to "feminize" James's style—or at least pose a gendered challenge to it—when in 1970 The Revue had a hit with a song called "Bold Soul Sister," an original Ike and Tina song that imitates—one might almost say rips off—James Brown's post "Cold Sweat" funk style. It comprises a two-measure riff that repeats throughout the song, no harmonic changes, only the addition of guitar fills and solo lines by Ike, the occasional drum fill to articulate the end of a measure, in imitation of, but not nearly as rhythmically intricate or intense as most of James's grooves. What is amazing about this song is Tina's vocal in which melody is completely subordinated to signature James Brown screeches, grunts, and squeals, articulated with as much intensity as the man himself. The lyric suggests an extraordinary "liberated" subject position for Tina: the bold soul sister, whom the Ikettes encourage to "do what you wanna, when you wanna, how you wanna, now, do your thing soul sister." I've never understood why this song received so little attention by journalists or cultural critics, or why Tina hasn't laid more claim to it throughout her solo career. Is it that it is just too derivative of James Brown, too much copying of a style that was associated so strongly with him, or was it that the style was too "black" for Tina, and too much tied up with the politics of the civil rights movement, and/or the black power movement at a particular historical moment? Does it associate her with African American culture too much—after all, she has openly embraced white pop and rock music and has been critical of R&B in the past.[64] Is it too "political" a song in terms of its gendered message for an artist like Tina, who has never been overtly associated with social politics, either in her music or in her public life as a celebrity (we don't

---

[63]   Robert Palmer, as quoted in Brackett, *Interpreting Popular Music*, p. 137.

[64]   For some discussion of this see Wynn. He discusses how disillusioned he was as a black man by Tina claiming white rock music as her generic home and her critical stance against R&B, pp. 17–18.

hear of her supporting particular charities, or, other than Live Aid, participating in benefit concerts)?

But "Bold Soul Sister" is an important musical moment. Tina once again signifies on James, this time on his style rather than covering a particular song. And there can be no question that it is, at least in part, a parody. Musically, she once again nearly outdoes James at his own, highly personal style; lyrically, Tina and the Ikettes signify in particular on James's tradition of self-reference, of his toasting/boasting practices. She is a "Bold Soul Sister," a "B.S.S." as she proclaims; the abbreviation makes it impossible not to imagine that she thinks this is, in some way, B.S. She proclaims that "It's my thing and I'm gonna do what I want to do," turning James's self-congratulatory sentiments into a motto for self empowerment (ironic, given the horrible, abusive circumstances of her personal life). And the first lyric she sings in the song is the line "Things and stuff and stuff and things and ... and stuff," pointing to the disjointed, sporadic, and sometimes nonsensical vocal interjections made by James: this is funny—and very bold— because she comments directly on James at the level of his style. I can't think of another instance of such irreverence towards James Brown, by a man, let alone a woman. Her mastery of the style, while consciously taking it apart, is what gives Tina her power in this song.

A tough girl as one of the boys[65]

Tina's real name is Anna Mae Bullock and in 1960 she was not married to Ike, not, in fact, intimately involved with him. According to accounts in both Tina's and Ike's autobiographies, Tina had no agency in her renaming, and while it gave her equal billing with Ike; pulling her out of the shadows of the Kings of Rhythm to become part of the headline, it also changed her identity and turned her into Ike's possession. While in other circumstances a show biz name change might be dismissed as fairly innocuous (many musicians and actors have stage names), in this case it needs to be taken up as a significant moment of erasure, as does her marriage to Ike. These moves were designed to make sure that Tina, the element that turned Ike and the Kings of Rhythm from a cover band into something artistically original, remained tied to him and reliant on him for her artistic success.[66]

It is, however, the image that Ike had in mind to go with this change that is ultimately of greater significance. Ike came up with the name "Tina" because it

---

[65] I take the title of this section from a chapter of Sherrie A. Inness's book *Tough Girls: Warriors and Wonder Women in Popular Culture* (Philadelphia, 1999).

[66] To put both the name change and the marriage in some perspective, it is instructive to note that according to Tina, when she expressed her reservations about the name change and staying with Ike and his band to him, he beat her for the first time. This instilled a profound sense of fear in her, which stayed with her throughout her years with Ike. See Turner with Loder, pp. 78–79.

sounded like "Sheena, Queen of the Jungle," a comic book character created in the 1930s, but one that Ike claims he remembered from Saturday movie matinee serials he watched as a child in Mississippi. Another example of the jungle goddess that Ike had grown up with was Nyoka; in particular, a fifteen-part movie serial called *The Perils of Nyoka* that was created in 1942 and that starred actress Kay Aldridge in the leading role. According to Tina's autobiography, Ike "[had] become fixated on the white jungle goddesses who romped through [these serials]—revealingly rag-clad women with long flowing hair and names like 'Sheena, Queen of the Jungle.'"[67]

bell hooks has noted about this story that "Ike's pornographic fantasy of the black female as wild savage emerged from the impact of a white patriarchal controlled media shaping his perceptions of reality."[68] While I agree with this analysis, it tells only part of the story.

Figures 8.2 and 8.3, show, respectively, depictions of the Hollywood Sheena and Nyoka. Sheena's provocative image is reminiscent of many typical Hollywood pin-up girls such as Betty Grable or Jayne Mansfield, respectable white women who served as models for the classic Hollywood idea of beauty in the 1950s. The animal skin worn by Sheena, and her bright, oversized "primitive"

Figure 8.2   Irish McCalla as *Sheena, Queen of the Jungle* (Nassour Studios, Inc., 1955)

---

[67] Ibid., p. 77.
[68] hooks, p. 67.

Figure 8.3   Kay Aldridge in *The Perils of Nyoka* (Republic Pictures, 1942)

jewellery conform to quite standard and facile Hollywood attempts to invoke the jungle (these are the only jungle signifiers in the picture, and they appear quite sanitized on this pristine, white, western body). There is a different kind of sexuality portrayed in the character of Nyoka: she is dressed in more practical enemy-fighting gear (khaki shirt, culottes and boots), which, interestingly for comparisons with Tina, draws the gaze to her bare legs as the primary sexual signifier (breasts are completely covered under a shirt that closes right up to the neck), as they were in so many photos of pin-up girls (so, again, Tina's image is linked to this white tradition).[69] These images suggest that Ike's initial idea was not at all about creating a pornographic fantasy of black female sexuality for Tina; it was about appropriating an image of middle-class white culture that would play into his desires for and fantasies about white women. That is, this was not about capitalizing on Tina's blackness in order to play into white male fantasies of black women, but rather to align her with a fantasy he took from white culture in order that *he* could live out *his* fantasy of access to such women (and by "such women" I mean not only access to the concept of white beauty and sexuality that they signified, but also access to their white, middle- or upper-class privilege). Both

---

[69]   For several good images go to http://www.imagesjournal.com/issue04/infocus/ perilsofnyoka.htm, http://nimst.tripod.com/cgi-bin/Nyoka.html and http://xoomer.virgilio.it/ amasoni2002/shl/independents/perils_of_nyoka_(1942).htm (accessed November 29, 2005).

Ike and Tina comment in their autobiographies on Ike's "taste" for white women; I imagine that part of the attraction was to align himself with the power of the dominant culture, with something that, as a poor man coming from the segregated South, was exotic to him (Anna Mae Bullock certainly wasn't—she was a poor black woman).[70]

Ike hints at this interpretation in an interview he gave in 2004. There, he states:[71]

> There was a woman called Nyoka, a white woman that used to swing through the jungle like Tarzan. When I was a small kid, I used to go to the movies. They didn't allow you to even look at a white woman in Mississippi back in them days ... .
> Boy, was I in love with that woman.

What is so striking and complex about this is that Tina's image of "primitive" black sexuality was born out of an idea borrowed from white, middle- or upper-class Hollywood. At the point of production, this image was racially and in terms of class constructed in one way (as an appropriation of something from white culture), while at the point of reception it came to be racially constructed in quite a different way (as a representation of black, lower-class "primitiveness"). This complexity brings us back to the whiteface cover of *Outta Season*, with its layers of racialized meanings. But the "jungle goddess" image that is associated with Tina did not emerge full blown when Ike renamed her; Figure 8.4 shows her in the early 1960s, a typical look that is replicated in, for example, her appearance on the television show *Shindig* from 1964 and the T.N.T. show from that same year.[72]

In the photograph, she is shown in a tailored knee-length white sparkly dress, white pumps and a stylish shoulder-length bob. She is even more conservatively dressed in the *Shindig* episode, where her hair is similarly styled, and she is dressed in a white, long-sleeved blouse and full skirt that comes just over the knee, a performance in which her movements are also highly restrained. This early Tina presents a picture of middle-class respectability that could be read as an attempt to assimilate into white culture. The more provocative image that we associate

---

[70] Ike's desire for white women is part of a problematic sexual politics in black culture. It has long been acceptable for black men to be with white women, but much less so for black women to be with white men. As Patricia Hill Collins explains, "One mark of hegemonic White masculinity lay in its ability to restrict the sexual partners available to black men. African American men were forbidden to engage in sexual relations with all White women, let alone marry them. In this context, any expansion of the pool of female sexual partners enhances African American men's standing within the existing system of hierarchical masculinities." Not so for black women: "Historically, good black women were those who resisted the sexual advances of White men, not those who invited them." *Black Sexual Politics*, p. 262.

[71] Interview with Rob Bowman for the liner notes to *Ike and Tina Turner Live in '71*.

[72] I want to thank Norma Coates for drawing my attention to the *Shindig* appearance and for loaning me a copy of the video.

Figure 8.4   Ike and Tina Turner in 1966

with her—halter tops, animal print rags for skirts, increasingly longer and wilder hair—developed over the course of the 1960s (see Figure 8.5), in sync, I would argue, with the progression of the civil rights movement, with the cultivation of "blackness" as increasingly desirable, both within black communities and within the white-controlled music industry, as young musicians and their audiences found raw versions of the blues and R&B to be "authentic" and otherwise hip.

Although no one has commented on the development of Tina's wardrobe choices before, it makes sense that these would play increasingly into the acceptance of certain kinds of black "authenticity" into white culture. Ike and Tina began receiving serious attention from superstar white artists in 1966—Phil Spector and The Rolling Stones—and later in the 1960s they tried to market themselves as "the original rock and roll," in an attempt to align themselves with more commercially successful white music. The *Outta Season* record cover from 1969 demonstrates their conscious understanding of racial politics in popular music at that time; it is not a huge leap to think that Tina's increasingly "primitive" self-presentation would form part of this paradigm.

In addition to it playing on ideas of black sexual "primitiveness," this image was sexually provocative in another way. It played on the idea of "tough girl" sexuality, which is what Kay Aldridge was also striving for with her Nyoka

Figure 8.5   Tina Turner in the late 1960s

character (this may be another way in which Tina's image is, in fact, more "white"—or whiteface—than "black"; see below). Writers have fleetingly pointed to Tina's tough girl persona as a given, but it has not been much analyzed.[73] In fact, little has been written about the subject of tough girls in general, although Sherrie Inness has made a useful first attempt to theorize the subject. "Toughness," she writes, "is perceived as the antithesis of femininity."[74] Although the markers of toughness are fluid, a common attribute is a "super-fit" physique, one that suggests "great powers of physical endurance." Physical control and endurance are then mapped onto the idea of emotional strength, and these qualities often lead the bearer of them to success and power. Inness points out that these attributes have, of course, "traditionally been associated with men, not women," although there are increasingly more tough girls in the media images we consume and she goes

---

[73]   See for example, Paul Grein's analysis in *Billboard* 96 (September 15, 1984), p. 42; Grein quotes Joan Baez in this article as saying that Tina "is the toughest broad that ever lived."

[74]   Inness, *Tough Girls*, p. 9.

on to scrutinize some in her book.[75] Interestingly, the majority of her tough girls, which come from television and film, are white. Inness problematizes this, writing, "tough women in the popular media typically are white, heterosexual and middle class, reflecting a culture in who these are the norms."[76] But I am uncertain that the absence of ethnic-other tough girls in the media is a product of those media choosing to represent the dominant culture. Rather, I would posit that at least in part it is because normative femininity—softness, passivity—is associated with middle-class whiteness; it is a fantasy of femininity constructed by middle-class white men for middle-class white women. It is this normative white femininity that is being transgressed in the tough girl images we get in the media. Hence, again, Tina's appropriation of the tough girl image might be seen as being linked to white culture.

The general signifiers of toughness spelled out by Inness certainly apply to Tina and also to the Ikettes. She is lean and muscular and the stage shows, with their energetic dancing from beginning to end, were an incredible test of endurance. Despite the revealing costumes worn by her and the Ikettes throughout the Revue's existence, there is a kind of energy that might be described as "masculine" in them. These are not voluptuous women's bodies, but rather taut, muscular, athletic bodies. There is a de-emphasis on curves in Tina's body type, which in addition to the often angular movements in the stage show, work against the softness associated with traditional femininity. Tina's is a hard body. She has acknowledged this, calling herself a "tomboy" on numerous occasions throughout her autobiography. The movements performed were almost always physically excessive, raucous, something entirely different than other girl performers in the 1960s, especially the kind of femininity being cultivated at Motown as acceptable for white consumption. Ike has recently commented on the choreography and costumes for the Ikettes, saying that they were inspired by majorettes he saw in a parade in his youth.[77] Elsewhere he has commented that some of the choreographed moves were inspired by his interest in karate. These associations would account for the angularity and athleticism of the choreography.

There is an enormous sexual energy in Tina's and the Ikettes' performances, a kind of foregrounding of the body both in terms of the amount of skin shown, and the constant "threat," if you will, of more being revealed (those tiny mini-skirts riding up at the crotch), as well as on movement of the body—frenetic movement of limbs and hips in particular, and of hair (the long wigs worn by Tina and the Ikettes were a conscious effort to incorporate more physical movement into the routines). Even though the movements are choreographed, suggesting a kind of physical discipline among the performers, the particular movements imply bodily freedom, freedom from social constraint. While the majority of other black women popular music performers at this time restricted themselves physically in order

---

[75] Ibid., p. 12.

[76] Ibid., p. 19.

[77] Ike Turner interview with Rob Bowman, *Ike and Tina Turner Live in '71*, p. 8.

to fit into white culture—where physical restraint and discipline was of utmost importance—Tina and the Ikettes were creating physical spectacle that made them culturally other—that made them black(er) and, I would argue, that also "masculinized" them, since some of their male counterparts—James Brown, Sam and Dave—engaged in similarly unrestrained physical movement. Perhaps it is, in fact, this emphasis on physical spectacle, this unrestrained bodily display, especially coming from women, that has led to the dismissal of Tina as a centrally important figure in the history of popular music. I've read two accounts, for example, in which Tina is mentioned briefly as someone with limited talent and then quickly compared to Aretha Franklin, who is held up as an icon of important black music. Nelson George writes that "Franklin expressed all a black woman could be, while her contemporaries (Diana Ross, Tina Turner, Dionne Warwick, [etc.]) … seemed trapped in one persona by the artistic decisions of male producers as well as by their own vocal limitations."[78] And bell hooks makes this same comparison, calling Tina's performances a "representation of wild animalistic sexuality," while Aretha sings songs of "resistance" calling her hit "Respect" an example of a song that "challeng[ed] black male sexism and female victimization, while evoking notions of mutual care and support."[79] Could it be that Aretha's larger, more matronly body and her physical restraint on stage make it possible for sole concentration to be placed on her voice, on the intellectual as opposed to the physical aspects of her performance—the mind over the body? Bodies in motion on stage seem to detract from the voice or from instrumental performance. (The question really becomes, how much movement, and of what kind, can a performer "get away with" before it becomes a distraction? Who else needs to be on stage—for example, virtuoso guitar players—for considerable movement to be acceptable, for the performance to be brought back to "the music?") Is the Ike and Tina show, perceived by these black intellectuals and others as minstrelsy barely disguised, a kind of caricature of black sexuality and hence to be dismissed?

But this analysis misses the point and in the process seeks to reinforce stereotypical notions of femininity and sexuality. I remember being slightly offended when I read Lucy O'Brien's characterization of Tina as "a rock chick parody" for the first time several years ago, but I now get it. This characterization brings the discussion back to Tina's powerful signifying practices. Throughout the 1960s, she began to understand that her power lay not only in claiming her wild image, but in self-consciously pushing this image into the realm of parody, thereby signifying on what her audience (including the many white, male rock stars who love her) thought she was/wanted her to be. When she left Ike in 1976 she worked hard to retain the stage name that he had given her, because she knew that it was this name and the act she had developed around it that gave her capital.[80] This knowledge she continued to use to cultivate her

---

[78] George Nelson, *The Death of Rhythm and Blues* (New York, 1988), p. 106.
[79] hooks, p. 69.
[80] Turner with Loder, p. 210.

"rock chick" voice and persona, even while often singing pop during her solo career. Her legacy from the 1960s lies in the ways she pushed the gendered and racialized boundaries around funk and rock and roll, especially the ways in which she claimed clearly defined "masculinized" musical territory for herself, problematizing the idea that these genres belong to men, even if they had been previously defined by them.

Response

Martha Mockus

In her account of lesbian diva-worship, Terry Castle recuperates the capacity to admire as a productive premise for feminist scholarly inquiry. She writes: "Intellectuals, on the whole, are not used to thinking of the 'capacity to admire' as a valuable human quality; indeed, so profound are our modern prejudices against anything smacking of enthusiasm or emotional excess, we are more likely to take such receptivity to others as a sign of moral and intellectual weakness."[1] However, loving another woman's singing voice is enriching and nourishing to the woman who admires, opening up greater epistemological possibilities for her. Castle continues, "In the same way that in a perfect world no shame would ever attach itself to the desire of woman for woman, no shame attaches—or should attach itself—to the adoration inspired by a passionate female voice."[2] In this volume, the admiration for girl singers that each author shows forms a vital part of the overall scholarly intervention of this project. Thankfully, these authors take their capacity to admire seriously and let it inspire their feminist analyses of girl singers.

These essays insist that girl singers and their music have a great deal to tell us about the complex social histories of gender in the UK and the US. The feminist intersectional paradigm for the analyses offered here present an exciting model for popular music studies, making it joyously impossible to accept the old failures of imagination that have routinely plagued androcentric histories of mid-century popular music. Furthermore, these authors present important narratives of female survival in music worlds that would too easily dispose of girl singers and in popular music histories that would omit them altogether.

It certainly is no coincidence that the version of womanhood envoiced by the girl groups and girl singers of the 1950s and 1960s was decried by Betty Friedan when she published *The Feminine Mystique* in 1963.[3] While girl singers and their music might seem to embody, even embrace, those features of domesticated heterosexual womanhood, cheerfully willing to dance right into marriage and motherhood, the essays in this volume show us just how contested that version of womanhood was and that female femininity was in fact a complex process of masquerade cross-cut by age, race (specifically blackness and whiteness), class, sexuality, and nation. In each essay, we encounter girl singers' multiple modes of

---

[1] Terry Castle, *The Apparitional Lesbian: Female Homosexuality and Modern Culture* (New York, 1993), p. 236.

[2] Ibid., p. 238.

[3] Friedan, *The Feminine Mystique* (New York, 1963).

masquerade: their motivations and effects, how they conceal and reveal certain constructions of femininity, and whose interests are served. When we listen closely, we can hear how girl groups and girl singers, effectively worked within and against the dominant ideology of womanhood, exposing it as a prescription, and producing perhaps a not so distant resonance with Friedan's critique of the "the problem that has no name."

Many a feminist and queer theorist have found Joan Riviere's highly influential essay from 1929, "Womanliness as a Masquerade," a useful starting point for theorizing female femininity and performance.[4] Riviere's claim that womanliness and masquerade are the same thing works to denaturalize female femininity and understand it as a kind of self-protective, compensatory charade within hetero-patriarchy. Specific elements of masquerade are open to some variation, especially between lesbians and heterosexual women, but the underlying concept of womanliness *as* masquerade has obvious advantages for feminist analyses of women performers on stage, on screen, and in the recording studio. It allows us to examine masquerade in more political terms: to identify the calculated artificiality of gendered performance, and to rethink female femininity as multivocal practices of creativity, conformity, resistance, or accommodation. In some cases, the masquerade of female femininity is consciously chosen, and foregrounded as such. In others, it is coercively enforced and results in dissemblance or self-injury. Throughout this volume, the authors compassionately and unromantically re-evaluate female femininity against the superficial charges of passivity, manipulation and straightness. Indeed, such masquerades—whether of Tina Turner or The Crystals, Brenda Lee or Mary Hopkin, Dusty Springfield or Marianne Faithfull— were forms of labor, a set of vocal performance practices that both concealed and revealed the social conditions under which those voices labored.

This work therefore raises additional questions about female femininity. How does "girlness" operate as both a body discipline and an ideological fulcrum in the institution of hetero-patriarchy? Given the limited materials and access to power available to them, how have some girl singers resisted self-destruction and other mechanisms of sexist and racist oppression? In what ways did their performances and other musical choices produce moments of rupture in the pretty girl surface of the masquerade itself?

Like most psychoanalytic theory, however, Riviere's work does not attend to other categories of experience, such as race or class. The essays here go to great lengths to show how masquerade itself is a multifaceted phenomenon in which female femininity is simultaneously constructed by race, class, age, sexuality and nation. In short, masquerade is fundamentally intersectional and each essay teases out the structural relationships among these categories. What's so exciting about these authors is that they also locate the intersectionality of masquerade in the music, and as primarily vocal. By "writing the voice" of each singer in question,

---

[4] Riviere, "Womanliness as a Masquerade," *The International Journal of Psychoanalysis* 10 (1929): 303–13.

we can *hear* how they sounded black, or middle class, or British, or older than their actual age. In other words, *vocal* masquerade played a leading role in these girl singers' musical achievements. Indeed, alongside visual image and behavior, the class, age, and racial crossings in their vocal masquerades constitute a primary ingredient in the micro-managed body disciplines of ideal girlness in the 1950s and 60s. The particular analyses of vocal masquerade offered here also reveal the deeply embedded racism, sexism and homophobia in the public perceptions and critical evaluations of these girl singers. At the same time, as these authors show, girl singers and girl groups offered a means by which the categories of class, race, age, and nation could actually be interrogated outside the borders of the traditional political sphere.

Such vocal masquerades point to the fraught relationship between agency and constraint as it functioned for these girl singers within the popular music industry and among their audiences. While each author identifies important instances of protest and resistance, to what extent are these instances contained, either by the internal mechanisms of masquerade itself or by some other social force? Why did these singers make certain vocal decisions about their music, and which decisions were theirs to make?

I heartily applaud the sophistication and nuance of these essays because they make it abundantly clear that not only were girl groups and girl singers as quintessentially 50s and 60s as Elvis Presley, The Beatles, and The Rolling Stones, but their finely detailed versions of female femininity taught all kinds of girls in the larger culture significant lessons about the power and the cost of masquerade. So many of these girl singers are remarkable figures of survival and reinvention, and we have been given new ways to listen to their own forms of resistance to mainstream gender codes. I am grateful to this work for expanding my own capacity to admire. But there is more to do. Although the fractured consciousness of girl singers' masquerades inspires feminist critiques, how can it produce feminist *subjects*? What does this marvelous work tell us about our lives today? At the very least, but perhaps most important, the new knowledge presented here allows us to take action toward liberating the lives and voices of our female students.

Select Bibliography

Aronowitz, Al, "The Dumb Sound: Pop Before the Beatles," *Saturday Evening Post*, August 1963; reproduced on *Rock's Back Pages*, http://www.rocksbackpages com/.

Auslander, Philip, *Performing Glam Rock: Gender and Theatricality in Popular Music* (Ann Arbor: University of Michigan Press, 2006).

———, "Watch That Man: David Bowie: Hammersmith Odeon, London, July 3, 1973," in Ian Inglis (ed.), *Performance and Popular Music: History, Place and Time* (Aldershot: Ashgate, 2006).

Banfield, Stephen, "Stage and Screen Entertainers in the Twentieth Century," in John Potter (ed.), *The Cambridge Companion to Singing* (Cambridge: Cambridge University Press, 2000).

Barkin, Elaine, and Lydia Hamessley, *Audible Traces: Gender, Identity, and Music* (Zürich and Los Angeles: Carciofoli Verlagshaus, 1999).

Barthes, Roland, "The Grain of the Voice," in Simon Frith and Andrew Goodwin (eds), *On Record: Rock, Pop and the Written Word* (London and New York: Routledge, 1990).

Bartky, Sandra Lee, "Foucault, Femininity and Patriarchal Power," in Katie Conboy, Nadia Medina, and Sarah Stanbury (eds), *Writing on the Body: Female Embodiment and Feminist Theory* (New York: Columbia University Press, 1997).

Betrock, Alan, *Girl Groups: The Story of a Sound* (London and New York: Omnibus Press, 1982).

Bordo, Susan, "The Body and the Reproduction of Femininity," in Katie Conboy, Nadia Medina, and Sarah Stanbury (eds), *Writing on the Body: Female Embodiment and Feminist Theory* (New York: Columbia University Press, 1997).

Bornstein, George, "Afro-Celtic Connections: From Frederick Douglass to *The Commitments*," in Tracy Mishkin (ed.), *Literary Influence and African-American Writers* (New York: Garland, 1996).

Bowman, Rob, liner notes to *Ike and Tina Turner Live in '71* (Reelin' in the Years Productions; Eagle Rock Entertainment, 2004).

Brackett, David, *Interpreting Popular Music* (Berkeley: University of California Press, 2000).

———, "Brown, James," *Grove Music Online*, L. Macy (ed.), http://www. grovemusic.com.

Bradby, Barbara, "Do-Talk and Don't-Talk: The Division of the Subject in Girl-Group Music," in Simon Frith and Andrew Goodwin (eds), *On Record: Rock, Pop and the Written Word* (London and New York: Routledge, 1990).

———, "She Told Me What to Say: The Beatles and Girl Group Discourse," *Popular Music and Society* 28/3 (2005): 359–90.

Breines, Wini, *Young, White and Miserable: Growing Up Female in the Fifties* (Chicago and London: University of Chicago Press, 1992).

Brodkin, Karen, *How the Jews Became White Folks and What that Says About Race in America* (New Brunswick, NJ: Rutgers University Press, 1998).

Brown, Lyn Mikel, *Raising Their Voices: The Politics of Girls' Anger* (Cambridge, MA: Harvard University Press, 1998).

Brown, Lyn Mikel and Carol Gilligan, *Meeting at the Crossroads: Women's Psychology and Girls' Development* (Cambridge, MA: Harvard University Press, 1992).

Brown, Mick, *Tearing Down The Wall of Sound: The Rise and Fall of Phil Spector* (London: Bloomsbury Publishing, 2007).

Budd, Elaine, *Your Hairdo* (New York: Scholastic Book Services, 1966).

Bufwack, Mary A. and Robert K. Oermann, *Finding Her Voice: Women in Country Music, 1800–2000* (Nashville, TN: The Country Music Foundation and Vanderbilt University Press, 2003).

Bunch, Merideth, *Dynamics of the Singing Voice* (Vienna and New York: Springer-Verlag, 1982).

Burnim, Mellonee V. and Portia Maultsby (eds), *African American Music: An Introduction* (New York: Routledge, 2004).

Burns, Lori, "'Joanie' Get Angry: kd lang's Feminist Revision," in John Covach and Graeme Boone (eds), *Understanding Rock: Essays in Musical Analysis* (Oxford: Oxford University Press, 1997).

Butler, Judith, *Undoing Gender* (New York: Routledge, 2004).

Carter, Angela, "Truly, It Felt Like Year One," in Sara Maitland (ed.), *Very Heaven: Looking Back at the 1960s* (London: Virago, 1988).

Castle, Terry, *The Apparitional Lesbian: Female Homosexuality and Modern Culture* (New York: Columbia University Press, 1993).

Chang, Jung, *Wild Swans: Three Daughters of China* (New York: Simon & Schuster, 1991).

Clemente, John, *Girl Groups: Fabulous Females That Rocked The World* (Iola, WI: Krause Publications, 2000).

Cleto, Fabio (ed.), *Camp: Queer Aesthetics and the Performing Self—A Reader* (Edinburgh: Edinburgh University Press, 1999).

Coates, Norma, "Teenyboppers, Groupies, and Other Grotesques: Girls and Women and Rock Culture in the 1960s and early 1970s," *Journal of Popular Music Studies* 15/1 (2003): 65–94.

Cohan, Steven, "'Feminizing' the Song-and-Dance Man: Fred Astaire and the Spectacle of Masculinity in the Hollywood Musical," Chapter 7 in *Hollywood Musicals: The Film Reader* (New York: Routledge, 2002).

Collins, Patricia Hill, *Black Feminist Thought: Knowledge, Consciousness and the Politics of Empowerment*, 2nd edn (New York: Routledge, 2000).

———, *Black Sexual Politics: African Americans, Gender and the New Racism* (New York: Routledge, 2004).

Crawford, Richard, *America's Musical Life: A History* (New York: Norton, 2001).

Cusick, Suzanne G., "On Musical Performances of Gender and Sex," in Elaine Barkin and Lydia Hamessley (eds), *Audible Traces: Gender, Identity and Music* (Zurich and Los Angeles: Carciofoli Verlagshaus, 1999).

Cyrus, Cynthia J., "Selling an Image: Girl Groups of the 1960s," *Popular Music* 22/2 (2003): 173–93.

Dame, Joke, "Unveiled Voices: Sexual Difference and the Castrato," in Philip Brett, Elizabeth Wood, and Gary C. Thomas (eds), *Queering the Pitch: the New Gay and Lesbian Musicology* (New York and London: Routledge, 1994).

Davis, Stephan, *Old Gods Almost Dead: The 40-Year Odyssey of the Rolling Stones* (New York: Broadway Books, 2001).

DeCurtis, Anthony, James Henke and Holly George-Warren (eds), *The Rolling Stone Illustrated History of Rock & Roll*, 3rd edn (New York: Random House, 1992).

DeNora, Tia, *Music in Everyday Life* (Cambridge: Cambridge University Press, 2000).

Doggett, Peter, "In Private: Peter Doggett Examines the Enigma That Was Dusty Springfield," *Record Collector* (May 1999): 70–73.

Doherty, Thomas, *Teenagers and Teenpics: The Juvenilization of American Movies in the 1950s* (Philadelphia: Temple University Press, 2002).

Douglas, Susan J., *Where the Girls Are: Growing Up Female with the Mass Media* (London: Penguin, 1995).

———, *Listening In: Radio and the American Imagination ... from Amos 'n' Andy and Edward R. Murrow to Wolfman Jack and Howard Stern* (New York: Random House, 1999).

Driscoll, Catherine, *Girls: Feminine Adolescence in Popular Culture and Cultural Theory* (New York: Columbia University Press, 2002).

DuBois, W. E. B., *The Souls of Black Folk* (1903), ed. Henry Louis Gates (New York: Bantam, 1989).

Dunn, Leslie C. and Nancy A. Jones (eds), *Embodied Voices: Representing Female Vocality in Western Culture* (Cambridge: Cambridge University Press, 1994).

Dyer, Richard, *White* (London and New York: Routledge, 1997).

Early, Gerald, *Tuxedo Junction: Essays on American Culture* (Hopewell, NJ: Ecco, 1989).

Endleman, Todd E., *The Jews of Britain* (Berkeley: University of California Press, 2002).

Evans, David, *Scissors and Paste: A Collage Biography of Dusty Springfield* (London: Britannia Press, 1995).

Faithfull, Marianne with David Dalton, *Faithfull: An Autobiography* (Boston: Little, Brown and Company, 1994).

Fast, Susan, *In the Houses of the Holy: Led Zeppelin and the Power of Rock Music* (New York: Oxford University Press, 2001).

Fischlin, Daniel (ed.), *The Other Side of Nowhere: Jazz, Improvisation, and Communities in Dialogue* (Middletown, CT: Wesleyan University Press, 2004).

Fiske, John, "The Popular Economy," Chapter 16 in *Television Culture* (London: Routledge, 1987).

242   *SHE'S SO FINE*

Floyd, Samuel, *The Power of Black Music: Interpreting Its History from Africa to the United States* (New York: Oxford University Press, 1995).

Foucault, Michel, *Discipline and Punish* (New York: Vintage, 1979).

Frankenberg, Ruth, *White Women, Race Matters: The Social Construction of Whiteness* (Minneapolis: University of Minnesota Press, 1993).

—— (ed.), *Displacing Whiteness: Essays in Social and Cultural Criticism* (Durham, NC: Duke University Press, 1997).

——, "Introduction: Local Whitenesses, Localizing Whiteness," in Ruth Frankenberg (ed.), *Displacing Whiteness: Essays in Social and Cultural Criticism* (Durham, NC: Duke University Press, 1997).

Freeland, David, *Ladies of Soul* (Jackson: University of Mississippi Press, 2001).

Friedan, Betty, *The Feminine Mystique* (New York: Dell, 1963).

Friedman, Susan Stanford, *Mappings: Feminism and the Cultural Geographies of Encounter* (Princeton, NJ: Princeton University Press, 1998).

Frith, Simon, "The Cultural Study of Popular Music," in Lawrence Grossberg, Cary Nelson and Paula Treichler (eds), *Cultural Studies* (London: Routledge, 1992).

Gaar, Gillian G., *She's a Rebel: The History of Women in Rock and Roll* (Seattle: Seal Press, 1992).

Gaines, Donna, *Teenage Wasteland: Suburbia's Dead End Kids* (New York: Pantheon, 1991).

——, "Girl Groups: A Ballad of Codependency," in Barbara O'Dair (ed.), *Troubled Girls: The Rolling Stone Book of Women in Rock* (New York: Rolling Stone Press, 1997).

Garland-Thomson, Rosemarie, *Extraordinary Bodies: Figuring Physical Disability in American Culture and Literature* (New York: Columbia University Press, 1997).

Garofalo, Reebee, *Rockin' Out: Popular Music in the USA* (Upper Saddle River, NJ: Prentice Hall, 2002).

Gates, Henry Louis, *The Signifyin(g) Monkey: A Theory of African-American Literary Criticism* (New York and Oxford: Oxford University Press, 1988).

——, *Figures in Black: Words, Signs, and the "Racial" Self* (New York and Oxford: Oxford University Press, 1989).

George, Nelson, *The Death of Rhythm and Blues* (New York: Pantheon Books, 1988).

George-Graves, Nadine, *The Royalty of Negro Vaudeville: The Whitman Sisters and the Negotiation of Race, Gender and Class in African American Theatre, 1900–1940* (New York: St Martin's Press, 2000).

Gill, Andy, "Ten Questions for Little Richard," in Kandia Crazy Horse (ed.), *Rip It Up: The Black Experience in Rock 'n' Roll* (New York: Palgrave MacMillan, 2004).

Gilligan, Carol, *In a Different Voice: Psychological Theory and Women's Development* (Cambridge, MA: Harvard University Press, 1982).

Gilroy, Paul, *The Black Atlantic: Modernity and Double Consciousness* (London and New York: Verso, 1993).

Goldin, Claudia and Lawrence F. Katz, "Why the United States Led in Education: Lessons from Secondary School Expansion, 1910 to 1940," Working Paper 6144, NBER Working Paper Series, [USA] (National Bureau of Economic Research, 1997).

Graddol, David and Joan Swan, *Gender Voices* (Oxford: Blackwell, 1985).

Greer, Germaine, *The Female Eunuch* (New York: McGraw Hill, 1971).

————— *The Whole Woman* (London: Anchor, 2000).

Greig, Charlotte, *Will You Still Love Me Tomorrow? Girl Groups From The 50s On ...* (London: Virago, 1989).

Gribin, Anthony J., and Matthew M. Schiff, *The Complete Book of Doo-Wop* (Iola: Krause Publications, 2000).

Griffin, Farah Jasmine, *If You Can't Be Free, Be a Mystery* (New York: Random House, 2002

Hawkins, Stan, *Settling the Pop Score: Pop Texts and Identity Politics* (Aldershot: Ashgate, 2002).

Helford, Elyce Rae, "'My Emotions Give Me Power': The Containment of Girls' Anger in *Buffy the Vampire Slayer*," in Rhonda V. Wilcox and David Lavery (eds), *Fighting the Forces: What's at Stake in* Buffy the Vampire Slayer (Lanham, MD: Rowman & Littlefield, 2002).

Hemming, James, *Problems of Adolescent Girls* (London, Melbourne and Toronto: Heinemann, 1960).

Herbert, Trevor and Peter Stead (eds), *Hymns and Arias: Great Welsh Voices* (Cardiff: University of Wales Press, 2001).

Hill, Sarah, *"Blerwytirhwng?" The Place of Welsh Popular Music* (Aldershot: Ashgate, 2007).

Hine, Thomas, *The Rise and Fall of the American Teenager* (New York: Perennial, 2000).

Hisama, Ellie, "Voice, Race and Sexuality in the Music of Joan Armatrading," in Elaine Barkin and Lydia Hamessley (eds), *Audible Traces: Gender, Identity and Music* (Zurich & Los Angeles: Carciofoli Verlagshaus, 1999).

hooks, bell, "Selling Hot Pussy: Representations of Black Female Sexuality in the Cultural Marketplace," Chapter 4 in *Black Looks: Race and Representation* (Boston: South End Press, 1992).

————, "Representing Whiteness in the Black Imagination," in Ruth Frankenberg (ed.), *Displacing Whiteness: Essays in Social and Cultural Criticism* (Durham, NC: Duke University Press, 1997).

Howes, Paul, *The Complete Dusty Springfield*, revised and expanded edn (London: Reynolds and Hearn, 2001 and 2007).

Ignatiev, Noel, *How the Irish Became White* (New York: Routledge, 1995).

Inglis, Ian (ed.), "'Some Kind of Wonderful': The Creative Legacy of the Brill Building," *American Music* 21/2 (2003): 214–35.

————, *Performance and Popular Music* (Aldershot: Ashgate, 2006).

Inness, Sherrie A., *Tough Girls: Warriors and Wonder Women in Popular Culture* (Philadelphia: University of Pennsylvania Press, 1999).

Irigaray, Luce, *This Sex Which Is Not One*, trans. Catherine Porter (Ithaca: Cornell University Press, 1985).

Jarman-Ivens, Freya (ed.), *Oh Boy! Masculinities and Popular Music* (New York and Abingdon: Routledge, 2007).

Jeffords, Susan, *Hard Bodies: Hollywood Masculinity in the Reagan Era* (New Brunswick, NJ: Rutgers University Press, 1994).

Kelly, Norman (ed.), *R & B, Rhythm and Business: The Political Economy of Black Music* (New York: Akashic, 2002).

Kincaid, James F., *Child-Loving: The Erotic Child and Victorian Culture* (New York: Routledge, 1992).

King, Florence, *Southern Ladies and Gentlemen* (New York: St. Martin's Griffin, 1975).

Kirk, Kris, "Going Back," *Gay Times* (September 1985); reproduced on *Woman of Repute*, http://www.cptelecom.net/mbayly/article-goingback.htm.

Koestenbaum, Wayne, *The Queen's Throat: Opera, Homosexuality and the Mystery of Desire* (New York, Poseidon Press, 1993).

Kofsky, Frank, *Black Nationalism and the Revolution in Music* (New York: Pathfinder Press, 1970).

Kort, Michele, "The Secret Life of Dusty Springfield," *The Advocate* (April 27, 1999): 50–55.

Lamb, Sharon and Lyn Mikel Brown, *Packaging Girlhood: Rescuing Our Daughters from Marketers' Schemes* (New York: St. Martin's Press, 2007).

Lebeau, Vicky, "The Unwelcome Child: Elizabeth Eckford and Hannah Arendt," *Journal of Visual Culture* 3/1 (2004): 51–62.

Lee, Brenda with Robert K. Oermann and Julie Clay, *Little Miss Dynamite: The Life and Times of Brenda Lee* (New York: Hyperion, 2002).

Leonard, Marion, "'Rebel Girl, You are the Queen of My World': Feminism, 'Subculture' and Grrrl Power," in Sheila Whiteley (ed.), *Sexing the Groove: Popular Music and Gender* (New York: Routledge, 1997).

Lerner, Harriet Goldhor, *The Dance of Anger: A Woman's Guide to Changing the Patterns of Intimate Relationships* (New York: Harper & Row, 2005).

Levy, Shawn, *Ready, Steady, Go! The Smashing Rise and Giddy Fall of Swinging London* (New York: Broadway Books, 2003).

Lewis, George, "Improvised Music After 1950: Afrological and Eurological Perspectives," in Daniel Fischlin (ed.), *The Other Side of Nowhere: Jazz, Improvisation, and Communities in Dialogue* (Middletown: Wesleyan University Press, 2004).

Linna, Miriam and Billy Miller, "Mary Weiss of the Shangri-Las," http://www.nortonrecords.com/maryweiss/index.html.

Lott, Eric, *Love and Theft, Black Face Minstrelsy and the American Working Class* (New York: Oxford University Press, 1993).

Lulu, *I Don't Want to Fight* (London: Time Warner, 2002).

Mahon, Maureen, *Right to Rock: The Black Rock Coalition and the Cultural Politics of Race* (Durham, NC: Duke University Press, 2004).

Mailer, Norman, "The White Negro: Superficial Reflections on the Hipster," *Dissent* 4 (Summer 1957): 276–93.

McPherson, Tara, *Reconstructing Dixie: Race, Gender and Nostalgia in the Imagined South* (Durham, NC, and London: Duke University Press, 2003).

Melnick, Jeffrey, "'Story Untold': The Black Men and White Sounds of Doo-Wop," in Mike Hill (ed.), *Whiteness: A Critical Reader* (New York and London: New York University Press, 1997).

Monks, Susan, "Adolescent Singers and Perceptions of Vocal Identity," *British Journal of Music Education* 20/3 (2003): 243–56.

Morgan, Prys, "From a Death to a View: The Hunt for the Welsh Past in the Romantic Period," in Eric Hobsbawm and Terence Ranger (eds), *The Invention of Tradition* (Cambridge: Cambridge University Press, 2000).

Mullings, Leith, "Images, Ideology and Women of Color," in Maxine Baca Zinn and Bonnie Thornton Dill (eds), *Women of Color in U.S. Society* (Philadelphia: Temple University Press, 1994).

Mulvey, Laura, "Visual Pleasure and Narrative Cinema," *Screen* 16/3 (1975): 6–18.

Neale, Steve, "Masculinity as Spectacle," *Screen* 24/6 (1983): 2–16.

Nelson, George, *The Death of Rhythm and Blues* (New York: Pantheon, 1988).

Nicholls, David (ed.), *The Cambridge History of American Music* (New York: Cambridge University Press, 1998).

Noble, David F., *A World Without Women: The Christian Clerical Culture of Western Science* (New York: Alfred A. Knopf, 1992).

O'Brien, Lucy, *Dusty: A Biography of Dusty Springfield* (London: Pan/Macmillan, 2000).

———, *She Bop II: The Definitive History of Women in Rock, Pop and Soul* (London: Continuum, 2002).

O'Dair, Barbara (ed.), *Trouble Girls: The Rolling Stone Book of Women in Rock* (New York: Random House, 1997).

Olwage, Grant, "Discipline and Choralism: The Birth of Musical Colonialism," in Annie Randall (ed.), *Music, Power, and Politics* (New York: Routledge, 2005).

———, "The Class and Colour of Tone: An Essay on the Social History of Vocal Timbre," *Ethnomusicology Forum* 13/2 (November 2004): 203–26.

Panfile, Greg, "Boys will be Girl Group, or the Johnettes," in *Soundscapes—Journal on Media Culture* (1999), http://www.icce.rug.nl/~soundscapes/.

Parker, Rozsika and Griselda Pollock, *Old Mistresses: Women, Art, and Ideology* (London: Routledge, 1981).

Patrick, Adele, "Defiantly Dusty: A (Re)Figuring of 'Feminine Excess'," *Feminist Media Studies* 1/3 (2001): 361–78.

Pavletich, Aida, *Rock-A-Bye, Baby* (Garden City, NJ: Doubleday and Company, Inc., 1980).

Pegley, Karen and Virginia Caputo, "Growing Up Female(s): Retrospective Thoughts on Musical References and Meanings," in Philip Brett, Gary Thomas and Elizabeth Wood (eds), *Queering the Pitch: The New Gay and Lesbian Musicology* (New York and London: Routledge, 1994).

Pipher, Mary, *Reviving Ophelia: Saving the Selves of Adolescent Girls* (New York: Ballantine, 1995).

Pope, Carole, *Anti Diva: An Autobiography* (Toronto: Random House of Canada, 2000).

Radano, Ronald, *Lying Up a Nation: Race and Black Music* (Chicago: University of Chicago Press, 2003).

Ramsey, Guthrie, *Race Music: Black Cultures from Bebop to Hip-Hop* (Berkeley: University of California Press, 2004).

Randall, Annie J., *Dusty! Queen of the Postmods* (New York and London: Oxford University Press, 2008).

Reeves, Martha, and Mark Bego, *Dancing in the Street: Confessions of a Motown Diva* (New York: Hyperion, 1994).

Rhodes, Lisa L., *Electric Ladyland: Women and Rock Culture* (Philadelphia: University of Pennsylvania Press, 2005).

Ribowsky, Mark, *He's a Rebel: Phil Spector—Rock and Roll's Legendary Producer*, 2nd edn (New York: Da Capo Press, 2007).

Riviere, Joan, "Womanliness as a Masquerade," *The International Journal of Psychoanalysis* 10 (1929): 303–13.

Roach, Hildred, *Black American Music: Past and Present*, Volume II (Malabar, FL: R.E. Krieger Pub. Co., 1985).

Roach, Joseph, *Cities of the Dead: Circum-Atlantic Performance* (New York: Columbia University Press, 1996).

Roediger, David, *Working Toward Whiteness: How America's Immigrants Became White* (New York: Basic Books, 2005).

Rogers, Mary F., *Barbie Culture* (London: Sage, 1999).

Ross, Andrew, "Uses of Camp," in Fabio Cleto (ed.), *Camp: Queer Aesthetics and the Performing Self—A Reader* (Edinburgh: Edinburgh University Press, 1999).

Sanjek, David, "Can a Fujiyama Mama be the Female Elvis? The Wild, Wild Women of Rockabilly," in Sheila Whiteley (ed.), *Sexing the Groove: Popular Music and Gender* (New York: Routledge, 1997).

Schloss, Joseph, *Making Beats: The Art of Sample-Based Hip-Hop* (Middletown, CT: Wesleyan University Press, 2004).

Shaw, Greg, "Leaders of the Pack: Teen Dreams and Tragedy in Girl Group Rock," *History of Rock* 29 (1982): 566–69.

Shaw, Sandie, *The World at My Feet: A Personal Adventure* (London: HarperCollins, 1991).

Shepherd, John, "A Theoretical Model for the Sociomusicological Analysis of Popular Music," *Theory and Method: Popular Music* 2 (1982): 145–77.

Shumway, David R., "Rock 'n' Roll Soundtracks and the Production of Nostalgia," *Cinema Journal* 38/2 (1999): 36–51.

Simmons, Rachel, *Odd Girl Out: The Hidden Culture of Aggression in Girls* (New York: Harcourt, 2002).

Slaven, Neil, liner notes to *Ike and Tina Turner Revue with the Kings of Rhythm Orchestra Live!!!* (Kent, CDKEND 102, 1993).

SELECT BIBLIOGRAPHY

Sloboda, John, "Mozart in Psychology." Paper read at *Mozart 2006: Classical Music and the Modern World*, British Library (London), January 28, 2006.

Smith, Patricia Juliana, "'Ask Any Girl': Compulsory Heterosexuality and Girl Group Culture," in Kevin Dettmar and William Richey (eds), *Reading Rock and Roll: Authenticity, Appropriation, Aesthetics* (New York: Columbia University Press, 1999).

———, "'You Don't Have to Say You Love Me': The Camp Masquerades of Dusty Springfield," in Patricia Juliana Smith (ed.), *The Queer Sixties* (New York and London: Routledge, 1999).

Smith, Suzanne, *Dancing in the Street: Motown and the Cultural Politics of Detroit* (Cambridge, MA: Harvard University Press, 2000).

Southern, Eileen, *The Music of Black Americans: A History* (New York: W.W. Norton, 1997).

Spector, Ronnie, *Be My Baby: How I Survived Mascara, Miniskirts, and Madness, or My Life as a Fabulous Ronette* (New York: Harmony Books, 1990).

Steedman, Carolyn Kay *Landscape for a Good Woman: a Story of Two Lives* (London: Virago Press, 1987).

Stilwell, Robynn, "Music of the Youth Revolution: Rock through the 1960s," in Nicholas Cook and Anthony Pople (eds), *The Cambridge History of 20th Century Music* (Cambridge: Cambridge University Press, 2004).

Stras, Laurie, "The Organ of the Soul: Voice, Damage, and Affect," in Neil Lerner and Joseph Straus (eds), *Sounding Off: Theorizing Music and Disability* (New York: Routledge, 2006).

———, "White Face, Black Voice: Race, Gender and Region in the Music of the Boswell Sisters," *Journal of the Society for American Music* 1/2 (2007): 207–55.

Strausbaugh, John, *Rock 'Til You Drop: The Decline from Rebellion to Nostalgia* (London: Verso, 2001).

Sweeney, Gael, "The King of White Trash Culture: Elvis Presley and the Aesthetics of Excess," in Matt Wray and Annalee Newitz (eds), *White Trash: Race and Class in America* (New York: Routledge, 1997).

Szatmary, David, *Rockin' in Time: A Social History of Rock and Roll* 5th edn (Upper Saddle River, NJ: Prentice Hall, 2004).

Taylor, Jill McLean, Carol Gilligan, and Amy M. Sullivan, *Between Voice and Silence: Women and Girls, Race and Relationship* (Cambridge, MA, and London: Harvard University Press, 1995).

Tawa, Nicholas, *Supremely American: Popular Song in the 20th Century: Styles and Singers and What They Said About America* (Lanham, MD: Scarecrow Press, 2005).

Toynbee, Jason, *Making Popular Music: Musicians, Creativity and Institutions* (London: Arnold, 2000).

Turner, Ike, *Takin' Back My Name: The Confessions of Ike Turner* (London: Virgin Books, 1999).

Turner, Tina with Kurt Loder, *I, Tina* (New York: Avon Books, 1986).

Twine, France Winddance, "Brown-Skinned White Girls: Class, Culture, and the Construction of White Identity in Suburban Communities," in Ruth Frankenberg (ed.), *Displacing Whiteness: Essays in Social and Cultural Criticism* (Durham, NC: Duke University Press, 1997).

Valentine, Penny, and Vicki Wickham, *Dancing With Demons: The Authorized Biography of Dusty Springfield* (New York: St. Martin's Press, 2000).

Walkerdine, Valerie, "Someday My Prince Will Come," Chapter 8 in *Schoolgirl Fictions* (London: Verso, 1990). First published in Angela McRobbie and Mica Nava (eds), *Gender and Generation* (London: Macmillan, 1984).

———, *Daddy's Girl: Young Girls and Popular Culture* (Cambridge, MA: Harvard University Press, 1997).

Wald, Gayle, "One of the Boys? Whiteness, Gender, and Popular Music Studies," in Mike Hill (ed.), *Whiteness: A Critical Reader* (New York: New York University Press, 1997).

———, "Just a Girl? Rock Music, Feminism, and the Cultural Construction of Female Youth," in Roger Beebe, Denise Fulbrook, and Ben Saunders (eds), *Rock Over the Edge: Transformations in Popular Music Culture* (Durham, NC: Duke University Press, 2002).

Walser, Robert, "Out of Notes: Signification, Interpretation and the Problem of Miles Davis," *The Musical Quarterly* 77/2 (Summer 1993): 343–65.

———, *Running With the Devil: Power, Gender and Madness in Heavy Metal Music* (Hanover, NJ: Wesleyan University Press, 1993).

Ward, Andrew, *Dark Midnight When I Rise* (New York: Farrar, Straus and Giroux, 2000).

Ward, Brian, *Just My Soul Responding: Rhythm and Blues, Black Consciousness, and Race Relations* (Berkeley, CA: University of California Press, 1998).

Warner, Jay, *American Singing Groups: A History 1940–1990* (New York: Da Capo, 1992).

Warwick, Jacqueline, "You're Going To Lose That Girl: The Beatles and the Girl Groups," in Yrjö Heinonen, Markus Heuger, Sheila Whiteley, Terhi Nurmesjärvi and Jouni Koskimäki (eds), *Beatlestudies 3. Proceedings of the Beatles 2000 conference*, Department of Music, Research Reports 23 (Jyväskylä: University of Jyväskylä, 2001): 161–67.

———, "'He's Got the Power': The Politics of Production in Girl Group Music," in Sheila Whiteley, Andy Bennett, and Stan Hawkins (eds), *Music, Space and Place: Popular Music and Cultural Identity* (Aldershot: Ashgate, 2004).

———, *Girl Groups, Girl Culture: Popular Music and Identity in the 1960s* (New York and London: Routledge, 2007).

Weatherall, Ann, *Gender, Language and Discourse* (New York: Routledge, 2002).

Weinstein, Deena, "The History of Rock's Pasts Through Rock Covers," in Thomas Swiss, John Sloop, and Andrew Herman (eds), *Mapping the Beat: Popular Music and Contemporary Theory* (Oxford: Blackwell, 1998).

Whitburn, Joel, *The Billboard Book of Top 40 Hits, 1955 to the Present* (New York: Watson-Guptill Publications, 1989).

————, *Top R&B Singles 1942–1999* (Menomonee Falls: Record Research Inc., 2000).

Whiteley, Sheila, *Women and Popular Music: Sexuality, Identity, and Subjectivity* (London and New York: Routledge, 2000).

————, *Too Much Too Young: Popular Music, Age and Gender.* (New York: Routledge, 2003).

Williams, Juan and the *Eyes on the Prize* Production Team, *Eyes on the Prize: America's Civil Rights Years, 1954–1965* (New York: Penguin Books, 1987).

Wilson, Mary, *Dreamgirl and Supreme Faith: My Life as a Supreme* (New York: Cooper Square Press, 1999).

Wiseman, Rosalind, *Queen Bees and Wannabes: Helping Your Daughter Survive Cliques, Gossip, Boyfriends and other Realities of Adolescence* (New York: Crown, 2002).

Wynn, Ron, *Tina: The Tina Turner Story* (New York: MacMillan, 1985).

Zanes, Warren, *Dusty in Memphis* (New York and Memphis: Continuum, 2003).

Song Title Index

A Fool in Love 205n, 206, 216–17
Alfie 141
Always Something There to Remind Me 140n, 141, 151, 152
Anyone Who Had a Heart 120, 121, 132–3, 141
Are You Ready to Be Heartbroken 155
As I Love You 176n
As Long as He Needs Me 176n
As Long as You're Happy 151
As Tears Go By 188
At My Front Door 122

Baby It's You 122n
Be My Baby 93, 118
Best of Both Worlds 145
Bigelow 6200 40, 75–6, 78
Bold Soul Sister 29, 209, 225–6
Boom Bang-a-Bang 145, 147
Brand New Me 140n
Break It To Me Gently 87n

Can I Get a Witness 146
Can't Hear You No More 146
Chains 97, 122n
Chariot 139
Come My Little Baby 47
Come Together 210, 220
Conversations 140n, 141

Da Doo Ron Ron 102, 103
Der Hölle Rache kocht in meinem Herzen (Queen of the Night's aria, *The Magic Flute*) 65
Di Fronte all'Amore 123
Do Re Mi 121
Don't Make Me Over 123
Don't Say Nothin' Bad About My Baby 94
Don't Sleep in the Subway 139
Don't Speak of Love 118

Don't You Know 121
Doodlin' 121
Downtown 139, 156, 160n
Dreaming My Dreams 198
Dynamite 79–80

For Emily, Whenever I May Find Her 2n
Frederick 155
Frosty the Snowman 51

Gee Whiz 85–6
Girl Don't Come 152
Give Him a Great Big Kiss 18, 52
Go Ahead On 133–4
Goldfinger 176n
Gonna Build a Mountain 134n
Good Girls 18

Hand in Glove (with the Smiths) 155
He Hit Me and it Felt Like a Kiss 102–7
He Like It, She Like It! 20–21
He's a Rebel 49–50, 103n, 146
He's Gone 45–6, 46ex
He's Sure the Boy I Love 103n, 146
Heatwave 142, 146n
Honky Tonk Woman 210, 220
Hound Dog 122

I Can Never Go Home Again 18
I Can't Hear You 121
I Can't Stay Mad at You 93
I Feel Love 1
I Had a Talk with My Man 121
I Have a Love 159n
I Idolize You 217n, 218
I Love a Piano 123n
I Only Want to Be with You 140n
I Saw A Tear 47–8, 48ex
I Want to Be Wanted 87n

I Want to Take You Higher (Ike and Tina Turner) 220
I Want Your Love Tonight 139
I Will Follow Him 50, 159
I'll Stop at Nothing 152, 153*n*
I'll Try Everything 153
I'm a Tiger 147
I'm Sorry 85–6, 87*n*
I've Been Wrong Before 120, 121, 135, 141
If It Don't Work Out 120, 121
In the Land of Make Believe 159*n*
It Was Easier To Hurt Him 121, 131–2
It's For You 142
It's My Party 93

Jambalaya 39*n*, 79, 82–5
Johnny Get Angry 100–102, 105, 131
Judy's Turn to Cry 93

Kiss Me, Honey, Kiss Me 176*n*
Knock, Knock, Who's There? 177

La Bamba 121
Lay Lady Lay 154
Layla 105
Leader of the Pack 21, 52
Leave a Little Love 145
Lemon Tree 149
Let's Jump the Broomstick 80
Locomotion 93
Long After Tonight is All Over 121
Long Live Love 149, 152
Love Me Do 154
Love's Just a Broken Heart 141

Mama Roux 154
Mama Said 120, 121
Maybe I Know 153
Maybe 1, 45
Message Understood 152
Mockingbird 120, 121, 131
Monsieur Dupont 152
Morning Dew 145, 147
Move It On Over 71
Mr. Lee 43
My Boyfriend's Back 7, 52
My Colouring Book 121

Needle in a Haystack 133, 134*n*
Nothing Comes Easy 152
Nothing Has Been Proved 113
Nothing 121
Nowhere to Run 26, 96–8, 105

Oh Gosh 159*n*
Oh Me Oh My (I'm a Fool For You Baby) 140, 147
Oh No He Don't 150
Oh No! Not My Baby 121
One Teenager to Another 79
Ooo Poo Pah Doo 219

Packin' Up 121
Party Lights 99–100, 105
Pilgrim's Chorus (*Tannhäuser*) 118
Pink Shoelaces 40–41
Please, Please, Please 209, 220–25
Pretty Baby 123*n*
Proud Mary 220, 222
Puppet on a String 152, 153–4
Push It To Make It Go 150

Que Sera, Sera 49

Relight My Fire 157
Remember (Walkin' in the Sand) 1, 52
Respect 221, 233
River Deep, Mountain High 207, 218, 219*n*
Rock the Bop 80
Rockin' Around the Christmas Tree 60, 80

Sailor 139
Shake, Rattle, and Roll 122
[S]he Will Only Break Your Heart 146
Shout 140, 145
Silver Threads and Golden Needles 123*n*, 138*n*
Sister Morphine 197, 199
Sleigh Ride 51
Sliding Through Life on Charm 201
Sound and Vision 179
Stay With Me 123
Step Inside Love 141
Stop Feeling Sorry for Yourself 152
Stop in the Name of Love 95
Sugar Sugar 54

SONG TITLE INDEX

Sun in My Eyes 154
Surprise, Surprise 146
Surround Yourself with Sorrow 141
Sweet Nothings 81, 144
Sympathy for the Devil 154, 198

Tell Him 123
That's How Heartaches Are Made 121
The Boat That I Row 145, 147
The End of the World 93n
The Love of the Loved 140, 142
The Man Who Sold the World 157
The Trouble with Boys 146
Then He Kissed Me 93
There's No Business Like Show Business 175
There's No Other Like My Baby 103
Those Were the Days 174
Till 49–50
To Sir With Love 147
Today 152
Tomorrow 152
Tonight in Tokyo 152
Tonight You Belong to Me 39–40
Tro, Tro, Tro 169–71, 170ex
Turn Me Loose 97
Turn, Turn, Turn 169–71, 170ex
Twenty-Four Hours From Tulsa 121

Uptown 103n

Watch That Man 157
What Have I Done to Deserve This? 113n
What's Easy for Two is So Hard for One 146
When the Lovelight Starts Shining Through His Eyes 120, 121, 132
When the Midnight Choo Choo Leaves for Alabam' 123n
White Christmas 51
Who Can I Turn To? 120, 121
Who Knows Where the Time Goes? 174n
Why'd You Do It 199
Will You Love Me Tomorrow 17, 34, 47, 48–9, 85, 93, 120, 121, 132
Winter Wonderland 52
Wishin' and Hopin 120, 121, 139, 145
Won't Be Long 121

Y Blodyn Gwyn (The White Flower) 175
Ya Ya Twist 139
You Are My Sweetheart 44, 45ex
You Can't Blame Him 153
You Don't Have to Say You Love Me 153, 158
You Don't Own Me 95, 121, 145
You'll Never Leave [Him] 146
You're My World 141–2
You've Not Changed 152
Your Cheatin' Heart 76–8

Subject and Name Index

abuse 103–4, 107, 131, 207, 211, 219, 222, 225; *see also* violence
accent (linguistic) 13–14, 20, 51–3, 170
ad libs, the 3
adolescence 10–12, 14, 16, 23, 25, 35–6, 41, 59, 69–70, 92, 99, 107, 151, 225; *see also* teenager
Aerosmith 1, 7
African American
   culture/tradition 27, 122, 124–9, 133, 203, 212, 225
   music 73, 114, 118–31, 144, 149, 155–6, 205–10, 212, 216–22, 225, 233; *see also* blues, call and response, calypso, funk, gospel, jazz, rhythm and blues, rockabilly, rock and roll, soul
   performance 59, 73, 191
   stereotypes 67, 207–8, 230
   singers 8, 25, 54, 73, 120–27, 49
   teenagers 16–18, 59, 89, 91–2, 97
agency 9, 11, 28, 60, 65, 69–70, 75, 128, 210–11, 214, 219, 237
Aguilera, Christina 27, 108
Albritten, Dub (manager) 81
All Saints 161
Alston, Barbara 102–3
Alston, Shirley 43, 54n
Altamont 172, 184, 198
Andrews, Chris (songwriter) 149, 152, 155
Andrews, Julie 38–9
Andrews Sisters, the 5, 20, 42
androgyny 59, 61, 63–4, 72, 87, 143, 157–9, 191
Angels, the 19, 49–50
anger/rage 26–7, 89–95, 99–101, 106–9, 199, 201
Anita Kerr Singers, the 87
Ann-Margret 24
Apartheid 128

appearance 18, 20, 50–51, 63–4, 67–9, 81–2, 86, 89, 95–9, 114–19, 143–4, 148–50, 157, 160n, 166, 172, 188–9, 208, 229; *see also* beauty, fashion
appropriation 122, 124, 191, 203–5, 210, 212, 220–21, 228–9, 232
Archies, the 54
Arendt, Hannah 89–90
Argent, Rod (songwriter) 120
Asbri, see music journalism
Atkins, Cholly 97, 104, 117n
Auslander, Philip 183, 188
authentic/authenticity 19n, 21–3, 26, 38, 40, 102, 118–19, 134, 184–5, 187–8, 199–200, 205, 220, 230

B*Witched 3
Baade, Christina 122n
baby-talk 72
Baby Washington 121
Bacharach, Burt (songwriter) 100, 133, 141, 149, 151
backing band(s) 3, 24, 129, 146
backing vocals/vocalist(s) 3, 25, 48, 50, 81, 93–4, 97, 99, 103, 122, 126, 130, 133–4, 152, 153n, 179
Baez, Joan 175, 231n
Ballard, Florence "Flo" 54
Barbie 15–17, 19
Bardot, Brigitte 116
Barr, Roseanne 66
Barry, Jeff (producer) 53–4
Barstow, Dick 73n
Bart, Lionel 188
Barthes, Roland *see* voice – "grain"
Bartky, Sandra Lee 98–9
Bassey, Shirley 176
BBC *see* British Broadcasting Corporation

256   *SHE'S SO FINE*

Beatles, the 7, 14, 50, 54, 74, 122*n*, 124, 138–9, 141–3, 149, 154, 156, 157*n*, 172, 175, 178, 190*n*, 191, 210, 220, 230
    Sgt. Pepper 172
beauty 15, 17, 29, 73, 160, 187, 207*n*, 208, 213, 227–8; *see also* appearance
Bee Gees, the 154
Bell, Madeline 25*n*, 113*n*, 119*n*, 125, 130, 133–4
Bell, Simon 113*n*, 122*n*
Bennett, Ronnie *see* Spector, Ronnie
Bennett, Tony 120–21
Beverley Sisters, the 20–21, 139
Billboard see music journalism
Black, Cilla (Priscilla White) 9, 24, 29, 120–21, 124, 135*n*, 137–8, 140–44, 147–9, 152, 155–8, 160, 166, 183
    background 141–3
    repertoire 141–2
    vocal qualities 142
blackface 73, 203–5; *see also* minstrelsy
    vocal blackface 124
blackness 19–21, 27–8, 52*n*, 124*n*, 126, 190, 203–5, 228–30, 235
Blossoms, the 3, 49, 146
Bluebelles, the *see* LaBelle, Patti
blues 21, 122, 164, 203–5, 210, 219, 230;
    see also rhythm and blues
    as a vocal style 48, 54, 73–4, 100, 123, 127, 213, 216, 221
    Chicago blues 188
    country blues 71–2
    southern blues 58–9
Bobbettes, the 43–5, 47
body 4*n*, 28*n*, 35, 37, 50, 63*n*, 64–5, 69– 73, 75–6, 80, 95–6, 98–9, 167–8, 205, 207*n*, 208, 211–12, 215, 222, 228, 232–3, 236–7
Boone, Pat 122
Boswell, Connie 42
Boswell Sisters, the 8, 52*n*
boyfriend(s) 18–19, 64, 94, 100–102, 131–2, 152–3
Bradley, Owen (producer) 58, 75, 85
Breakaways, the 17, 24
Brel, Jacques (songwriter) 149
Bricusse, Leslie (songwriter) 134

Brill Building 51, 100
Britain
    in the 1950s and 60s 12–15, 20–21, 91, 98, 116–17, 122, 137–49, 158, 189, 191, 201
    ethnicity in 12–15, 20–21, 27–8, 63, 66*n*, 155–6
    (male) musicians in/from 54, 128, 137, 151, 157, 190–91, 208
British Broadcasting Corporation (BBC) 4, 20, 65*n*, 122, 124, 131, 134, 144, 145, 154, 177, 196*n*
British invasion 54, 137, 156, 157*n*, 167*n*, 183
Brooks, Dolores "LaLa" 103
Brown, James 29, 52*n*, 129, 209, 210*n*, 212, 217, 220–26, 233
    Live at the Apollo 209, 220–22
Brown, Maxine 121
Brown, Ruth 127, 216
Brox Sisters, the 8
Bowie, David 145, 147, 157, 179–80
Boy George (George O'Dowd) 149*n*
Buffy the Vampire Slayer (TV series) 107
Bush, Kate 149, 155, 161
Butler, Jerry 146
Butler, Judith 193
Byrds, the 169

Calder, Tony (manager) 188
call and response 126, 133–4, 212, 216, 222
calypso 20, 149
Carlisle, Belinda 55
Cash, Johnny 59, 72
Cassidy, David 55
Celtic ethnicities 12, 16, 27, 144, 149, 155;
    see also Ireland, Scotland, Wales
Chang, Jung 95*n*
Chantels, the 1, 42–7, 130
Charles, Ray 86, 121
Charles, Tina 55
Charlie Is My Darling (film) 190–91
Cher (Cher Bono) 4, 9, 24, 54
Cherry, Neneh 4
child/children/childhood 4, 13, 26, 34–6, 39–41, 44, 57–66, 68–77, 81–2, 86–7, 90, 95*n*, 108, 122, 128, 139,

144, 148, 158, 172, 177–8, 218–19; *see also* girl(s)

child prodigy *see* prodigy

child star 39, 58, 60–65, 73, 76, 86, 108, 139

Chiffons, the 24

Chordettes, the 42

choreography 26, 43, 97, 104, 116*n*, 210, 232

civil rights movement (US) 14, 16–17, 58, 89–90, 127, 221, 225, 230

Church, Charlotte 73

Clapton, Eric 105

Clark, Claudine 99–100

Clark, Petula 124, 137, 139, 156, 160, 167*n*
background 139

Clarkson, Kelly 55, 108

class 7–8, 10–15, 17, 20–21, 22*n*, 28, 61, 90–92, 95–6, 98, 107, 116–17, 148, 161, 193–4, 202, 215*n*, 218, 228–9, 232, 235–6
comparison between US and Britain 12–15, 20–21
in the US 12–15, 20–21, 59, 63*n*, 64, 66–9, 71, 86–7, 210
in Britain 12–15, 20–21, 66, 98, 122, 127, 189–91, 193–4, 201

Clary, Julian 21

Cline, Patsy 42, 87*n*

clique *see* friends/friendship

Clooney, Rosemary 4*n*, 9, 72

Cobain, Kurt 105

Cochran, Eddie 64, 72

Cocker, Jarvis 200–201

Cogan, Alma 24, 130

Coleman, Gary 66

Coley, Doris 47–8, 50

Collier, Mitty 121

Collins, Lorrie (the Collins Kids) 60, 68–9

conformity 10–11, 17, 22, 23, 236; *see also* friends/friendship, peer groups

Cooder, Ry 197

Cookies, the 94, 97, 122*n*

Corrs, the 5

Costello, Elvis 136

counterculture 22, 186, 191, 202

country music/country singers 8, 21–2, 42, 48*n*, 57–8, 71–3, 76, 85–6, 93*n*, 149

cover versions 1, 29, 51, 76, 79, 82, 118, 120–24, 131–3, 141, 144–6, 149,

151–2, 155, 157–8, 159*n*, 169, 165, 175, 188, 203, 209–10, 219–26

Crystals, the 3, 9, 49, 93, 102–5, 146, 236

Culture Club 157

Cusick, Suzanne 28, 42*n*, 167–9, 171, 176

Cyrus, Cynthia 17–18, 20

Daae, Christine (*The Phantom of the Opera*) 36

Dansettes, the 8

Darin, Bobby 86

David, Hal (lyricist) 100, 133, 141, 151

Davis, Sammy, Jr. 66

Davis, Skeeter 93

Day, Doris 9, 19, 49, 53, 64*n*

De Leath, Vaughn 42

Deltairs, the 43

Deneuve, Catherine 116

Denny, Sandy 174*n*, 176*n*

DeShannon, Jackie 149

Diamond, Neil (songwriter) 145

Dido 161

difference 6, 7, 11, 21, 61, 66, 118, 149, 212, 214

Disney 7, 108
Hercules (film) 7

Dixie Cups, the 24

Dixon, Reather 43, 45

doo-wop 42–9, 51, 52, 105–6

Donegan, Lonnie 171*n*

Donovan 159*n*, 175, 180

Dorsey, Lee 121, 139

"double consciousness" 124, 127

Douglas, Susan 19, 34–5, 41, 53
Where The Girls Are 19, 34–5

doxa 10–21, 23, 26, 27; *see also* conformity, respectability

dress 17–19, 20, 43, 54, 61*n*, 63*n*, 67–9, 72, 75, 80–82, 89, 95–8, 117–18, 134, 143, 159–60, 160*n*, 172, 193, 227–9; *see also* appearance, fashion

Dr. John 154

drag 63–4*n*, 117, 160*n*

Dreamgirls (musical) 7

DuBois, W.E.B. 127

Duffy, Aimée Ann 7

Dunbar, John 187, 198

258   SHE'S SO FINE

Duncan, Leslie 130, 134
duos/duets, male-female 4, 8, 25, 131, 166, 176*n*
Durbin, Deanna 38–9, 73
Dylan, Bob 154

Echoes, the (Dusty Springfield's backing band) 129
Eckford, Elizabeth 89–93
Ed Sullivan Show, The (TV programme) 124
Eisteddfod 164–5, 167, 172, 178
El Dorados, the 122
Ellison, Lorraine 123
empty/emptiness 57, 61–5, 66, 70, 71, 74*n*, 75, 87
Epstein, Brian (manager) 142–3, 183, 190*n*
Essex, the 3
ethnicity 11–12, 16, 28, 66, 74*n*, 91, 148–9, 155–6; *see also* race
Etting, Ruth 8
Eurovision Song Contest 27, 147, 153–4, 177, 179, 180
Everett, Betty 121, 146
Exciters, the 3, 123

Fabian 97
Faithfull, Marianne 28, 140, 156, 158, 159*n*, 160, 175, 183–202, 236
    background 187, 189, 190
    Broken English 195, 199–200
    Faithless 198
    Kissin' Time 201
    Love In A Mist 197
    press treatment of 186, 191–2, 194–5
    Rich Kid Blues 198
    vocal qualities 159*n*, 189, 197, 199
Fairport Convention 174*n*, 176*n*
Famous Flames, the (James Brown's backing band) 129
fan(s) 5, 6, 19, 22–3, 26, 27, 29, 53, 58, 114–17, 119, 122, 123*n*, 124, 128*ex*, 131, 135, 142, 143, 157, 175, 184–5, 191, 198, 200
fashion 4, 8, 26, 41, 117–18, 143, 150, 158, 159–60, 189, 193; *see also* appearance, dress
Faith, Adam 151

Faye, Alice 65, 72
femininity 10–11, 13–14, 17–19, 29, 72, 92, 95–8, 106, 116–17, 128, 145, 157, 159, 161, 193–4, 208*n*, 213, 217, 232–3, 235–7
feminism/feminist 5–6, 8, 19, 22–3, 29, 59, 66, 99–101, 106, 138, 160, 199–201, 211, 235–7
    protofeminism 144, 153
Fisk Jubilee Singers 122
Fitzgerald, Ella 8, 42, 127, 135
Floyd, Samuel 125–6, 211–12
Foley, Red 75–6
folk 22, 54, 86, 116, 123, 145, 149, 163, 165–9, 171, 179*n*
folk-pop 188, 189, 198
folk-rock 145, 169, 175, 176*n*
Foucault, Michel 98
Foxworthy, Jeff 66
Foxx, Charlie and Inez 120–21, 131
Francis, Connie 24, 85, 87*n*
Frankenberg, Ruth 11, 12, 126
Franklin, Aretha 10, 24, 50–51, 54, 121, 183*n*, 210, 221, 233
Franz, John (producer) 130
Friedan, Betty 14, 117, 235–36
    The Feminine Mystique 14, 235
Friedman, Susan 11, 21
friends/friendship 2, 3, 18, 58*n*, 94, 103–4, 106*n*, 158; *see also* conformity, peer groups
Frusciante, John 1–2
Funicello, Annette 85
Funk 1, 209, 225, 234
Funk Brothers (Motown backing band) 129
Future Sound of London 180

Gaar, Gillian 102, 138
Ganser, Marge and Mary Ann 52
Garland, Judy 38–9, 40, 53, 62*n*, 73–4, 75, 81*n*, 135, 172*n*
Garland–Thomson, Rosemarie 95
Garner, Kay 134
Gates, Henry Louis 125–6, 211–12
Gaye, Marvin 146
gaze 60, 62*n*, 176, 188, 193, 228
gender 1, 7, 10–11, 15, 20–21, 23–5, 27–8, 57–8, 85, 86, 90, 92, 96, 120, 166,

171, 186, 187, 193, 202, 212, 221, 224, 235–57

gender ambiguity/gender bending 62*n*, 63, 64*n*, 67–8, 72, 157, 159

gender boundaries/norms 15, 124, 128, 130, 131, 165, 187, 189, 191, 193–4, 198, 205

gender roles/gendered behaviour 100, 101, 114, 118, 146, 153, 154, 157, 161, 201, 205, 213

gendered voices 126, 131, 159, 167, 213–17, 219, 224–6

gender in rock 1, 187, 213–17, 219

in songs 131–2, 146, 152–3, 206, 224–6

gender studies 6

genre 21–2, 24, 33, 35, 54, 61, 93, 165, 171, 185, 214, 221, 225, 234

Gibb, Maurice 158

Gibson, Debbie 55

Gilligan, Carol 70, 91, 99

Gilroy, Paul 124*n*, 126

The Girl Can't Help It (film) 19, 70

girl(s)/girlhood (*guide only*) 8, 9, 10–17, 21–3, 24, 59, 61, 63–72, 79, 85, 87, 89–100, 101, 102, 105–9, 114, 116–17, 128, 138, 140, 156, 158, 161, 186, 191, 236

girl talk 8, 79, 133, 158, 224, 225

girls' voices 24, 25–6, 33–42, 59, 94, 168

girl groups

and collective identity 17–21, 93–5

careers of 9–10, 24

definition of 2–3

influence on male musicians 1–2, 7, 122*n*, 157

manipulation of 3*n*, 9, 24, 54, 97–8

mixed-race 25

singing technique and 33–55

British covers of repertoire 130, 132, 145–6, 152

girl singers

careers of 8–10, 24

definition of 3–4

in Britain 113–80, 183–202

influence on male musicians 74, 157

in popular culture 5, 7–8

in popular music studies 6–7, 23

in the US 33–109, 138, 203–34

technique and 33–55

vocal decorum and 72–5

"girl power" 22, 117, 140, 145, 161

Goffin, Gerry (songwriter) 48*n*, 85, 93*n*, 94, 102–3, 106

Goodrich, Sandra *see* Sandie Shaw

Gordy, Berry (producer) 9, 97, 116, 183

Gore, Lesley 24, 93, 95, 121, 145, 153

gospel 72, 122, 210, 216–18

as a vocal style 44, 49, 51, 54, 65, 73, 125, 131, 134, 216–18

Grand Ol' Opry 68, 85

Green, Hughie (presenter) 169*n*, 177

Greenwich, Ellie (songwriter) 24, 53

Greer, Germaine 22, 117

Grieg, Charlotte 20, 41, 150

Griffin, Farah Jasmine 128

Haley, Bill 122

Haley, Jack 65

Hairspray (musical) 7

Harrison, George 149*n*

Harvey, PJ (Polly Jean) 185, 200–201

Hearts, the 49

Hendrix, Margie 121

Hole (band) 105–7

Holiday, Billie 8, 127–28, 135

Holland-Dozier-Holland (songwriters) 97, 132

Hollies, the 156

Holly, Buddy 59, 74, 216

The Honeymooners (TV series) 104

hooks, bell 90, 227, 233

Hopkin, Mary 28, 149*n*, 159*n*, 163–80

as "England's sweetheart" 166–8

Earth Song/Ocean Song 179

image 171–3, 177–9

Paul McCartney and 166, 168–9, 174–6, 177

Post Card 169, 174–6, 179*n*

repertoire 169, 174–5

vocal qualities 171, 175

Hullabaloo (TV series) 104

Hynde, Chrissie 161

Ian, Janis 10, 24

identity 4*n*, 10–11, 15–21, 26, 35, 41–2, 53, 54, 95, 107, 114*n*, 115, 126,

131, 134, 188, 205, 215, 226; *see also* persona
Ignatiev, Noel 126–7
Ikettes, the 210–11, 225–6, 232–3
image 9, 17–20, 25–9, 39, 41, 43, 53, 67*n*, 71, 82, 96, 115–19, 138–9, 143, 145, 148, 158, 159, 166, 171–3, 176, 177, 179*n*, 186–90, 197–200, 207–10, 213–14, 217, 219*n*, 222, 225; *see also* appearance
imprisonment 97
indie rock 185, 200–201
Inness, Sherrie A. 231–2
Ireland/Irish/Irishness 15, 16–17*n*, 116, 118, 127, 142, 149*n*, 155*n*, 177*n*
Irigaray, Luce 3*n*, 4*n*
Isley Brothers, the 145
Iwan, Dafydd 172

Jackson, Mahalia 73, 74, 80, 216
Jackson, Michael 66
Jackson, Wanda 10, 60, 68–9
Jagger, Mick 28, 146*n*, 183, 185–6, 192–9
    relationship with Marianne Faithfull 187–8, 190–91, 197–8, 199
Jankowski, Linda 49
jazz 42, 51, 54, 114, 122, 124, 126, 142, 149
Jefferson Airplane 176*n*, 183
John, Elton 134
Johnson, Lou 151
Johnson, Plas 40
Jones, Brian 184, 192*n*, 196, 198
Jones, Caryl Parry 179*n*
Jones, Heather 179*n*
Jones, Tom 130, 149*n*
Joplin, Janis 172, 183*n*
Josie and the Pussycats (TV series) 25, 29

Kallen, Kitty 121
kazoo 101–2
Keating, Ronan 10
Kid Galahad (film) 100
Khan, Chaka 25n
Kincaid, James F 57, 60–64, 66, 73*n*, 87
King, Carole 24, 48*n*, 85, 93*n*, 94, 102, 103*n*, 106, 117
    Tapestry 117
King, Florence 66, 73–4

Kings of Rhythm, the (Ike and Tina Turner's backing band) 206, 218, 219, 22, 226
Kinks, the 153*n*, 156
Knight, Marie 121
Knowles, Beyoncé 3
Kramer, Billy J. 142*n*
Krasnow, Bob (producer) 203
Kubrick, Stanley 70

LaBelle, Patti 3, 9*n*, 24
Laine, Frankie 76
Lamont, Lena (*Singing In The Rain*) 36
Lana Sisters, the 123
lang, kd 63, 100–101
Lauper, Cyndi 55
Lavigne, Avril 108
Led Zeppelin 176*n*
Lee, Brenda 10, 24, 26, 38, 39–40, 44, 57–87, 144, 236
    background 58, 75, 81, 86
    vocal performance 75–87
Lee, Peggy 73, 127, 135
Lennon, John 142, 149
Lennox, Annie 64*n*, 149*n*, 161*n*
lenticular logic 18–21, 23, 26, 27, 29
Lewis, Emmanuel 66
Lewis, George 125–26
Lewis, Jerry Lee 59, 64, 72, 80
Lincoln, Abby 127
Little Anthony 46
Little Eva 93, 102, 146*n*
Little Orphan Annie 64
Little Rock Nine 89–92
Little Richard 213, 214, 216–17
Liverpool 142–3, 155, 166, 167*n*, 190*n*
Loder, Kurt 206
Lolita (film and book) 26, 70–71, 79, 81, 87
London (city) 1, 8, 13–14, 16*n*, 20, 116, 119, 129–30, 132, 134*n*, 137, 139, 143, 144, 148, 149, 156, 166, 167*n*, 175, 176*n*, 177–9, 187, 189–90, 193, 196, 199
London, Julie 73
Looking Glass 1
Love, Courtney 105–9
Love, Darlene 10, 23, 24, 49–52, 54*n*, 103*n*, 146

SUBJECT AND NAME INDEX

Lulu (Marie Lawrie) 9, 24, 29, 117, 124, 130, 137–41, 144–9, 155–61, 166
background 144
repertoire 145–7
Something to Shout About 145
vocal qualities 145
Luvvers, the (Lulu's backing band) 146
Lymon, Frankie 46
Lyne, Adrian 70
Lynn, Vera 138
Lynne, Shelby 8

Maddox, Rose 60
Madonna 6, 9, 55, 161
Mansfield, Jayne 4, 70, 72, 227
March, Little Peggy 50, 159
market/marketing 17, 21, 39, 57, 60, 70–71, 79, 81, 108–9, 113, 147, 163, 167*n*, 168, 171, 179, 187–8, 208, 219, 221, 230
Marr, Johnny 152, 155
marriage 13, 16–17*n*, 19, 41*n*, 70, 86, 95–6*n*, 139, 148, 158, 179, 199, 206*n*, 219, 223–4, 226, 229*n*, 235
Martin, George (producer) 142
Martin, Janis 60, 68
Marvelettes, the 5
masculinity 1, 63, 72, 101, 105, 191, 200, 214–15, 225, 229*n*
masochism 103, 189
masquerade 18–20, 27, 101, 160*n*, 235–7
Massey, Marion (manager) 146
Maultsby, Portia 125
McCartney, Paul 142, 149*n*, 166, 168–9, 174–6, 177
McCrea, Earl-Jean 94
McPherson, Tara 19–20, 26
media, *see* press
Melly, George 143*n*
Melnick, Jeff 209
melody 26, 49, 51–2, 65, 76, 83, 85, 97, 100, 103, 106, 129, 165*n*, 216–18, 225
Melody Maker, see music journalism
Memphis Minne 216
Merman, Ethel 175
Mimms, Garnett 121, 131
Minogue, Kylie 55

minstrelsy 126, 203–5, 233; *see also* blackface
Miracles, the *see* Robinson, Smokey, and the Miracles
misogyny 95, 102, 106, 186
Mitchell, Joni 54, 179*n*
mixed-sex groups 2–3, 4*n*, 25
Mods/Mod revolution 114, 116–17, 139, 148, 150, 158–60
Monroe, Marilyn 70, 72
Morissette, Alanis 108
Morrison, Van 149*n*
Morrissey 148, 149*n*, 152, 155, 157
Morton, George "Shadow" (producer) 54*n*, 183
Most, Mickie (producer) 146–47
mother/motherhood 4, 13–14, 17*n*, 18, 41*n*, 65, 68–9, 72,74*n*, 81, 89, 95–6*n*, 99–100, 107, 117, 139, 189, 190, 198, 208, 235
Motown 21, 27, 54, 55*n*, 64*n*, 104, 114, 116*n*, 124, 129, 132–3, 163, 232
Artist Development Program 54, 97–8
Moyet, Alison 4*n*, 161
Mozart, Wolfgang Amadeus 65
MTV Unplugged (television series) 105
Mulvey, Laura 60, 62
Murray, Anne 134
Murray, Juggy 206
Murray, Ruby 139
music journalism 113, 186, 194–5; *see also* press
Asbri 172–3, 180
Billboard 104
Melody Maker 116, 123*n*, 190
Rolling Stone 172, 175, 179n, 186
musicology 6, 23

Napier-Bell, Simon 118
Newley, Anthony (songwriter) 134
Newman, Randy (songwriter) 135
newspapers, *see* press
Nico 201–2
Nirvana 105
Nitzsche, Jack 197
Nolan Sisters, the 55
Novak, Kim 116
Nunley, Louis 81

262   *SHE'S SO FINE*

Nyoka (*The Perils of Nyoka*) (TV series)
227–30

O'Brien, Lucy 138, 212, 233
O'Brien, Margaret 62*n*
O'Brien, Mary *see* Springfield, Dusty
O'Connor, Sinead 161
O'Day, Anita 8
Oermann, Robert 57, 69, 71, 79, 87
Oldham, Andrew Loog 187–90
Olsen twins, the 66
opera 34, 39*n*, 65, 73, 118*n*, 133, 159
Opportunity Knocks (TV series) 169, 177,
180
Orbison, Roy 72
Ordettes, the, *see* Patti LaBelle
Owens, Shirley 34, 47–9, 85

parody 2, 29, 64*n*, 117, 185, 203–5,
212–13, 217, 226, 233
Parton, Dolly 66, 69–70, 180
passive/passivity 28, 61, 63, 91, 93, 101,
158, 161, 166–68, 174, 176–7, 188,
232, 236
Patience and Prudence 39–40, 41, 43
Pavletich, Aida 33–5, 38, 46*n*, 51–3
peer groups 19*n*, 94; *see also* conformity,
friendship
Performance (film) 198
performance (live) 28–9, 50–51, 75–6, 80,
105–7, 131, 134, 151, 209–11, 213,
220–26, 232–3
vs studio recording 209
performance studies 28, 187
Perkins, Carl 59
Peter, Paul and Mary 149
Pet Shop Boys, the 9, 13*n*, 152, 157
Pfaff, Kristen 105
The Phantom of the Opera (film) 36
Pink (singer) 108
Pipettes, the 8
Pitney, Gene 121
Pop Idol (TV franchise) 169*n*
posture 80, 95–100
Pought, Emma 43, 45
Powell, Jane 73
Powell, Maxine 97–8, 117*n*

Presley, Elvis 59, 64, 67, 68, 72, 80, 100,
122, 124, 216, 237
press, 68, 107–8, 113–14, 176*n*, 179*n*, 184,
186, 192–3, 195–7, 199; *see also*
music journalism
News of the World 192
New York Times 199
tabloid press 153, 192, 197
The Times 144, 192–4
primitiveness 227–30
prodigy/prodigiousness 26, 39, 47, 57–62,
72–3, 76, 81
producer 4, 23, 26, 47, 52, 54*n*, 55, 58, 75,
85, 102, 108, 116, 124, 130, 132,
137, 142, 145, 146, 175, 179, 203,
233; *see also* record production
psychomachia 150
psychotherapy 160–61
puberty 19, 35 36, 38, 40, 41, 42*n*, 59,
69–70, 73, 86, 168
prepubescence 58, 87, 168
Pulp, see Cocker, Jarvis
Pussycat Dolls, the 25*n*

Quant, Mary 160

race 7, 10–15, 17–21, 22*n*, 24–5, 27–8,
59–60, 63, 66–7, 85–7, 89–92,
114, 118–20, 125–30, 161, 189,
194, 210, 212, 214–15 227–30,
235–7; *see also* African American,
blackness, white culture, whiteness
racialization 52*n*, 67, 124, 205, 218, 221
racial purity/superiority (concept of)
118, 189
Radcliffe, Jimmy 121
radio 9, 42, 53, 58, 114*n*, 120, 122, 123*n*,
124, 126, 200
rage *see* anger
Raincoats, the 199
Ramsey, Guthrie Jr. 125
Randolph, Boots 85
record companies 4n, 9 50–51, 71, 85, 117,
140
Ace 8
Apple 169, 178–9
Atlantic 54, 147, 183, 197
Cambrian 169

SUBJECT AND NAME INDEX

Columbia 51, 146, 183
Decca 58, 78, 140, 197
Philips 120, 130, 140
Pye 140, 153*n*
Rhino 8
Sain 169, 172
Stax 85
Sue 206
Sun 71
record production 24, 25, 40, 39, 51–2,
    103, 130, 132–4, 141, 142, 171,
    179, 207, 218
    double–tracking 39–40, 43, 48–9, 50,
    52, 53
Red Hot Chili Peppers, the 1, 7
Reece, Douggie 131
Rees-Mogg, William 193
Reeves, Martha, and the Vandellas 10, 54,
    96–8, 104, 116–17*n*, 118, 124, 125,
    142, 146*n*
relationships 4, 18, 28–9*n*, 64–5, 74, 94,
    158, 186, 190–91,219, 222–4;
    see also boyfriend(s), friends/
    friendship, marriage, peer groups
    in songs 76, 79, 93, 94–5, 97, 99–105,
    108, 131–3, 146, 152–4, 158, 222–4
repression 26, 69, 95–9
respectability 12–19, 21–2, 68–9, 91–2,
    223, 227–30
Reynolds, Debbie 36*n*
rhythm and blues (R&B) 58, 72, 86, 101,
    147, 149, 203, 219–26
Richards, Keith 146*n*, 188, 190–98
Riley, Billy Lee 72
Rimes, LeAnn 73–4
Riot Grrrl movement 6, 27, 105–8
Riviere, Joan 236
Robinson, Smokey, and the Miracles 124
rockabilly 21, 26, 40, 46, 57–61, 64,
    67–74, 86–7
rock and roll 4, 8–9, 19, 20, 29, 58, 59*n*,
    69–71, 86, 93, 101, 137, 171*n*, 209,
    212–14, 216–17, 219–21, 230
Rock and Roll Hall of Fame 10, 213
"rock chick" 213, 233–4
rock culture 28, 185–7, 194–9, 202
rock journalism; *see* music journalism
Rodgers, Jimmie 71

Roediger, David 126
Ronettes, the 10, 17–18, 23, 24, 51, 53,
    93, 183
Rolling Stone, see music journalism
Rolling Stones, the 28, 146, 154, 156,
    183–200, 210, 220, 230, 237
    Beggar's Banquet 198
    Exile on Main Street 198
    Goat's Head Soup 198
    Let It Bleed 197
    Sticky Fingers 197
Rose Marie, Baby 39
Ross, Annie 42
Ross, Diana 3, 7, 9, 24, 54, 132, 233
Rossum, Emmy 36*n*

Santiglia, Peggy 50, 52
Sassoon, Vidal 159–60
Saturday Night Fever (film) 63*n*, 67
saxophone 40, 79, 85, 99, 100, 101
Scotland/Scottishness 144, 146, 149*n*
Searchers, the 153*n*, 156
Seeger, Pete (songwriter) 169*n*, 170*ex*
Seldon, Cathy (*Singing In The Rain*) 36*n*
self-mutilation 95, 99
Sesame Street (TV series) 7
sexuality 19, 21, 27, 41, 57–75, 81–2, 86–7,
    113, 120, 146*n*, 152–3, 158–60,
    176*n*, 185–91, 193–5, 207–8, 215,
    219, 227–30, 232–3, 235–7
    bisexuality 113, 120, 128, 167*n*, 191
    heterosexuality 13*n*, 21, 41*n*, 58, 101,
    120, 158. 185–7, 195, 223, 232,
    235–6
    homosexuality 16*n*, 143, 155, 157, 193
    lesbianism 113, 158, 160*n*, 235–6
Scott, John 72
Shangri-Las, the 1, 3, 18, 24, 52–4, 93, 183
Shapiro, Helen 24
Shaw, Sandie (Sandra Goodrich) 10,
    137–8, 140–41, 143, 144, 147,
    148–61
    background 148
    Choose Life 154
    Hello Angel 155
    post–music career 160–61
    press treatment of 153–4, 158
    repertoire 149–55

Reviewing the Situation 152, 154
vocal qualities 150–51
Sheena (*Sheena, Queen of the Jungle*) (TV series) 227–28
Shindig! (TV show) 96–7, 104, 229
Shirelles, the 10, 17, 19, 24, 34, 43, 47, 85, 93, 120, 121, 122*n*, 130, 132, 157
Shirley and Lee 4
Shumway, David 184
"signifyin(g)" 27, 29, 125–30, 133, 203–5, 211–13, 217, 219, 233
Simon and Garfunkel 2*n*
Simone, Nina 127
Simpson, Ashlee 108–9
Simpson, Jessica 108
Sindy 15, 17, 19
Singing In The Rain (film) 36*n*
singing technique *see* vocal technique
skiffle 21, 171
Slick, Grace 176*n*, 183
Sloboda, John 81
Sly and the Family Stone 220
Smashing Time (film) 137, 141, 143*n*, 150, 152–3*n*
Smith, Arlene 2, 42, 43, 44–7, 50, 51, 54*n*
Smith, Bessie 122–3, 127, 213, 216
social realism 16
Soft Cell 157*n*
song form 48–50, 79–80, 97, 99–105, 218
soul 5*n*, 21, 27, 54, 119*n*, 120–24, 134, 145, 146, 147, 166–7*n*, 221
Sounds of Motown (TV special) 124
South, the (the southern United States) 12, 14, 15*n*, 17*n*, 63, 69, 73–4*n*, 86–7, 89
southern culture 20, 26, 52, 58–9, 67*n*, 71–4
southern stereotypes 68
Southern, Eileen 125
Spears, Britney 27, 55, 67*n*, 108
Spector, Phil 3*n*, 9, 23–4, 51–2, 54*n*, 102–4, 106, 116, 132, 146*n*, 183, 207*n*, 218, 219, 230
A Christmas Gift To You From Phil Spector 51–2
Spector, Ronnie (Ronnie Bennett) 7, 10, 23, 51
Spice Girls, the 3*n*, 5, 6, 22–3, 25*n*, 55, 140, 161

Springfield, Dusty (Mary O'Brien) 7, 8, 9, 10, 27, 29, 54, 113–36, 138–41, 147, 148, 149*n*, 152, 153, 156, 158–61, 167*n*, 236
appearance 29, 114–20, 136, 159
arrangements, musical 129–34
as backing singer 134
background 116, 122–3, 127
Dusty in Memphis 147, 159*n*
Ev'rything's Coming Up Dusty 120–22
identification with African American music and musicians 27, 114, 120–31
range, vocal 123, 135–6, 159, 167*n*
record production and 130
repertoire, choice of 27, 120–24, 134
sexuality 27, 113, 117, 120, 128, 158, 160n, 167n
Thong, Gladys (pseudonym) 134*n*
vocal technique ("Dustifying") 130–36
Springfields, the 116, 123, 138*n*, 140*n*
Stefani, Gwen 108
Stewart, Sandy 121
Steve Allen Show, The (TV series) 76
Stevens, Dodie 40–41, 44
Stock, Aitken and Waterman (producers) 55
Strausbaugh, John 184
Stredder, Maggie 134
Styrene, Poly 199
Sugababes, the 25*n*
Sumac, Yma 42
Summer, Donna 1
Summers, Joanie 100–102
Supremes, the 3, 5, 8, 9, 10, 20, 24, 54, 55*n*, 95, 98, 120, 121, 124, 134, 183
Sweeney, Gael 67
Sweet Honey in the Rock 3

tabloid press *see* press
Take That 9, 157
A Taste of Honey (film) 16
Taylor, Eve (manager) 151, 154
teenager(s) 2, 8–23, 41, 59, 65, 67*n*, 69, 70, 79, 85, 86, 89–108, 114, 117, 132, 133, 148, 156, 158, 175, 179, 186, 188; *see also* adolescence
anger and 26–7, 99–109

conformity and 10–23, 26, 91, 95–6, 98, 100
education of 12, 22
race and 12–13, 15–22, 89–93
respectability and 12–15, 91, 95–8, 100, 174
singers/singing and 2, 9, 26, 33–55, 68, 123, 141, 151, 152n
self-monitoring and 95–9
Temple, Shirley 39, 62n, 64–6, 75, 81, 86
Temptations, the 124
Tharpe, Sister Rosetta 216
Thatcher, Margaret 143, 155
Thomas, Carla 5n, 44, 85–6
Thornton, Big Mama 122, 127, 216
Tiffany (Tiffany Darwisch) 55
Tin Pan Alley 39, 49, 51, 73, 85, 123n
Ting Tings, the 4n
Tomos, Rhiannon 179n
Top of the Pops (TV show) 4, 29, 122, 196n
"tough girl," toughness 68, 209–10, 217, 226, 230–32
traditional song 165, 171
transformation 62, 98, 108, 116, 140, 143, 156
Travolta, John 67
tropes/troping 57, 68, 106n, 126, 129, 131, 212, 216–17, 222
Troy, Doris 125, 130
Tucker, Tanya 73
Turner, Tina (Anna Mae Bullock) 10, 24, 28–9, 127, 188n, 203–34, 236
appearance 208, 226–33
Ike and Tina Turner Live in '71 219
Ike and Tina Turner Revue, the 203, 206–7, 209–11, 232
The Ike and Tina Turner Revue Live with the Kings of Rhythm 218–19, 222
Live! The Ike and Tina Turner Show 219
music historiography and 205–10
Outta Season (Ike and Tina Turner) 203–5, 229, 230
relationship with Ike 207, 208n, 210–11, 217, 224, 226, 228, 233
signifying and 203–5, 211–13, 217, 219, 233
vocal qualities 208, 216–18

Turner, Ike 203–14, 219–21, 224–30, 232–3
claims of control over Tina's performances 210–11, 224, 226–28, 232
Turner, Joe 122
Twiggy 169, 178

United States of America
in the 1950s and 60s 12–20, 58–60, 69–71, 124, 219
and ethnicity 12, 16–17, 58–60, 63, 66–9, 72, 74, 89–90, 92–3; *see also* civil rights movement

Valens, Ritchie 121
Vandellas, *see* Reeves, Martha, and the Vandellas
Velvelettes, the 130, 133
Vernon Girls, the 24
Vincent, Gene 59, 64, 72
Visconti, Tony 179, 180
Vitti, Monica 116
violence 15, 17, 63n, 148, 167, 191
in girl group songs 26, 99–108
domestic 222, 224
vocal decorum 72–5, 76, 79
vocality/vocal identity 26, 41, 42, 46, 53, 54–5, 126, 131, 215
teen vocality/ teen voice 26, 33–55, 68, 91
vocal blackface 124
vocal gender 126, 131, 159, 167–8, 214–16, 219, 236–7
vocal stereotypes 36, 215; *see also* baby-talk
vocal labor 212, 236, 142, 151, 175
voice
damage 135
"grain" (Barthes) 35n, 114, 130, 135, 220
noise 126, 135
pitch 37, 42, 43, 49–50, 51, 52, 75, 79, 217n
quality 34, 35, 39, 49, 50, 79, 99, 101, 103, 131, 153n, 171, 174, 214–16
range 34, 36, 37, 42–5, 48–52, 72, 126, 131, 135, 142, 150–51, 159, 167n, 174, 197, 215–17
rasp 135

register 36, 37, 40, 42–5, 48, 80, 85, 131, 142, 145, 150, 168
timbre 75, 78, 135, 141, 150, 159, 214, 215, 217*n*
vocal style 26, 40, 50, 51, 75–80, 86–7, 123, 130–36, 144, 161, 165–6, 171, 179*n*, 189, 198, 213–19, 225–6; *see also* blues, doo-wop, gospel, rockabilly
vocal technique 25–6, 33–55, 153*n*, 221
  abuse 38
  attack 75, 132
  belting 37, 44*n*, 74, 85, 123, 143, 216, 218
  crooning 37, 51, 139
  distortion 106, 216–18
  embellishment 33, 131
  falsetto 1, 40, 42, 44, 45, 142, 159, 216
  growl 44, 72, 73, 75, 79, 83, 85, 99, 100, 107, 217
  hiccup 47, 49, 72, 75, 76, 79, 83
  hypervocalization 46, 49
  improvisation 78, 126, 130, 134, 165*n*, 218
  intonation 35, 36, 40, 42–4, 48, 49, 50, 51–2, 72, 150
  shout 4, 48, 49, 65, 73, 123, 12, 216, 217, 218
  support 37, 39, 50–51, 136
  placement 36–7, 52, 151, 159
  vibrato 35, 72, 135, 150, 171, 176, 197, 216, 218
  yodel 42, 80

Wadsworth, Derek 113*n*, 129–30
Wagner, Richard 118
Wald, Gayle 189, 219
Wales 122, 163–7, 172–8
  language 28, 163–5, 167–9, 174–5, 176*n*, 179*n*
  popular culture in 163–6, 176
  popular music in 163–8, 171, 176, 179*n*
  role of chapel in 164–5, 168, 171, 172, 177–8
  vocal style 165–6, 171, 179*n*
  Welshness 164, 167, 169, 172, 174, 176
Walkerdine, Valerie 61, 64, 66, 91, 109
Ward, Clara 216

Warwick, Dionne 24, 54, 120, 121, 123, 132, 141, 233
Waters, Ethel 8, 42
Weill, Kurt 185, 200
Weiss, Betty 52
Weiss, Mary 52–3, 55
Weinstein, Deena 20
Wexler, Jerry (producer) 183*n*
white culture 12, 29, 208, 210, 228–30, 232–3; *see also* whiteness
whiteface 203–5, 229, 231
Whitehead, Peter (director) 190, 196
Whiteley, Sheila 71, 79, 87, 166, 168, 171
whiteness (*guide only*) 10–21, 28–9, 48*n*, 55, 59–61, 66, 73, 86, 87, 90, 92, 117, 126, 127, 129, 203–5, 218, 219, 228–9, 232, 235
white supremacy/white privilege 189, 194
white trash 12, 59, 66–9, 72, 74*n*, 86
Wilde, Oscar 196
Williams, Hank 39*n*, 71, 74, 76–9
Williams, Marion 216
Wilson, Mary 54, 55*n*, 98–9
Winehouse, Amy 7
woman/women 8–9, 12–15, 16–17*n*, 20, 22*n*, 54, 67, 72–4, 82, 86, 90, 95–9, 101, 102, 104, 105–9, 116, 126, 131, 132, 133, 141, 146, 148, 151, 154, 158–61, 176*n*, 189, 193–4, 207–8, 212, 223–4, 226, 229, 235–36
  (as singers) in music 2–5, 21–2, 24, 27, 28*n*, 29, 33, 59–60, 63, 68–70, 127–8, 138, 156, 163, 166, 167*n*, 168, 208–11, 213, 216, 217, 219*n*
  in rock culture 183–8, 195, 198–201
womanhood 15, 144, 151, 189
The Women of Rockabilly: Welcome to the Club (film) 57, 59, 68, 76
Wynn, Ron 210

Yardbirds, the 156
Yazoo 4*n*
Yuro, Timi 5*n*, 24

Zavaroni, Lena 36
Zombies, the 156